U.S.
vs.
THEM

J. Peter Scoblic

U.S.
vs.
THEM

**How a Half Century of Conservatism
Has Undermined America's Security**

VIKING

VIKING
Published by the Penguin Group
Penguin Group (USA) Inc., 375 Hudson Street,
New York, New York 10014, U.S.A.
Penguin Group (Canada), 90 Eglinton Avenue East, Suite 700,
Toronto, Ontario, Canada M4P 2Y3 (a division of Pearson Penguin Canada Inc.)
Penguin Books Ltd, 80 Strand, London WC2R 0RL, England
Penguin Ireland, 25 St. Stephen's Green, Dublin 2, Ireland (a division of Penguin Books Ltd)
Penguin Books Australia Ltd, 250 Camberwell Road, Camberwell,
Victoria 3124, Australia (a division of Pearson Australia Group Pty Ltd)
Penguin Books India Pvt Ltd, 11 Community Centre,
Panchsheel Park, New Delhi–110 017, India
Penguin Group (NZ), 67 Apollo Drive, Rosedale, North Shore 0632,
New Zealand (a division of Pearson New Zealand Ltd)
Penguin Books (South Africa) (Pty) Ltd, 24 Sturdee Avenue,
Rosebank, Johannesburg 2196, South Africa

Penguin Books Ltd, Registered Offices: 80 Strand, London WC2R 0RL, England

First published in 2008 by Viking Penguin, a member of Penguin Group (USA) Inc.

1 3 5 7 9 10 8 6 4 2

Copyright © J. Peter Scoblic, 2008
All rights reserved

LIBRARY OF CONGRESS CATALOGING IN PUBLICATION DATA
Scoblic, J. Peter.
U.S. vs. them : how half a century of conservatism
has undermined America's security / J. Peter Scoblic.
p. cm.
Includes bibliographical references and index.
ISBN 978-0-670-01882-6
1. United States—Foreign relations—1945–1989. 2. United States—Foreign
relations—1989– 3. United States—Politics and government—1945–1989. 4. United States—
Politics and government—1989– 5. Conservatism—United States—History—20th century.
6. Conservatism—United States—History—21st century. 7. National security—United States—
History—20th century. 8. National security—United States—History—21st century.
I. Title. II. Title: Us vs. them. III. Title: Us versus them.
E840.S387 2008
327.73009'04—dc22   2008001770

Printed in the United States of America   Set in Minion

To my mother and father

CONTENTS

"When I was coming up, it was a dangerous world. And we knew exactly who the 'they' were. It was us versus them, and it was clear who 'them' was. Today we're not so sure who the 'they' are, but we know they're there."

—George W. Bush, January 21, 2000

INTRODUCTION

THIS IS A BOOK about a mystery.

It started not long after the September 11 attacks, when George W. Bush redefined the war on terrorism. From a targeted effort to prosecute al Qaeda and its sponsors, the president broadened the war's scope to include rogue states seeking chemical, biological, and nuclear weapons. During his January 2002 State of the Union address—in which he famously dubbed Iran, Iraq, and North Korea an "axis of evil"—the president stated, "By seeking weapons of mass destruction, these regimes pose a grave and growing danger. They could provide these arms to terrorists, giving them the means to match their hatred." Bush repeatedly reaffirmed this priority—in a speech at West Point that June, when he said, "The gravest danger to freedom lies at the crossroads of radicalism and technology," and later that year, in the National Security Strategy, which said, "[I]n an age where the enemies of civilization openly and actively seek the world's most destructive technologies, the United States cannot remain idle while dangers gather."

Many Americans welcomed these statements of resolve, as did I—to an extent. Admittedly, they were broad, but I believed they contained a more specific message. I assumed that, despite his rhetoric about "weapons of mass destruction" and "rogue regimes," the president was chiefly concerned about *nuclear* weapons in the hands of terrorists. (And, in fact, the president did later acknowledge that *nuclear* terrorism was his greatest concern.) I made that assumption because nuclear weapons can do far more damage than either chemical or biological ones. It takes a great many chemical weapons to hurt a large number of people, and although a potent biological agent could kill thousands, it is also extremely difficult to culture a virulent disease and deliver it effectively. Moreover, germ weapons can be fought with preventive steps, vaccines, and even cures. Nuclear weapons, by contrast, can be fairly simple devices, technologically speaking, and even a small atomic bomb can instantly wipe out a large section of a city, killing hundreds of thousands and causing trillions of dollars in damage.

This was a prospect more sobering than even the smoking ruin of Ground Zero. After September 11, one rabbi said that the only way to truly comprehend the devastation of that day was to take one death you had personally mourned and imagine reliving it thousands of times. Well, imagine reliving the destruction of that September morning many times over. Or imagine the chaos following Hurricane Katrina multiplied a thousandfold. What's more, consider the steps the government took domestically after the 9/11 attacks—concerning homeland security, civil liberties, immigration— and magnify them to nearly authoritarian levels. Civilization—even American civilization—is a fragile thing. A nuclear 9/11 could be a catastrophe so great as to render the postattack United States unrecognizable—politically, economically, sociologically, and psychologically. In that sense, a nuclear terrorist attack is an *existential threat*—the only immediate one we face.

In ostensibly pursuing the specter of nuclear-armed terrorists, the Bush administration was aggressive. Quickly choosing to focus on Iraq, it rejected the tools of diplomacy. It went only grudgingly to plead its case before the United Nations and then mocked the competence of weapons inspectors, questioned the utility of the Security Council, and brushed off the concerns of allies. Repeatedly, the president insisted that no other country could be given control over our national security. Time after time, he asserted that we could not wait for a threat to manifest before acting—that we must not let the smoking gun become a mushroom cloud. Soon, impatient to remove Saddam Hussein from power, he ordered the invasion of Iraq.

Witnessing the speed of this process, the dismissal of the international community, and the emphasis on force as the prime tool of U.S. foreign policy, national security analysts agreed that something major was taking place. But what exactly was that something? To many, the administration seemed to have broken with decades of foreign policy precedent. Lacking a frame of reference, some called it a "revolution."

Anthropologists of the Bush administration soon developed a lexicon to describe its behavior. They first classified the Bush team as unilateralist— that is, they noted that it preferred to act alone, unconstrained by treaties, institutions, or partners. This, they said, contrasted sharply with a bipartisan Cold War foreign policy based on alliances such as NATO; the grand Gulf War coalition of George H. W. Bush; and Bill Clinton's emphasis on globalization. Its unilateralism was accompanied by a particular form of arrogance and self-righteousness, a sense that American intentions must never be questioned. And it was backed by a militarism that not only ele-vated preventive strikes to the level of a publicly declared national security doctrine, but suggested that force was the administration's preferred modus operandi—not its option of last resort. Once it became clear that Iraq had neither weapons of mass destruction nor meaningful links to al Qaeda, crit-ics accused the administration of being deceitful as well.

Each of these adjectives provided some insight into the administration. But, however accurate these pejoratives, each was largely descriptive, not explanatory. That is, calling the Iraq war a unilateral, military adventure justified by cherry-picked intelligence may be an accurate assessment, but it does not tell us *why* the Bush administration pursued such a war. *Why* was the administration inclined toward unilateralism, militarism, and deceit?

That was the mystery—a mystery made infinitely more puzzling by the fact that, on more than one occasion, the administration behaved in pre-cisely the *opposite* fashion. For example, as the White House was warning of Iraq-generated mushroom clouds, as it was rewriting military doctrine to emphasize preventive war, as it was embracing unilateralism and brush-ing off allies like fleas, it was simultaneously downplaying nuclear threats from North Korea and Iran. In late 2002, as North Korea tore the covers off its previously mothballed nuclear program, the Bush administration insisted the situation was not a crisis. In fact, it explicitly foreswore military strikes, even though Bill Clinton—not renowned in conservative circles for his martial seriousness—had considered the same North Korean actions a casus belli. Bush, in contrast, argued not only that North Korea's nuclear program must be stopped diplomatically, but that it must be halted by mul-tilateral diplomacy led by another country (China). When Iran revealed at about the same time that it had a secret uranium-enrichment program, Bush officials maintained that the UN Security Council should resolve the problem. Which is to say, the administration went from being unilateral, militaristic, and assertive to being multilateral, pacifistic, and resigned.

What was going on? This was supposedly a clear-headed, decisive admin-istration, led by a straight-shooting Texan who stated over and over again, "When the American president says something, he better mean what he says." But when it came to the single greatest existential threat to the United States of America, Bush seemed to mean very little of what he had said.

To be sure, there were differences between the situations in Iran, Iraq, and North Korea—differences that the administration insisted required individual approaches. The most salient difference, however, was that Iraq was the one member of the axis of evil *without* a nuclear program. Even if you assumed the very worst about Iraq's atomic capabilities before the invasion, the worst still wasn't as bad as what was publicly verifiable about North Korea and Iran at the same time. The Iraq war, then, was not undertaken to guarantee America's nuclear security.

Other administration initiatives gave the lie to Bush's counterproliferation rhetoric even more compellingly. After 9/11, for example, the administration tried to cut funding for a program that secured loose fissile material in the former Soviet Union, one of the richest potential sources for a terrorist trying to build an atomic bomb. In addition, it set about dismantling the decades-old web of nonproliferation treaties and norms, going so far as to declare that U.S. nuclear weapons should have not only a deterrent role but a tactical military one—and that it hoped to build new warheads for use on the battlefield. Then, in 2005, the administration promised to ship nuclear technology to India, thus enabling it to build more nuclear weapons, a development that was certain, in turn, to motivate Pakistan, an unstable state with a not-insubstantial al Qaeda presence, to do the same.

What sort of counterproliferation effort was this? At times, watching the Bush administration was like trying to understand quantum mechanics, where light could be both a wave and a particle, causality ceased to apply, and the same starting variables could produce wildly different outcomes. Frustrated by such uncertainty, Albert Einstein had once complained that God does not play dice with the universe, but that's precisely what George W. Bush seemed to be doing with U.S. foreign policy. And by 2007—with Iraq in flames, North Korea testing nuclear weapons, and Iran starting to enrich uranium—it had become a game he was losing, badly.

But George W. Bush was not playing dice with U.S. foreign policy. There was no "revolution." The mystery was not intractable. His foreign policy was simply conservative.

If describing Bush's foreign policy as "conservative" seems self-evident and explaining it that way seems tautological, that is only because conservative heritage is poorly understood. "Conservative," used in its historical sense, has a far richer meaning than "hawkish" or "hard-line." For decades, it was by no means equivalent to "Republican." And although the term is used today by a variety of people to describe a variety of attitudes and positions—from libertarianism to authoritarianism—the fact is that conservatism has a distinct lineage in American intellectual history, albeit one with a bewildering number of offspring and a trinity of great-uncles rather than a single forefather.

Most observers looking to explain the administration's behavior in terms of an ideology that accounts for unilateralist, militarist, propagandist behavior have turned to *neo*conservatism. Neoconservatives originally comprised a group of fervently anti-Soviet liberals who in the 1970s grew increasingly uncomfortable with the Democratic Party and ultimately abandoned it for President Ronald Reagan. After the Cold War, these neoconservatives became obsessed with a sort of American messianism involving the proactive spread of democracy. There are, or were, many neoconservatives in the Bush administration, and clearly they had an impact, particularly on the decision to invade Iraq, an action they hoped would help liberalize the Middle East. But their policies alone cannot fully account for its behavior. Most Bush officials, including many who are often labeled neoconservative—Dick Cheney, Donald Rumsfeld, and John Bolton, for example—have little connection to neoconservatism. They are simply standard-issue conservatives, whose ideological genealogy can be traced to the mid-1950s, when economic libertarians, religious traditionalists, and militant anticommunists united to oppose a bipartisan coalition that supported New Deal policies at home and containment of the Soviet Union abroad.

In foreign policy, "conservative" describes a distinct attitude in which the world is conceived in terms of "us versus them" or "good versus evil," with the United States assuming the role of a righteous protagonist facing a monolithic enemy. It is often an explicitly religious vision, with frequent allusions not only to good and evil, but also to God, Satan, and Armageddon. If virtually all American officials during the Cold War were anticommunist, this religious worldview made conservative anticommunism particularly potent and uncompromising. Characterizing the Soviet Union as an earthly manifestation of evil, rather than simply as an antagonistic nation-state, convinced conservatives that Moscow could not be reasoned with. The forces of good could not—and should not want to—coexist with the forces of evil. Conservative anticommunists rejected the bipartisan policy of containment, dismissed negotiation with the Soviet Union as appeasement, and even insisted that a nuclear war was winnable. George W. Bush is the direct descendant—indeed, the ultimate product—of this movement.

Admittedly, modern conservatives—that is, post–World War II conservatives—are not the first to cast American foreign policy in a moral framework. America itself was conceived in oppositional terms: It was the New World, as distinct from the Old World of Europe. It was to be a "New Israel," in which settlers who had a covenant with God would be the vanguard of political and religious liberty on earth. Even as this explicitly religious narrative gave way to a more secular version in which the forces of liberty fought the forces of tyranny, America's inherent Manichaeanism—its tendency to see the world in dualistic terms—remained operative for concrete as well as abstract reasons. After all, the new America was in fact surrounded by enemies—unfriendly Native Americans and competing European imperialists. The colonists had to rely on themselves for protection, and neutrality was the safest means of avoiding European conflicts. These foundational influences—an exceptionalism comprising both a moralism and a nationalism—represent enduring traditions in U.S. foreign policy.

What, then, distinguishes contemporary conservatism? Why is it useful to explain Bush's foreign policy as conservative rather than simply as American? The answer is that the fundamental traditions of American foreign policy can be combined in a variety of ways, with a variety of strengths. Think back a moment to high school chemistry: Atoms are composed of protons, neutrons, and electrons. An atom of oxygen is not made of different basic stuff than an atom of lead, but they have entirely different properties. It is the number and arrangement of those building blocks that makes an element harmless, or useful, or dangerous. What is more, certain elements may be helpful in certain circumstances and harmful in others. Uranium, for example, can be used in both medical research (that is, to cure disease) and in nuclear weapons (to murder millions of people). So it is with the building blocks of a foreign policy and its suitability for a particular situation.

By the mid-twentieth century, the American exceptionalism of the eighteenth and nineteenth centuries had become untenable. The threat from the Axis powers, the horrors of World War II, and the essential contribution of the United States to victory made it clear that American security was now bound up with the security of others. The development of nuclear weapons in the 1940s was the final blow, rendering the old moralist and nationalist conception of foreign policy irrelevant—or worse, dangerous. Cold War conservatism, initiated as a response to the perceived excesses of liberalism at home and the dangers of communism abroad, combined exceptionalist ideas into a particularly extreme form at a particularly fraught time. Whatever its benefits in the Republic's first century, the belief that the world was divided into us and them, good and evil—indeed, us *versus* them, good *versus* evil—was a terribly inappropriate one for the U.S.-Soviet conflict. For one thing, it did not accurately describe the world, for as we later learned, communism was not monolithic, the Soviets could be negotiated with, and containment was possible. Most important, nuclear weapons had rendered traditional forms of military competition obsolete. Instead, international security required reaching some sort of modus vivendi with the enemy so that the world did not suddenly end in nuclear holocaust. Conservatives were not only ill suited to this task; they rejected its very premise.

The first half of this book is devoted to showing how, at the precise time when we needed to engage our enemies and to deemphasize military confrontation, conservatives promoted the opposite tack, deriding containment as appeasement, rejecting mutual assured destruction, and preparing to fight and win a nuclear war. The Cold War ended peacefully not because Ronald Reagan "won" it, but because Reagan, having taken the superpowers to the brink of nuclear war in his first term, stepped back in his second and reopened arms control negotiations, cooperating with a Soviet leader who, fortunately, had decided the USSR needed fundamental reform.

For better or worse, American security has only become more dependent on cooperation since the September 11 attacks. Although today a global thermonuclear war is unlikely, staying the threat of nuclear terrorism will require an intense degree of international coordination and, yes, negotiation with the evil empires of the post–Cold War world—states like Iran and North Korea. We simply cannot adequately protect ourselves by ourselves.

The Bush administration has rejected this conclusion precisely because it is conservative. Its insistence on seeing the world in Manichaean terms has led it, like its Cold War forebears, to refuse coexistence with evil regimes, to emphasize military solutions to problems, to shun diplomacy as "appeasement," to scorn international institutions as unwelcome checks on American power, and even to view truth as relative. From its selection of Iraq as a primary target to its fumbling of the North Korean and Iranian crises, to its renewed emphasis on the utility of our own nuclear weapons, to its inexplicable apathy toward safeguarding loose nuclear material, to its willingness to sell nuclear technology to India, the administration has exacerbated the threat we face from nuclear terrorism. Its one inarguable success—the abolition of the Libyan nuclear program—was achieved only because it violated the very principles that have guided the rest of its policies.

The solution to the mystery, then, lies in ideology, and the second half of the book examines the Bush administration's paradoxical behavior through the lens of conservatism. It quickly becomes clear that protecting ourselves from nuclear terrorism demands that we abandon a binary, oppositional view of the world. The Bush administration may be almost over, but conservatism is not. Republicanism was once distinct from conservatism, but they have become increasingly synonymous. The disaster of the Iraq war has apparently forced something of a reconsideration— the Bush administration has lately dabbled in talks with Iran and signed a deal with North Korea (alienating, it should be noted, many conservatives)— but one need only listen to the campaign rhetoric of the Republican presidential candidates to realize that the good-versus-evil worldview is now firmly entrenched in the GOP. Although the Bush administration is almost certain to leave office with abysmally low approval ratings, the American people's susceptibility to a conservative conception of U.S. foreign policy will remain high because, culturally, exceptionalism is part of our heritage and because, psychologically, humans are hardwired to think tribally in times of danger.

Ideological conflicts are, by nature, fought at the conceptual level, often deteriorating into a cacophony of isms that obscure more than they clarify. Post-9/11 debates about foreign policy, in which neoconservatism (and any number of proffered alternatives) has received so much attention, have been no different. By contrast, debates over nuclear policy are usually narrowly focused, and its practitioners conceive of problems in programmatic terms—another weapon system, another arms treaty. Even during the Cold War, when debates about deterrence reached an almost theological level of abstraction, nuclear issues occupied their own niche, away from debates about human nature and our role in the world. Perhaps that is why we now find ourselves in grave nuclear danger with little idea of what to do next, given that the only way to overcome the danger is to understand the role that ideology played in cultivating it. We need to map how ideas have had consequences. Then—and only then—can we solve the mystery of the Bush administration and of national security in a transnational world.

PART ONE

IDEAS

Chapter One

WORLDVIEW

IT MADE FOR an unusual Cold War battlefield. Far removed from the streets of Budapest, the plains of North Korea, or the shores of Quemoy, Carnegie Hall typically played host to the world's great musicians. On the evening of September 17, 1959, however, it was the site of an impassioned demonstration against communism. Taking the stage the night before an orchestra was to perform an arrangement of Bach were representatives of the hastily constituted Committee Against Summit Entanglements. The occasion was the visit of Soviet premier Nikita Khrushchev, whom President Dwight D. Eisenhower had invited to the United States in hopes of easing Cold War tensions.

Relations between the nations—allies during World War II—had turned frigid after the surrenders of Germany and Japan, once it became clear that the Soviet Union was not going to give up control of Eastern Europe. By Ike's second term, they were openly hostile. In 1956, Khrushchev ordered the Red Army to crush a Hungarian movement for independence from the Soviet bloc, killing thousands of aspiring democrats. Throughout the mid-1950s, Khrushchev repeatedly claimed that the Soviet Union possessed an atomic advantage, and in 1957 a presidential commission reported that the Soviets might soon be able to launch a disarming nuclear strike against the United States. Then, in late 1958, Khrushchev triggered a crisis over the Allied occupation of West Berlin, which lay 110 miles inside Red Army–controlled East Germany. In a desperate attempt to stanch the embarrassing annual exodus of three hundred thousand impoverished East Germans to the economically booming West, Khrushchev gave the United States six months to remove its forces from the city so that the communists could take over.

Eisenhower, however, was not riled by Soviet claims of nuclear dominance or the domestic fear they engendered. He ignored Khrushchev's ultimatum over Berlin, refusing to be goaded into increasing the size of the military or confronting the Red Army in Germany. ("We are certainly not

going to fight a ground war in Europe," he declared.) Instead, Eisenhower
followed the advice of former British prime minister Winston Churchill,
who had been urging the American and Soviet leaders to hold a summit to
air their differences. Nearing his final year in office and looking to leave a
legacy of peace, Eisenhower invited Khrushchev for a visit.

To thirty-three-year-old William F. Buckley, Jr., the public face of the
Committee Against Summit Entanglements, the thought that America
could make peace with the Soviets was a "hallucination." Buckley's looks
were boyish, but his mind was that of a man in his intellectual prime.
By the time of Khrushchev's visit, he had already written two books and
founded *National Review* magazine. When he took the stage at Carnegie
Hall that September evening, he did not simply speak; he orated. His voice
marked by hints of a British accent that he had picked up (or cultivated)
during time he spent in England as a teenager, Buckley laid out a case
against Eisenhower's invitation to the Butcher of Budapest. He mocked the
popular notion that the visit would open Khrushchev's eyes to the wonders
of capitalism, derided the American public's unquestioning faith in Eisenhower, and took a token shot at liberal hypocrisy. The Democratic mayor
of New York City, Buckley noted, had once refused to meet with a visiting
Saudi royal because his kingdom discriminated against Jews, and yet here
was the president fawning over the arrival of a man who not only discriminated against Jews, but killed them. Of course, he murdered Catholics and
Protestants, too. Could *that,* Buckley asked, be the difference? "Khrushchev murders people without regard to race, color, or creed . . . and, therefore, whatever he is guilty of, he is not guilty of discrimination?" The
audience laughed and applauded.

Buckley was not worried that the president would concede some crucial point during negotiations; rather, he felt that the communist-in-chief's
mere presence on American soil constituted appeasement, the dirtiest
word in international politics ever since 1938, when British prime minister Neville Chamberlain had claimed to have secured peace by grant-
ing Adolf Hitler the Sudetenland. In the face of Soviet belligerence—in
particular Khrushchev's threats to absorb West Berlin into the Eastern
bloc—Buckley saw the summit as an act of "diplomatic sentimentality"
that would only confirm for Khrushchev America's weakness, allowing
him to hear "with his own ears the death rattle of the West." National support for the summit indicated a "lapse of our critical and moral faculties."

To Buckley, the Cold War was not merely a struggle between nations, or even between ideologies. It was a struggle between faiths, and in such a struggle the ultimate weapons were moral in nature. By inviting Khrushchev to America, Eisenhower and all who supported him had committed the cardinal sin of blurring the line between good and evil.

Buckley's view of the Cold War is important because he was not simply a protester or a journalist; he was a revolutionary, the vanguard of the modern conservative movement. His 1951 book, *God and Man at Yale*, was one of the first works to blend the different strains of postwar conservatism, enabling it to become a viable force in American politics. His *National Review* would provide conservatives an intellectual town hall where they could make sure they were all on the same page, literally and figuratively. For example, James Burnham, who wrote a column titled "The Third World War" for the magazine, would do more than any other individual to articulate the foreign policy of the Cold War Right. As George H. Nash wrote in his seminal book *The Conservative Intellectual Movement in America Since 1945*, "[I]f *National Review* (or something like it) had not been founded, there would probably have been no cohesive intellectual force on the Right in the 1960s or 1970s. To a very substantial degree, the history of reflective conservatism in America after 1955 is the history of the individuals who collaborated in—or were discovered by—the magazine William F. Buckley, Jr. founded."

Conservatives themselves agree with that assessment. As columnist George F. Will wrote in 1980, when Ronald Reagan was elected president and the conservative revolution seemed to have reached its apex, "[A]ll great Biblical stories begin with Genesis. . . . And before there was Ronald Reagan, there was Barry Goldwater, and before there was Barry Goldwater there was *National Review,* and before there was *National Review* there was Bill Buckley with a spark in his mind, and the spark in 1980 has become a conflagration." Or, as President Reagan himself would say in 1985 at a banquet honoring *National Review*'s thirtieth anniversary: "I think eventually the pundits and analysts are going to catch on to the enormous force and deep roots of the conservative movement. . . . And, when that happens, they are going to realize something not only about this journal, but about its founder and editor: that Bill Buckley is perhaps the most influential journalist and intellectual in our era—that he changed our country, indeed our century."

But back in 1959, Buckley and his ideological brethren had a long way to go before they would be feted by a sitting president. Despite his ultimate influence—indeed, despite the brisk sales of anti-Khrushchev stickers and tickets to his Carnegie Hall event that September morning—Buckley's conservatism was sharp fare for the bland palate of postwar America. It was certainly not synonymous with the ideology then prevalent in the GOP. Eisenhower and his advisers espoused a "modern Republicanism" that was, in essence, a blend of Rooseveltian policies at home and Trumanesque confrontation of the Soviet threat abroad. In other words, the president's governing philosophy was simply a modestly more conservative version of that of his Democratic predecessors, which is why, in 1952, Democrats had implored him to run on *their* ticket. By contrast, the ideology of Buckley and his comrades was a radical blend of libertarian economic philosophy and religious traditionalism, combined with an unflinchingly aggressive anticommunism that was diametrically opposed to the Right's earlier isolationist tendencies and at odds with the bipartisan doctrine of "containment."

Conservative anticommunism's absolutist understanding of the Cold War transformed foreign policy from a morally neutral attempt to defend the country into a religious crusade. The Soviet Union was not simply a powerful state whose interests clashed with those of the United States; it was the embodiment of satanic forces. Containment, the strategy of limiting Soviet influence to its existing sphere of influence, was unacceptable because it implied long-term coexistence with those forces. The same objection was levied against negotiations aimed at achieving a modus vivendi. Given such beliefs, it is hardly surprising that inviting hell's earthly ambassador for a tour of the Midwest and some chitchat in the White House was more than conservatives could stomach. (Buckley actually threatened to dye the East River red so that Khrushchev would arrive in New York to a coursing channel of "blood.") The Cold War was first and foremost a fight against evil, and the forces of good did not make deals with the devil.

The Fall of the Old Conservatism

Citizens of the George W. Bush era may have to strain to imagine a time in which conservatism did not have so tight a grip on American politics. But in the period after World War II, conservatism as a coherent ideological force did not exist. Republicans had controlled the White House from 1921 to 1933 and during that time had managed to erode the American public's trust in their ability to manage the economy, in part because conventional economic wisdom had held that the government *shouldn't* manage the economy. Markets were supposed to be self-regulating, and laissez-faire capitalism had steadily increased living standards and economic power to the point that America had become the world's leading industrial player. Calvin Coolidge—who presided over most of the Roaring Twenties—thus happily and consistently supported business with low taxes, deregulation, and high tariffs (laissez-faire applying only to the American economy, not the global one).

But in 1929, the stock market crashed, the banking system failed, and unemployment skyrocketed, leaving Republicans flummoxed. Their economic doctrine held that thrift was essential—the man who saved today could invest his capital and spur long-term growth, whereas consumption only satisfied short-term appetites and made little contribution to the economy. It was a moral as well as an economic argument. American tradition valued individualism and self-reliance: Thrift was virtuous, profligacy was indulgent, and debt was sinful. The same principles were applied to government, where they effectively dictated that federal expenditures should never exceed tax revenue.

Herbert Hoover, the president tasked with righting the economy, was a GOP star whose earlier tour as secretary of commerce had been widely applauded. But as economic depression set in and the number of unemployed soared by millions, he lamely touted personal charity as the path to relief. When an emergency committee on joblessness recommended a more ambitious program of public works and a national employment service, Hoover rejected its findings. The head of a subsequent commission more to his liking testified to Congress that the federal government should not worry that its antipoverty effort was inadequate "unless it is so bad it is obviously scandalous, and even then we would not be obliged to be concerned." "There is grave danger in taking the determination of these things into the Federal Government," it cautioned. To compensate for anticipated government shortfalls from the slowing economy, Hoover actually raised taxes, increasing the burden on an already beleaguered populace.

In 1932, voters revolted, overwhelmingly turning Hoover out of the

White House in favor of Franklin Delano Roosevelt and his plans to radically overhaul the government's role in the economy. In his first inaugural address, Roosevelt called for direct hiring by the government to ease
unemployment, national planning for utilities, and federal consolidation
of relief activities. Republicans had dominated the White House for most
of the last seventy years, but now liberalism, with its belief that government could serve as a force for good in the economic and social lives of
American citizens, would get its chance. For six years Republicans watched
as the "creeping socialism" of the New Deal devoured the economic liberty of which they were so protective. Then, in 1938, just as it seemed the
American public might be wearying of the Roosevelt administration, the
nation was confronted with a crisis in Europe.

European affairs had traditionally repelled Americans. As Thomas
Paine wrote in *Common Sense,* "[T]his new world has been the asylum
for the persecuted lovers of civil and religious liberty from *every part*
of Europe. Hither they have fled, not from the tender embraces of the
mother, but from the cruelty of the monster." The monster was not simply
the oppression of European tyrants, but the oppression of the European
system itself, a balance-of-power structure in which colonies—including
the American ones—were mere pawns in the great power conflicts that
had obsessed Europe for centuries. Americans had greater ambitions for
their new country.

Early in the Republic's history the Founding Fathers concluded that
the best way to ensure American liberty—to ensure that America grew
into an independent power rather than remaining a plaything of the Old
World—was to remain neutral in European affairs. The founding text for
this idea was George Washington's Farewell Address, in which the first
president warned America against international alliances: "Europe has a
set of primary interests which to us have none or a very remote relation.
Hence she must be engaged in frequent controversies, the causes of which
are essentially foreign to our concerns." Later this injunction was reinforced by Thomas Jefferson's admonition against "entangling alliances"
in his first inaugural address. Then, in what was essentially the converse
of Washington's warning, James Monroe declared in an address to Congress on December 2, 1823, that the Americas—that is, the entire Western
Hemisphere—were off limits to European power politics. There were to
be no new colonies, no transferring of colonies between European powers,

and no reimposition of colonial rule once independence had been secured. At the same time Monroe stressed that the United States would not "interfere in the internal concerns of any of [Europe's] powers." It was a promise he kept: When Latin American colonies rebelled and looked to the United States for encouragement in their democratic endeavor, Monroe refused them even moral support.

American foreign policy of the eighteenth and nineteenth centuries is often described as "isolationist" because the United States consciously divorced itself from European affairs. Other observers, noting that the young country traded with Europe, expanded westward, and eventually acquired colonies of its own abroad, have dubbed its foreign policy "unilateralist," meaning that America sought chiefly to maintain its liberty through freedom of action. One term suggests a reactive posture, the other a proactive one, and both seem appropriate characterizations of different eras. But whatever term one prefers, U.S. foreign policy was clearly created *in opposition to* the rest of the world—not only the world across the ocean but the world in the immediate vicinity. If the United States was to remain exceptional, it had to maintain that attitude. In its early years America was surrounded by enemies: Native Americans constantly assaulted the colonial intruders, as did the imperialist European powers that held New World territories. Nationalism—an us-versus-them worldview—was therefore a critical part of the American experience and psyche.

Woodrow Wilson was the first to explicitly reject this solipsistic attitude. To be sure, he was promoting his own brand of exceptionalism, in which Americans were to defend not only their own liberty but the liberty of others as well. That was the rationale Wilson gave for America's entry into World War I, and when it was over, he sought to involve the nation in a permanent structure for peace, a collective security organization that would require its members to come to the defense of others. The League of Nations was utopian, expecting far too much of the realpolitik-oriented Europeans and asking far too much of Americans, who still fiercely guarded their sovereignty. But its sharp departure from us-versus-them principles changed the nature of American foreign policy, and even skeptics had to acknowledge that World War I had left the United States in a far stronger position relative to Europe and thus bequeathed it the capacity for world leadership.

When the GOP reclaimed the White House after the war—via Warren

Harding, then Coolidge and Hoover—the strict nationalism of the eighteenth and nineteenth centuries was tempered by a new, more global outlook. Many Republicans did not support the League; at the same time, a faction of internationalists realized that the United States had outgrown its provincialism. As a result, during the 1920s, three Republican presidents led the nation in a sort of compromise neoisolationism, in which the United States promoted peace abroad while carefully avoiding any formal commitment to preserve that peace. When Harding negotiated the Washington Naval Treaty (which limited the possession of warships by the United States, Britain, Japan, France, and Italy), he had to assure the Senate that "there is no commitment to armed force, no alliance, no written or moral obligation to join in defense." When the Senate considered U.S. involvement in the Permanent Court of International Justice, it did so only under the condition that America's role be limited. And the Kellogg-Briand Pact, an attempt to actually outlaw war, while superficially a symbol of international cooperation, was in fact just a way of striving for peace while avoiding all responsibility for maintaining it.

In the late 1930s, however, as the Nazi army swallowed Czechoslovakia, invaded Poland, and swept west toward France, this neoisolationist consensus on the right fractured. Republican internationalists wanted to help Britain and the other countries fighting Germany. These men were often from the more cosmopolitan East Coast, with closer personal and business ties to Europe, and they believed that unless the United States helped the Allies defeat the Nazis, American interests would suffer. They were pragmatists, not Wilsonians, but they clearly understood that the United States could no longer stand apart from the conflicts of Europe. These men would become the moderate Republicans of the Cold War—men like McGeorge Bundy—but their influence would be far outshone by the heirs of another prewar faction.

In sharp contrast to Republican internationalists were conservatives who clung determinedly to their nationalism. For them, World War I had demonstrated neither America's increasing interdependence with Europe nor its greater role in the world, but rather the futility of intervention itself: Wilson had called for making the world safe for democracy and had instead fostered a resurgent German militarism. These conservatives were culturally as well as politically distinct from their more worldly fellow Republicans. Often from the Midwest, they were suspicious not only of internationalism but of all things internationalist—such as Wall Street banks. Their leader was Robert A. Taft, an Ohio senator and the son of the twenty-seventh president, who argued that World War II was just another of Europe's incessant internecine bloodlettings and need not stain American shores. Their resistance only strengthened after Hitler invaded Russia, since that meant that aid to the Allies would aid the communists as well. Hoover and fourteen other top Republicans even issued a statement condemning Churchill's alliance with Joseph Stalin. Outside the Beltway these conservatives drew strength from publications like the *Chicago Tribune* and grassroots organizations like America First, which advocated withdrawal behind impregnable defenses, arguing that intervention abroad would undermine democracy at home. The conservative position boiled down to one fundamental belief: As Taft put it, "We would be worse off entering the war than if Hitler occupied all of Europe."

The ultimate battle came in early 1941 over FDR's proposal to aid the Allies in their struggle against Hitler, even though the United States had yet to officially enter the war. The Lend-Lease Act empowered Roosevelt to give Great Britain and other Allied nations billions of dollars in materiel. Conservatives fought the measure for two months, recognizing that the fate of their movement was at stake. When the measure passed, conservative Republican senator Arthur Vandenberg noted sadly in his diary, "We have tossed Washington's Farewell Address into the discard. We have thrown ourselves squarely into the power politics and the power wars of Europe, Asia, and Africa. We have taken the first step upon a course from which we can never hereafter retreat." He was right. On December 7, 1941, the Japanese bombed Pearl Harbor and the United States entered World War II. Four years later, having played the essential role in defeating Germany and Japan, the United States was the most powerful country on the planet, with interests and responsibilities around the globe.

The Great Depression and World War II and its aftermath had, in effect, validated both liberalism and internationalism, leaving the Grand Old Party looking old but rather less than grand, at least in ideological terms. Indeed, it is difficult to imagine a set of circumstances that could have more thoroughly repudiated the big-business, America-first conservatism of the interwar years. In 1950 Lionel Trilling famously wrote, "In the United States at this time liberalism is not only the dominant, but even the sole intellectual tradition. For it is the plain fact that nowadays there are no conservative or reactionary ideas in general circulation."

To be sure, the Republican Party itself remained a powerful force. Capitalizing on anti-Truman sentiment in the 1946 midterm elections, for example, Republicans won both houses of Congress with the refrain "Had Enough?" while the quip "To err is Truman" made the rounds of Republican cocktail parties. But the GOP's national candidates were moderates whose views differed little from Truman's own. Thomas Dewey, the former New York governor who was the Republican presidential nominee in both 1944 and 1948, was a member of the GOP's East Coast establishment, accepted most premises of the New Deal, and supported American involvement in World War II and the reconstruction of Europe. Eisenhower, who won election in both 1952 and 1956, called people who wanted to abolish New Deal programs "stupid"; he went on to create the department of Health, Education and Welfare; and he declared the necessity of a "gradually expanding federal government." And, as befitted a man who had commanded Allied forces in Europe during World War II, he was strongly committed to the defense of the Continent.

After the war, Taft continued in the role of patron saint of the Republican right wing, a bulwark of anti–New Dealism, to whom true conservatives turned when men like Dewey were selected to represent the GOP. He could not, however, provide the intellectual foundation for a new conservatism. Asked by a reporter if he had read Russell Kirk's sweeping intellectual history, *The Conservative Mind,* Taft just laughed and said, "You remind me of [James] Thurber's *Let Your Mind Alone.* There are some questions that I have not thought very much about, but I'm a politician, not a philosopher." More important, while paying lip service to the need to combat communism abroad, Taft could not let go of his isolationist tendencies and sought to reduce reconstruction aid to Europe under the Marshall Plan while opposing the creation of NATO. In 1952, Eisenhower offered to stay out of the presidential race—effectively ceding the Republican nomination to Taft—if the senator would agree that the United States had to play a larger role in Europe, but Taft refused and died soon thereafter.

Without a coherent creed or a patron, conservatives of the period were defined principally by their discontent. Unhappy with the existing order—the growth of government, the encroachment of modernity, the rise of communism—they constituted what Albert Jay Nock, in his book *Memoirs of a Superfluous Man,* would call "the Remnant." But dissatisfaction was hardly a sufficient basis for an ideological movement capable of challenging liberalism. Conservative angst needed an intellectual framework. In the late 1940s and early 1950s, that framework began to emerge in the publications of a small group of academics and, more significantly, in the unorthodox ideas of one young man with particular journalistic flair.

The Rise of the New Conservatism

Most modern American conservatives arrived at ideological maturity only after a tortuous intellectual adolescence—one that for many included a flirtation with socialism. William F. Buckley, Jr., by contrast, was raised a conservative by his father. A devotee of free enterprise who believed, even during the depths of the Depression, that ambition and hard work could raise anyone from poverty, the elder Buckley made his own fortune lawyering for the oil business in Mexico. His emotional engines were his devout Catholicism and fierce anticommunism, both of which were strengthened by the revolution that swept Mexico in the early part of the twentieth century, threatening the church and infecting the locals with Bolshevist notions. Will Buckley's anticommunism was itself fundamentally religious in nature—according to his son John, he saw communism as the "anti-Christ." He even initially opposed American intervention in World War II because he hoped Nazi Germany would defeat the Soviet Union and crush Bolshevism.

Will Buckley's children readily absorbed his politics. At the age of thirteen, young Bill was already an ardent anti–New Dealer, and in the summer of 1939 he and his siblings started a newspaper titled the *Spectator,* which became the local organ of America First and argued against joining Britain in its fight against Germany. (Bill even named his first sailboat "Sweet Isolation.") In liberal internationalist Sharon, Connecticut, where the family had its estate, Great Elm, the Buckleys were anomalous. Noted Bill's sister Patricia, "You'd find us in every corner surrounded by controversy because we were the only conservatives and America Firsters." Albert Jay Nock, a friend of Will Buckley's, occasionally visited Great Elm for lunch, and Bill read *Memoirs of a Superfluous Man* in his senior year of high school, becoming immediately taken with its notion of the Remnant.

By the time Buckley matriculated to Yale in 1946, he was thus possessed of a peculiar ideology. Although Yale's students on the whole considered themselves fairly conservative, theirs was a literal conservatism that preferred gradual to dramatic change, slow evolution of the status quo to upheaval. In practice, this meant they subscribed to a moderate Republicanism that accepted the existing welfare state because it neutralized radical challenges to the capitalist system. Buckley, by contrast, could only be characterized with oxymoron: He was a revolutionary conservative, a radical traditionalist. He wanted little state and a lot of religion.

Communism, which represented the opposite—a lot of state and no religion—was the enemy. As the chairman of the *Yale Daily News*, Buckley inveighed against what he saw as the socialism of the university's economics department and the atheistic spirit that pervaded campus. Invited by the Yale administration to give the Alumni Day oration, he wrote a speech attacking the "laissez-faire theory of education" that put socialists on par with capitalists. As a remedy, he suggested the university declare "active Christianity the first basis of enlightened thought and action" and "communism, socialism, collectivism, government paternalism inimical to the dignity of the individual."

Whether he realized it or not, Buckley personified two emerging schools of thought bubbling up within academic circles—though clearly not at Yale—that would give rise to important strands of modern American conservatism. The first of these was libertarianism. In 1944, Friedrich A. Hayek, an Austrian émigré to Great Britain, published *The Road to Serfdom,* in which he argued that there was an essential link between political liberty and economic liberty. In itself, this idea was not new; Herbert Hoover had made the same point. But Hooverism had been thoroughly displaced by the New Deal, and Hayek was a serious economist at a time when other serious economists were following John Maynard Keynes toward the consensus that government ought to regulate the economy. What's more, Hayek took his premise to its logical end, concluding that state interference in economic affairs inevitably led to dictatorship. For years, conservative politicians like Taft had been tarring the New Deal as "collectivist," "communist," and even "fascist." Now Hayek's polemic lent their ravings intellectual heft.

Hayek's ideas soon made a splash among the broader public. As postwar economic growth washed over America, more and more people had begun to question whether the massive expansion of government in the 1930s and 1940s had now gone far enough. As the Depression receded into memory, Roosevelt's dramatic, sometimes intrusive changes no longer seemed quite as necessary. Although it was an academic tract whose projected audience was sufficiently limited that the University of Chicago Press printed only two thousand copies, *The Road to Serfdom* catapulted to popular and widespread review attention. *Reader's Digest* condensed it, and the Book-of-the-Month Club distributed more than one million copies of the article. Just as notable was the seriousness with which the book was considered by the liberal intellectual establishment. A front-page article in the *New York Times Book Review* judged *The Road to Serfdom* "one of the most important books of our generation."

Just as libertarians were rebelling against the increasing regulation of the economy, so were so-called traditionalists rebelling against what they perceived as the troubling soullessness of American society. Over the preceding decades, modernity had undermined the individual's place in the world. Industrialization and urbanization had displaced workers from their communities and deposited them in assembly lines and office jobs. The popular culture of the late 1940s—from television to pulp novels—with which people distracted themselves from this alienation was growing increasingly crude. Meanwhile, social science had flourished and had begun to treat humans as if they were just another form of machine. America was booming, and yet in the race to progress, it was not clear what it was racing toward—except, perhaps, Soviet-style regimentation and atheism.

In 1948, Richard Weaver, a disillusioned history professor with a penchant for the old South, thought he had discovered the source of this postwar American malaise. It lay, unexpectedly, in the fourteenth century, when the English philosopher William of Occam had rejected the notion of "universals," or moral truths. Weaver wrote a book arguing that this idea had had a domino effect on Western thought over the subsequent centuries. Occam's rejection of universals led to the fallacy that experience, not transcendence, was paramount and that man could understand nature through science. When man began to probe his own nature scientifically—through biology, economics, and psychology—"religion [began] to assume an ambiguous dignity. . . . Man created in the divine image, the protagonist of a great drama in which his soul was at stake, was replaced by man the wealth-seeking and -consuming animal." In the modern age, Weaver argued, man had traded wisdom for knowledge, truth for facts, and in the process started a slide toward crudity, anomie, and materialism. If we did not regain our moral sense, we would find that we had taken the short step from Occam's rationalism to communism. Weaver titled his book *Ideas Have Consequences.*

For traditionalists, then, religion was not simply a balm for the ravages of the twentieth century, but a bulwark against totalitarianism. Just as libertarians saw a connection between liberalism and communism, traditionalists believed that atheism empowered communism. Conversely, liberty was the product of morality. Gordon Keith Chalmers, then president of Kenyon College, argued in his book *The Republic and the Person,* "[W]hat has really made possible the liberty of the individual has been not only its root in truth but the constancy of human agreement about the relation of men to God, right and wrong, good and evil." In his 1953 book *The Conservative Mind*—a 150-year history of thinkers from Edmund Burke to T. S. Eliot that established a pedigree for the burgeoning conservative movement—Russell Kirk, another history professor with a nostalgia for the antebellum South, argued that natural law and transcendence were the solution to America's postwar ills: "Political problems, at bottom, are religious and moral problems."

It is not hard to see how traditionalists, who believed in rules, and libertarians, who opposed them, might have trouble coexisting, let alone joining in an ideological vanguard. In fact, in 1957, Hayek delivered a paper to the libertarian Mont Pelerin Society titled "Why I Am Not a Conservative"—he considered himself an "Old Whig"—and invited Kirk to defend his definition of conservatism immediately afterward, which Kirk did. In the coming years, the libertarian and traditionalist strains of conservatism would be reconciled by the argument that the ultimate goal of man was virtue (thus pleasing the traditionalists) but that virtue was worthless unless man chose it of his own free will (thus pleasing the libertarians). But before such philosophical finesse could fuse the movement's church with its lack of state, the precocious William F. Buckley, Jr., effortlessly held those two ideas in his mind simultaneously, and with brilliance, charisma, and ambition translated them into a movement.

After review, the Yale administration did not let Buckley give his feisty Alumni Day speech attacking New Haven's moral and intellectual degradation; so, after graduation, he channeled his ideas into a book. *God and Man at Yale* was a devastating critique of the modern university and its tolerance—indeed, its promotion—of ideas that Buckley considered nothing less than an attack on traditional Judeo-Christian values. *God and Man at Yale,* though the work of a twenty-five-year-old, showcased the themes that would suffuse Buckley's later work: Free enterprise is good; individual morality is important; religious truth is not debatable; communism, liberalism, and moral relativism are wrong. Those were the same themes that would come to define the modern American conservative movement.

God and Man at Yale became a *New York Times* bestseller and made Buckley a celebrity—though not a universally beloved one. (McGeorge Bundy, a Yale alumnus and establishment Republican who would later become President John F. Kennedy's national security adviser, wrote in the *Atlantic Monthly* that *God and Man at Yale* was "dishonest in its use of facts, false in its theory, and a discredit to its author.") The book led to job offers from the *American Mercury* and the *Freeman,* right-leaning magazines. But Buckley was keen to start his own publication, and his interest came at a propitious time. In 1952, the *American Mercury* lost its funding and was forced to turn for cash to Russell Maguire, a millionaire and noted anti-Semite, whose support led to the defection of almost all its senior staff. The *Freeman,* too, had been beset by mass resignations, and in 1954, the libertarian Foundation for Economic Education bought it and turned it into a monthly. "What is needed," one conservative said, in response to this newly gaping intellectual hole on the right, "is a weekly, something that, like *The Nation* and the *New Republic* of the '30s, would be on the desks of professors, bureaucrats, editorial writers, legislators, in short, of opinion-makers all over the country every week."

Buckley was only too eager to oblige. In November 1955, not yet thirty, he founded *National Review* and recruited both Kirk and Weaver to write for him. In its first issue, the magazine published its "credenda," or fundamental principles. First were its libertarian bona fides: "The growth of government—the dominant social feature of this century—must be fought relentlessly." When it engaged in anything beyond protecting the lives, liberty, and property of its citizens, *National Review*'s editors explained, the "activities of government tend to diminish freedom and hamper progress." They also warned of an intellectual and cultural "menace" in America, the purveyors of which sought to "impose upon the nation their modish fads and fallacies." If the credenda did not explicitly mention God, they neverthe-less made it clear that *National Review* was a magazine of, by, and for tradi-tionalists: In "the conflict between the Social Engineers, who seek to adjust mankind to conform with scientific utopias, and the disciples of Truth, who defend the organic moral order," there was no doubt on which side *National Review* stood.

Conservative Anticommunism

However forceful the magazine's libertarianism and traditionalism, it was anticommunism that became *National Review*'s hallmark. By the begin-ning of 1947, the Soviet Union had reneged on its promise to hold free elections in Warsaw; communist satellite governments had taken power in Poland, Romania, and Bulgaria; and a communist insurgency threat-ened Greece's royalist government. In February 1948, a Soviet-supported coup ousted the Czech president, bringing the last free country in Eastern Europe under Soviet control. Just a few months later, the Red Army cut off access to West Berlin. In September 1949, whatever security Americans had taken from their monopoly on nuclear weapons evaporated as U.S. planes detected an unusual concentration of radioactive isotopes over the Pacific Ocean, confirming that the Soviets, too, now had the bomb. The following month, having finally crushed the Nationalist government, communist rebel Mao Tse-tung established the People's Republic of China.

These developments were startling for all Americans, but for conser-vatives particularly so: Communism was the ultimate expression of the trends they feared in American liberalism. Government had reached mon-strous proportions in the Soviet Union; there were no more zealous social engineers than communists, who believed they could fashion a utopian society—and at the expense of religious truth. As Buckley had written, "I myself believe that the duel between Christianity and atheism is the most important in the world. I further believe that the struggle between individ-ualism and collectivism is the same struggle reproduced on another level." The Cold War was nothing less than the ultimate battle against the forces that libertarians and traditionalists most feared.

Anticommunism therefore served a practical as well as an existential function for the conservative movement, uniting libertarians and tradi-tionalists in a common cause. It also served to distinguish postwar conservatism from prewar conservatism, as the Cold War forced conservatives to permanently give up their insistence on isolation from Europe. Many conservatives still felt that American involvement in World War II had been a mistake—had not our intervention empowered the communists, just as men like Taft had warned?—but in the face of communism's viral spread across Europe and Asia, the neutralism of the past was no longer an option. The Cold War was not simply another instance of Europeans fighting among themselves for control of Western civilization; rather it was a fight for the existence of Western civilization itself. As one *National Review* contributor put it, "To advocate isolationism today, therefore, is to aid, albeit unconsciously, the Communist grand design of world domination."

While this recognition that American security was intertwined with that of other nations was a philosophical shift from the exceptionalism of earlier conservatives, it did not mark a complete break. In the postwar world, after all, America's power was so great relative to Europe's that there was no danger of the New World's sovereignty being subordinated to that of the Old. There was no risk that America would become the instrument of European machinations, as Washington and Jefferson had feared. NATO, for example, was unquestionably an entangling alliance, but because American troops comprised the bulk of its forces, and its supreme commander was to be an American, conservatives could rationalize it as an extension, not a dilution, of American power. Faced with an existential threat to the Republic, then, most conservatives were able to flip their isolationism inside out, transforming it into a unilateralism that was more suited to the times and nearly as psychologically satisfying as their earlier avoidance of European conflict. They were able to maintain an us-versus-them dichotomy even as the United States became the guarantor of not only its own security, but that of the entire free world.

Indeed, even as conservatives were redefining their foreign policy dichotomy they were also amplifying it. The centuries-old notion of American exceptionalism that had made conservatives wary of intervention in European affairs had originally been based not simply on practical considerations but on *moral* initiative. When the settlers landed on American soil, they had conceived of themselves as a divinely ordained beacon of liberty. One preacher said, "Here has our God . . . prepared an asylum for the oppressed in every part on Earth." As historian Walter McDougall has written, "Americans were a chosen people delivered from bondage to a Promised Land," which was nothing less than a "New Israel." This remarkable self-conception had profound theological implications. The mission of the colonists was millennial—to bring about a thousand-year-long Kingdom of God on Earth that would defeat the Antichrist.

After the American Revolution, this Manichaeanism became secularized, with the emphasis on the conflict between the liberty of the New World and the tyranny of the Old. But after World War II, conservatives resurrected the earlier religious aspect, painting the Cold War not only as a struggle between freedom and despotism, but as an apocalyptic battle between good and evil. The threat to the United States was not simply the Soviet Union, a country; it was communism, an ideology of godlessness whose collectivism diminished the value of the individual soul. This division of the world was reinforced by the orthodox Christianity of conservatism's intellectual leaders, for whom any political goal to create the perfect society represented the work of the Antichrist. As Buckley's *National Review* cofounder Brent Bozell explained, "The Christian eschaton is post-human"—or, in plain English, heaven can wait.

Conservative anticommunism was rife with religious language and imagery. In their premiere issue, *National Review*'s editors declared that the United States was "irrevocably at war" with "satanic" communism. Indeed, communists were ascribed many of the same traits as Satan; they were princes of lies with superhuman powers of deceit and manipulation. Apocalyptic rhetoric was de rigueur in the magazine's pages, with contributors even embracing the risk of all-out nuclear war if it would push back the Soviet devil.

Frank Meyer, one of *National Review*'s most prominent contributors, knew whereof he spoke. Like many of the magazine's writers and editors, he was an ex-communist who had seen the error of his ways. Born in New Jersey in 1909 and educated at Oxford University, Meyer was a severe-looking man who—as the title of his column, "Principles and Heresies," suggested—served as the arbiter of ideological and philosophical disputes within the conservative movement. It was his thinking and writing that eventually made it possible for traditionalists to philosophically lie down with libertarians based on the idea that, in order to promote virtue, man must have the freedom to seek his own salvation. ("The belief in virtue as the end of man's being," Meyer wrote, "implicitly recognizes the necessity of freedom to choose that end.") Meyer himself, though, leaned toward the traditionalists, dubbing *Ideas Have Consequences* the "fons et origo of the contemporary American conservative movement." His conservatism and his anticommunism stemmed principally from his belief in the transcendent. *"Effective* anti-Communism," he wrote—emphasizing the word "effective," because "of course everybody is 'against Communism'"—"requires an uncompromising understanding that Communism is evil, in comparison with which and against which our heritage, despite all its imperfections, is good." For Meyer, this Manichaeanism was the essential truth of the Cold War: Such moral clarity was essential to defending the United States.

The link between conservatism's religiosity and its anticommunism was epitomized in the figure of Whittaker Chambers. Short, heavy, and habitually ill clad (a Soviet spy once gave him fifty dollars to buy a decent suit), Chambers had been a member of the American Communist Party in the 1920s, writing first for the *Daily Worker* and then serving as editor of the *New Masses*. But just as his position in New York's burgeoning bohemian literary subculture was blooming, Chambers was summoned to a meeting with the Communist Party's national secretary, who told Chambers that he had been selected for "underground work." "What," Chambers asked, "does 'underground work' mean?" "They will tell you" was the only reply. "They" were the directors of the Soviet espionage apparatus, and ultimately, they would assign Chambers to serve the Glavnoye Razvedyvatelnoye Upravlenie, or GRU, the Red Army's intelligence unit. For the next five years, Chambers lived a life of aliases, clandestine rendezvous, and dead drops, eventually moving to Washington, where he photographed stolen government documents and relayed them to handlers in Moscow.

But as news of Stalin's purges seeped out of the Soviet Union in the late 1930s, Chambers experienced a profound crisis of conscience. In 1937 and 1938, he grew increasingly distraught as he contemplated the moral consequences of the crimes committed in the name of communism. Reading the autobiography of a Soviet technocrat who had been dragged off to the gulag for no apparent reason and later escaped to Finland, Chambers came to an inescapable conclusion: "This is evil, absolute evil. Of this evil I am a part." Accusing the revolution of immorality—indeed, conceiving of morality as anything other than what was good for the Communist Party—was heretical, but Chambers could not help himself. He began to pray. And then, as he walked toward a dark hall in his house one day, he was enveloped by an all-consuming silence that brought him to a halt. "In this organic hush," he later wrote, "a voice said with perfect distinctness: 'If you will fight for freedom, all will be well with you.'" It was as though a dam had burst: "There tore through me a transformation with the force of a river." Having heard the voice of God, Chambers was reborn a devout Christian—and a rabid anticommunist.

By the time his memoir, *Witness,* was published in 1952, Chambers was already a celebrity, having testified to the House Un-American Activities Committee against Alger Hiss, a former State Department official and alleged Soviet spy, in an attempt to inspire the nation to anticommunism. *Witness* itself became an instant bestseller and a touchstone of the Right. (Buckley, who was deeply moved by the book, would beg Chambers to join the staff of *National Review,* which he did, though only briefly.) It argued that the United States was at a "turning point in history." The book characterized the Cold War as a clash between "the two irreconcilable faiths of our time—Communism and Freedom," in which it would be "decided for generations whether all mankind is to become Communist, whether the whole world is to become free, or whether, in the struggle, civilization as we know it is to be completely destroyed or completely changed." At the core of America's struggle with communism lay the issue of faith; for the Cold War was not merely a struggle between superpowers, but a struggle between "irreconcilable opposites—God or Man, Soul or Mind, Freedom or Communism." As Chambers biographer Sam Tanenhaus has written, *Witness* was a call "not merely to arms but to Armageddon."

Containment

Standing in sharp contrast to the messianic, binary foreign policy of Whittaker Chambers and his right-wing devotees was that of George F. Kennan. A career Foreign Service officer who had joined the State Department after graduating from Princeton in 1925, Kennan was also fiercely anticommunist, having soured on Stalinism early in his training as a Sovietologist. Based in Riga, Latvia—the closest post the State Department had to Russia in the early 1930s—Kennan even opposed Roosevelt's diplomatic recognition of the communist regime in 1933, arguing that there could be no compromise between the United States and the Soviet Union and that "within twenty or thirty years either Russia will be capitalist or we shall be communist."

By the beginning of the Cold War, Kennan was one of the U.S. government's top Soviet experts. In February 1946, while temporarily in charge of the American embassy in Moscow, he received a State Department cable asking why Soviet leaders persisted in making anti-American statements. Kennan responded with a five-thousand-word telegram which argued that Russia had long been motivated by national insecurity—an insecurity it traditionally redressed through the destruction of its enemies. Marxism, which called for global revolution, had become the "perfect vehicle" for rationalizing this antagonistic relationship with the outside world. His conclusion was dire: "[W]e have here a political force committed fanatically to the belief that with the U.S. there can be no permanent modus vivendi, that it is desirable and necessary that the internal harmony of our society be disrupted, our traditional way of life be destroyed, the international authority of our state be broken if Soviet power is to be secure." The following year, he wrote, under the pseudonym "X," a widely read article for the journal *Foreign Affairs* that seemed to propose a global war on communism: "Soviet pressure against the free institutions of the Western world is something that can be contained by the adroit and vigilant application of counterforce at a series of constantly shifting geographical and political points, corresponding to the shifts and maneuvers of Soviet policy, but which cannot be charmed or talked out of existence."

On the surface, this sounded little different from the conservative analysis, and indeed, when Truman adopted Kennan's principle of "containment," he used absolutist language to support it. In March 1947, the president asked Congress for four hundred million dollars to help Greece and Turkey fight communist insurgencies. His speech painted a Manichaean picture in which "totalitarian regimes imposed upon free peoples, by direct or indirect aggression, undermine the foundations of international peace and hence the security of the United States." In what would become known as the Truman Doctrine, the president declared that "it must be the policy of the United States to support free peoples who are resisting attempted subjugation by armed minorities or by outside pressures." Subsequently, the administration pledged to fund the reconstruction of Europe via the Marshall Plan and to defend it militarily through NATO. In 1950, Truman commissioned a review of defense planning, known as NSC-68, which concluded that the Soviet Union is "animated by a new fanatic faith, antithetical to our own, and seeks to impose its absolute authority over the rest of the world."

Despite their own messianic rhetoric, liberals did not consider the Cold War a fundamentally religious conflict. They, too, believed the Soviet Union was tyrannical, but when they spoke of a grand battle between good and evil, they did so conscious that they were oversimplifying the nature of the Cold War. In an America that was tired of war, that had voted Republicans into control of Congress because of their promise to reduce taxes, liberals needed to garner support for a robust international presence, a draft, and billions of dollars in military expenditures to make containment credible. As Dean Acheson, then Truman's undersecretary of state, said in a speech to the Maryland Historical Society in November 1945: "I can state in three sentences what the 'popular' attitude is toward foreign policy today: 1. Bring the boys home. 2. Don't be a Santa Claus. 3. Don't be pushed around." The administration's problem was that it could not accomplish the first two goals while guaranteeing the third.

Rhetoric thus became vital to selling the administration's postwar foreign policy, and Acheson was one of its best practitioners. A graduate of Groton, Yale, and Harvard Law, he came to Washington in 1919 to clerk for Supreme Court Justice Louis D. Brandeis. Appointed secretary of state in 1949, Acheson would become a pariah to conservatives for the supposedly insufficient zeal of his anticommunism, for his defense of his friend Alger Hiss following Whittaker Chambers's accusations, and for his upper-crust manner, which offended the right wing's populist sensibilities. (One colleague told Acheson to shave off his bristly guardsman's mustache, whose tips were cantilevered over the corners of his mouth, just to improve his relations with conservative congressmen.)

Acheson had learned from his government service that it was often necessary to make arguments "clearer than truth" and that the fear of communism was one thing that motivated Congress to act. Truman had asserted, without qualification or caveat, that the United States must support free peoples under communist threat, suggesting that he would fight communism everywhere in a global ideological crusade. Acheson, however, did not take this promise literally; as he testified to Congress, he did not interpret the Truman Doctrine as a "crusade against ideology," nor did he think the United States should indiscriminately intervene in the affairs of other nations.

The president himself viewed his speech as a political sales pitch as much as a statement of American strategy. When Truman and his aides had briefed members of Congress three weeks earlier on the need to spend millions combating communism in the Mediterranean, Senator Arthur Vandenberg, who had recently converted to internationalism, had said, "Mr. President, the only way you are ever going to get this is to make a speech and scare the hell out of the country." Truman took the advice—and Acheson drafted the speech. Clark Clifford, a close Truman adviser, had sharpened the rhetoric, all the while asking himself, "Is this speech saleable?" Finally, the president removed any vestige of equivocation, changing "I believe it should be the policy of the United States . . ." to "I believe it *must* be. . . ." When Secretary of State George Marshall and Chip Bohlen, a top Soviet expert, objected to an advance copy of the address, complaining that there was "too much rhetoric," Truman responded that, unless he framed the four-hundred-million-dollar request as a matter of life or death, Congress would not approve it.

NSC-68 was similarly exaggerated. Acheson later explained that the goal of the document had been "to bludgeon the mass mind of 'top government' so that not only could the president make a decision, but that the decision could be carried out." The document that resulted was just as stark in its portrayal of a perilous global landscape as the Truman Doctrine speech had been. It made statements like: "The implacable purpose of the slave state is to eliminate the challenge of freedom." Seeing a draft of NSC-68, Bohlen again complained about the language, but Acheson dismissed his concerns. If the document's tone was apocalyptic, so be it; the important thing was to provoke action.

There was enormous risk in overselling the anticommunist cause. As the mass mind of top government was bludgeoned, it was damaged, losing whatever modest ability it had had to distinguish rhetoric from reality. Taken at face value, the notions that America was obligated to help free peoples everywhere resist subjugation (as per the Truman Doctrine) and that containment should be a chiefly military enterprise (as per NSC-68) meant that the United States would commit itself to deploying troops to any country that threatened to go communist, whether or not the United States had any vital interest there. In the 1960s, that absolutism led two Democratic presidents to involve the United States in Vietnam. But containment as a policy was intended to be nuanced, not absolutist. It was not meant to be applied universally, and the Truman administration did not use it in that fashion.

Take China, for example. For more than twenty years the Nationalist government, led by Chiang Kai-shek, had been trying to eradicate a persistent and growing communist rebellion led by the popular Mao Tse-tung. After Japan surrendered in August 1945, President Truman had hoped to reconcile the Nationalists and the communists in a coalition government, but continued U.S. aid to the Nationalists antagonized Mao while convincing Chiang he could win the civil war. He could not. By 1948, Mao had mustered a revolutionary army of two million men, and Chiang's repeated military blunders assured a communist victory. On October 1, 1949, Mao founded the People's Republic of China, and Chiang fled to Taiwan.

Conservatives were aghast; hundreds of millions of people and an enormous part of Asia had suddenly gone communist. Truman, by contrast, was relieved. To him, China was a peripheral concern compared with Europe, and for several years he had wanted to cultivate an alliance with Mao in order to pressure Stalin, but congressional conservatives like Senator Bill Knowland had insisted on sending Chiang massive quantities of economic and military aid. On March 3, 1949, Truman approved a National Security Council paper that advocated the restoration of "ordinary economic relations between China on the one hand and Japan and the Western world on the other" in order to "exploit frictions between the Chinese Communist regime and the USSR should they arise." In contrast to conservatives, the Truman administration would engage evil if it served America's strategic interests: "If the Devil himself runs China, if he is an independent devil, that is infinitely better than if he is a stooge of Moscow, or China comes under Russia," Acheson said.

A similar realism perfused Truman's policy after North Korea invaded the South in June 1950. Truman quickly decided that the United States would intervene militarily to push back Kim Il Sung's troops, but he wanted to limit the war to the Korean peninsula. In August 1950, he sent Averell Harriman to Tokyo with a message for General Douglas MacArthur, who was overseeing the reconstruction of Japan and would command the American response: "Tell him two things. One, I'm going to do everything I can to give him what he wants in the way of support; and, secondly, I want you to tell him I don't want to get into a war with the Chinese communists." MacArthur agreed, but Harriman noted that he wanted to involve Chiang Kai-shek in the fight: "He has a strange idea that we should back anybody who will fight Communism, even though he would not give an argument why the Generalissimo's fighting Communists would be a contribution toward the effective dealing with the Communists of China." Indeed, as Harriman was leaving, MacArthur said, "We should fight Communists everyplace—fight them like hell!"

Once he had driven back North Korean troops, MacArthur was briefly allowed to pursue his dream of a war against communism when Truman gave him permission to push north of the 38th parallel—the dividing line between North and South Korea that Kim's forces had violated. The results were disastrous. Despite Truman's admonitions and Chinese premier Chou En-lai's warning that U.S. troops should keep their distance, MacArthur surged north to the Yalu River, North Korea's border with China. In response, three hundred thousand Chinese troops stormed into Korea, routing the American forces, which fled the onslaught.

Truman, having learned from MacArthur's overzealousness, wanted to hold the South and declare the purpose of the war essentially fulfilled. But MacArthur was insistent on widening the war to attack mainland China, a tactic he felt would "doom Red China to the risk of imminent military collapse." He advocated using Chiang's Nationalist forces to reinforce his own in South Korea, blockading the coast, and bombing Chinese communications, transportation, and industrial nodes. Perhaps Nationalist forces could even invade the PRC, MacArthur suggested. "There is," he famously said, "no substitute for victory." Truman ultimately fired MacArthur—who quickly became a hero to conservatives—clearly demonstrating that the White House's vision of the Cold War was more limited than the messianism of the right wing.

This must have come as a relief to George Kennan, who had worried that his *Foreign Affairs* article had poured gasoline on the administration's smoldering anticommunism. In 1947, although he supported aid to Greece and Turkey, Kennan objected to Truman's address to Congress because of the speech's black-and-white dichotomies. Dividing the world "into communist and 'free-world' components [avoided] specific recognition of specific differences among countries," he complained. Kennan had never conceived of containment as a global doctrine, but rather had intended it to protect Western Europe and Japan—he did not, for instance, consider the "loss" of China to be catastrophic. Kennan also insisted that he had envisioned containment as primarily a psychological and economic, not military, campaign against the Soviet Union. As anti-Soviet rhetoric grew and the country armed for confrontation, he worried that the United States, as a democracy, was particularly ill suited to conduct this kind of nuanced effort; instead, vulnerable to demagoguery, it was likely to turn to war, the ultimate expression of absolutism. War with the Soviets, he felt, was unnecessary.

Key to this optimism was Kennan's interpretation of the role that ideology played in Soviet foreign policy: Although Marxism was an integral part of that policy, it had essentially become a justification for the power sought by the regime. It was, he wrote, a "fig leaf" covering the naked totalitarianism of Stalin's dictatorship and the legacy of Russian expansionism, which long preceded the Bolshevik Revolution. Power, not ideology—and certainly not "evil"—was the ultimate force driving the Soviet Union. According to Kennan, "It is a matter of indifference to Moscow whether a given area is 'communistic' or not. All things being equal, Moscow might prefer to see it communized, although even that is debatable. But the main thing is that it should be amenable to Moscow's influence." In 1947, he went so far as to argue that, even if American communists took over the United States, "the only reaction of the men in the Kremlin would be to stamp it as a form of fascism" unless the revolutionaries were under their direct control.

The distinction between Marxism and Russian nationalism was lost on minds less supple than Kennan's, but it had enormous ramifications. If ideology was not going to force the Soviet Union into a "do or die" confrontation with the United States, Kennan argued, then "[t]here is no reason, in theory, why it should not be possible for us to contain the Russians indefinitely by confronting them firmly and politely with superior strength at every turn." Such coexistence might not be amicable—Russia would remain a "rival not a partner"—but it need not be bloody. The Cold War could just as well be a cold peace.

Liberation

To conservatives, this was nothing less than apostasy: If communism was evil, then coexistence was a moral impossibility and containment a sin, effectively a truce with the devil. "[E]vil is not something that can be condescended to, waved aside or smiled away," Chambers wrote in *Witness*. "Evil can only be fought." Similarly, *National Review*'s editors declared, "We consider 'coexistence' with communism neither desirable nor possible, nor honorable." In *The Shame and Glory of the Intellectuals*, conservative philosopher Peter Viereck wrote, "For the millions of slaves behind the Iron Curtain, 'peaceful' coexistence means not peace but a continuation of torture and murder. . . . How long today can the Christian-Judaic moral basis of American freedom survive . . . 'containment'?"

But if containment was morally defective, what was the alternative? Save preventive nuclear strikes during the brief period when the United States had an atomic monopoly (an option advocated by some conservatives), war was not an option—not a wise one, certainly. The Soviet Union had armed forces posted in Europe, and the American public had no appetite for a remobilization that would undermine the postwar economic boom, plunge the country once again into privation, and likely kill hundreds of thousands, if not millions.

The conservative retort to containment was proposed by James Burnham, a professor of philosophy at New York University. Like many of his fellow conservatives, he had once been a socialist, working in the 1930s with communist unions in Detroit and with Trotsky's Fourth International. And like many others, he had left the movement after becoming disillusioned by Stalin's crimes and the Soviet Union's alliance with Nazi Germany. In the early 1940s, he wrote two thoughtful books, *The Managerial Revolution* and *The Machiavellians,* in which he wrestled with socialism's role in the world. As he studied the Soviet Union during the war, however, his views took a turn toward the paranoid and the absolute, and as one war ended, he primed himself for another. In 1947, he published *The Struggle for the World,* in which he argued that the Soviet Union was bent on world domination, with only the United States blocking its path. The struggle would be one to the death: "You can get along with communism in only one way: by capitulating to it."

Having decided that "the Third World War had begun," Burnham became a crusader, and Kennan, as the de facto author of containment, became his chief target. Kennan's problem, according to conservatives, was that he saw the Cold War in traditional, realpolitik terms, in which international relations could be understood as the struggle among states for power. Such a model, they argued, accounted for neither the importance of morality nor the importance of ideas. In *The Struggle for the World,* Burnham wrote that, while Kennan might have been the Truman administration's top Sovietologist (he "has read an unusual amount for an active member of a government Department," Burnham condescended), he did not appreciate that communism invalidated traditional models of international relations.

Containment was unacceptable to Burnham because it essentially allowed for no change in the status quo; it was a defensive strategy. While containment did seek to limit the further expansion of Soviet power, it acceded to its presence in areas that were already under communist domination, in particular Eastern Europe. It was, in effect, a policy of "heads we tie, tails you win." Worse, Burnham felt that it wasn't working. "It is hard," he wrote, "to see even what it means to try to 'contain' a universalistic, militant, secular religion, based on a vast land mass inhabited by 800 million humans, which has irrevocably set itself the objective of monolithic world domination, and which already exists and acts inside every nation throughout the world." Containment, according to Burnham, was simply appeasement.

By using the word "appeasement," Burnham was tapping a powerful rhetorical vein. "Appeasement" was, of course, the term used to describe Neville Chamberlain's 1938 agreement with Hitler at Munich. When Hitler did not adhere to the pact, Chamberlain was tarred by history as the incarnation of weakness in the face of aggression. Later, Burnham would up the ante by describing containment as a "Yalta strategy," referring to the 1945 meeting between Roosevelt, Churchill, and Stalin at which the Soviet Union was allowed control of Eastern Europe in exchange for promising to hold free elections, which it did not. Yalta was thus a symbol of, at best, gullibility and, at worst, the liberal willingness to appease tyrants. Any form of negotiation with the Soviets, Burnham wrote, constituted a Yalta strategy.

Instead of containment, Burnham proposed liberation. He believed that, if the United States had just set itself to the task after World War II, even a "mild initiative" could have prevented the Soviets from maintaining control of Eastern Europe (an optimistic view, given the millions of Red Army troops stationed there as of May 1945). Now, he insisted, we must not simply contain communism; we must roll it back. We must aim to secure "freedom for all the peoples and nations now under communist domination, including the Russian people." Where containment was defensive, liberation would be offensive. It would be not just an economic or military effort, though it would be those, but a *political* effort: one that would include supporting exile governments, outlawing communism domestically, and fomenting unrest and harassing communists in Eastern

Europe. There would be no compromise, no negotiation, no attempt to achieve a modus vivendi with the Soviets. The aim was regime change—not just in Eastern Europe, but in the Soviet Union itself.

William Buckley loved Burnham's work, and in the summer of 1950 while his bride, Pat, basked in the Hawaiian sun, he had spent his honeymoon reading Burnham's latest book. So when he was assembling a masthead for *National Review,* Buckley went to recruit Burnham at his pre–Revolutionary War house in Kent, Connecticut. Burnham readily agreed to write a column, which he called "The Third World War"—emphasizing the totality of the conflict and the need for victory.

The "Failures" of Containment

By that standard, of course, the Truman administration had been a miserable failure. Not only had it lost China, it had accepted stalemate in Korea. But the Republicans were no more successful. Initially, it seemed that the Eisenhower administration would take up the cause of liberation because its Secretary of State was the moralistic John Foster Dulles. Dulles was an establishment sort—a graduate of Princeton, senior partner at Sullivan & Cromwell, member of the Council on Foreign Relations and the Century Association—who had even served as a foreign policy adviser to Truman. But he was also the son of a minister who, in 1937, had reembraced his faith. In many ways, he was closer to Whittaker Chambers than to Dean Acheson, for from its beginning, Dulles saw the Cold War in religious terms. In 1950, he published *War or Peace,* in which he argued that "Soviet Communism starts with an atheistic godless premise. Everything else flows from that premise."

In 1952, Dulles wrote an article for *Life* magazine titled "A Policy of Boldness" in which he argued that, despite enormous expenditures and military commitments, the Truman administration was devoted merely to holding the line against communism. "We are not working, sacrificing, and spending in order to be able to live *without* this peril," he wrote, "but to be able to live *with* it, presumably forever. . . . Ours are treadmill policies which, at best, might keep us in the same place until we drop exhausted." In place of the reactive "emergency measures" of containment, Dulles urged a political offensive backed by nuclear weapons. "There is a moral or natural law not made by man which determines right and wrong. . . . This law has been trampled by the Soviet rulers, and for that violation they can and should be made to pay." He argued that the United States should make clear its goal of "liberation" of the peoples under communist rule.

In 1952, Dulles was asked to write the GOP's foreign policy platform. Robert Taft thought that because Dulles was a moralist advising the moderate Eisenhower, he would be able to identify areas of agreement between the conservative and pragmatic wings of the party. The result, however, was a lot of moralism and very little moderation. Eschewing the bipartisan approach to foreign policy that had marked the Republican platform during the 1944 and 1948 Dewey races—and, indeed, his own career to date—Dulles targeted all the Democratic weak spots softened by conservative attack. The final document declared that Republicans would "repudiate all commitments contained in secret understandings such as Yalta which aid communist enslavement." It, too, advocated a strategy of liberation: "[W]e shall again make liberty into a beacon light of hope that will penetrate the dark places. . . . It will mark the end of the negative, futile and immoral policy of 'containment' which abandons countless human beings to a despotism and godless terrorism."

Despite what Dulles or his platform advocated, however, the chief goal of the man who had led Allied forces during the last world war was to keep the United States out of another one. President Eisenhower made explicit his preference for containment over liberation only a few months after he took office. In July 1953, he convened the "Solarium Exercise," in which three teams were assigned to argue for different approaches to the Soviet Union: Team A for containment; Team B for an aggressive push against communism in China and the Eastern bloc; and Team C for full rollback, even at the risk of nuclear war. The exercise was supposedly an open policy debate, but Eisenhower stacked the deck in favor of Team A. Dulles had recently fired George Kennan, yet Eisenhower brought him back to lead the procontainment team and praised him in front of his competitors. The exercise demonstrated to senior administration officials that liberation was an extraordinarily risky venture and they agreed to continue a policy of containment.

Buckley soon concluded that Eisenhower had a "deficient understanding" of communism. On New Year's Eve 1955, Brent Bozell wrote that, after Eisenhower's inauguration, he had believed "that the new Eisenhower administration means to anchor its foreign policy to a firm moral foundation: it intends to encourage liberation operations against the Communist empire." However, the tally of Eisenhower's accomplishments three years later made him reach for a stiff drink: Ike had agreed to an armistice that left North Korea in communist hands; he had ceded North Vietnam to Ho Chi Minh; his spokesmen were twittering about peaceful coexistence; and he had said, with regard to Taiwan's aims to "liberate" mainland China, that "the United States is not going to be a party to an aggressive war." By 1958, *National Review*'s Meyer wrote that we had been yielding to the Soviet Union for ten years, "step by step and point by point."

Nowhere was this made clearer than in Hungary. In February 1956, Khrushchev had taken the dramatic step of secretly denouncing Stalin and his crimes at the Communist Party Congress. Seeing a ripe opportunity for a little psychological warfare, the CIA, having obtained a copy, disseminated the speech widely. Khrushchev's renunciation of Stalin's policies emboldened democrats throughout Eastern Europe, and in October 1956, Hungarian students began demonstrating, demanding that the Soviet Union withdraw its troops from the country and allow Hungarian statesman Imre Nagy to assume power. Khrushchev agreed, but when, on October 31, Nagy declared that Hungary would withdraw from the Warsaw Pact, the Soviets moved in, tanks rolling through the streets of Budapest. As the hopelessly outgunned Hungarian rebels desperately radioed for help, the United States did nothing, having determined that no country in Eastern Europe was worth the risk of a nuclear World War III. The dream of liberation, along with thirty thousand Hungarians, died in Budapest. Conservatives were aghast: Apparently, Buckley wrote, nothing could disturb the "tranquil world of Dwight Eisenhower."*

Worse, following a scare in which the United States nearly went to war with China over a few tiny islands, Eisenhower agreed to meet with Khrushchev. In July 1955, the two leaders convened in Switzerland for the first U.S.-Soviet summit since the Potsdam Conference in 1945. From the summit emerged the "spirit of Geneva," a hope that peaceful coexistence could be achieved. Burnham, however, insisted that the Soviets interpreted Eisenhower's willingness to meet as evidence of "imperialist disintegration" and that they were merely making a "tactical move . . . designed to

---

*Ironically, Burnham, who had done more than anyone to advance the doctrine of liberation, balked at intervening in Hungary—a stance that caused substantial uproar at *National Review*.

disarm" the United States. Summits, according to Burnham, were a "barbarous practice" that served only to legitimate communist rulers. "Any gangster's rule is strengthened if he can get his picture taken along with the Mayor, the Chief of Police, and the Parson," he wrote. (Meyer put the very term "summit meeting" in scare quotes.) Yet Eisenhower persisted in his policies, meeting with Khrushchev several more times. By 1959, when Khrushchev actually came to the United States itself, conservatives had had enough—and William F. Buckley, Jr., took to Carnegie Hall.

Conclusion

The new conservatism crafted by Buckley and his cohort was historically unique, in part because it was defined so heavily by its anticommunism, an imperative that had only seized American foreign policy in the mid-1940s. Anticommunism, combined with Buckley's intellectual dexterity and the ideological stylings of Frank Meyer, also made it possible for the contradictory impulses of libertarianism and traditionalism to be fused with it into a stable and potent trinity. The new conservative approach to foreign policy nevertheless drew heavily on a traditional American exceptionalism, with its strong tendencies to see the world in terms of us versus them and good versus evil. While that exceptionalism had waxed and waned over the years as it was tested and altered, in the new conservatism, it was resurrected in a form at least as potent as the original.

The moralism that underlay it was a potent draught. In moderation, it could motivate and even embolden. It was in such fortifying doses that the Truman administration presented a moral view of the Cold War to the American people, as a means of securing their approval for aid to Greece and Turkey, the formation of NATO, and the funding of the Marshall Plan. But, in excessive quantities, "moral clarity" was intoxicating, blurring reality, and conflating different actors and their disparate motivations. Conservatives viewed communism as monolithic, which prevented them from predicting, or capitalizing on, events like the split between China and the Soviet Union.

Conflation was not a problem to which liberals were immune: U.S. involvement in Vietnam was, in large part, a function of the belief in the indivisibility of communism, which led us to regard Ho Chi Minh as a tool of Moscow and Beijing. But if liberals later vulgarized the carefully calibrated anticommunism of the Truman years—in part out of fear that they would be charged with losing another country to communism—they also, as we shall see, ultimately renounced their flirtation with absolutism. More important, though, moralism never led liberals, even hawkish ones, to the extreme conclusions adapted by conservatives.

For one thing, liberals never abandoned the idea of coexistence. Speaking at the National War College in late 1949, Dean Acheson said, "Today, you hear much talk of absolutes . . . that two systems such as ours and that of the Russians cannot exist in the same world . . . that one is good and one is evil, and good and evil cannot exist in the world. . . . [But] good and evil have existed in this world since Adam and Eve went out of the garden of Eden. . . . That is what all of us must learn to do in the United States: to limit objectives, to get ourselves away from the search for the absolute." Nor did liberals abandon negotiation as a viable tool of U.S. foreign policy. Even NSC-68, a militaristic document whose purpose was to prepare the United States for war with the Soviet Union, acknowledged that "it is essential . . . that we always leave open the possibility of negotiation with the U.S.S.R. A diplomatic freeze . . . tends to defeat the very purposes of 'containment' because it raises tensions at the same time that it makes Soviet retractions and adjustments in the direction of moderated behavior more difficult."

By contrast, conservatives thought that it was "silly, of course, to discuss peace with communists," as Burnham dismissively wrote. A willingness to negotiate with the Soviets was a sign of the liberal "syndrome"—that is, it was a symptom of a disease. Conservatives found little purpose in conducting diplomatic relations with communist states. They did not want negotiation, they did not want coexistence, and they did not want a modus vivendi. What they wanted, in the phrase of Robert Strausz-Hupé, was a "forward strategy for America," an offensive spirit. "Containment or liberation?" as Burnham put the question in the title of his popular 1952 book, was in fact no question at all. The only true question was whether Americans were strong willed enough to do the job. Burnham lamented that the nation possessed a strong "anti-ideological tendency," a preference for pragmatism. This would not do in the face of communism. This was no simple matter of conflict and cooperation in international relations; we were met at Armageddon.

None of conservatism's critiques might have mattered, but for two factors that made its rejection of coexistence vitally important. The first was that the conservative movement was about to move from the intellectual fringe to the political mainstream, enabling it to translate theory into action. The second was that the stakes of the Cold War were too high to be reduced to a hotheaded moralistic dispute between good and evil. In the nuclear age, it would be all too easy for Armageddon to morph from religious metaphor into earthly reality.

Chapter Two

CANDIDATES

McGEORGE BUNDY, the president's national security adviser, was hosting a dinner party when the call came. At about 8:30 P.M. on the evening of Monday, October 15, 1962, Ray Cline, the CIA's Deputy Director for Intelligence, phoned to report that American U-2 planes flying over Cuba the previous day had spotted newly constructed launch pads for Soviet nuclear missiles. The deployment was a brazen bit of saber rattling—President John F. Kennedy had warned the Soviets against doing this very thing the previous month—and Bundy would spend the next thirteen days debating how to parry the move. For the moment, however, he faced a more immediate question, one presumably unique in the annals of political and social etiquette: Should he interrupt his dinner and rush to inform President Kennedy that the Soviets were on the verge of deploying nuclear weapons a mere ninety miles from American soil, or should he return to his guests and do his best to maintain a genial sangfroid, saving the news for the morning?

Bundy decided to wait. For one thing, the surveillance photographs taken by the U-2s were not yet ready for Kennedy. For another, a hastily called evening meeting was sure to raise eyebrows. If he abruptly left for the White House with guest and Soviet expert Chip Bohlen in tow, the other foreign policy hands at the table would certainly know something was up. And this needed to be kept quiet, at least until Kennedy had a chance to think through the ramifications. Besides, Bundy knew that Kennedy was tired, having just returned to Washington from a congressional campaign swing through New York. The coming days promised to be some of the most trying for an administration that had already been challenged by several high-profile foreign policy crises. The president, he thought, would need his rest.

As the Cuban missile crisis entered its first day, the arms race was proceeding at full tilt. The Soviets had exploded their first atomic bomb in August 1949, followed in 1953 by their first thermonuclear device.* By the time Kennedy assumed the presidency, the Russians had enough weapons to inflict a retaliatory strike even if we launched our entire arsenal at them first. Indeed, Kennedy had ridden to the presidency in part by stoking fears that the United States had fallen behind the Soviet Union in the development of missile technology. On taking office, he ordered a dramatic buildup not only of America's conventional forces but of its nuclear arsenal as well, adding to the fleet of bombers, intercontinental ballistic missiles (ICBMs), and submarine-launched ballistic missiles (SLBMs).

The Cuban missiles did not really give the Soviets a military advantage over the United States. (As Kennedy himself prodded his advisers, "What difference does it make? They've got enough to blow us up now anyway.") But they *looked* bad, and in the superpower contest, a contest fought largely through symbols and proxies, appearances mattered greatly—both abroad and at home. Kennedy had already suffered one humiliation in Cuba with the failed Bay of Pigs invasion the previous year, and he feared not only the strategic consequences of the crisis but also the political impact on his presidency and the midterm congressional elections, which were only three weeks away. On October 22, 1962, Kennedy addressed the nation live on television, announcing a blockade of the island and demanding that Soviet premier Nikita Khrushchev remove the missiles.

On the tensest day of the crisis, a Soviet surface-to-air missile shot down an American U-2 plane over Cuba, killing the pilot, and the Joint Chiefs of Staff demanded retaliatory air strikes. A few hours later, another U-2 strayed into Soviet airspace near Siberia, in an area where the Soviets based many of their ICBMs, suggesting that we were scouting for a first strike. At one point, a U.S. spy in Moscow telephoned his American handlers to warn that war was imminent. Neither side wanted war over Cuba, but any of these incidents could have triggered a response that could in turn have quickly escalated to a nuclear exchange. As Khrushchev wrote to Kennedy during this period, "Should war indeed break out, it would not be in our power to contain or stop it, for such is the logic of war."

---

*Whereas some nuclear weapons (including the first U.S. and Soviet bombs) generate their explosive power by splitting atoms—a process known as fission—thermonuclear weapons use a fissile explosion to compress a core of hydrogen isotopes, releasing energy in a process known as fusion. Fusion weapons can have far greater power.

Kennedy himself estimated the chances of war to be between one in three and one in two. As a precaution, he recalled his traveling wife and children to Washington so they could join him in an underground bunker should Moscow launch its nuclear arsenal. The U.S. military went to DEFCON 2—its highest level of alert short of actual war—for the first, and only, time during the Cold War. The American public was riveted on the drama, and Billy Graham preached about "the end of the world." With good reason: A nuclear exchange could have killed one hundred million Americans, ending, if not the world, certainly the United States.

In the end, war was averted only by compromise. Kennedy publicly promised not to invade Cuba if the Soviets removed their missiles. And he sent his brother, Attorney General Robert F. Kennedy, to tell the Soviet ambassador that we would quietly reciprocate by withdrawing U.S. missiles from Turkey, near the Soviet border. In a remarkable success for U.S. foreign policy, the president had thus prevented a nuclear conflict with little cost to the United States—he had wanted to replace the missiles in Turkey with the new submarine-based Polaris, in any case.

At least one man, however, thought that Kennedy's "resolution" of the crisis was a national travesty. Barry Goldwater, an aggressively anticommunist Republican senator from Arizona, was appalled that the president had made any sort of concession to the Soviets (and he likely wasn't even aware of the secret quid pro quo to remove missiles from Turkey) and angry that we had forfeited our right to invade Cuba. "We locked Castro's Communism into Latin America and threw away the key to its removal," Goldwater said. To the senator, the boy president had appeased the communist regime, just as he had the year before when he had offered Castro five hundred bulldozers if he would release prisoners captured during the Bay of Pigs fiasco—a trade Goldwater had called "surrender to blackmail."

This was the standard conservative take on the resolution of the most dangerous episode in human history. Goldwater's conservative bona fides were without parallel among national politicians. He was a libertarian who believed that "man's political freedom is illusory if he is dependent for his economic needs on the State," and he was a traditionalist who venerated "revealed truths." He had close ties to conservative intellectuals: Brent Bozell (William F. Buckley, Jr.'s Yale debate partner, *National Review* cofounder, and brother-in-law) ghostwrote Goldwater's right-wing manifesto *The Conscience of a Conservative*. That book, buoyed by a growing

malaise about the country's moral direction during the calorie-free politics of the Eisenhower years, sold millions of copies, making Goldwater
a household name and pushing conservatism into the American political bloodstream. Aided by demographic shifts in the South and West that
helped the conservative wing of the Republican Party, Goldwater rode his
growing fame to the 1964 GOP convention, where he defeated moderate
Nelson Rockefeller to win the party's nomination. For the first time, the
conservative movement had a real political leader.

Like the conservatives who worshipped him, Goldwater embodied
the new American exceptionalism. In the 1960s and 1970s, the ramifications of that worldview—the hatred of containment and the status quo,
the emphasis on rollback and victory, the rejection of negotiations—came
to rest particularly heavily on arms control. The Cuban missile crisis
was a crucial case test: If conservatives rejected accommodation with
the Soviets simply because it allowed a modest threat like Fidel Castro to
remain in power, even when the very existence of the United States was
at stake, it was doubtful they would condescend to negotiation under any
circumstances. It demonstrated that, to conservatives, the rollback of
communism mattered more than controlling nuclear weapons or preventing their use.

As moderate Democrats and Republicans alike sought to stabilize the
nuclear relationship between the superpowers, Goldwater and other conservatives consistently objected. While they often targeted their arguments
at a particular agreement, the treaties themselves were never the issue;
their true aim was to halt any steps toward coexistence with the Soviet
Union. Regime change would always be more important than nuclear
security, and nothing quite said "victory is impossible" like "mutual
assured destruction."

Goldwater and Arms Control

Goldwater, like his fellow conservatives, was an absolutist. His most famous
quote, delivered at the 1964 Republican Convention—"[E]xtremism in
the defense of liberty is no vice . . . moderation in the pursuit of justice is
no virtue"—cast both the ends and the means of politics in moral terms. It
was a philosophy Goldwater applied abroad as well as at home. He saw the
"Communist War"—not the "Cold War"—as a fight against an ideological

movement, not a nation. In such a conflict, there could be no neutrality, and there could be no compromise. "We are at war with an evil, and the evil is communism."

The reason that the United States was not winning this war—the reason America had "lost" China, abandoned Hungary, and accepted stalemate in Korea—was that it had not grasped the true nature of the threat. Just as it was to William F. Buckley, Jr., and his colleagues at *National Review*, the status quo was unacceptable to Goldwater, and therefore so was the strategy of containment. Victory was the only acceptable goal in any conflict, and he was flabbergasted that anyone would think otherwise with respect to a struggle as epochal as the Cold War. "I doubt if any United States Senator or government official—ever before in the history of our Republic—has been called upon to make a *case for victory* in a conflict where everything that the United States stands for today—or ever stood for in the past—is at stake." In 1962, Goldwater wrote a book in response to a George Kennan–like defense of containment made by Senator J. William Fulbright, fittingly titled *Why Not Victory?*

In *Why Not Victory?* Goldwater argued that merely "daring to win" would take the United States a long way toward defeating the Soviet Union. Our greatest handicap was that we simply did not believe that the struggle against communism was the "central political fact of our time." Often, however, Goldwater contradicted himself. For example, although he reassured readers that nuclear war with the Soviets was unlikely—Moscow would attack only if it thought the USSR was losing the Cold War—he wanted America to strive for victory, and by that logic, a successful foreign policy would lead to war. At another point, Goldwater wrote that U.S. policy was intended to protect America and advance freedom; because communism prevented the advance of freedom, he continued, America would not be safe until it defeated the communist threat. At the same time, he cautioned that we ought not support self-determination in third world countries when a fair election would produce a communist regime. In other words, we must support freedom except when it advanced communism, because communism retards the spread of freedom.

If some of his reasoning was tortured, Goldwater was certain of one thing: In the quest for victory, negotiation was anathema. Indeed, in *The Conscience of a Conservative*, he surrounded the word itself with quotation marks—"negotiation"—as though the very concept were suspect. Not

only did Goldwater oppose talks on specific issues, such as the status of
Berlin; he wanted to cut off all diplomatic ties with communist countries
because those relations provided "moral support to the very regimes we
mean to defeat." U.S.-Soviet summits were therefore the ultimate sign not
only of weakness, but of moral cowardice. Referring to the same Khrushchev visit that had rendered Buckley apoplectic in 1959, Goldwater wrote,
"A craven fear of death is entering the American consciousness; so much
so that many recently felt that honoring the chief despot himself was the
price we had to pay to avoid nuclear destruction"—phrasing which suggested that Goldwater would rather be dead than even talk to a Red.

Soon these convictions manifested in opposition to Kennedy's efforts
at nuclear diplomacy. John F. Kennedy was an unlikely arms control pio-
neer. In the 1960 campaign, the young Massachusetts senator had tried to
run to Richard Nixon's right on foreign policy issues, bemoaning the loss
of China, warning of a missile gap with the Soviets, and accusing Nixon of
ceding Cuba to the communists. His rhetoric was absolutist: The United
States would "pay any price" and "oppose any foe" to further the cause
of freedom. Upon taking office, he engaged in an immense buildup of
military might—including nuclear might. And, of course, one of his first
foreign policy ventures was an attempt to roll back communism in Cuba
via the ill-fated Bay of Pigs invasion. It was under Kennedy that the line
between Truman's targeted anticommunism (which differentiated vital
American interests from peripheral ones) and the Right's quasireligious
view of the Cold War (which recognized no distinction between communism in Russia and that in China or Yugoslavia) began to blur. President
Kennedy and Vice President Lyndon B. Johnson, put on the defensive by
conservatives' incessant accusations of communist appeasement, eventually forgot that much of Truman's rhetoric about a global showdown
between good and evil was just that. Applied literally, as conservatives
demanded, it led us into Vietnam.

Even at its most extreme, however, the anticommunism of liberals like
Kennedy and his establishment compatriots, including Republicans like
Bundy, never rejected negotiation. Kennedy attacked the idea that "we
have only two choices: appeasement or war, suicide or surrender, humiliation or holocaust, to be either Red or dead." The Cold War, he believed,
was marked by such complexity that it sometimes shaded into paradox.
He was a pragmatist who believed that negotiation with the Soviets could

be fruitful because "national interest is more powerful than ideology," thereby rejecting one of conservatism's central Cold War tenets. In a September 1963 speech seen as an attack on Goldwater, Kennedy said, "We must recognize that foreign policy in the modern world does not lend itself to simple black-and-white choices of good or evil." Because he regarded the Cold War as a traditional power struggle, not an apocalyptic moral showdown, he did not feel the need to overthrow the USSR before he could talk to it. After all, the two countries shared a pressing interest: avoiding nuclear war.

The superpowers' competition in atomic weapons disturbed Kennedy deeply. In December 1959, he gave a speech lamenting that the United States and the Soviet Union together were "in a position to exterminate all human life seven times over." From this somber truth he concluded, "Both sides in this fateful struggle must come to know, sooner or later, that the price of running this arms race to the end is death—for both." Kennedy devoted a quarter of his inaugural address to calling for a "quest for peace" in which the United States and the Soviet Union would "formulate serious and precise proposals for the inspection and control of arms—and bring the absolute power to destroy other nations under the absolute control of all nations." In September 1961, he signed legislation—legislation he had first championed as a senator—establishing the Arms Control and Disarmament Agency, which gave those who sought to constrain the arms race an official voice in policy making. And that same month, he gave a speech on disarmament to the United Nations in which he called for a "peace race," promising that "we shall never negotiate out of fear, [but that] we shall never fear to negotiate."

Kennedy's chief arms control goal was a treaty banning the testing of nuclear weapons. He believed that a test ban would not only discourage the Soviets from trying to match the size of our nuclear arsenal by demonstrating our willingness to end the arms race, but would also dissuade other countries from developing nuclear weapons. He was also gravely concerned about the environmental and health effects of the hundreds of U.S. and Soviet nuclear tests that had already been conducted. The human cost of testing had been growing as a political issue since March 1954, when a fifteen-megaton American H-bomb explosion in the Western Pacific produced unexpectedly high fallout, poisoning those nearby, triggering a panic in Japan, and increasing radiation levels as far away as

Nevada. Just three weeks after his inauguration, Kennedy flew by helicopter to the Maryland headquarters of the Atomic Energy Commission for a briefing on nuclear issues, and by March, the administration was holding high-level meetings to formulate a negotiating position from which to approach the Soviets.

President Eisenhower had first pursued a test ban in 1958, but negotiations had broken down after CIA pilot Francis Gary Powers's U-2 plane was shot down over the Soviet Union. Kennedy was able to restart talks on the issue, but the two sides ultimately deadlocked over the question of inspections. While tests in the atmosphere, in outer space, or underwater were easily observed, tests conducted underground were difficult to distinguish from natural seismic events, such as earthquakes. That meant that underground tests—particularly small ones—might be concealable, allowing a country to violate the test ban undetected and thereby to improve its nuclear arsenal while its opponent's arsenal remained technologically static.

Because Kennedy officials could not simply accept Moscow's word that it was abiding by the treaty, they suggested that when an unidentified seismic event occurred, a scientific team be sent to inspect the area. It was a reasonable suggestion, but the Soviets, obsessed with secrecy, were convinced that such inspections were really a ruse to enable the Americans to spy on them. Ultimately, it became clear that there would be no agreement on a *comprehensive* test ban treaty, or CTBT—that is, one banning all tests—because the Soviet resistance to on-site inspections could not be overcome. Instead, on August 5, 1963, the two parties signed the *Limited Test Ban Treaty*, or LTBT, prohibiting nuclear weapons tests in the atmosphere, in outer space, and underwater, but allowing them underground.

Although the treaty's scope was thus decidedly modest, conservatives predicted apocalypse. They objected that the Soviets would cheat on the agreement, conduct clandestine tests, and use the information they gleaned to build a bigger and better arsenal. The U.S. arsenal, meanwhile, would stay the same size and quality, or perhaps even deteriorate, because the United States would honestly abide by the terms of the treaty. Eventually, the conservatives argued, the United States would lose its nuclear superiority over the Soviet Union and ultimately the Cold War. As Goldwater melodramatically declared on the Senate floor, "If it means political suicide to vote for my country and against this treaty, then I commit it gladly." He then tried to scuttle the LTBT by offering a so-called killer amendment that would have tied the treaty's approval to Soviet withdrawal of its military forces from Cuba—a condition the Soviets would never have accepted. Ultimately, he was one of only nineteen senators to vote against the accord.

In truth, nuclear scientists had assured the Senate that underground testing would enable the United States to maintain its arsenal—and, just to be certain, Kennedy ordered a robust round of tests after the treaty took effect. Ironically, for conservatives, the best way to have ensured U.S. nuclear superiority would have been to support a treaty that was *more* restrictive—that is, a CTBT—because it would have slowed or stopped Soviet warhead development at a time when American technology was much more sophisticated. Ambassador Averell Harriman, who led the LTBT delegation to Moscow, later complained that the United States should have tried harder for a comprehensive ban: "When you stop to think what the advantages were to us of stopping all testing in the early 1960s, when we were still ahead of the Soviets, it's really appalling to realize what an opportunity we missed." We missed that opportunity in part because Kennedy was well aware that conservatives would balk at a CTBT without inspections, even though Glenn Seaborg, who headed the Atomic Energy Commission from 1961 to 1971, later said that on-site inspections probably weren't essential to verification anyway—technological advances soon allowed us to more accurately identify underground nuclear tests from afar.

The specifics of the treaty were really beside the point anyway—Goldwater objected not just to the LTBT, but to negotiation in any form. Negotiations were suspect, he believed, because there was always the danger that we would "lose" rather than "win." Even if we did "win," the Soviets would never abide by an agreement unless it was in their interest to do so; and if it was in their interest, they would do it regardless of whether or not there was an agreement. "[I]f that is the case," Goldwater concluded, "then why bother to 'negotiate' about it?" Arms control itself was simply a "cute" term, he wrote, for disarmament, and he mocked the "bewildering" array of proposals being considered to prevent the use of nuclear weapons. At one point in *Why Not Victory?* Goldwater actually seemed to suggest that negotiations were part of a nefarious Soviet strategy to bore us to death, drawing out talks with proposal and counterproposal until we lost our minds: "They are masters at this type of protracted intrigue," he warned. In the ultimate expression of his hatred for engagement, Goldwater even opposed the eminently sensible Hot Line Agreement, which established a communications link between Moscow and Washington so that leaders could talk directly during emergencies like the Cuban missile crisis.

Goldwater's governing assumption was that all international interaction was zero-sum—that there had to be a winner and a loser. The very concept of negotiation—in which both sides benefit in the same way that trading partners benefit from exchanging goods—therefore eluded him. When he did consider the unlikely possibility of a mutually beneficial arrangement, he could not understand why one party's interests might be contingent on the other's behavior, even though such reciprocity is a fundamental basis of many human interactions.

Unfortunately, the nuclear age required not only an appreciation of how negotiations were non-zero-sum, but also an acceptance of the idea that warfare, in which there had traditionally been winners and losers, was no longer zero-sum. But Goldwater did not accept the notion of a nuclear "revolution": "I do not subscribe to the theory that nuclear weapons have changed everything," Goldwater asserted. But they had: Nuclear weapons meant that military victory was no longer possible in a great power conflict. Despite conservatives' insistence that the Cold War was different from past conflicts, they did not seem to comprehend just how much had changed.

No Such Thing as Victory

One of the first men to grapple with the significance of nuclear weapons was Bernard Brodie. Brodie had enrolled at the University of Chicago in the early 1930s with the intention of becoming a meteorologist. Soon, however, he became absorbed in the study of international relations, specifically the causes and conduct of war, and he stayed on at the university to complete a Ph.D. The book that grew out of his dissertation, *Sea Power in the Machine Age,* and his follow-up volume, *A Layman's Guide to Naval Strategy,* were instantly adopted by the navy, which was being forced to quickly turn out new officers to meet the demands of World War II. Brodie spent 1943 and 1944 working for naval intelligence and soon made a name for himself in the world of military affairs. In 1945, Brodie joined the Yale University faculty, and it was as a newly minted professor that he walked in to a local drugstore near New Haven on the morning of August 7 to buy a copy of the *New York Times*. The headline that day was one of the century's most dramatic: FIRST ATOMIC BOMB DROPPED ON JAPAN; MISSILE IS EQUAL TO 20,000 TONS OF TNT. Farther down the column was a smaller heading underscoring for readers what to Brodie was immediately obvious: NEW AGE USHERED. Overnight, his life's writing had been rendered obsolete.

So Brodie began writing anew, publishing in 1946 one of the first volumes to systematically dissect the military and political ramifications of the bomb. He came to two important conclusions. The first was that military superiority no longer mattered: "Superiority in numbers of bombs does not endow its possessor with the kind of military security which formerly resulted from superiority in armies, navies, and air forces"; now one had to destroy only a certain number of enemy cities before one reached the point of diminishing returns. The second was that the chief purpose of the bomb was to *deter* an enemy attack: "Thus far the chief purpose of our military establishment has been to win wars. From now on its chief purpose must be to avert them. It can have almost no other useful purpose." The development of the H-bomb only reinforced his beliefs, forcing him to consider that Karl von Clausewitz's famous dictum—"War is an extension of politics by other means"—had been overturned. The Prussian strategist had meant that military action was never an end in and of itself, but rather a tool to advance the national interest. But if a nuclear attack would result in strategic retaliation, how could we rationally use nuclear weapons? After all, Brodie wrote, "It is self-evident that national objectives in war cannot be consonant with national suicide."

These conclusions were not immediately accepted in Washington. Neither President Eisenhower nor Secretary of State John Foster Dulles nor the military brass initially viewed nuclear weapons as revolutionary, even after the development of the H-bomb. (And Brodie himself spent decades mulling the utility of nuclear weapons, changing his mind several times in the process.) Eisenhower's military priorities were to avoid another war like Korea and to constrain the Pentagon's budget, as he didn't want to spend vast sums trying to match the much larger Red Army. For his part, Dulles lamented what he saw as the Truman administration's reactivity—its willingness to wage the Cold War on Soviet terms, responding to crises the communists had instigated—and he thought nuclear weapons would enable a bolder stance. In January 1954, in a speech at the Council on

Foreign Relations, he said that the United States would "depend primarily upon a great capacity to retaliate, instantly, by means and at places of our choosing." However efficient this sounded in theory, the practice of massive retaliation, as it came to be known, would have been horrifying. Plan 1-A of the Single Integrated Operations Plan, developed during Eisenhower's last year in office, called for the use of more than three thousand nuclear weapons against the USSR, China, and Eastern Europe if the Soviets invaded Western Europe—or even if we thought they were about to do so. Hundreds of millions of people in a dozen countries would have died almost instantly.

The air force, which was in charge of most nuclear weapons at the time, was greatly enthused about such power—the ability, as General Curtis LeMay put it, to kill a nation. But to the Kennedy administration, which was briefed on the plan in 1961, it seemed grossly immoral. Certainly it was disproportionate to vaporize millions of Soviet civilians before the Red Army had killed a single American. Worse, the plan called for killing millions of Chinese and Eastern Europeans, regardless of whether they had participated in a Soviet attack, simply because they were part of the communist bloc. The air force wasn't bothered by such concerns. As General Tommy Power joked to Robert McNamara, whom Kennedy had tapped to lead the Pentagon, "Mr. Secretary, I hope you don't have any friends or relations in Albania, because we're just going to have to wipe it out."

McNamara was disgusted with Power and horrified by the SIOP, but his chief objection to massive retaliation was strategic, not moral. After all, once the Soviets had developed nuclear weapons, there was little expectation that we would be able to destroy all their nuclear forces in a first strike. They would retaliate in some fashion, crippling the United States even if only with a few dozen warheads. McNamara, a whiz kid whose analytic skills had propelled him to the head of the Ford Motor Company, believed there must be a more controlled approach to nuclear war—a more *logical* approach. As journalist Fred Kaplan has chronicled, that instinct brought him into the welcoming arms of a group of mathematicians, logicians, and economists at a new think tank called the Research and Development Corporation, or RAND—the "wizards of Armageddon"—who were trying to reason how the United States could pull the nuclear trigger without blowing out its own brains.

The "solution" that many analysts embraced was to *limit* a nuclear war. The United States should not plan, per the SIOP, to launch the entirety of the nuclear arsenal in what Herman Kahn, one of RAND's leading theorists, dubbed a "war orgasm." Instead, if it had to use nuclear weapons first in a conflict—say, because the Red Army invaded Western Europe, overwhelming American troops—it should first target Soviet military forces. Nuclear weapons might stop a conventional assault, and if the United States also targeted Soviet nuclear forces, they would impede Moscow's ability to retaliate in kind. The United States could then hold Soviet cities hostage to a second U.S. strike, meaning that in the best case the Soviets might be deterred from retaliating at all. In this way, RAND analysts theorized the United States might actually be able to win a nuclear war against the Soviet Union. Resorting to his own sexual metaphor, Brodie likened the SIOP to orgasmic intercourse, whereas the RAND strategy was equivalent to withdrawal before ejaculation. More formally, this approach was known as counterforce.

Counterforce was a highly imperfect response to an impossible situation. For one thing, even a strike restricted to military targets—many of which were located near civilian centers—would still kill millions of Russians. For another, it greatly increased our need for nuclear weapons, which cost money and were likely to provoke the Soviets. Whereas the SIOP was aimed principally at hard-to-miss and easy-to-destroy civilian and industrial targets (similar to the strategic bombing campaigns of World War II), counterforce required targeting specific—often very small—military ones. Destroying such targets was hard to do with confidence, so multiple weapons had to be deployed for each particular site. The Soviets would respond to our deployment by building more weapons, which in turn generated more targets for us, and an arms race would ensue. Most problematic, though, counterforce did not convincingly lower the risk of retaliation. If the United States used nuclear weapons against the USSR, the Soviets were almost certain to respond in kind even if we targeted "only" their military facilities. Cold, rational calculation of the type practiced at RAND would likely vanish along with the first target.

Yet faced with the alternative—a spasm involving most or all of our nuclear forces—McNamara decided it was better to have options. In a crisis or during a war, we could launch as many or as few weapons as we wished against any variety of targets. A counterforce strategy would enable us to scale our nuclear use to any possible Soviet attack, a notion that meshed with Kennedy's vision of "flexible response" for the conventional military. So on June 17, 1962, McNamara delivered what has to be one of the least uplifting commencement addresses in the history of higher education; it would come to be known as his "No Cities" speech. Speaking at the University of Michigan, he declared that nuclear weapons served the same purpose as conventional weapons and should be used the same way: "[Our] principal military objectives, in the event of a nuclear war stemming from a major attack on the Alliance, should be the destruction of the enemy's forces, not of his civilian population." The implication was that a nuclear war might be winnable. After all, if we could destroy all of the enemy's forces, then we would be safe from retaliation.

It was not long, however, before McNamara realized that a counterforce strategy did not in fact reverse the nuclear revolution in warfare as Brodie had described it—that is, it did not mean that nuclear weapons could be used to achieve national objectives. Counterforce could provide us with options, but it could never make a nuclear war winnable, as some of its more enthusiastic proponents suggested. (Kahn, for example, in a dark tome called *On Thermonuclear War*, wrote that life after a holocaust in which twenty million perished could actually be marked by a renewal of American society—sentiments that made him the model for Peter Sellers's Dr. Strangelove.) No strategy could limit damage to America in any meaningful way because the Soviets would never let themselves be put in a position in which the United States could knock out *all* their weapons. And it took very few nuclear weapons to inflict unacceptable damage.

On December 3, 1964, McNamara sent President Johnson a memo elaborating on his realization and what it meant for the U.S. nuclear posture. The United States needed the capacity to absorb an enemy's nuclear strike and still have enough weapons left to inflict sufficient damage on the Soviets—to destroy, say, a handful of cities—so that they would not contemplate an attack in the first place. McNamara called this an assured-destruction capability. The reason that victory would never be possible was that limiting damage to one's own country meant undermining the enemy's assured destruction capability—and the enemy would always take steps to ensure its own retaliatory capability while limiting damage to itself. Or, as McNamara summed up, "Our damage limiting problem is their assured destruction problem, and our assured destruction problem is their damage limiting problem." A counterforce strategy just led to an action-reaction cycle that spurred the arms race while making neither side any safer.

McNamara's conclusion was supported by analysis showing that, in a nuclear conflict, defenses were of little utility. In theory, if you could defend against nuclear weapons, then Brodie's belief that nuclear war was national suicide could be overturned: A nuclear war would be fightable and winnable. To be sure, bombers could be shot down, and, in the 1940s, the United States began studying how to defend against missiles—the delivery vehicle of choice for nuclear warheads. There was also a push for civil defenses—in the form of shelters to protect Americans from the blast, heat, and fallout of a nuclear explosion. The problem was that nuclear weapons were so destructive that any countermeasures had to be nearly perfect, and all the Soviets had to do to overcome them was to build a few more missiles. A thorough Pentagon study led by General Glenn Kent concluded in 1964 that no combination of civil defenses, missile defenses, and counterforce targeting could efficiently and affordably protect America from new Soviet deployments. For every dollar the Soviet Union spent on offense, the United States would have to spend at least three just to protect 50 percent of its industry and 60 percent of the population. And the imbalance would only grow worse as the United States tried to save a greater percentage of Americans. Even if we preemptively destroyed many Soviet weapons on the ground, intercepted many of the remaining on their way here, and sheltered our citizens underground, we still couldn't adequately defend ourselves. Nuclear war *was* national suicide unless you considered millions of dead and the end of civilization acceptable.

That convinced McNamara that rather than pursuing counterforce—or missile defense or civil defense, both of which had passionate backers—the United States ought to simply maintain an assured destruction capability, which he somewhat arbitrarily defined as being able to wait out a first strike and still have enough nuclear weapons remaining to destroy 30 percent of the Soviet Union's population and 50 percent of its industry. On September 18, 1967, McNamara gave a speech very different from his No Cities address, arguing, "The cornerstone of our strategic policy continues to be to deter nuclear attack upon the United States or its allies. We do this by maintaining a highly reliable ability to inflict unacceptable damage upon any single aggressor or combination of aggressors at any time during the course of a strategic nuclear exchange, even after absorbing a surprise first strike. This can be defined as our assured-destruction capability." That did not mean we would now target only cities—we continued to aim our nuclear forces at the enemy's nuclear forces—but the Johnson administration recognized that assured destruction was a fact of life.

That acknowledgment was crucial. Assured destruction was not a policy choice; it was simply a condition. But what if one side thought that it *could* win? Or what if one side believed that the *other* thought that? The best course of action might be to strike first out of a rational desire to avoid the worst case. This quandary was represented by a classic exercise in game theory known as the prisoner's dilemma. Game theory is an analytic tool developed by mathematician John von Neumann to predict rational behavior in situations marked by uncertainty. Formally, it comprises often complex equations and matrices, but some of its essential lessons can be conveyed by analogy. Imagine that two men are arrested for armed robbery and placed in separate holding cells. Because the police don't have enough evidence to prosecute them for the robbery, they offer each man a deal: If you confess and your partner stays silent, we will let you go free and he will receive the maximum sentence of ten years. If you both confess, you'll both be convicted but will receive a lesser, but still harsh, sentence of five years for cooperating with the police. If you both stay silent, we'll be able to convict you only of the lesser charge of weapons possession, and you'll each get six months in prison.

The "best" result—that is, the one that minimizes the total time spent in prison—would be for both to stay silent. But in this situation, each robber must ask himself: Should I keep my mouth shut and hope my partner does the same? Or should I confess and protect myself from a possible ten-year sentence, with a chance at immunity? The interesting thing about the prisoner's dilemma is that, assuming you have no particular loyalty to your accomplice, it always makes sense for you to rat him out. Consider: If you knew that he was going to confess, then you should do the same in order to avoid the maximum sentence. Likewise, if you knew that he was going to stay silent, you should confess so that you get off scot-free. Unfortunately, if both prisoners act in their self-interest, each will spend five years in prison, when they could have gotten off with six months apiece. Contra Goldwater, the prisoner's dilemma demonstrated that interactions were not necessarily zero-sum—there was not always a winner and a loser. Trying to win, even if rational, could lead to mutual loss.

The prisoner's dilemma is most often used as an analogy for arms races, in which each decision to build more weapons represents an iteration of the game: At each point it seemingly makes sense to build more because if your enemy doesn't reciprocate, you will have an advantage, and if he does, you'll need to be prepared. However, if both parties follow this logic—which the prisoner's dilemma says they will—both will end up worse off than if they had simply called a truce at some point.

With some tweaking, the prisoner's dilemma can also be used to highlight the danger of a conflict like the Cuban missile crisis. Ultimately, war did not erupt during that incident because neither side wanted it—that is, both sides perceived the payoff of staying mum as greater than ratting out the other. That was because neither side really wanted to murder millions of people, but also because neither Khrushchev nor Kennedy believed that the other side would "stay quiet" in the face of betrayal. They would see missiles and bombers coming over the horizon and respond in kind, or they would absorb a first blow and retaliate with their remaining forces. Thus, unlike in the prisoner's dilemma, each side had an incentive to cooperate with the other.

But returning to the what-ifs, what if one or both sides believed that a disarming first strike was possible? It might decide to launch during a crisis, rationally concluding (assuming it could overlook the deaths of millions of civilians) that the best possible outcome was to destroy the enemy and be left standing. In other words, what if it thought that victory was possible? Or, perhaps worse, what if one side believed that *its enemy* thought a disarming first strike was possible? That perception, correct or not, would also encourage it to launch first to preempt an expected attack. Suddenly, a crisis begins to look like a game of prisoner's dilemma, where the temptation to rat out your accomplice exceeds your temptation to stay quiet and ostensibly rational behavior leads to an irrational outcome—in this case, a mutually destructive nuclear war. That problem was only exacerbated by the fact that—despite the Kent study showing that damage-limitation efforts like missile defense were useless at the margins—launching first would give the attacking state *some* advantage. In taking out many enemy weapons, an attacking state might not avoid a retaliatory strike, but it might save a few of its cities from destruction by destroying the weapons its adversary had aimed at them. Wouldn't that be worth it?

McNamara and others eventually concluded that, no, it wouldn't: With each side having thousands of warheads, the destruction would inevitably be unacceptable. It wouldn't matter who launched first. In prisoner dilemma terms, it would be like the difference between a one-hundred-year sentence and a two-hundred-year sentence: Either way, you'd die behind bars. But if that was not clear to both sides, or if it was not clear to each that the other also believed it, each side would arm itself in preparation for the worst-case scenario, and the spiraling uncertainty could lead to what game theorists would call, with some understatement, a suboptimal outcome.

It was into this quandary that arms control stepped. Just as the prisoners could change their behavior if they were allowed to communicate and reassure each other that they would stay quiet, so could the superpowers reassure each other that they agreed they were living in a world governed by the prospect of assured destruction. By structuring their nuclear forces in a way that signaled this and by reducing the incentives to strike first, they could make nuclear war, which no one wanted, less likely. As Thomas Schelling and Morton Halperin wrote in their classic study *Strategy and Arms Control,* "The essential feature of arms control is the recognition of the common interest, of the possibility of reciprocation and cooperation even between potential enemies with respect to their military establishments."

The UN and the NPT

Unfortunately, that sort of non-zero-sum thinking was antithetical to conservatism, which rejected it not only in U.S.-Soviet relations but also in multilateral venues. Following World War I, conservatives had opposed the League of Nations in no small part because it established a collective security arrangement in which an attack on one member was considered an attack on all. And collective security was nothing more than a global exercise in non-zero-sum thinking.

After World War II, conservatives had been forced to abandon their strict unilateralism to fight communism. Still, their distrust of cooperative engagement was able to hibernate comfortably just beneath the surface for the simple reason that the United States dominated many of the nominally international organizations in which it participated. For example, NATO, ostensibly a shining example of America's Cold War multilateralism, was driven by U.S. priorities. After all, Europe didn't have a hope of fending off an attack by the Soviet empire without the support of the United States.

When it came to truly international organizations like the United Nations, however, the traditional conservative nationalism resurfaced because conservatives could not see how such institutions were capable of undercutting communism; all they did was threaten American sovereignty. Conservatives made it clear that they saw their more limited version of internationalism as far more realistic and concerned with the security of the United States than that of liberals, which was little more than a vague, unrealistic, and ultimately dangerous "one-worldism." In other words, the new conservative internationalism was not all that different from the old conservative nationalism. And combined with a moralistic view of the Cold War, it led to one of the conservatives' more bizarre and foolish stands: opposition to the Nuclear Nonproliferation Treaty.

Since World War I, non-zero-sum thinking had increasingly molded liberal ideas about security policy. As international conflicts became ever more destructive, cooperation became ever more crucial. Although Wilson's League of Nations had failed, FDR believed that, in the wartime alliance between the United States, Britain, China, and the Soviet Union, he had found a model for maintaining the peace. This concept of the "four policemen" was intended as a more practical vision of collective security, in which the peace was kept by a small concert of great powers. It formed the basis for the United Nations Security Council.

It was the arrival of the nuclear age, however, that made the principle of interdependence essential. World War I had killed twenty-four million people; World War II had killed fifty million; but a conflict involving thousands of nuclear weapons would obliterate civilization. As the ramifications of the nuclear revolution became clear, cooperation went from humanitarian ideal to human necessity. In his September 1963 speech to the United Nations, President Kennedy explained, "The science of weapons and war has made us all, far more than [the founding of the United Nations] 18 years ago in San Francisco, one world and one human race, with one common destiny. In such a world, absolute sovereignty no longer assures us of absolute security. The conventions of peace must pull abreast and then ahead of the inventions of war. The United Nations, building on its successes and learning from its failures, must be developed into a genuine world security system."

Conservatives, predictably, rejected such notions. As *National Review* put it in 1955: "No superstition has more effectively bewitched America's Liberal elite than the fashionable concepts of world government, the United Nations, internationalism, international atomic pools, etc. Perhaps the most important and readily demonstrable lesson of history is that freedom goes hand in hand with a state of political decentralization, that remote government is irresponsible government. It would make greater sense to grant independence to each of our 48 states than to surrender U.S. sovereignty to a world organization."

The actual operation of the United Nations did little to quiet such skepticism. Because both the United States and the Soviet Union had veto power, the UN Security Council was able to accomplish little. Increasingly, the body's work shifted to the General Assembly, where each nation had one vote, where there were no vetoes, and where the number of member states was growing rapidly as former colonies availed themselves of the postwar principle of self-determination. In the General Assembly, the United States was but one among many, and conservatives feared it would be tied down by lilliputian states—that the organization could handicap the exercise of American power, as James Burnham put it. Of course, the United Nations could not *force* the United States to do anything, but conservatives feared its influence nonetheless—in part because they felt America paid too much attention to world opinion.

As one *National Review* contributor wrote, "You and I, dear reader, may think world opinion means one thing, but when the phrase comes prancing toward us dressed fit to kill in capital letters, World Opinion is identical with the policy of a global apparatus lightly but skillfully manned by an informal staff of political, journalistic, and academic brainwashers and con men comprising what might be called the Liberal International. If it so please you, the Libintern." The American foreign policy establishment believed the UN essential, and the Libintern believed that the UN had supranational authority, that nation-states were "fossils of modern history." The United Nations aimed to curtail national liberty just as American liberals sought to curtail individual liberty at home via the government. A nationalist policy abroad was thus a natural extension of a libertarian policy at home.

Goldwater, a staunch libertarian, shared this concern with infringe-ments upon American sovereignty. He believed that, even if world govern-ment per se was not imminent, the United Nations and its spawn—groups like the International Labour Organization; the General Agreement on Tariffs and Trade; and the UN Educational, Scientific and Cultural Orga-nization (UNESCO)—were "designed to control and supervise many of our essentially domestic concerns." Goldwater had particular scorn for the World Court, which he believed had the power to declare the Bill of Rights illegal if it chose to. More important, when America acted through the United Nations—as it had, for example, in the Korean War and the Suez crisis—its ability to fight the war on communism was inevitably con-strained by the participation of others and by even nominal deference to their opinions. We must at all costs, Goldwater believed, preserve our free-dom to fight for freedom.

And therein lay Goldwater's second concern: The problem with the United Nations was not only that it infringed on America's *means* to act, but that it had different *ends*. The purpose of international organizations was not to promote freedom or to fight communism. Rather, they were concerned with vague concepts like peace, law, and justice—concepts on which there was little international consensus. The world was divided, and it was imperative that America remember that. When it acted through the United Nations, it inevitably was obliged to subordinate its interests to those of neutralist, and even communist, nations. The United States, Goldwater wrote, "must avoid complete reliance on any organization whose total interest does not coincide with freedom. The United Nations is one of these."

It was such thinking that led conservatives to oppose the Nuclear Non-proliferation Treaty (NPT), a crucial agreement that involved commu-nist and neutral states, whose purpose was to enhance not only American security but also that of the Soviet Union and the third world, and that did so by constraining U.S. freedom of action.

Until the mid-1960s, preventing the spread of nuclear weapons to other countries had been a goal but not a priority of U.S. foreign policy. The United States had even helped Britain with its nuclear program, and turned a blind eye when France built atomic weapons. The conventional wisdom was that it would not threaten U.S. security if selected allies had nuclear weapons. The Soviet Union felt the same way, helping communist

China with its nuclear program. When the Chinese tested their first nuclear weapon in 1964, however, it served as a wake-up call for the United States, which suddenly found itself facing another nuclear-armed communist country. As scholar Francis J. Gavin has written, China was the ultimate rogue state. It was doing everything it could to disrupt the status quo, aiding North Vietnam, threatening Taiwan, and even invading India. It also seemed a less rational actor than the Soviet Union. Mao, for example, had commented, "If the worst came to the worst and half of mankind died, the other half would remain while imperialism would be razed to the ground and the whole world would become socialist."

U.S. officials came to believe that the world had reached a nuclear tipping point. A number of nations—Argentina, Brazil, Mexico, Sweden, Switzerland, Japan, Italy, Israel, Egypt, India, Japan, Canada, South Africa, Czechoslovakia, Romania, East Germany, West Germany, Yugoslavia— either had the ability to make nuclear weapons, were close to being able to do so, or were considering developing such an ability. It was more than likely that further proliferation would upset whatever nuclear balance existed between the superpowers and replace it with competing clusters of nuclear states, decreasing the relative influence of the United States, holding its citizens hostage, and perhaps triggering nuclear war. So in 1964, President Johnson appointed a committee led by Roswell Gilpatric, the deputy secretary of defense, to study the potential consequences of proliferation and what the United States should do about it.

The Gilpatric Committee, initially divided about the seriousness of proliferation, produced a report that argued the United States should make nonproliferation a top foreign policy priority. Notably, the committee concluded that "the Soviet Union, because of its growing vulnerability to proliferation among its neighbors, probably shares with us a strong interest in preventing the further spread of nuclear weapons." In other words, the committee recognized that the world was more complex than us versus them and saw the potential for cooperation with our enemy. It recommended, among other things, a comprehensive test ban treaty, nuclear weapon–free zones, and, most important, a nonproliferation agreement.

President Johnson accepted the committee's recommendations and began negotiation of the NPT, which, much to conservatives' horror, necessitated direct talks with the Soviet Union. Ultimately, the treaty established a two-tiered system: On one side were the five states that had developed nuclear weapons before the treaty was signed (Britain, France, China, the United States, and the Soviet Union), and on the other was the rest of the world. Countries that had not already built nuclear weapons pledged never to do so; countries that had nuclear weapons pledged never to build them for anyone else. In exchange, the nuclear-weapon states agreed to help nonnuclear states develop nuclear power, and nuclear states agreed "to pursue negotiations in good faith on effective measures relating to cessation of the nuclear arms race at an early date and to nuclear disarmament."

Conservatives charged that the treaty violated America's sovereignty, while Goldwater worried that it would force the United States to defend those without nuclear weapons. *National Review* wrote that "the Treaty may make us more of a world policeman than ever, while denying us the opportunity to decide whom we will protect and how, and denying to us, too, the opportunity to consider our own interests." The need to link U.S. security to that of Western European countries had been traumatic enough for the conservative movement; extending entangling alliances to a gaggle of states across the globe was a bridge too far, even if it did stem the spread of nuclear weapons. If the Senate was to support the NPT, Goldwater felt it should do so only with the understanding that "nothing in the treaty is to be construed to create or give rise to any new commitment by the United States to provide military assistance to any country attacked, or threatened with an attack, by nuclear weapons."

Even more injurious from the conservative standpoint, the treaty prevented us from giving nuclear weapons to allies, even if doing so might help us defend against the Soviet Union. This meant that the treaty, like the UN, not only impinged on our freedom of action, but also distracted us from our anticommunist mission by failing to observe the clear moral demarcation between friends and enemies. For example, in the 1960s, West Germany was actively considering a weapons program to defend itself against the Soviet Union. Because it was a member of NATO, West Germany was technically under the U.S. nuclear umbrella—that is, we were committed to defending it with nuclear weapons, if necessary—but some analysts and politicians questioned the credibility of that deterrent. If the Soviets attacked, say, Bonn, would we really retaliate on Germany's behalf, knowing that the Soviets might then launch a nuclear missile at

New York? Why would we not want to shore up the power of our friends at the expense of the communists?

It was a reasonable question and one the Gilpatric Committee had considered at length, ultimately deciding that allowing more nuclear powers would just be too risky: "New nuclear capabilities, however primitive and regardless of whether they are held by nations currently friendly to the United States, will add complexity and instability to the deterrent balance between the United States and the Soviet Union, aggravate suspicions and hostility among states neighboring new nuclear powers, . . . and eventually constitute direct military threats to the United States." The vision of the world in which a gain for one side was a loss for the other simply did not apply in this situation. Nonproliferation was a non-zero-sum problem. Gilpatric, for one, found it "implausible that additional proliferation could be compartmentalized, quarantined, or regionalized." Instead, proliferation was likely to come in clusters. If India developed nuclear weapons, for example, then so would Pakistan and perhaps others. (Which, of course, is exactly what later happened.) Gilpatric found it even less likely that a regional nuclear conflict—which became more likely as more nations developed nuclear weapons—would not affect U.S. security. If a single bullet in Sarajevo could trigger World War I, what would be the ramifications of even a small nuclear exchange? A nationalistic approach to the problem, one committee member noted, was simply not feasible. American interests were broader than the U.S.-Soviet conflict, and in this instance we shared interests with the Soviets and others.

Conservatives thought we were being duped. They believed the Soviets supported the treaty only because it prevented us from arming our allies, while in effect not preventing them from doing anything—after all, Moscow was not about to give nukes to discontented Warsaw Pact states like Poland or Czechoslovakia. William Henry Chamberlin—in what *National Review*'s editors said was his finest piece for the magazine—wrote, "United States ratification of the nonproliferation pact means commitment to a policy that is immoral, foolish, and most probably impractical, a policy that makes nonsense of our defensive alliance in Europe, that favors our enemy and slights our allies." The NPT, according to Chamberlin, was little more than a nuclear Yalta. John G. Tower, a popular conservative Republican senator from Texas, introduced reservations to the NPT that would have allowed us to retain the "option to establish Atlantic nuclear defenses," by which he meant the option to give nuclear weapons to friendly Europeans.

Contrary to the emerging wisdom that proliferation of nuclear weapons would result only in the proliferation of threats to America, conservatives could not fathom why more weapons for our side was not worse for their side—why more weapons might not just be worse, period.

Nixon the Arms Controller

Rather unexpectedly, the leader who did the most in this period to further arms control and undermine the conservative position on nonproliferation and arms control was Richard Nixon. Barry Goldwater had been trounced in the 1964 election, as the American public was apparently less enamored of his conservatism than the delegates who had chosen him to be the GOP's presidential nominee. That loss effectively ended his hopes for the White House, but in 1969, conservatives believed that another one of their own had ascended to the Oval Office.

Nixon ran as a conservative and was certainly known as one, having been a chief pursuer of Alger Hiss and, rather less justifiably, having accused actress-turned-politician Helen Gahagan Douglas of being a communist ("pink right down to her underwear," as he put it) in his successful campaign against her for a California Senate seat. Nixon detested the Eastern establishment, which he felt had always snubbed him (despite high achievement in law school, Nixon had failed to be accepted at prestigious New York City law firms), and seemed to enjoy taunting liberals. And liberals, for their part, loved to hate Nixon, whose campaign played to white, working-class fears about race and law and order. He supported the Vietnam War, nuclear superiority, and missile defense.

But whatever Nixon's past demagoguery and whatever his campaign promises, he was also a realist—that is to say, he viewed international politics fundamentally as a struggle among nations for power. He did not see the Cold War, as most conservatives did, as a quasireligious conflict, but instead thought that national interests could be served by dealing with one's enemies, or even by turning one's enemies into friends. Nixon was confident that he could advance American interests by establishing a relationship with the Soviets—and the Chinese—perhaps even securing their help in ending the Vietnam War.

In his quest for détente, he found common cause with Henry Kissinger, a Harvard professor who would serve as his secretary of state and
national security adviser and who would come to epitomize American
foreign policy realism. In his 1954 book, *A World Restored*—an admir-
ing history of Prince von Metternich's efforts to establish a balance of
power in nineteenth-century Europe—Kissinger wrote, "Moral claims
involve a quest for absolutes, a denial of nuance, a rejection of history." He
later rejected the notion that U.S. foreign policy was "a struggle between
good and evil, in each phase of which it is America's mission to help defeat
the evil foes challenging a peaceful order." As he would explain in a 1975
speech somewhat misleadingly titled "The Moral Foundations of Foreign
Policy," nuclear weapons demanded that Americans and Soviets "seek a
more productive and stable relationship despite the basic antagonism of
our values." Coexistence was an "imperative."

Nixon distinguished himself from conservatives immediately upon
assuming office, calling in his inaugural speech for "an era of negotiation." In his first term, in an effort to improve relations with the communist world and ease the burden on American foreign policy, Nixon
declared that we no longer sought victory in Vietnam, he increased trade
with the Soviet Union, and he welcomed Ostpolitik (which promised change
through rapprochement) in Germany. Nixon began withdrawing troops
from Vietnam and encouraging the Vietnamization of the war. Particularly offensive to conservatives were Nixon's overtures to China, beginning with the June 1971 lifting of a trade embargo on the People's Republic
that had been in place since the communist takeover in 1949. Then, in
February 1972, the president actually visited the mainland for a summit with Mao Tse-tung himself, producing the Shanghai Communiqué,
which announced that the two countries would move toward normalizing relations. For conservative commentators, relations with China not
only legitimized communist tyranny over hundreds of millions of people
but meant the abandonment of Taiwan, which lost its seat at the United
Nations when the People's Republic of China was admitted.

The vanguard of détente, however, was arms control. Although he had
run for president demanding that the United States maintain a nuclear
advantage over the Soviets and had, in 1969, fought for a missile defense
system to protect against Soviet attack, Nixon soon changed his approach.
In his first press conference as president, he rejected the principle of nuclear

superiority in favor of nuclear "sufficiency"—a strategy with which Kissinger agreed. In 1957, Kissinger had published a bestselling book on nuclear weapons in which he argued that "the destructiveness of modern weapons deprives victory in an all-out war of its historical meaning," a conclusion that mirrored those of Brodie and McNamara. True, that book had also argued that it might be possible to *limit* a nuclear war—and therefore that atomic weapons could have some use on the battlefield—but Kissinger soon changed his mind. By 1969, he and the president both saw advantage in an agreement that limited defenses and established strategic parity—that is, rough equivalence in nuclear forces. Parity would deny advantage to either side, making a nuclear strike undertaken out of hubris or fear less likely. To that end, missile defense was more valuable as a bargaining chip than as a weapons system. American negotiators thus began meeting with their Soviet counterparts in 1969 to hammer out a treaty limiting offensive and defensive weapons in a process known as the Strategic Arms Limitation Talks, or SALT. At the same time, Nixon pushed the NPT through the Senate, believing that it, too, would further détente.

The SALT negotiations dragged on for three years, but on May 26, 1972, Nixon and Leonid Brezhnev (who had wrested control of the Soviet Union from Khrushchev in 1964) met at a summit in Moscow and signed two agreements: the Anti-Ballistic Missile (ABM) Treaty and the Interim Agreement on the Limitation of Strategic Offensive Arms. The Interim Agreement froze the existing number of ICBMs and SLBMs at their 1972 levels—2,347 for the Soviets and 1,710 for the Americans. The apparent numerical disadvantage was offset by the fact that American forces were more technologically advanced, that the United States had nuclear weapons in Europe that could hit the USSR but that were not covered by the agreement, and that America had significantly more nuclear-armed bombers, which also lay outside the treaty's scope. The Interim Agreement marked a first step in limiting offensive weapons, but it proved to be a modest one, because both signatories were on the verge of deploying a new technology—multiple independently targetable reentry vehicles, or MIRVs—which enabled several warheads to be placed on each missile and aimed at different locations. Because the Interim Agreement limited the number of missiles, not the number of warheads on them, MIRV technology allowed both sides to continue to expand their arsenals. (Nixon and Kissinger considered but ultimately made little effort to include MIRVs in the discussions, believing it would be too difficult to win military and right-wing support for such a ban.)

The ABM Treaty, by contrast, was paradigm-shifting, as it forbade the United States and the Soviet Union from deploying nationwide missile defenses. McNamara and the Kent study had already ascertained that missile defenses could not limit damage to an acceptable level if the Soviets were determined to overcome them. But missile defenses were worse than useless; they were destabilizing. Logically speaking, any defense we built would be more effective at handling fewer missiles than at handling more, meaning that a missile defense was most useful in rebutting a retaliatory attack carried out after we had already launched a counterforce attack. In other words, missile defense was an excellent adjunct to a first-strike offensive force. Although missile defense itself seemed intuitively harmless and even commonsensical, in a nuclear standoff defenses could be as dangerous as offenses.

By outlawing national missile defenses, then, the ABM Treaty was making a profound statement about the futility of nuclear competition. It enshrined McNamara's realization that a nuclear war could not be effectively fought, in essence codifying the concept of assured destruction, while rejecting the logic of counterforce. As Nixon would later write, a "major effect of the ABM Treaty was to make permanent the concept of deterrence through 'mutual terror': By giving up missile defenses each side was leaving its population and territory hostage to a strategic missile attack. Each side therefore had an ultimate interest in preventing a war that could only be mutually destructive." While the United States did continue to target the Soviets' nuclear forces in the event that war broke out, the ABM Treaty suggested an official understanding that such plans were a façade. After all, McNamara never welcomed assured destruction; he simply acknowledged that, whatever America's stated intentions, that was the nature of the U.S.-Soviet nuclear relationship. The United States couldn't redefine that through new weapons systems, nuclear superiority, or a defensive capability. It had to accept the fact that victory was not possible, that America and the Soviet Union needed to stabilize the nuclear balance and coexist.

Conservatives Reject Nixon, Détente, and Arms Control

For conservatives, containment had at least sought to maintain the status quo, but détente represented a regression, for far from attempting to secure victory—moral, political, or military—over communism, it sought to warm relations with Moscow. As Cold War historian John Lewis Gaddis has written, a "fundamental premise of détente" was that "the West would not seek to alter the internal character of Marxist-Leninist regimes." For men like Buckley and Goldwater, regime change was the whole point of the exercise. The ideological and moral character of states *mattered*. "It is not the case that KGB repression and the absence of freedom of movement for persons and ideas—to take two key examples—are merely 'domestic questions,'" James Burnham wrote. "They are of the totalitarian essence; they make normal relations with the Soviet Union impossible. The Nixon-Kissinger speak-no-evil version of détente implies acceptance of Soviet totalitarian practices."

By the summer of 1971, conservatives had lost faith in Nixon. The hard-line anticommunist they had elected president seemed to have been replaced with a liberal doppelgänger. In July, twelve leading lights of the conservative movement, including Tom Winter and Allan Ryskind of the right-wing magazine *Human Events*, Randal Teague of Young Americans for Freedom, and John Jones and Jeff Bell of the American Conservative Union, met in William F. Buckley's townhouse on the Upper East Side of Manhattan and announced their "suspension of support" for Nixon. Their disillusionment only grew when Nixon promoted the Family Assistance Plan, which included a guaranteed income, and announced wage and price freezes, the kind of government meddling that rankled conservatives. With the presidential visit to China, the conservatives had had enough, and that December, the "Manhattan Twelve" decided they would oppose Nixon in the 1972 Republican presidential primaries. Although they knew they had little chance of unseating him, they wanted to send a message, and their chosen messenger was an Ohio congressman named John Ashbrook.

Ashbrook had little recognition outside conservative circles—*Time* magazine called him an "unknown"—but his ideological credentials were sterling. Along with Clif White, a public relations consultant, and William Rusher, the publisher of *National Review*, Ashbrook had helped launch the Draft Goldwater movement in 1961. He was a founder of the American Conservative Union and a leader of the Committee of One Million Against the Admission of Red China (to the United Nations). He considered détente an illusion and Nixon's openness to communists an "apostasy," and he denounced the president's summit meetings in Beijing and Moscow.

This approach resonated on the right. A poll of the thirty-one thousand members of the Conservative Book Club found that Ashbrook was the fifth most popular politician in the country, trailing only such heavyweights as Goldwater, Buckley, Ronald Reagan (then the governor of California), and John Tower (the Republican senator from Texas). Reagan and Tower, however, were already lined up behind Nixon, and Goldwater, though he had long been more conservative than the GOP, was a Republican loyalist who refused to participate in "party-wrecking." Even though he noted that some of the administration's policies, including its overtures to China, "violate my basic concept of conservative government," he would not tolerate Nixon bashing. So, in 1972, as détente came to a head with the signing of the SALT accords, John Ashbrook became the face of the conservative movement.

For men like Ashbrook, SALT was a double blow. As a product of détente, the Strategic Arms Limitation Talks were offensive in and of themselves, the manifestation of Nixon's misguided belief that he could "somehow cut a deal" with communists. The ABM Treaty and the Interim Agreement were particularly objectionable because they not only signaled the administration's lack of interest in winning the Cold War politically, but they also, conservatives believed, prevented us from winning it militarily, should it ever come to that. SALT officially established not only nuclear coexistence, but nuclear vulnerability.

This left Ashbrook sputtering with incomprehension. He felt it was "close to clinical lunacy" to "make certain our population is not protected from enemy attack, while simultaneously ensuring that our own weapons cannot inflict too much damage on the enemy." In his mind, there was no reason to abandon the hope of winning a nuclear war. "When a strong man armed keepeth his palace," he righteously intoned, "his goods are in peace." To Ashbrook, assured destruction was not a fact of life; it was a liberal construct designed by men like McNamara, who had stood idly by, unilaterally disarming the United States while the Soviets had deployed missile system after missile system.* He found the coalescing nuclear orthodoxy, with its warning against destabilizing force structures and missile defenses,

---

*In fact, the Kennedy and Johnson administrations greatly expanded the U.S. nuclear arsenal, deploying 997 new ICBMs and 576 new SLBMs—adding 2,459 missile-delivered warheads and another 505 deliverable by bomber.

utterly nonsensical: "Everyone knows that the United States will never strike first."

Donald Brennan, a defense analyst at the Hudson Institute, took aim at that orthodoxy in an article for *National Review* that gave the Cold War one of its most iconic terms. Placing "mutual" before McNamara's "assured destruction," Brennan wrote, "The concept of mutual assured destruction provides one of the few instances in which the obvious acronym for something yields at once the appropriate description for it; that is, a Mutual Assured Destruction posture as a goal is, almost literally, mad. MAD." Brennan was a scholar, and his arguments against the ABM Treaty and the Interim Agreement were considerably more sophisticated than Ashbrook's. But like other conservatives, he foundered on the misimpression that MAD was a "philosophy," a "sophomoric ideology and fashion" that McNamara had imposed on the Pentagon. Even though he acknowledged that "victory" in a nuclear war would be "altogether Pyrrhic," Brennan simply refused to accept mutual assured destruction.

Increasingly, grassroots conservatives—the people Goldwater had galvanized several years earlier—were cottoning to the idea that America's leaders were waving a white flag in the face of Soviet nuclear aggression. They were led by a woman named Phyllis Schlafly, who in 1952 had captured a GOP congressional nomination by campaigning as a straight-talking—and fiercely anticommunist—housewife. She lost the election, but her profile as a conservative grew, and a decade later she gained national attention when she published *A Choice, Not an Echo,* a pro-Goldwater book that sold millions in the run-up to the 1964 Republican convention. Later, she would become famous for her opposition to the Equal Rights Amendment, but Schlafly first focused her lobbying efforts against arms control. She assailed the Kennedy administration for the LTBT, for its handling of the Cuban missile crisis, and for "unilaterally disarming" in the face of the Soviet nuclear threat. "Our goal must be victory—not containment, coexistence, disengagement, or stalemate," she declared. When the Nixon administration opened the SALT process, she lamented that "the Nixon administration has done nothing to change the disastrous course of nuclear disarmament carried out for seven years by McNamara."

Conservatives were at least as angered by the Nixon administration's unwillingness to defend the country as by the limits on our offensive

systems. Because of the ABM Treaty, Ashbrook complained, "[w]e no longer have the power to protect our country from nuclear missiles, which
can kill scores of millions of Americans. All President Nixon can do is call
up on the hot line and say, 'Please, Mr. Brezhnev, don't fire.'" Of course,
the United States had never had that power in the first place. True, in 1967
Johnson announced plans for a limited system to protect major cities by
detonating nuclear explosions near enemy warheads as they entered the
atmosphere, and in 1969 Nixon reoriented this system to protect U.S. missile fields. But these efforts were rudimentary. Nevertheless, conservatives
were confident that missile defense would enable us to transcend the limitations of a nuclear world. Just as the isolationists and neo-isolationists
of the interwar period had hoped that geography could insulate America
from European wars, conservatives in the Cold War believed that technology could protect America from dealings with communists. A missile
defense was not only a physical shield; it was a moral prophylactic against
the temptation to negotiate with communists in the nuclear age.

Ultimately, conservative objections to SALT boiled down to the
familiar argument that good could not coexist with evil. Any genuine discussion regarding peace could only take place once the underly-
ing ideological conflict had been resolved—once communism had been
defeated and there had been regime change in the Soviet Union. According to Goldwater, arms control and disarmament would be appropriate
only "when the cause for arms is removed." Another *National Review*
correspondent wrote that "the United States can agree to limitation of its
strategic arms only when the Soviet Union proves by its deeds that it has
abandoned all thought of using force to dominate free societies." As Ashbrook put it: "The total history of man indicates we can place very little
reliance on treaties or written documents. This is especially true when
the agreements are with nations or powers which have aggressive plans.
Hitler had plans. Chamberlain's Munich served only to deaden the free
world to reality. The communists have plans. SALT will merely cause us
to lower our guard, possibly fatally." James Burnham, who by now was
calling his *National Review* column "The Protracted Conflict," wrote, "I
repeat: The nature of the regime is the heart of the matter. And this is precisely the factor which, in their discussions of the SALT accords, the President, Henry Kissinger, and all the other official spokesman have resolutely
ignored."

Conclusion

Conservatives were correct in their assessment that arms control would not solve our problems with communism or the Soviet Union: Weapons were the effect, not the cause, of conflict. But that observation missed the point. Nuclear weapons were unlike any form of arms the world had known. Their ability to destroy an entire society in a matter of minutes generated a paranoia in decision makers that could bring about war even if neither side wanted it. Strategic stability therefore had to be the priority: After all, America could not fight an ideological battle if it no longer existed. But nuclear stability required negotiations; it helped if the product of those negotiations was formalized in treaties; and it was likewise essential that each side accepted the other's right to exist. Arms control might not on its own produce détente, but that was irrelevant. In fact, the worse relations got, the more important arms control became: As paranoia increased, the potential for apocalyptic miscalculation did as well.

Conservatives refused to recognize that, in the nuclear age, U.S. security was dependent in some measure on perceptions and actions in Moscow. Psychologically, conservatives could not accept the fact that they could not control this situation. And so they looked to unilateral measures, such as missile defense, that not only allowed them to preserve their belief that victory was attainable but also put them directly in charge of their fate, without having to engage evil. Conservatives failed to prioritize the goal (nuclear security) and the means to achieve it (diplomacy), because to them nothing was more important than regime change.

In the short term, however, conservative distaste for the SALT agreements was of little consequence. The Senate approved the ABM Treaty and the Interim Agreement in August 1972 by the overwhelming majority of 88–2. (Only two senators voted against the treaties—one of whom was James Buckley, Bill's brother. Barry Goldwater was absent but indicated that he would have voted against.) In the House, which had been asked to consider the Interim Agreement because it was a resolution rather than a formal treaty, Ashbrook was joined in opposition by only a few colleagues. He was simply a man ahead of his time, for the ABM Treaty would become a persistent boogeyman, nipping at Reagan's efforts to develop Strategic Defense Initiative (SDI) and the Republican Congress's push for a limited system in the 1990s. Ultimately, George W. Bush would withdraw from the treaty in 2002. After Ashbrook's death ten years later, President Reagan would eulogize him, saying that conservative "principles are in the ascendancy today in large part due to his efforts."

Why, given the fundamental challenge that the ABM Treaty in particular represented to their worldview, did conservative politicians let it pass in 1972? For one thing, a contentious 1969 vote on missile defense had demonstrated that the country was barely willing to spring for a limited system, let alone a more ambitious one that could plausibly provide an advantage in a nuclear war. Indeed, the hearings preceding the 1969 vote had significantly undermined confidence in the technological feasibility of missile defense. Furthermore, Nixon, whatever his liberal heresies, was a Republican president. Conservatives' power was growing within the party and across the country, but few were willing to deal Nixon an enormous defeat in the summer of 1972, when the GOP convention was only weeks away and Democratic challenger George McGovern was still considered a threat. Whatever the growing power of conservatives, opposition to arms control was still a fringe view in the early 1970s. The SALT process was popular, for after years of war in Vietnam, the American public had tired of conflict with the communists.

To encourage Senate ratification of the SALT accords, Nixon linked the vote to increased funding for the B-1 bomber and MIRV systems. This placated conservatives by suggesting that whatever the philosophical implications of SALT, the United States would continue to seek nuclear advantage over the Soviets. White House officials reassured the concerned that America would retain a large lead in warheads deployed. Victory could still be ours.

Conservatives were also soothed by legislation from Senator Henry "Scoop" Jackson of Washington State. Jackson had chafed at the apparently unequal limits set for U.S. and Soviet launchers, fearing the treaty codified not parity but inferiority. The only explanation, he suggested, evoking Yalta, was that Nixon had reached some secret agreement with Moscow in exchange for SALT—perhaps a promise to help end the war in Vietnam. True, we were ahead technologically and we did have more bombers, but, whereas we could not deploy any more ICBMs, the treaty allowed the Soviets to deploy as many more bombers as they wanted. Jackson led the charge against the treaty's "inequality," ultimately championing an amendment demanding that, in future treaties, all numerical limits be equal. Of course, the senator wasn't interested in equality. As his top arms control aide later acknowledged, "Our real preference was not parity, but victory. You don't get a victory out of parity." It was a classically conservative statement. The only problem was that Jackson was a Democrat, as was his aide, Richard Perle. They would be at the vanguard of a new addition to the conservative movement, and the Right was about to get a whole lot more powerful.

Chapter Three

MOVEMENT

ON NOVEMBER 12, 1979, several hundred concerned Americans descended on the nation's capital. They checked into the Hotel Washington, where a block of rooms had been reserved for them, and the next morning headed to One Constitution Avenue, the site of the Reserve Officers Association Memorial Building, just feet from the U.S. Capitol and the Senate offices. There, after coffee and donuts, they were briefed on their mission: to convince one hundred senators to vote against the SALT II treaty, which Jimmy Carter had signed five months earlier. Although the treaty set equal limits on the number of launchers the United States and the Soviets were allowed, its opponents felt that it merely enshrined American weakness in the face of a growing Soviet nuclear threat. They called their efforts Peace Through Strength Week, incorporating a phrase that Ronald Reagan (who was announcing his candidacy for the presidency that very day in New York) would use often to explain his unique approach to arms control. But Peace Through Strength Week was also a show of force in and of itself—domestic political force, wielded by a new conservative coalition.

The four-day event was the brainchild of an organization called the American Security Council. Founded in the 1950s with the McCarthyite goal of ferreting out communists in the business community, the ASC had, by the 1970s, broadened its focus to a more general assault on détente and arms control. In 1978, it formed the Coalition for Peace Through Strength, an alliance of 148 members of Congress, led by Senator Robert Dole, who opposed Carter's foreign policy and insisted that the United States maintain nuclear superiority over the Soviet Union—repudiating the notion of the stable nuclear balance that Robert McNamara and Henry Kissinger had advocated and that SALT II was supposed to reinforce. The coalition touched a nerve in the military and political establishment, and within a year it had signed up another 43 U.S. senators and representatives and 2,400 retired or reserve generals and admirals, all of whom opposed the treaty on the grounds that it was a "symbol of phased surrender" to the Soviet Union.

In addition to this official firepower, the coalition boasted a wealth of "member organizations" that brought its message to the American people. These included dozens of conservative groups—the American Conservative Union, Young Americans for Freedom, and Phyllis Schlafly's Eagle Forum, to name but a few—but, interestingly, also something called the Coalition for a Democratic Majority, whose stated goals were to return the Democratic Party to the principles of Harry Truman (who, of course, had not been a conservative).

The centerpiece of the Coalition for Peace Through Strength's outreach effort was a half-hour film called *The SALT Syndrome*. Set to a soundtrack fit for a horror movie, it featured image after image of missiles launching, submarines creeping, and nuclear weapons exploding, punctuated by commentary from retired generals and intelligence officials. The "syndrome" was the American tendency to "unilaterally disarm," which had gripped Washington policy makers after the United States decided to follow "McNamara's theory of 'no defense,' which is called 'Mutual Assured Destruction.'" The movie was a concise, vivid statement of conservative nuclear thought: MAD was a choice. As the narrator explained, "You play an important role in U.S. strategy—that of nuclear hostage." Meanwhile, the Soviets had proceeded to pursue a war-winning capability, producing many times more missiles, submarines, and bombers than we had, as well as missile defenses, air defenses, and civil defenses, all of which would allegedly enable the Soviets to coerce us into doing whatever they wanted.

The movie was a remarkable, and remarkably effective, piece of propaganda. It combined fact, exaggeration, and outright nonsense—one interviewee claimed the Soviet Union was on the verge of deploying particle beams that would shoot down all incoming missiles—to argue that the United States had left itself nearly helpless against a Soviet behemoth bent on world domination. Ultimately, it was shown on television more than two thousand times; the ASC's chairman, John Fisher, estimated that by the 1980 election, the council's messages would have reached at least 137 million Americans. An 800 number that ran during the movie solicited donations, and the coalition would earmark millions of dollars for the defeat of SALT II, ultimately outspending protreaty forces by fifteen to one. The American Security Council also sponsored mailings to ten million households and ran ads in papers across the country, accusing Carter of allowing the United States to militarily fall behind the Soviet Union.

Only seven years earlier, the Senate's 88–2 passage of the ABM Treaty and the SALT I Interim Agreement had demonstrated that politicians of both parties, as well as the foreign policy establishment—that is, the elite and largely nonpartisan group of decision makers who ran policy from administration to administration—broadly supported Nixon, arms control, and détente. Conservative outliers who opposed accommodation with the Soviet Union had little power, while hard-line policy makers who were squeamish about parity with the Soviets were appeased by Nixon's promise that the U.S. arms buildup would continue despite the Interim Agreement's strictures. The ABM Treaty might have embraced mutual assured destruction, but development of multiple-warhead systems suggested that the United States would still try to win a nuclear war. For their part, the American people were eager to ease Cold War tensions, skeptical of missile defense, and hopeful that arms control could prevent an apocalypse.

By 1976, however, dissatisfaction with détente had spread beyond conservative circles, with 60 percent to 70 percent of Americans believing that the Soviet Union had benefitted more from rapprochement than we had. Even though the Soviets had promised to help reduce tensions in the Middle East and Southeast Asia, they had tolerated an Egyptian attack on Israel in 1973 and continued to aid the North Vietnamese, doing nothing to stop them from overrunning the South in 1975. They had aided communists in Portugal after its revolution in 1974 and used Cuban troops to impose a Marxist regime in Angola in 1975. Détente increasingly seemed to be a one-way street, with the United States restraining itself while the Soviet Union continued an unchecked military buildup in support of ever-increasing expansionist aims.

Despite these disappointments, President Gerald Ford hewed closely to the realpolitik of his predecessor, appointing the liberal Nelson Rockefeller as vice president and keeping Henry Kissinger as his secretary of state and national security adviser. Ford's moderate position, however, only spurred greater levels of foreign policy radicalism. *National Review* was relieved at the tension that resulted. For the previous several years, it opined, "Diogenes couldn't find an admitted cold warrior in Washington . . . even with a pack of bloodhounds added to his lantern." Now, however, a split was opening between "hards" and "softs." The former, the editors noted approvingly, stressed the importance of the "free movement of people and ideas across national borders, insisting that this is not merely an 'internal question' but a precondition for genuinely friendly relations among nations. They criticize SALT I for having conceded the Soviet Union quantitative superiority in strategic weapons and fear SALT II will concede qualitative superiority also." In other words, the character of the regime mattered more than nuclear stability. Interestingly, *National Review* noted, those who were "hards" did not overlap precisely with those who were Republicans or even those traditionally classified as conservatives.

National Review was on to something. In the mid-1970s, hawks—that is, establishment policy makers who placed a higher premium on confrontation and the use of military force than did their more "dovish" colleagues—who had long nested comfortably within both Republican and Democratic administrations, became increasingly wary of our relationship with the Soviet Union. They did not believe that détente had borne the fruits that Nixon and Kissinger had promised and feared that we were lulling ourselves into a dangerous complacency as Moscow's power, particularly its nuclear arsenal, grew stronger and stronger. This growing concern brought them into alignment with the acolytes of Barry Goldwater, who had rejected accommodation with the Soviets since the Eisenhower administration. At the same time, a faction of liberal intellectuals dissatisfied with the pacifistic post-Vietnam tenor of the Democratic Party found that their militant anticommunism brought them closer to the right than the left side of the political spectrum, leading them to be dubbed "neoconservatives."

Like sheets of ice calving from a glacier, the hawks and the neoconservatives fell away into the sea of conservative discontent that had been lapping at Washington's centrist foreign policy establishment for decades. These converts shared the conservative belief that, in the Soviet Union, the United States faced an ideological enemy with messianic goals. The neoconservatives, particularly, subscribed to the simplistic good-versus-evil, us-versus-them schema that animated the Right. They believed that there were clear sides in the Cold War and worried that Democrats had forgotten this defining principle. The hawks were less moralistic but no less explicit in their assessment of the Soviet threat. They agreed that MAD was a choice, that nuclear war fighting was a better strategy, and that negotiation was of little value—and in doing so they effectively accepted the Manichaean worldview that had led conservatives to the same conclusion.

The collapse of the détente consensus not only led to a new political alliance but also yielded a new intellectual tactic, as the neocons brought a sense that their convictions about Soviet perfidy painted a more accurate picture of Soviet intentions and capabilities than the data and analysis of American intelligence agencies. In essence, they argued that the nature of the Cold War was something to be morally intuited, not empirically observed. They painted a horrifying picture of the Soviet threat, lent gravitas by the support of establishment figures who played on the fears of average Americans. Thus, at the same moment that the conservative movement got an infusion of brains from the hawks and neocons, it got an infusion of brawn from the grass roots.

The Hawks Fly Right

Within the Washington establishment, two incidents in particular catalyzed growing opposition to accommodation with the Soviets. First was the visit of exiled Soviet dissident Alexander Solzhenitsyn, who stopped in the capital during the summer of 1975 to speak at an AFL-CIO dinner. Freshman senator Jesse Helms—an absolutist who saw the Cold War as a struggle being waged on "every continent" and who was eager to speak up "in favor of freedom and against Communism, wherever it was found"—tried to arrange for Solzhenitsyn to meet with the president in early July, but Ford demurred. The president was about to visit Brezhnev in Moscow, and Kissinger feared a formal meeting with the author of *The Gulag Archipelago* would sour the trip. Conservatives were outraged by the amorality of this calculation. How was it that the United States had so lowered its standards that an American president would shun a heroic dissident to placate a communist regime? George F. Will, who had begun his journalistic career at *National Review* and was now writing for the *Washington Post* as well, opined that Ford aides were "showing a flair for baseness that would have stood them in good stead with the previous administration."

Weeks later, Ford further angered the Right by endorsing what was known as the Helsinki Final Act. The measure was the product of two years of negotiation by the Conference on Security and Cooperation in Europe to settle various issues that had remained outstanding since World War II. Among other things, it officially sanctioned the postwar national borders, a move that effectively legitimized Soviet control over the Baltic states. Despite the fact that the agreement was a consensus document signed by thirty-five nations, most of them noncommunist, conservatives declared the Final Act another Yalta. Solzhenitsyn himself denounced the conference as "the betrayal of Eastern Europe" and noted, to make sure his point had not been missed, that "an amicable agreement of diplomatic shovels will bury and pack down corpses still breathing in a common grave."

Although conservatives had warily eyed Nixon's rapprochement with the USSR and China, most right-wing officials, such as Barry Goldwater and John Tower, had refused to break with the GOP, whatever their ideological qualms. In the mid-1970s, their loyalty proved justified when a politician named Ronald Reagan saw a chance to capture the Republican Party for conservatives. Reagan, a former actor and charter subscriber of *National Review,* had been a leading conservative since he stumped for Goldwater in 1964, delivering a carefully developed speech articulating conservative principles—moral virtue, rollback of government, inveterate hostility to communism—more compellingly than Goldwater himself could. The success of "The Speech" catapulted him to the governorship of California, where he quickly became a top contender for the GOP presidential nomination, coming in second to Nixon in 1968. By the time Nixon resigned, Reagan was nationally recognized, popular for reforming California's welfare system, and untarnished by Watergate—leaving him ready to challenge Ford in the name of Goldwater's ideals.

That meant, in no small part, promoting the conservative view of the Cold War—including moral condemnation of the Soviet regime—and the policies that stemmed from it. Reagan, beginning his 1976 run for the Republican presidential nomination, attacked Ford's coldness toward Solzhenitsyn ("one of the great moral heroes of our time") and his signing of the Helsinki Final Act (placing "the American seal of approval on the Soviet empire in Eastern Europe"). Indeed, Reagan's campaign was relentlessly antidétente, opposing the Nixon-Kissinger-Ford policies of realpolitik. Reagan's popularity—he almost defeated Ford in the New Hampshire primary, and ultimately won twelve states—revealed that the antinegotiation attitude once the exclusive province of conservatives now appealed to rank-and-file Republicans.

By early 1976, conservative pressure had grown so intense that Ford stopped using the word "détente" altogether, and although he won the nomination, the policy was effectively dead. At the convention, Reagan supporters introduced a "Morality in Foreign Policy" plank to the GOP platform that explicitly repudiated détente, praised Solzhenitsyn by name, and criticized the Final Act, even repeating the accusation that it was a Yalta-like secret accord—a shocking rebuke to a sitting U.S. president from his own party. Ford was furious but was persuaded not to challenge the plank by his thirty-four-year-old chief of staff, Dick Cheney, who had also (unsuccessfully) pressured him to meet with Solzhenitsyn.

The Right attacked Ford's arms control overtures as well. Richard Nixon had resigned the presidency in August 1974, having made little progress on a SALT II Treaty, with negotiations hamstrung by the question of how to limit MIRVs and by the president's increasing attention to Watergate. Eager to meet Brezhnev and move SALT II forward, Ford flew on November 23, 1974, to Vladivostok, where he found the premier willing to make a deal. Brezhnev offered Ford a choice between equal ceilings (meaning each side would have the same number of ICBMs, SLBMs, and heavy bombers) and "offsetting asymmetries," by which the United States would be allowed more MIRV missiles while the Soviets would be allowed more launch vehicles. Though both options represented progress, offsetting asymmetries made more sense for the Americans, as it left the Soviets with fewer MIRV launchers, less overall throw weight (that is, missile payload capacity), and fewer warheads. True, they would have more missiles, but their arsenal would be a more stable one, geared more toward deterrence than toward war fighting. Ford, however, knew that he would have to sell the agreement on the Hill, and with Scoop Jackson's popular call for numerical equality in SALT II on his mind, he and Brezhnev agreed that the United States and the Soviet Union would each be allowed 2,400 long-range delivery systems, only 1,320 of which could be MIRVed.

The deal represented yet another instance of right-wing opposition to arms control undermining not only nuclear stability but the stated goals of conservatives—in this case, a U.S. advantage in MIRVs. Worse, Ford's decision did not placate the Right. Having demanded equality in the number of launch vehicles, conservatives now complained that the Vladivostok deal, which provided just that, left the United States in an inferior position. Senator James L. Buckley—William F. Buckley, Jr.'s brother and one of the two senators to vote against the SALT I accords—delivered a speech warning of just this eventuality. James Burnham explained that, although there was equality in types of missiles, the Soviet ICBMs had far greater throw weight, and therefore "the agreement recognizes and in effect freezes Soviet superiority in nuclear firepower." And Reagan noted that "the major drawback of the proposed SALT agreement announced by Messrs. Ford and Brezhnev at Vladivostok last fall is its failure to provide for parity in missile payloads." The United States was already at a four-to-one disadvantage, he said, and could soon be at a ten-to-one disadvantage unless it acted quickly.

Far more interesting was the fact that hawks within the administration were beginning to sound increasingly like conservatives. In early 1974, Secretary of Defense James Schlesinger had pushed the development of a new nuclear weapons doctrine that would give the president a greater range of nuclear options in the event of a confrontation with the Soviet Union—that is, he would be able to attack anything from a few Soviet military bases to the country's entire economic infrastructure. In and of itself, this provision fit with Robert McNamara's conclusion that, while a limited nuclear war was unlikely to stay limited, it was better to have options—which is why both Nixon and Kissinger approved the plan. But Schlesinger put a different spin on it, explaining at a luncheon press conference at the Overseas Writers Association that he was effecting a "change in targeting strategy" so that the United States had alternatives to "initiating a suicidal strike against the cities of the other side." MAD, he said, was bad; we needed more flexibility. Schlesinger was essentially parroting the conservative line, implying that MAD was a policy that could be rejected—as opposed to a condition—and that he was the one who had done it.

Schlesinger himself was not part of the conservative movement. Rather he was an economist who had worked for several years at RAND and served the Nixon administration in several capacities before being appointed secretary of defense, growing increasingly concerned as the Soviets approached nuclear parity with the United States. Whereas Kissinger argued that "military superiority has no practical significance . . . under circumstances in which both sides have the capability to annihilate one another," Schlesinger worried that the Soviets might gain some sort of counterforce advantage. While his announcement about targeting had the effect of chilling U.S.-Soviet negotiations, given that MAD was the basis for SALT, he also tried to scuttle the talks directly. At a June 20, 1974, meeting of the NSC, Schlesinger told Nixon that his Pentagon would not support any SALT agreement that did not guarantee U.S. superiority. He wrote Senator Scoop Jackson a letter advocating Jackson's hardline approach to SALT, effectively undermining the president's. And in the run-up to Vladivostok, he encouraged Ford to hold out for an equal number of launchers—in part because he believed the Soviets would never accept it (foreshadowing a tactic that would be used by arms control opponents in the Reagan and George W. Bush administrations).

On November 2, 1975, as part of a shake-up of his national security staff, Ford fired Schlesinger, who left office complaining about the illusions of détente and Kissinger's softness toward the Soviets. His dismissal became something of a cause célèbre on the right, with Reagan claiming that Ford had fired Schlesinger because the president was afraid to admit "the truth about our military status." But as it happened, conservatives needn't have worried about Schlesinger's replacement. Donald Rumsfeld, a congressman from Illinois and then head of Nixon's Office of Economic Opportunity, had been a proponent of disengaging from Vietnam. But he had always had hawkish leanings; as a freshman representative he had tried to sabotage the confirmation of Kennedy's secretary of the navy by insinuating that he supported nuclear disarmament in the face of the Soviet threat. Tapped to represent the United States at NATO headquarters in 1973, he pivoted further rightward, most notably on arms control issues, becoming increasingly concerned with the loss of American nuclear superiority.

Within weeks of his appointment to the Pentagon, Rumsfeld began attempts to thwart the SALT II talks. In December, Ford and Kissinger left on a tour of Asia, after which Kissinger planned to fly to Moscow with suggestions for addressing issues. But during the trip, Rumsfeld cabled Kissinger aboard Air Force One to complain that he had not been consulted about the proposal, forcing Kissinger to abandon his trip. When Kissinger finally did go to Moscow, Rumsfeld opposed the deal he reached, effectively killing it, because, as Ford later noted, the Senate would never ratify an arms treaty that did not have the support of the secretary of defense: "The attitude in the Defense Department made it impossible to proceed in the environment of 1976." Hawks were beginning to flock to a perch that had been the exclusive province of conservatives.

Perhaps the most conspicuous defection was that of Paul Nitze, investment banker-turned-public servant. Nitze was one of the seminal figures in the creation of the Cold War containment consensus. He had written NSC-68 and helped draft the Gaither Committee report, which had warned of the nonexistent "missile gap" that Kennedy highlighted during the 1960 election. While in the Kennedy administration, he had favored air strikes during the Cuban missile crisis, and in the late 1960s he had lobbied Congress in support of missile defense. Nitze had always been gravely concerned that the Soviets would gain military superiority over the United States, but he balanced that fear with a desire to create global stability and prevent nuclear war. At an academic conference in 1960, Nitze had speculated that the safest approach to nuclear weapons might be to put them under NATO, and then UN, control. And when Nixon appointed him to the SALT I delegation he became a committed arms control negotiator, helping forge the ABM Treaty and the Interim Agreement. Although these actions left him open to attacks from the Right—it was Nitze whose appointment to the navy Rumsfeld had tried to sabotage—Nitze's anticommunism had always been quite hawkish. Conflicting impulses had always rent Nitze, and it now seemed that the more pessimistic had taken hold.

In June 1974, Nitze resigned from the SALT II delegation, believing that Nixon had been so weakened by Watergate that he was apt to cave to Soviet pressure. The deal Ford struck at Vladivostok did nothing to reassure him, and in an article in the January 1976 issue of *Foreign Affairs*, Nitze made a striking break with his past approach to arms control, which had welcomed the principles of parity and nuclear stability. Now he argued that "there is every prospect that under the terms of the SALT agreements the Soviet Union will continue to pursue a nuclear superiority that is not merely quantitative but designed to produce a theoretical war-winning capability." The Soviets, he wrote, might wish to avoid a war, but they did not believe it unthinkable, as the United States did—hence their ambitious civil defense efforts. While we had pursued policies designed to reinforce MAD, the Soviets had pursued a nuclear advantage, believing it would give them a political advantage. According to Nitze, the terms of the Vladivostok agreement would eventually enable the Soviets to launch a first strike that took out our ICBMs—the chief component of our deterrent force—leaving us with only less accurate submarine-launched missiles. The United States could use those to retaliate against Soviet cities, but, Nitze argued, we would be reluctant to do so because the Soviets could then destroy American cities in a third strike.

Nitze attacked not just Vladivostok but the arms control process in general: "Unfortunately, I believe the record shows that neither negotiations nor unilateral restraint have operated to dissuade Soviet leaders from seeking a nuclear war–winning capability—or from the view that with such a capability they could effectively use pressure tactics to get their way in crisis situations." Détente itself was useless: "[I am] skeptical that the Soviet leaders are in fact moving toward any lasting reduction in tensions, or any abandonment of expansionist aims." The only solution was to increase our own war-fighting capability by making our missiles less vulnerable and, if possible, creating a viable civil defense system.

The *Foreign Affairs* article was a shocking piece of work. Here was a charter member of the Cold War foreign policy establishment—a man who had been a lead negotiator of the SALT I accords—taking the conservative line on the very utility of arms control. Nitze was an expert, not just another ideologue. The war-winning strategy he encouraged became a touchstone for conservatives, as to them it made perfect sense. Conservatives, by supporting Nixon, had largely ignored the SALT I accords, allowing the idea of coexistence to be enshrined in a nuclear treaty. With Nitze's objection to the SALT II negotiations, they were given a second chance to reject MAD in favor of victory. So was Scoop Jackson.

Enter the Neocons

Scoop Jackson, like conservatives, believed in the existence of evil. In 1945, as a congressman, he had visited the Buchenwald concentration camp just days after its liberation from the Nazis, an experience which had cemented his conviction that American power should be used to fight totalitarianism. Throughout his service in Congress, Jackson consistently championed a strong defense, lambasting Eisenhower for spending too little on weapons, spearheading congressional support for the Vietnam War, and later opposing those who wanted to "cut and run," as he put it. He distrusted the concept of mutual assured destruction, advocating in its stead missile defenses to shield the nation from Soviet attack. And he was convinced that arms control threatened to give the communists a decisive nuclear advantage; it was his amendment to the SALT I Interim Agreement that called on future treaties to set "equal" limits, perversely pushing Ford to accept a less favorable agreement at Vladivostok.

It was hardly surprising, then, that during the Nixon administration Jackson tried to undermine détente. In 1972, he proposed an amendment that would have denied normal trade relations with certain countries that did not freely allow emigration, a shot at the Soviet refusal to allow Jews to leave the country without paying an "exit tax." When Kissinger complained that Jackson was hurting the administration's attempts to secure Moscow's cooperation, he sneered, "Wouldn't it be nice to have a secretary of State who doesn't take the Soviet point of view?" Jackson's focus on the evil of the Soviet Union and his distaste for amoral realpolitik would have put him squarely in the conservative camp, except for the fact that he was a Democrat with a strong attachment to New Deal policies. Such liberal economic leanings put him at odds with the *National Review* crowd, but they dovetailed nicely with a movement gaining momentum in intellectual circles in the late 1960s and early 1970s.

The ideology that became known as neoconservatism had its origins in prewar New York, where the American Left comprised not only Rooseveltian liberals, but communists and their assorted fellow travelers, who believed that the Soviet Union provided a feasible alternative to the democratic, capitalist system that had failed so many during the Depression. By the late 1940s, these radicals had largely been purged from respectable public discourse—or at least from the Democratic Party. But that national reckoning had in fact been preceded in the 1930s within the cafeteria alcoves of the City College of New York, where, as the world was engulfed in a titanic struggle against fascism, two groups of Jewish students—among them Irving Kristol, who would become neoconservatism's leading figure—debated the morality of the Soviet state. Both groups were Marxist, but while one was tenaciously pro-Soviet, the other had come to believe that Stalin had betrayed the ideals of the Russian Revolution and spawned a moral monstrosity. This conviction was soon reinforced by news of Stalin's show trials against scores of Soviet revolutionaries, thinkers, and artists, and confirmed by his 1939 pact with Hitler. Kristol and his friends concluded that the regime was poisoned, and so was the ideology it had used to justify its crimes.

It is difficult to understate the disillusionment of these nascent intellectuals—and the vitriol with which they viewed the Stalinists. Their rejection of communism was a defining choice, decisively splitting them from all who harbored sympathy for the Soviet regime, and it was replaced by an ardent nationalistic Americanism, the product of their realization that the United States, whatever its flaws, had defeated fascism in World War II and now provided the only feasible counterweight to the Soviet monster. They adopted what Norman Podhoretz, editor of the neoconservative journal *Commentary,* would later call a "hard anti-communism" defined by two propositions: "(1) the Soviet Union was a totalitarian state of the same unqualifiedly evil character as Nazi Germany, and as such could not be expected to change except for the worse . . . ; (2) the Soviet Union was incorrigibly committed to the cause of world revolution. . . . [O]nly American power stood in the way of this fanatical ambition to destroy freedom all over the world, and only American awareness of the threat could generate policies that would threaten it."

As the conservative movement took root in the mid-1950s, then, these intellectuals adopted a strict good-versus-evil outlook—and a scorn for radical elements of the American Left—that was not unlike that of the ex-communists in *National Review*'s orbit who were defining modern conservatism. But, like Jackson, these men retained a yearning for social justice that did not comport with the libertarianism of the Right; they distrusted utopian visions as much as conservatives did, but not the welfare state itself. Harry Truman, with his commitment to New Deal principles and his aggressive anticommunism, made for a better fit.

But as the uproar of the 1960s tore liberalism apart, they moved right. The catalyst was the New Left, the student movement that challenged the Democratic establishment: the party hierarchy, its failure to redress economic and racial inequality, and, ultimately, its complicity in the Vietnam War. The New Left riled neoconservatives on a number of levels. Tom Hayden, the lanky, intense leader of Students for a Democratic Society, and his radical comrades reminded the CCNY alums of the Stalinists they had faced thirty years earlier. In his calls for participatory democracy, they

detected a revolutionary utopianism, a mass politics that was at best hope-
less and at worst dangerous. In the New Left's association with the counter-
culture of the sixties, they perceived a lack of respect for traditional values.
The SDS protests of 1968, in which radicals seized university buildings,
evoked for neoconservatives the American communists of 1948, who had
seized control of unions and the Progressive Party. Moreover, Kristol and
his comrades were, first and foremost, intellectuals; the attack on institutions dedicated to the free exchange of ideas—institutions that many had
made their homes—smacked of totalitarianism.

But it was the New Left's refusal to condemn the evils of communism—
its anti-anticommunism—that truly animated the neoconservative movement. Defeating communism was the top priority for these onetime
Marxists, and though not all of them supported the Vietnam War, they were
horrified by the antiwar movement, which attacked not only American
involvement in Southeast Asia, but the struggle against communism writ
large, and even America itself. It was undoubtedly true, as the New Left
insisted, that U.S. power could be used for ill as well as for good, but some
protesters turned that observation into the argument that America was
invariably imperialist and militarist. Other protesters added severe insult
to injury by adopting the converse position, venerating Mao Tse-tung, Fidel
Castro, and Ho Chi Minh.

The New Left, of course, was not speaking for the Democratic foreign
policy establishment, but Vietnam was forcing first Johnson and then his
would-be successors in 1968 and 1972 to question exactly how the United
States should contain the Soviet Union. In 1967, McGeorge Bundy, the
former national security adviser, published an article titled "The End of
Either/Or," which argued that however tempting it was to view the fight
against communism as a cartoon war of good guys versus bad guys, the
United States had to acknowledge the limits of its power while also fulfilling its global responsibilities. In truth, Truman, Eisenhower, and Kennedy
had never seen the Cold War in terms of black and white, but Bundy and
fellow members of the Vital Center were making a serious effort to reap-
praise the purposes of American might. It was an eminently sensible
move, but neoconservatives were convinced that it meant the party was
abandoning anticommunism in favor of isolationism or a naive moral
relativism. For neoconservatives, the United States was the only thing
standing between the free world and communism. What made their

anticommunism "hard" was its division of the world into good and evil. Indeed, perhaps the most salient tendency these intellectuals took from their CCNY years was an all-consuming oppositionalism—it was Alcove 1 versus Alcove 2; Trotskyists versus Stalinists; liberals versus communists; good versus evil; us versus them.

When procedural changes took the power to choose candidates away from party bosses and placed it in the hands of primary electorates and interest groups, traditional Democratic politics collapsed. The SDS principles of "participatory democracy" tipped the scales of the presidential nomination process away from its traditional base of working-class voters—voters who favored a strongly anticommunist foreign policy—toward progressive movements that could turn out greater numbers of voters. The result was the nomination in 1972 of George McGovern, who wanted to reduce America's global presence. Neoconservatives were stunned; no one whose campaign slogan was "come home America" could conceivably fight communism. They felt that an ideological minority had hijacked the Democratic Party. If this was the New Left, Kristol, Podhoretz, and their fellow neocons would head right.

The Republican Party, however, did not offer obvious sanctuary. Realists of the Nixon-Kissinger stripe did not care about the character of the Soviet regime; indeed, their philosophy of international politics denied that such things mattered. So after Nixon defeated McGovern in 1972, neoconservatives formed the Coalition for a Democratic Majority (CDM) to rescue the Democratic Party from the antiwar, radical Left and pull it back toward a militant anticommunism. Its members— intellectuals such as Jeane Kirkpatrick, Midge Decter, Eugene Rostow, Richard Pipes, and others—saw themselves as the heirs of Truman. They didn't seem to realize, however, that Truman's anticommunism, while moral, was not moralist—that is, while it confronted the Soviet Union, it never reduced that fight to black and white terms. The neocons did—and, as a result, came to the same conclusions that conservatives had.

The CDM argued that détente was a false peace. Whereas Americans defined détente as a state of genuinely peaceful relations, the Soviets defined it simply as the absence of direct aggression between the superpowers while "ideological struggle" persisted. In other words, the CDM vilified détente because it *only* helped us avoid nuclear war, while taking no steps toward true peace. Like *National Review* and Barry Goldwater, the CDM argued that the free movement of people and ideas was a precondition for friendly relations among nations. That might be true, but it was most certainly not a precondition for preventing nuclear war, and preventing nuclear war was no small accomplishment. For neoconservatives, as for conservatives, regime change was more important than nuclear stability.

Somewhat confusingly, the CDM believed that, although the Soviets were pursuing détente in order to avoid a major war while continuing ideological combat, they were also pursuing a nuclear first-strike capability, a capability they might well achieve if America pushed ahead with SALT II. The only solution was to prepare for confrontation. As one CDM policy brief declared, "As they did in the Truman years, liberals and Democrats must again take the lead in rallying America to increase our defense capabilities, both nuclear and conventional." The CDM's political representative was Scoop Jackson, whom it supported in his 1976 bid for the Democratic presidential nomination. Ultimately, Jackson would fall to Jimmy Carter in the primaries, but his influence would be significant, as his acolytes bridged the gap between the intellectual world of the neoconservatives and the policy makers of Washington.

The alignment of the hawks and neocons with the conservatives represented in some respects a second wave of the fusionism that had brought together the traditionalists, libertarians, and anticommunists in the 1950s. Just as suspicion and hatred of the Soviet Union had united those seemingly disparate groups into a coherent ideological movement, so did a strong suspicion of the Soviet Union and of détente and arms control unite 1970s contrarians, sublimating their differences under a shared fear of American weakness and Soviet strength.

While conservatives welcomed the company ("Come on in, the water's fine," *National Review* beckoned to the neocons), there was no individual like Frank Meyer to formally bless this union, and no single magazine like *National Review* to lend the nascent assembly a patina of ideological coherence. Together, these factions would soon erupt with monstrous political force, but to ignite, they needed a catalyst. That catalyst—a small exercise in "competitive intelligence" known as Team B—would not only fuse a new conservative movement but would provide it with an insidious tool that would be wielded during the Carter administration (and to devastating effect decades later by the George W. Bush administration): the politicization of truth.

The Nature of Truth

Conservatives had long distrusted the CIA. The Agency was a bastion of East Coast elitism with a tendency to hire from Wall Street and the Ivy League, and its leaders tended to be liberal. Worse than its sins of breeding and political affiliation, however, was the CIA's intellectual foundation. The Central Intelligence Agency was, after all, built not only on the derring-do of Cold War spies, but also on the empiricism of desk-bound analysts who believed that most variables could be measured and that hard data could ultimately paint an accurate picture of reality. The Agency's motto—"And ye shall know the truth and the truth shall make you free"—might have been taken from the Gospel according to John, but the CIA was most certainly not a faith-based institution. Quite the opposite. Sherman Kent, a Yale historian who became the director of the Agency's Office of National Estimates, wrote in his textbook on intelligence: "[W]e insist, and have insisted for generations, that truth is to be approached, if not attained, through research guided by a systematic method. In the social sciences, . . . there is such a method."

To conservatives, this creed was not as inoffensive as it might seem. Traditionalists like Richard Weaver distrusted the Enlightenment itself, because its embrace of secular rationalism displaced God from human affairs. During the Progressive Era, the idea that economic, political, and even cultural phenomena were the products of measurable forces bred ranks of social scientists and government experts who were confident they could solve problems such as poverty and crime. By contrast, traditionalists believed that social science—with its notion that quantitative analysis could improve the human condition—was a step toward communism, with its goal of *perfecting* the human condition. The scientific method was fine for physics, but metaphysics should be left to the divine. As *National Review* had explained in its first issue, "The profound crisis of our era is, in essence, the conflict between the Social Engineers, who seek to adjust mankind to conform with scientific utopias, and the disciples of Truth, who defend the organic moral order." It did not help that a belief in the utility of government led to the expansion of government, which offended libertarians as well.

Whatever the CIA's ideological and methodological sins, for the first decades of the Cold War conservatives left the Agency alone because it played a vital role in fighting Soviet influence.* The CIA's covert and counterrevolutionary activities comprised the only efforts to roll back, rather than just contain, communism. By the late 1960s and 1970s, when the CIA gained notoriety for those very activities, antagonism toward the Agency became a left-wing cause and its defense therefore a badge of honor for the Right. But just beneath the surface lay an ideological time bomb. How, after all, could conservatives, who believed that the essential character of the Soviet Union had to be understood at a visceral, even religious, level, trust white-jacketed men with calipers to measure the communist threat?

It was the neoconservatives who ultimately brought this skepticism to the fore. Many of the first neocons were social scientists themselves, but they knew that even well-meaning programs could have perverse effects. Welfare, for example, while providing an economic safety net, could also encourage dependency on the government and cultivate a permanent underclass. In the mid-1960s, as President Johnson pursued the Great Society, neoconservatives became concerned about overreach—that "big ideas" to improve material conditions were in fact fostering crime, riots, and social distortion. As Irving Kristol wrote, "[W]e certainly do have it in our power to make improvements in the human estate, but to think we have it in our power to change people so as to make the human estate radically better than it is . . . [is an] arrogant assumption. . . . [B]y acting upon this assumption we shall certainly end up making our world worse than it need have been." Kristol explained that problems of social policy were issues "of political philosophy, not of economics or sociology or public policy in the conventional sense of that term"—a belief that mirrored Russell Kirk's conviction that "political problems, at bottom, are religious and moral problems." When activist government programs failed, the neoconservative contributors to the *Public Interest* concluded that they

---

*In fact, William F. Buckley, Jr. himself briefly served as a spy in Mexico City in the early 1950s, providing information on left-leaning student groups.

did so because they failed to factor values, morality, and culture into the equation.

Neoconservatives originally intended to improve social policy, not subvert it, but, as journalist Franklin Foer has written, their critique opened the door to a wholesale skepticism of scientifically discoverable truth. In this Kristol and other neoconservatives were profoundly influenced by Leo Strauss, a philosopher who preferred the received wisdom of the Greeks to Enlightenment-style inquiry. Strauss embraced terms like "good" and "evil" at a time when moral relativism pervaded the academy, and he reinforced the neoconservative conviction that morality mattered in public policy. Straussianism was similar to the traditionalism of the Right, and it also helped fertilize conservatism. One of Strauss's most famous students was Harry Jaffa, who wrote speeches for Goldwater during the 1964 campaign and argued that American government was based on the idea of natural law. William F. Buckley, Jr., noted that Strauss was important because he taught that "scientific approaches to epistemology" were "terribly misleading."

The neocon critique thus metastasized from constructive criticism of social programs to an assault on those programs and on the bureaucrats, intellectuals, and experts who administered them. In 1966, political analyst David T. Bazelon published an essay in *Commentary* observing that, in postindustrial America, universities were churning out a "new class" of highly educated workers, who, needing outlets for their expertise, flocked to jobs in government, think tanks, academia, and journalism. Bazelon's article was more descriptive than critical, but over the following decade neoconservatives employed his analysis to explain why American policy continued to move toward the political left via the Great Society, increased business regulation, and détente: The new class was using its so-called expertise not to advance the national interest but to advance liberal political causes—and its own professional fortunes. An unrepresentative subset of the population was steering the ship of state, and it would be the job of an even smaller and less representative subset of the population to warn the country of this danger: "It is the self-imposed assignment of neoconservatism to explain to the American people why they are right and to the intellectuals why they are wrong," Kristol wrote.

Much of this animus was initially directed against government regulation—the consumer and environmental protection efforts gaining strength in the early 1970s. Kristol believed that the new class had been imbued with the "anti-capitalist aspirations of the left": "The simple truth is that the professional classes of our modern bureaucratized societies are engaged in a class struggle with the business community for status and power." He worried that regulation was slowly strangling free enterprise. Throughout the late 1960s and 1970s, the number of federal employees and the number of government departments grew—a massive expansion of federal power that made libertarians cringe and that bolstered neoconservative claims about the appearance of a new class. In 1979, Robert L. Bartley, editor of *The Wall Street Journal*'s editorial page, wrote, "When business finds it has problems in the regulatory or public arena, its instinctive response is to seek out 'the experts.'" But the experts, Bartley warned, "have the skills of the New Class and are thus the people most likely to share its outlooks, interests, and agendas."*

If the establishment's experts could not be trusted, neoconservatives would have to provide their own, creating a counternew class and arguing, in effect, that two analytic wrongs make a right. Thus, while the centrist Brookings Institution had been established, in its founder's words, to produce scholarship "free from any political or pecuniary interest," the purpose of the neoconservative American Enterprise Institute was explicitly to promote the political and pecuniary interests of business. The Heritage Foundation had even fewer pretensions to disinterested social-scientific inquiry, producing right-wing background papers on foreign and domestic policy issues to influence politicians and journalists. As its director of research, Burton Pines, said, "We're not here to be some kind of Ph.D. committee giving equal time. Our role is to provide conservative public-policy makers with arguments to bolster our side." The problem, as journalist John B. Judis has written, was that in adopting this ideologically adversarial approach to policy, conservatives and neoconservatives had essentially abandoned the very idea of dispassionate analysis.

This was the situation in 1974, when a logician and mathematician named Albert Wohlstetter fired a broadside against Sherman Kent's bastion of social science, the Central Intelligence Agency, charging it with consistently underestimating the threat from the Soviet nuclear arsenal.

---

*President George W. Bush would award Kristol, Podhoretz, and Bartley the Presidential Medal of Freedom, the nation's highest civilian honor.

Team B and the First Casualty

Albert Wohlstetter was obsessed with U.S. nuclear preparedness. He had joined RAND in 1951 and soon published a famous study allegedly demonstrating the vulnerability of U.S. bombers to a Soviet first strike. Wohlstetter detested mutual assured destruction and promoted counter-force doctrine. In 1969, he brought two young graduate students, Richard Perle and Paul Wolfowitz, to Washington as manpower in his effort to identify and lobby politicians sympathetic to his fight for missile defenses. Then, in 1974, Wohlstetter wrote two articles for *Foreign Policy,* arguing that the CIA had *underestimated* Soviet ICBM deployments from 1962 to 1972 because it had *overestimated* the Soviet threat in the past—a mistake that had led us to increase our military spending. Essentially, Wohlstetter said, liberals at the CIA were blaming the United States for the arms race and were now trying to slow America down by soft-pedaling the Soviet threat.

With its formidable byline and charts of previously classified data, Wohlstetter's articles did show that the CIA had in fact underestimated Soviet missile strength—but it failed to demonstrate that liberal bias was responsible. Wohlstetter was arguing against a straw man; no one at the CIA believed the United States had consistently overstated the Soviet threat. Often the United States had not taken it seriously enough, being surprised by the first Soviet atomic and hydrogen bomb tests and by the launch of Sputnik, which demonstrated Russia's advanced rocketry. The recent miscalculation regarding ICBMs was better explained not as an attempt to rectify past hawkishness, but rather by the incorrect, but hardly liberal, assumption that the Soviets would retire their older missiles as they deployed new ones, just as the United States did. Besides, CIA predictions had been quite accurate about qualitative advances, such as Soviet MIRV development, which constituted the most significant threats to the U.S. nuclear force.

Nevertheless, Wohlstetter's conclusions shocked the conservative members of an obscure governmental body, the President's Foreign Intelligence Advisory Board. The PFIAB was composed of about a dozen prominent citizens nominally charged with keeping an eye on the intelligence agencies. President Nixon used the board as a holding pen for prominent conservatives whom he wanted to keep quiet; membership gave them the illusion of influence. (Physicist Edward Teller, for example, a missile defense advocate and opponent of both the Limited Test Ban Treaty and the ABM Treaty, served on the board in the mid-1970s.) In the early and mid-1970s, in other words, the PFIAB was staffed by precisely the sorts of people who worried that détente had lulled the nation into a false sense of security while the Russians prepared for nuclear war. In Wohlstetter's article, these conservatives believed their fears had been quantified, and they began agitating for an independent review of Soviet intelligence that would serve as a counterpoint to the CIA's rose-tinted estimates. To placate them when he found himself under withering fire from Ronald Reagan during the 1976 primaries, President Ford green-lighted what would be known as the Team B exercise.*

The man appointed to lead Team B was Richard Pipes, a professor of Russian history at Harvard University and, more importantly, a man who had the ear of neoconservative standard-bearer Scoop Jackson. Pipes was fiercely anticommunist—a view less and less acceptable in the post-Vietnam, leftward-drifting academy—and his worldview meshed cleanly with that of his senatorial patron. Pipes's hatred of the Soviet Union, like that of many early *National Review* conservatives, stemmed in part from personal encounters with the ravages of totalitarianism—in his case, as a young Jew in Nazi-occupied Warsaw. To Pipes, the barbarity of totalitarian systems was a tactile thing, whereas to most Americans, he felt, it was merely an abstraction. As he settled into his work at Team B, Pipes's critique mirrored that of the conservatives: America simply didn't understand the evil it faced. And he followed that belief to the same conclusion the conservatives did: The Soviet regime had to be overthrown. As he would later say of his support for the Iraq war, "destroying this invasive evil" was the right thing to do.

Team B was designed to be prejudiced. That is, its members were chosen precisely because they believed that the CIA did not accurately represent Soviet intentions and nuclear capabilities. Six other outsiders, including Nitze, were selected to serve with Pipes on Team B, as were five government employees, including Wolfowitz, then on staff at the Arms Control and Disarmament Agency. Most were known hard-line cold warriors and

---

*There were actually three B teams: one to look at Soviet air defenses, one to look at Soviet ICBM accuracy, and one to evaluate Soviet strategic objectives. It was this last team that proved controversial and has gone down in history as "Team B," and it is the one that we will be concerned with here.

critics of the Agency. When asked why Team B had been stacked this way, Pipes explained matter-of-factly, "There is no point in another, what you might call, optimistic view." Indeed, when Pipes approached Nitze to serve on the group, Nitze was left with the impression that its task was not to offer a fresh assessment of Soviet strategy, but to determine why past National Intelligence Estimates (NIEs) had been "consistently wrong"— an odd objective, given that Pipes had yet to examine the past estimates. Team B, in short, begged the question. Its members saw the Soviet threat not as an empirical problem but as a matter of faith. Leo Cherne, the PFIAB's chairman, acknowledged this explicitly: "We are in the midst of a crisis of belief, and a crisis of belief can only be resolved by belief." For three months, the members of Team B pored over the CIA's raw intelligence data—and used them to reaffirm their beliefs.

In the early 1960s, the United States had believed that the Soviet Union would build a minimum deterrent force—that is, one that could survive a first strike and then retaliate with a few dozen warheads against American cities. But as the Soviets deployed more and more ICBMs, American intelligence revised its view: The Soviets appeared to want parity with the United States or perhaps even a slight lead, which would confer no military advantage, but might lend them some prestige. It was these assumptions, in part, that had led the CIA to underestimate Soviet ICBM deployments. To be fair, the assumptions were reasonable and widely shared by hawks and doves alike, based on the available data. Even General Daniel Graham—a vociferous critic of the CIA and a member of Team B, who had served as deputy director of the national intelligence community—noted in response to Wohlstetter's *Foreign Policy* article that, "in the mid-1960s, . . . the only logical Soviet force level that anyone could prognosticate was a numerical equality with the United States (based on political urges), or a minimum deterrent of some 350 Inter-Continental Ballistic Missiles (ICBM) plus Sea-Launched Ballistic Missiles and bombers."

Team B scoffed at the notion that the Soviets wanted only a deterrent capability. The very first sentence of its report stated that the intelligence community had "substantially misperceived the motivations behind Soviet strategic programs, and thereby tended consistently to underestimate their intensity, scope, and implicit threat." In truth, concluded Team B, détente and arms control were merely elements of the Soviet drive for global hegemony. "Soviet leaders are determined to achieve the maximum attainable measure of strategic superiority over the U.S., a superiority . . . which is measured not in Western assured destruction terms but rather in terms of war-fighting objectives of achieving post-war dominance and limiting damage to the maximum extent possible." To accomplish this, the Soviets were building up offensive and defensive forces, including a "massive civil defense" program. The Soviets, Team B warned ominously, worshipped military power "to an extent inconceivable to the average Westerner." In other words, not only did Team B believe, like conservatives, that Soviet ideology precluded coexistence and negotiation, but it was convinced that the Soviets were preparing to fight and win a nuclear war. Worse, they were frighteningly close to being able to do so: "*Within the ten year period of the National Estimate the Soviets may well expect to achieve a degree of military superiority which would permit a dramatically more aggressive pursuit of their hegemonial objectives* [emphasis in original]."

Team B's members were even more blunt in discussing their ostensibly classified findings with the press. Major General George Keegan told the *New York Times,* "I am unaware of a single important category in which the Soviets have not established a significant lead over the United States. . . . [This] grave imbalance in favor of Soviet military capability had developed out of a failure over the last 15 years to adjust American strategic thinking to Soviet strategy, and out of the failure of the leadership of the American intelligence community to 'perceive the reality' of the Soviet military build-up." William van Cleave agreed that "overall strategic superiority exists today for the Soviet Union" and went so far as to say, "I think it's getting to the point that, if we can make a trade with the Soviet Union of defense establishments, I'd be heartily in favor of it." When asked if the United States should try to rectify the situation by seeking superiority over the Soviet Union, rather than establishing the rough parity that had been the goal of the Johnson, Nixon, and Ford administrations, General Graham, replied, "The question was, 'Do I advocate superiority for the United States?' I say, 'Yes.'"

The report was a blow to the CIA. As they conducted their study, the members of Team B had met with the members of Team A—that is, the professional CIA analysts preparing the annual National Intelligence Estimate on Soviet strategy—in the hope that this adversarial process would sharpen the final intelligence community product. What many had not expected was just how adversarial it would be: one CIA participant described it as a "zero-sum discussion," with Team B out to defeat and humiliate Team A. According to a story that ran in the *Washington Post*, "[N]umerous sources on all sides agree that the 'peer pressures' on the insiders were great. Graham was reported to have said to the CIA group at one point: 'I don't want to tell you guys you're going to lose your jobs if you don't get on board, but that's the way it is.'" Team A apparently did heed the warning and got on board. In the *New York Times*, "high-ranking officials of the Central Intelligence Agency" were quoted as saying the 1976 National Intelligence Estimate on Soviet strategic forces was "more somber than any in more than a decade."

In truth, the official intelligence estimates had been getting increasingly pessimistic for several years before Team B arrived on the scene. The 1975 NIE, for example, acknowledged that the Soviets were "probably striving for a strategic posture which has some visible and therefore politically useful advantages over the U.S. and which would give the USSR better capabilities than the U.S. to fight a nuclear war." In other words, there was reason for increasing concern about Soviet intentions. But whereas official estimates arrived at their conclusions on the basis of new data, such as increased ICBM deployments, Team B operated in the opposite way, beginning with its beliefs about the nature of Soviet society and intentions and interpreting the data to reinforce them. The result was not only a more apocalyptic view of Soviet intentions, but also a number of embarrassingly wrong predictions about Soviet capabilities.

For example, Team B argued that the Soviets would extend the range of their Backfire bombers by giving them a midair refueling capability (which would enable them to attack the United States) and would build five hundred of them by 1984. But intelligence in the mid-1980s revealed that fewer than half that number were built, none of which could refuel in flight. General Keegan claimed that a Soviet facility at Semipalatansk was designed to test directed-energy weapons, such as lasers and particle beams. It turned about to be a test site for nuclear-powered rocket engines. In one bizarre instance, Team B even cited its failure to find a nonacoustic antisubmarine system (that is, a way of tracking enemy subs with means more sophisticated than sonar) as evidence that it might exist: "[T]he absence of a deployed system by this time is difficult to understand. The implication could be that the Soviets have, in fact, deployed some operational non-acoustic systems and will deploy more in the next few years." The most egregious error, however, was Team B's overestimation of Soviet military spending: According to the report, there had been "an intense military build-up in nuclear as well as conventional forces of all sorts, not moderated either by the West's self-imposed restraints or by SALT." In fact, growth in Soviet military spending had slowed the previous year—the year Team B was supposed to be analyzing—and would remain flat for the next five years.

Team B was not the first extragovernmental review group to exaggerate the Soviet threat, but it was the first to attack the very methodology used to assess that threat. In addition to its reliance on preconceived notions, Team B criticized the CIA for committing an analytical sin known as "mirror-imaging"—that is, assuming your enemy has the same principles and goals as you do. But in rejecting this approach, they threw out the entire system of inductive reasoning and substituted their own beliefs. In so doing, they placed a greater emphasis on intentions than on demonstrated capabilities. For one thing, it was easier to make a case against the Soviets through assertions about intentions than through testable predictions. More important, however, a discussion of intentions allowed Team B to emphasize the moral component of Soviet behavior that they felt was essential to understanding the communist enterprise. Pipes and his colleagues criticized the intelligence community as mechanistic in its focus on measuring weapons via satellite data and the like: "Because the Soviet Union ultimately wishes to destroy not merely its opponents' fighting capacity but their very capacity to function as organized political, social, and economic entities, its strategic arsenal includes a great choice of political, social, and economic weapons besides the obvious military ones. For this reason, Soviet strategic objectives cannot be accurately ascertained and appreciated by an examination of the USSR's strategic nuclear or general purpose forces alone." According to Team B, the intelligence community did not spend enough time on the enemy's "ideas, motives and aspirations." The CIA focused too much on so-called hard data and not enough on "soft factors." Team B examined both and managed to see the worst case no matter what the data suggested.

Each of these methodological tics hacked away at the very foundations of objective analysis—of truth itself. Team B was correct to recognize that faulty assumptions could produce faulty estimates, but, rather than eschew assumptions, they simply embraced their opposites. According to John Prados, an expert on intelligence and Soviet strategic forces, whereas the CIA believed in "an objective discoverable truth," Pipes and his colleagues engaged in an "exercise of reasoning from conclusions" that they felt was justified in "moral and ideological terms." Furthermore, assuming the worst in any given estimate, which might be superficially prudent, meant Team B had essentially given up trying to uncover the truth. Finally, it embraced an adversarial process of truth-finding—as in a courtroom, Team B believed that analysts should formulate a best-case scenario and a worst-case scenario and let the policy maker choose whichever he found most convincing. Of course, in a courtroom, a judge and jury are meant to be impartial, whereas the president, or any other political appointee, is by definition ideologically partial. Team B, however, wanted to continue the adversarial process, in effect recommending that policy makers be allowed to choose whichever truth they found most convenient.

While not all Team B members actively subscribed to the new class critique or an anti-Enlightenment philosophy, many persisted in doing so even years later, after the Soviet Union had collapsed and Team B's analyses were shown to have been seriously flawed. Pipes, for example, gave this explanation of why Sovietologists had failed to predict the fall of communism: "[T]he failure of the profession was also and perhaps most of all due to a 'social-scientese' methodology which ignored history, literature, witnesses' testimonies, and all else that could not be explained in sociological jargon and buttressed with statistics. . . . Being imponderable and hence unquantifiable, the peculiar features of national culture escaped their attention. So, too, did the moral dimension of human activity inasmuch as scientific inquiry was expected to be 'value-free.'" The CIA could not paint an accurate picture of the Soviet Union because the most basic colors—black and white, good and evil—were not in its palette. In trying to be objective, they missed the true nature of the enemy. It was the essence of the new class critique, tied intimately to an older conservative critique that bristled at treating people as physical quantities rather than metaphysical entities. "Science in our day enjoys well-deserved prestige," Pipes continued, "but its methods cannot be applied to human affairs." Russell Kirk could not have put it better himself.

The Committee on the Present Danger

Team B would have an extraordinary intellectual impact on conservatives, becoming a model for right-wing dissent regarding intelligence findings.

Its denigration of experts, its emphasis on moralism, and its embrace of politicized truth were in keeping with a conservative and neoconservative tradition and ultimately provided much of the rationale for the Iraq war. In the interim, however, it had significant political ramifications, bringing conservatives, neoconservatives, and hawks together in an organization called the Committee on the Present Danger (CPD).

The committee was a follow-on to the Coalition for a Democratic Majority and was based on the intellectual foundations laid by Team B. But led by Eugene Rostow, who had also headed the CDM's foreign policy task force, the Committee on the Present Danger had a far broader membership. It included not only neoconservatives like Richard Pipes, Midge Decter, Norman Podhoretz, and Jeane Kirkpatrick, but also establishment Democrats like Paul Nitze and Dean Rusk (Kennedy's and Johnson's secretary of state), establishment Republicans like David Packard (Nixon's deputy secretary of defense) and Andrew Goodpaster (Eisenhower's top national security adviser), well-known military officers like General Maxwell Taylor and Admiral Elmo Zumwalt, and traditional conservatives like Congresswoman Clare Booth Luce, millionaire Richard Mellon Scaife (one of Barry Goldwater's earliest backers), and Donald Brennan (the Hudson Institute analyst who had coined the term "MAD" in the pages of *National Review*).

Like the Coalition for a Democratic Majority and Team B, the Committee on the Present Danger believed that détente had failed and that the Soviet Union was an ideological beast bent on world domination. As conservatives had stressed for decades, it could not therefore be understood as a traditional nation-state: Its goals and methods were alien. But it was the specter of nuclear inferiority that most focused the minds of the committee's 141 founding members. Although the SALT I agreements had codified mutual assured destruction by eliminating defenses and capping offenses, the CPD insisted that the Soviets had not slowed their nuclear deployments at all. On the contrary, they had fielded new missiles with even greater capabilities. In this buildup, and in alleged Soviet efforts at civil defense and hardened command-and-control centers, the CPD saw evidence of a war-fighting—not a deterrent—strategy. That meant the United States needed to be prepared for a first strike. Evoking the now-standard conservative specter of appeasement, the CPD wrote, "The Soviet military build-up of all its armed forces over the past quarter century is, in part, reminiscent of Nazi Germany's rearmament in the 1930s." The CPD saw itself as a collection of Churchills facing a country of Chamberlains.

One did not have to be an appeaser or a communist sympathizer, however, to dispute their analysis. For one thing, the SALT agreements had not slowed U.S. deployments, either. America had already begun deploying MIRV technology when the agreement was signed and, between 1972 and 1977, had deployed an additional three thousand warheads—hardly an indication of strategic restraint. (Indeed, the United States went from being able to target 1,700 Soviet sites in 1970 to 7,000 sites less than ten years later.) Moreover, when the United States signed the Interim Agreement, the Soviets had made it clear that they planned to upgrade their missiles. Though the CPD sometimes suggested that they had violated the accord by increasing the size of their silos, the truth was that the issue simply had not been covered by the treaty. Indeed, by MIRVing its warheads first, America looked as though *it* was preparing for a first strike. MIRVs were first-strike weapons, both because they could take out several targets with a single missile and because they were themselves valuable targets, meaning we'd be more inclined to launch them first in a crisis rather than lose them to a Soviet first strike.

Nevertheless, the CPD was convinced that the Soviets did not believe in mutual assured destruction and, therefore, that we could not adhere to the idea of "nuclear sufficiency" despite the fact that we had enough atomic firepower to destroy the Soviet Union many times over. As the CPD said, "In the nuclear age, 'enough' may not be enough." CPD members believed that a nuclear war was most likely to start during a crisis, at which point one side or the other would begin using nuclear weapons against military targets, avoiding population centers. They found the possibility of such a war not at all unthinkable; indeed, it would be fought like any other war, with the victor being the one who could take out more of the enemy's forces. According to the CPD, the United States was falling so rapidly behind the Soviets that, within a few years, it might well lose a nuclear war and, worse, might not be able to retaliate at all. As it wrote in a brief called "Is America Becoming Number Two?": "The early 1980's threaten to be a period of Soviet strategic nuclear superiority in which America's second-strike capacity will become vulnerable to a Soviet preemptive attack without further improvements in U.S. weapons." The CPD was stuck in the same zero-sum logic that had bedeviled Goldwater, only now it was becoming mainstream.

Paul Warnke Unites the Right in Action

It was not surprising, then, that one of the Committee on the Present Danger's first targets was Paul Warnke. Like many in the foreign policy establishment, Warnke was a lawyer by training, and in the mid-1950s, he had become a partner in Dean Acheson's law firm. During the late Johnson administration, he was general counsel to the secretary of defense, serving both Robert McNamara and his successor, Clark Clifford. A strong critic of the Vietnam War who did not subscribe to the idea that by losing Saigon we would lose all of Asia, Warnke rejected the monolithic vision of communism that had led us into the war. Instead, Warnke argued that the United States needed to prioritize its interests. Like George Kennan, he believed our enemy was a country, not a global ideological movement: "We face a single military threat," he wrote, "not a hostile world."

Warnke's most salient intellectual contribution, however, was to question the need for U.S. nuclear superiority. In 1975, he wrote an article for *Foreign Policy* magazine attacking the call for increased military spending to offset the growing Soviet nuclear arsenal. Warnke acknowledged that the Soviets might well be building more nuclear weapons, but he maintained that it did not matter. Like McNamara and Kissinger before him, he saw no value to so-called strategic superiority. The only result of building more and more weapons was that the Soviets would build more weapons in response. The two countries were, he wrote, like "apes on a treadmill" in a race to nowhere.

Warnke's arguments appalled the CPD, and when Jimmy Carter nominated him both to head the Arms Control and Disarmament Agency and to lead the SALT II negotiating team, the committee mobilized for battle. First came the neoconservative assault: Penn Kemble (founder and cochairman of the Coalition for a Democratic Majority) and Joshua Muravchik (son of coalition member Emanuel Muravchik) anonymously circulated a critique of Warnke on Capitol Hill shortly after the 1976 election. Kemble and Muravchik's memo accused Warnke of advocating "unilateral abandonment by the U.S. of every weapons system which is subject to negotiation at SALT." And it assaulted his *Foreign Policy* article, insisting that Warnke was wrong to claim that nuclear superiority was meaningless. Kemble and Muravchik used the Team B analysis to validate their critique.

More interesting, however, was the grassroots second wave, which came in the form of a group founded specifically to stop Warnke's nomination. The Emergency Coalition Against Unilateral Disarmament was linked with the Coalition for a Democratic Majority and actually worked out of the CDM's offices in Washington. But the Emergency Coalition was loaded with conservatives, including James Roberts, executive director of the American Conservative Union; Charles Black, campaign director for the Republican National Committee; and Howard Phillips, director of the grassroots Conservative Caucus. The directors of Young Americans for Freedom, the Young Republican National Federation, and the American Security Council were on the steering committee. The Emergency Coalition's executive director was Morton Blackwell, a hard-right conservative who worked for two publications produced by Richard Viguerie, a leader of the grassroots conservative force that would come to be known as the New Right. Thus were the views of neoconservatives, hawks, and traditional conservatives given a populist base.

The New Right comprised voters angry with what they saw as the disenfranchising of white, blue-collar America. The catalysts for this new movement, wrote Kevin Phillips, one of its leaders, included "public anger over busing, welfare spending, environmental extremism, soft criminology, media bias and power, warped education, twisted textbooks, racial quotas, various guidelines, and an ever expanding bureaucracy." An important subset of the New Right that would become known as the Moral Majority fixated on traditional values. There was no shortage of issues in the 1960s and 1970s to incite these voters, including gay rights, feminism (Schlafly's anti-SALT Eagle Forum was also known as Stop ERA, as it was simultaneously dedicated to scuttling the Equal Rights Amendment), and, of course, abortion, spurred by the 1973 *Roe v. Wade* decision. The issue that perhaps inflamed them most— government interference with Christian schools—gave them common ground with libertarians, even though they were not disciples of laissez-faire economics.

The New Right's ideology was not an intellectual conservatism, and its decidedly populist bent distinguished it from the *National Review* orthodoxy. As Phillips wrote, "Most of the 'New Conservatives' I know believe that any new politics or coalition has to surge up from Middle America . . . not dribble down from Bill Buckley's wine rack and favorite philosopher's shelf." The distrust was mutual. Sniffed Buckley, "I have simply nothing to say to someone who is proud of his ignorance of [philosopher Eric] Voegelin. I am ashamed of my superficial knowledge of him." But the *National Review* contingent recognized common ground between the Right it had cultivated since the mid-1950s and the movement rising from the heartland. As Russell Kirk wrote, the most salient characteristic of the Moral Majority was that "they take a religious view of the human condition" and "believe in a moral order of more than human contrivance."

The New Right arose in response to domestic concerns—another factor that differentiated it from the communist-driven conservatives— and when its members did address foreign policy, they were more likely to emphasize nationalism over anticommunism—more us-versus-them, than good-versus-evil—a leaning that was persuasively illustrated in the 1977 battle over the Panama Canal Treaty, by which the United States ceded control of the waterway back the Panama. Unlike Buckley, who supported local jurisdiction over the canal in the belief that a bit of Latin goodwill would help buttress support for the United States and therefore opposition to communism in Central and South America, the New Right saw the Panama Canal as undeniably belonging to America (it was not the "Panama Canal" but the "American Canal in Panama"). The canal controversy did demonstrate, however, that the New Right could be mobilized for foreign policy battles; and as Jerry Sanders writes in *Peddlers of Crisis*, in the confirmation battle over Paul Warnke, the New Right joined *National Review* conservatives, as well as their new fellow travelers, the hawks and the neoconservatives.

That battle was vicious. At Warnke's confirmation hearings, Nitze, in an unestablishment display of emotion, dismissed Warnke's ideas as "absolutely asinine" as well as "screwball, arbitrary, and fictitious." Daniel Patrick Moynihan—the most prominent neoconservative politician, after Scoop Jackson—devoted his first speech on the floor of the United States Senate to savaging the Warnke nomination. One conservative congressman accused Warnke of being in collusion with "the World Peace Council, a Moscow-directed movement which advocates the disarmament of the West as well as support for terrorist groups." Meanwhile, the

New Right provided populist muscle. Paul Weyrich, who had founded the Heritage Foundation, was also on the Emergency Coalition's steering committee. Using mailing lists provided by Viguerie—who said his idols were "the two Macs" (that is, Senator Joseph McCarthy and General Douglas MacArthur) and who would go on to become a direct-mail baron with a fifteen-million-name database of conservatives by 1980—Weyrich sent out six hundred thousand letters urging voters to tell their senators to oppose Warnke.

Ultimately, the Senate confirmed Warnke 70–29 for the ACDA post. The Senate confirmed him to the SALT post as well, but only by a vote of 58–40—a relative victory, some conservatives argued, because Carter would need 67 votes to ratify any new treaty. The whole spectacle suggested that broad dissatisfaction with the direction of U.S. foreign policy was brewing. As Anthony Lewis of the *New York Times* wrote, there was "a peculiar, almost venomous intensity in some of the opposition to Paul Warnke; it is as if the opponents have made him a symbol of something they dislike so much that they want to destroy him. . . . [I]t signals a policy disagreement so fundamental that any imaginable arms limitation agreement with the Soviet Union will face powerful resistance. And it signals the rise of a new militant coalition on national security issues."

SALT II Dies and the Conservative Coalition Rises

The attack on Warnke was but a warm-up for the eventual assault on SALT II two years later, by which time conservatives had solidified their alliance with the hawks and neocons, perfected the tactic of gross intellectual distortion, and more effectively harnessed the muscle of the New Right. Jimmy Carter, who came to Washington a less militant anticommunist than any of his postwar predecessors, didn't stand a chance. Speaking at Notre Dame's graduation in May 1977, Carter bemoaned the "intellectual and moral poverty" of the Vietnam War. For years, Carter said, "We've fought fire with fire, never thinking that fire is better quenched with water." But now that we were "free of that inordinate fear of communism," things could change. Interdependence, not Manichaeanism or nationalism, would be the foundation of his foreign policy.

Such progressive views were reflected in his nuclear ambitions. A few days before his inauguration, Carter mused to the Joint Chiefs of Staff that he could envision the United States and the Soviet Union having only two hundred submarine-launched nuclear missiles each—in other words, a purely deterrent force. The comment was immediately leaked to conservative columnists Rowland Evans and Robert Novak who, under the headline "Nuclear Blockbuster," recounted, "Stunned speechless, General George Brown, chairman of the Joint Chiefs, stared at the man about to be his commander-in-chief." In his inaugural address, President Carter called for nuclear disarmament: "We pledge perseverance and wisdom in our efforts to limit the world's armaments to those necessary for each nation's own domestic safety. And we will move this year a step toward the ultimate goal—the elimination of all nuclear weapons from this Earth." Then, in June 1977, he canceled the B-1 bomber program, arguing that it was both expensive and unnecessary, since the development of cruise missiles would enable the older B-52s to deliver nuclear weapons just as effectively, if not more so. Critics tarred Carter as a "unilateral disarmer," and by now even the Soviets were annoyed. Vladimir Semenov, the head of the USSR's SALT delegation, told Warnke that Carter should have given up the B-1 during U.S.-Soviet negotiations—"So that we could both have gotten credit."

Carter's first formal arms control overture to the Soviets foundered as well. Ford had left Carter with the framework agreement for a SALT II Treaty that he had signed at Vladivostok, which stated that the United States and the USSR would deploy a total of no more than 2,400 ICBMs, SLBMs, and bombers. Of those 2,400 "strategic nuclear delivery vehicles," no more than 1,320 would be allowed to carry multiple warheads. The Vladivostok accord was a positive step, but Carter felt that it was not ambitious enough, for while it required the Soviets to modestly reduce their deployed forces, it still allowed for an enormous number of nuclear weapons. (The United States did not even *have* 2,400 delivery vehicles.) In March 1977, just two months after taking office, Carter therefore proposed significantly lower numbers. But Brezhnev, who had already expended significant political capital convincing his more hawkish colleagues to accept the Vladivostok limits, decried the move as a propaganda step. Negotiations proceeded fitfully from there. The SALT II Treaty took an additional two years to negotiate—Carter and Brezhnev finally signed it in Vienna on June 18, 1979—but its ultimate outline resembled the framework reached by Ford.

In response, Scoop Jackson bluntly charged Carter with "appeasement in its purest form." The case against the SALT II Treaty had been building since the critiques of Albert Wohlstetter and Paul Nitze, the conclusions of Team B, and the arguments of the Committee on the Present Danger. Now, CPD members appeared seventeen times before Senate committees to lambaste the accord. Donald Rumsfeld also testified against it, calling instead for a $44 billion increase in defense spending: "Our nation's situation is much more dangerous today than it has been at any time since Neville Chamberlain left Munich, setting the stage for World War II." And the American Security Council launched Peace Through Strength Week.

The arguments now being advanced were essentially the same as the ones the Right been making for the past five years. The Soviet Union did not believe in mutual assured destruction. It might not want to fight a nuclear war, but, in the event that a crisis escalated, it was preparing to fight and win. Even worse, it had the ability to do so. Because of its development of MIRVs and its significant advantage in throw weight—an advantage preserved by SALT II—the Soviet Union would be able to destroy American ICBMs on the ground. The United States would then be deterred from retaliating because its SLBMs were only accurate enough to target cities, and, if the United States hit Soviet cities, the USSR would use its remaining forces to take out American cities in a third strike. Moreover, the Soviet population would be protected by its extensive civil defense program; America would not be able to inflict "unacceptable damage." In a crisis, the United States would have to meekly submit to Soviet will, painfully conscious of its nuclear inferiority and the potential costs of brinksmanship. As the CPD had written, the Soviet goal "is not to wage a nuclear war but to win political predominance without having to fight." An argument that had started on the fringes of the far Right was now being made with total seriousness by a strong cross section of foreign policy experts, backed by significant public support.

The only problem was that it was a fatuous argument, grounded in zero-sum thinking. Numerically, the CPD had a superficial case. If the Soviets had some two hundred ICBMs with ten warheads each, then they might well be able to destroy America's one thousand nuclear missile silos. But the notion that the Soviet Union could—let alone would—do so, believing that the United States would not retaliate, was fantastical.

The Soviets would have to be 100 percent certain of our surrender, since if they were wrong, their civilization would be destroyed. And they simply couldn't be certain. For one thing, an attack involving thousands of warheads against our ICBM force would be initially indistinguishable from an all-out offensive, as opposed to "just" a disarming strike. It is entirely possible that, upon detecting such a large Soviet launch the United States might immediately retaliate rather than leave its missiles vulnerable on the ground. Moreover, if two thousand one-megaton warheads detonated on U.S. soil—that is, weapons with a total explosive force of 160,000 Hiroshima-sized bombs—the casualties would be enormous, despite the remote location of our silos: up to twenty million fatalities, according to the Office of Technology Assessment. It is almost impossible to imagine a U.S. president not responding after an attack that had killed so many Americans. As Robert McNamara put it:

> The idea that, in such a situation, we would sit here and say, "Well, we don't want to launch against them because they might come back and hurt us," is inconceivable! And the idea that the Soviets are today sitting in Moscow and thinking, "We've got the U.S. over a barrel because we're capable of putting 2,000 megatons of ground-burst on them and in such a situation we know they will be scared to death and fearful of retaliation; therefore we are free to conduct political blackmail," is too incredible to warrant serious debate.

The Right's faith in the efficacy of Soviet civil defenses was remarkably credulous of Soviet propaganda, especially given America's own civil defense efforts, which only demonstrated just how difficult it would be to protect any part of the population. Even assuming that the Soviets were able to evacuate their cities, an Arms Control and Disarmament Agency study found that U.S. retaliation would still kill twenty-five million Russians—and the Soviet Union would cease to be an urban society because there would be no cities left. If the United States was concerned that even that did not constitute "unacceptable damage," it could set the weapons to detonate on the ground (instead of in the air), maximizing the radioactive fallout from the blast, thereby killing forty to fifty million Soviets. Or it could simply target the evacuated populations directly and kill seventy to eighty-five million Soviets. Millions more would die from starvation, disease, and the lack of organized medical care. If we were not confident that even these options would kill enough people, we could always target the cities when the evacuation began—evacuating millions of people takes a while, after all.

Even if one ignored these arguments, the notion that the United States would be forced to bow before a Soviet Union granted free global reign because of its nuclear superiority does not stand the test of history. In the 1970s, conservatives liked to argue that we had "won" the Berlin crisis of 1961 and the Cuban missile crisis of 1962 because we had obvious nuclear superiority. By contrast, they say during the 1973 crisis in the Middle East, both sides compromised because there was nuclear parity. To the new conservatives, there was an obvious correlation between our loss of superiority and a loss of influence. But even discounting the fact that at the time many conservatives thought we had "lost" the Cuban missile crisis, there is the not insignificant counterargument that even when we had a nuclear *monopoly* in the 1940s the Soviets had acted very aggressively. Military power did not automatically translate into political power.

Conservatives had once made this very point themselves: "What fire power did the Bolsheviks have prior to 1917? A few hundred revolvers, and a little home-made dynamite," James Burnham wrote in 1956. "The basic question is not who is ahead in bombers, missiles, A and H-bombs. We have been, and it has made no difference." Between 1945 and 1950, the Soviets reneged on promises to allow free elections in Eastern Europe, installed communist puppet governments, backed a coup to oust the Czech president, and even encouraged Kim Il Sung to attack South Korea. During the Eisenhower administration, after the Soviets had tested nuclear weapons but before they had a reliable second-strike capability, John Foster Dulles's policy of brinksmanship and massive retaliation worked only sporadically. Burnham's point was that political will could be more important than military might, and he was right: Given that deterrence is a psychological condition, not an immutable law of physics, we could always choose to act in the face of Soviet aggression, regardless of the nuclear balance.

But in their insistence that the Soviets were seeking a war-fighting capability, did not believe in MAD, and were therefore dangerous, the new conservatives were themselves calling for a nuclear war-winning strategy. For example, Nitze wrote, "A responsible objective of military strategy . . . would be to bring the war to an end in circumstances least damaging to the future of our society." That was simply a wordy way of saying that, if it came to war, the United States should try to win.

That wasn't such a crazy idea, which is why it was *already* our policy: Even after McNamara concluded that a nuclear war was not winnable, the Johnson administration continued to target Soviet nuclear forces, because it was better to have the option of trying to control and win a nuclear war than not to have the option at all. That policy was continued and expanded by both the Nixon and Ford administrations. So not only were Nitze and his CPD colleagues arguing against a straw man when they criticized our allegedly naive policy of "deterrence"; they were criticizing the Soviets for a strategy we ourselves were pursuing.

Besides, we now know that the CPD analysis of Soviet nuclear intentions was wrong. From 1989 to 1994, American experts on the Soviet Union, led by researcher John Hines, interviewed twenty-two senior Soviet military personnel. They found that, by the early 1970s, the Soviet leadership realized that a nuclear exchange would be so devastating that there could not be a winner in any meaningful sense. Although they did not adopt MAD as official policy, their doctrine was based on deterrence through the threat of retaliation. They believed that any "limited" nuclear exchange in Europe would quickly escalate; nevertheless, they planned for it because they needed a strategy for conflict in Europe. While there was a civil defense program in the USSR, no one in the leadership considered it an element of an offensive strategy. In short, Soviet nuclear doctrine was remarkably like our own.

Conclusion

In the fall of 1979, SALT II stalled in the Senate as several events further challenged détente, chief among them the "discovery" of a brigade of Soviet troops in Cuba. Though the force had been there since 1962, the Carter administration mistakenly charged that its presence was a violation of the agreement that ended the Cuban missile crisis, suggesting that the Soviets could not be trusted. Moreover, Carter had by then expended much of his political capital to pass the Panama Canal Treaty. When the Soviet Union invaded Afghanistan that December, Carter withdrew SALT II from Senate consideration.

There was no reason why Soviet troops in Cuba, or even the invasion of Afghanistan, should have affected SALT II. Détente, it was true, had not delivered the peace for which many had hoped. But arms control was not—or should not have been—treated as a reward for good behavior. The United States pursued arms control because constraining the Soviets' nuclear capabilities and reassuring them about American intentions was in the national interest. If anything, the less the United States trusted the Soviets, or the more aggressive the Soviets were, the more important arms control became.

Remember that the "dilemma" of the prisoner's dilemma arises precisely because each prisoner is afraid he cannot trust the other. If Moscow was as benign as London, there would have been no need for dialogue. Most Americans intuitively understood this. They realized that, no matter our hopes for banishing communism, we first had to control the nuclear danger; the Soviet threat was first and foremost a nuclear threat. That general understanding explains why rejection of arms control had been a fringe position in the early 1970s. But by the time of the SALT II ratification debate, the lonely voices of John Ashbrook and Phyllis Schlafly had been joined by those of neoconservative intellectuals and establishment elites, backed by a chorus of grassroots conservatives.

Conservatives' insistence on seeing the Cold War in terms of good versus evil had led them to reject the notion of coexistence and with it the value of negotiation. In the 1960s, it became clear that that ideological rigidity applied regardless of the nuclear revolution. Zero-sum thinking precluded any understanding that the concepts of victory and defeat could not be applied to the conflict with the Soviet Union without endangering the very existence of the United States. Thus conservatives rejected MAD, which they viewed as simply nuclear coexistence, and arms control, which was merely nuclear negotiation. In the 1970s, conservatives and their neoconservative and hawkish brethren justified this position by arguing that it was the Soviets who had rejected deterrence and meaningful reductions in nuclear weapons. Likewise, they argued, it was the Soviets who failed to recognize the implications of the nuclear revolution, which meant the United States was in danger of losing a nuclear war. America needed to strengthen its moral clarity, its will to fight, and its nuclear arsenal in order to convince the Soviets that it would win an atomic exchange.

It was a shoddy analysis, but it was backed by powerful forces.

Conservative political pressure was enormous, and, by the end of his term, President Carter had strayed far from the ideals expressed in his inaugural. His nuclear policies increasingly resembled those of Team B, the Committee on the Present Danger, and groups like the Emergency Coalition Against Unilateral Disarmament. Carter had achieved a SALT II agreement, but he himself had pulled it from consideration. He had agreed to deploy intermediate-range missiles in Europe, approved development of the mobile MX land-based missile to replace the silo-based Minuteman (which essentially signaled acceptance of the CPD's argument about ICBM vulnerability), and signed Presidential Directive Number 59, or PD-59, which expanded counterforce options.

Yet Carter's CPD-like moves were not guided by the mores of the new conservative coalition. His deployment of missiles in Europe, for example, was accompanied by a decision to pursue negotiations limiting those very weapons. PD-59, though it reaffirmed counterforce doctrine, was never meant to suggest that a nuclear war was winnable. It did not countenance counterforce strikes against the Soviet homeland, but advised limited strikes as a last resort against Soviet theater forces should they invade Europe, in an attempt to limit any general war for as long as possible. Moreover, Harold Brown, Carter's secretary of defense, said he believed that even limited nuclear strikes on Soviet forces would escalate to general nuclear war, meaning that PD-59 was less a rejection of MAD than it was a worst-case option. And, even in the wake of the invasion of Afghanistan, Carter held up nuclear stability as the most important goal of foreign policy: "Especially now, in a time of great tension, observing the mutual constraints imposed by the terms of these treaties, [SALT I and II] will be in the best interest of both countries and will help to preserve world peace. . . . That effort to control nuclear weapons will not be abandoned." Unfortunately, his successor had different ideas.

Chapter Four

PRESIDENT

THE FUNERAL OF an American president is a magnificent sight. The power of the office is only amplified by the solemnity of death and reinforced by all the symbolic trappings granted the commander in chief, as if an inaugural, Veterans Day, and Memorial Day were combined in a single ceremony. It was so even for Richard Nixon, who left the presidency in disgrace. And it was so for Gerald Ford, whose most memorable act in his abbreviated term was pardoning Richard Nixon. It was inevitable, then, that the funeral of Ronald Reagan, whom many credit with nothing less than winning the Cold War and banishing the threat of communism that had loomed over America for generations, would bring the capital to a halt and rivet the public.

Reagan's death on June 5, 2004, provided in some ways a temporary respite from the deep partisan division that had opened in Washington during the George W. Bush presidency. The National Cathedral, with its ability to seat four thousand, proved a tent big enough for administration officials and their fiercest critics. Former presidents Jimmy Carter and Bill Clinton sat with former presidents Gerald Ford and George H. W. Bush. Former vice president Al Gore took his place in front of Republican super-strategist Karl Rove. The new joined the old. Margaret Thatcher, Mikhail Gorbachev, and Václav Havel sat with Hamid Karzai and the interim Iraqi president at the ceremony.

But if Reagan's funeral was a signal moment of national and even international mourning, it was especially a moment of conservative mourning, for the fortieth president was, as *National Review*'s editors put it, "one of ours." Reagan had strode onto the conservative stage in 1964 when he recorded a campaign spot for his good friend Barry Goldwater, which *Washington Post* reporter David Broder called "the most successful political debut since William Jennings Bryan electrified the 1896 convention with the 'Cross of Gold' speech." The advertisement, a version of the speech Reagan had been delivering across the country as a spokesman for

General Electric, was a pithy brief for conservatism, in which he said that "government does nothing as well or as economically as the private sector"; heaped scorn on Washington intellectuals; linked liberalism to communism; and painted the Cold War as a quasireligious struggle in which we would either triumph over "the most evil enemy mankind has known" or sentence our children to "a thousand years of darkness." Reagan's 1980 campaign for the presidency was built upon the same themes, with an emphasis on the doom that would result if America did not assert itself militarily vis-à-vis the Soviet Union.

It was not surprising that Reagan epitomized the libertarianism, traditionalism, and anticommunism that had fused in the 1950s to create the modern conservative movement, for he had learned his conservatism from *National Review,* which he called his "favorite magazine." During his presidency, he would award Russell Kirk the Presidential Citizens Medal, the second-highest honor a president can bestow on a civilian, and would give James Burnham the Presidential Medal of Freedom, the nation's highest civilian honor. Reagan was close to Bill Buckley, and Bill's brother James joined Reagan's State Department as undersecretary for security affairs. Reagan was close to neoconservative intellectuals as well. Norman Podhoretz liked to brag that most top officials in the Reagan administration were *Commentary* readers and that several of them, including UN ambassador Jeane Kirkpatrick, were *Commentary* writers. (Indeed, it was Kirkpatrick's famous *Commentary* essay "Dictatorships and Double Standards" that first brought her to Reagan's attention.) When Scoop Jackson died in 1983, President Reagan awarded his friend the Medal of Freedom, declaring how proud he was that a number of the senator's followers had "found a home" in his White House. Hawks and neoconservatives from the Committee on the Present Danger, including Richard Pipes, Paul Nitze, and Eugene Rostow, joined his administration.

Reagan also capitalized on the Right's grassroots nationalism, matching its fear of Soviet evil with an idealized view of American good. Here he tapped the rich tradition of American exceptionalism that stretched back to the seventeenth century, when Dutch and English Protestant settlers sought to establish a "new Israel," far removed from the sins of the Old World, in which they would struggle for redemption and salvation. Reagan never tired of reminding Americans, à la John Winthrop, that their country was a "shining city on a hill," that it had a "rendezvous with destiny."

Such missionary rhetoric was a welcome tonic for Americans after the
malaise of Vietnam and the Carter years. It resonated particularly with
the nationalists on the right, many of whom were former isolationists and
had long distrusted foreign entanglements and international institutions.
Reagan was able to leaven their inherent pessimism—their nightmares of
Reds and the decline of Western civilization—with the optimism inherent
in the idea of America as God's chosen nation.

During the Reagan years, for the first time since World War II,
conservatism began to seem natural to the American people. The civil
rights movement had pushed the South firmly into Republican hands,
and the white working class, generally left-leaning on economic issues,
found itself increasingly disturbed by the liberal stand on crime, busing,
and war. At the same time, a grassroots New Right had mobilized millions
of voters concerned about "moral issues" such as abortion, school prayer,
and homosexuality. Stagflation had opened the door for new ideas on
managing—or not managing—the economy. And the rise of New Right
institutions had created an organizational machine and populist base that
spread what had once been an elite (and elitist) movement around the
country. With the ascension of Reagan, conservatives finally controlled
the Republican Party—and the country. As George F. Will wrote, "It took
approximately 16 years to count the votes in the 1964 election, but finally
they all came in, and Goldwater won."

It was only natural, then, that when the Soviet Union collapsed shortly
after Reagan left office, conservatives concluded that they were responsible, that it was their understanding of the Cold War as a struggle between
good and evil that had generated Reagan's foreign policies—an uncompromising stand against the Soviets, buttressed by an arms buildup; a missile
shield to supplant the hated mutual assured destruction; and rollback
to replace the morally bankrupt containment—and ultimately ensured
victory, just as they had always insisted it would. When Vice President
Dick Cheney spoke over Reagan's body as it lay in state under the Capitol
rotunda, he said, "More than any other influence, the Cold War was ended
by the perseverance and courage of one man who answered falsehood
with truth, and overcame evil with good." In George W. Bush's eulogy at
the National Cathedral the following day, he agreed that "Ronald Reagan
believed in the power of truth in the conduct of world affairs. When he
saw evil camped across the horizon he called that evil by its name." For

conservatives, Reagan—specifically Reagan's foreign policy—was a paragon of moral clarity.

In truth, President Reagan was less paragon than paradox. If he embodied conservatism's belief that the Cold War was an apocalyptic showdown between good and evil, he also believed that he could avert that Armageddon by meaningful discussion with the Soviet Union. Although he accepted the premise of conservative foreign policy, he did not accept its ramifications. While it is true that Reagan rejected coexistence with communism and mutual assured destruction, he also embraced a working relationship with Soviet leaders. He believed in American military power, but he also believed in reducing that power through arms control. Above all, in marked contrast to the conservative emphasis on war-fighting—an emphasis that had become a symbol of the conservative worldview—Reagan believed that nuclear war was unthinkable, a position routinely mocked as soft-headed by men like Buckley, Burnham, Nitze, Pipes, and Jackson. Instead, Reagan wanted to abolish nuclear weapons, a desire that put him not only to the left of the conservative coalition, but also to the left of the liberal nuclear freeze movement. For Reagan, the evil of nuclear weapons clearly outweighed the evil of communist states.

Reagan's ideologically—and often logically—conflicted worldview was mirrored in his ideologically heterodox staff. As Reagan biographer Lou Cannon describes it, the administration was in a constant battle between "pragmatists" or "realists" (known to their opponents as "accomodationists" and "one-worlders") and "conservatives" or "Reaganauts" (more derisively known as "hard-liners" and "crazies"). While all were anticommunist and supported increased defense spending, the pragmatists saw benefit to negotiation with Moscow where the conservatives saw only appeasement. From 1981 to 1983, the Reaganauts had the upper hand as the president tried to pressure the Soviet Union via his military build-up. This period marked the closest conservatives came during the Cold War to seeing their principles translated into policy. The result was nearly a nuclear war with the Soviet Union. During the latter five years of his presidency, due to staff changes as well as a tactical shift by Reagan, the pragmatists held the upper hand and violated conservative principles on a regular basis. The result was dramatically reduced tensions with Moscow and a treaty eliminating an entire class of nuclear weapons. By the end of Reagan's term, conservatives felt betrayed. The leader of their movement had begun by talking about rearmament but was now proposing full disarmament; Reagan had gone from advocating rollback to engaging in détente. The patron saint had become a fallen angel.

It was not until the collapse of the Soviet Union that he was resurrected as the movement's idol. But to make that resurrection intellectually and psychologically palatable, conservatives had to forget that they had rejected Reagan by the end of his term in 1988. In fact, they had to construct a simplified image of him, in which his Manichaean worldview had led him to eschew containment for a policy of rollback that, combined with economic, military, and psychological pressure, forced the communists to call an end to their revolution and admit defeat. Instead of acknowledging Reagan's penchant for negotiation and hatred of nuclear weapons, they focused on Reagan's simplicity and deduced that, to defeat an enemy, one needs nothing more than moral clarity and military might. They decided not only that Reagan was ideologically pure, but that his purity was effective. For conservatives, Reagan validated conservatism.

Reagan in the Garden of Good and Evil

There were few signs that President Reagan was a nuclear abolitionist during his first years in office. The problem was that his particular brand of antinuclearism was, at first blush, indistinguishable from virulent militarism.

Addressing West Point's graduating class in 1981, Reagan said, "I am told there are links of a great chain that was forged and stretched across the Hudson to prevent the British fleet from penetrating further into the valley. Today, you are that chain, holding back an evil force that would extinguish the light we've been tending for 6,000 years." He spoke not of carefully nurturing the status quo, but rather of overturning it, telling an audience at the University of Notre Dame, "The West won't contain communism, it will transcend communism." On June 8, 1982, Reagan promised the British Parliament that "the march of freedom and democracy . . . will leave Marxism-Leninism on the ash-heap of history as it has left other tyrannies which stifle the freedom and muzzle the self-expression of the people." Reagan reiterated that the "forces of good [would] ultimately rally and triumph over evil," and he suggested that coexistence with communism was unacceptable: "Must freedom wither in a quiet, deadening accommodation with totalitarian evil?"

Likewise, the primary purpose of Reagan's famous "evil empire" speech—delivered on March 8, 1983, to the National Association of Evangelicals—was to dissuade evangelicals from supporting a freeze on the production and deployment of nuclear weapons, as the Conference of Catholic Bishops had done. The speech, written by Buckley protégé Anthony Dolan, was a model conservative blend of religious traditionalism and anticommunism, replete with quotes from Whittaker Chambers. It also made explicit the link between Manichaeanism and nuclear war fighting. "We must never forget," Reagan said, "that no government schemes are going to perfect man. We know that living in this world means dealing with what philosophers would call the phenomenology of evil or, as theologians would put it, the doctrine of sin. There is sin and evil in the world, and we're enjoined by Scripture and the Lord Jesus to oppose it with all our might." To support the freeze movement, Reagan suggested, was to commit the grave sin of moral relativism. "I urge you to beware the temptation of pride—the temptation of blithely declaring yourself above it all and label both sides equally at fault, to ignore the facts of history and the aggressive impulses of an evil empire, to simply call the arms race a giant misunderstanding and thereby remove yourself from the struggle between right and wrong and good and evil."

Reagan was certainly not going to remove himself from that struggle, and, like the Committee on the Present Danger, he believed that the Soviets were so much stronger than us that we might not even be able to retaliate after a first strike. In a crisis, Reagan said, this superiority would enable the Soviets to just "take us with a phone call," by which he meant they could deliver an ultimatum: "Look at the difference in our relative strengths. Now, here's what we want . . . Surrender or die." Reagan thus came into office pledging to "halt the decline in America's military strength" and to replace it with "strategic superiority," as the 1980 GOP platform had promised. Defense Secretary Caspar Weinberger, whose earliest foreign policy experience was as an intelligence officer for General Douglas MacArthur in the Pacific, announced a major military buildup in 1981, saying, "I look forward with great enthusiasm and eagerness as we begin to rearm America."

Of course, President Carter had never *dis*armed America; he had backed the MX missile and steadily increased spending on conventional arms, raising the Pentagon's budget significantly during his last year in office. Reagan, however, embarked on the largest peacetime military buildup in U.S. history, proposing to more than double the defense budget by 1986, from $171 billion to $368 billion. He wanted more of everything—more tanks, more warships, more jets, and, of course, more nuclear weapons. In 1981, Reagan reauthorized two strategic programs canceled by Carter: the B-1 bomber and the so-called neutron bomb, a nuclear weapon designed to reduce collateral damage by delivering a smaller blast but higher doses of radiation.* He authorized the deployment of three thousand nuclear cruise missiles aboard aircraft and accelerated development of the Trident II SLBM, nuclear-capable sea-launched cruise missiles, and the B-2 stealth bomber. This orgy of procurement hardly seemed the indulgence of a nuclear abolitionist.

Reagan not only embraced the arms race but rejected arms control as well. As a member of the Committee on the Present Danger, he had fought the SALT II Treaty, calling it "fatally flawed." His disapproval was hardly limited to that hapless accord: Reagan had opposed the Limited Test Ban Treaty in 1963, the Nuclear Nonproliferation Treaty in 1968, the ABM Treaty and the SALT I Interim Agreement in 1972, and the Vladivostok Accord in 1974. In other words, Reagan had opposed every major Cold War arms control agreement, whether negotiated by a Republican or a Democrat. In a September 1979 radio address, he asked his audience, "Do arms limitation agreements—even good ones—really bring or preserve peace? History would seem to say, 'No.'" His evidence was *The Treaty Trap*, a book by his friend, Hollywood lawyer Laurence Beilenson, who wrote, "Diplomacy and treaties have coexisted happily with war all through the ages. If they could prevent war, why haven't they?" Reagan praised *The Treaty Trap* as "the best book written on defense," and his message seemed clear: arms, not arms control, were America's best defense.

The men Reagan appointed to key arms control positions in his administration did little to dispel this conclusion. President Kennedy had created the Arms Control and Disarmament Agency to promote nuclear stability and balance the Pentagon's incessant call for more weapons. To

---

*Reagan called the neutron bomb a "moral improvement" over other nuclear weapons. Detractors dubbed it the "Republican bomb" because it killed people without damaging property.

head ACDA Reagan named Eugene Rostow, a man who believed that arms control had no place in U.S. foreign policy. Rostow had led the CPD's fight against SALT II and told the Senate Foreign Relations Committee that the last arms control treaty worth supporting was the Rush-Bagot Agreement of 1817, under which the United States and Canada had agreed to demilitarize the Great Lakes. "Arms control thinking," Rostow averred, "drives out sound thinking."

Reagan named Richard Burt to head the State Department's Bureau of Politico-Military Affairs. Intelligent and articulate, the thirty-three-year-old Burt had been a national security reporter for the *New York Times* and one of the few journalists sympathetic to the Committee on the Present Danger. He dubbed the SALT process a "favor to the Russians," arguing, like Goldwater, that even talking with Moscow legitimized the communist regime. Just months before joining the Reagan administration, Burt wrote a piece for the journal *Daedalus* in which he argued against further restraints on nuclear weapons: "Arms control has developed the same kind of mindless momentum associated with other large-scale government pursuits. Conceptual notions of limited durability, such as the doctrine of mutual assured destruction, have gained bureaucratic constituencies and have thus been prolonged beyond their usefulness. There are strong reasons for believing that arms control is unlikely to possess much utility in the coming decade." It was a sign of the administration's aversion to diplomacy in the early 1980s that Burt would emerge as a moderate.

The standard against which he would be measured was set by Richard Perle, the assistant secretary of defense for international security affairs. Perle, too, was young and brilliant, only thirty-nine when he took his post. He had spent the past thirteen years as national security assistant to Senator Scoop Jackson, in which capacity he had been one of the most conspicuous opponents of détente. At one point, a frustrated Henry Kissinger had screamed, "You just wait and see! If that son of a bitch Richard Perle ever gets into an administration, after six months he'll be pursuing exactly the same policies I've been attempting and that he's been sabotaging." In fact, he would not, but would instead become the administration's chief arms control obstructionist, dubbed "the Prince of Darkness" by his enemies. Perle believed that the only worthwhile U.S.-Soviet agreement had been the Austrian State Treaty of 1955, which ended the Soviets' postwar occupation of the country. Arms control, Perle once said, "does violence to our ability to maintain adequate defenses." "The sense that we and the Russians could compose our differences, reduce them to treaty constraints, . . . and then rely on compliance to produce a safer world," he said, "I don't agree with any of that."

Nor did many of the administration's higher-ranking officials. Perle's immediate superior was Fred C. Iklé, who had taken over ACDA in 1973, when Jackson had forced Nixon to purge the SALT I delegation, and subsequently opposed Kissinger's efforts to reach a SALT II agreement. Caspar Weinberger, like all good conservatives, viewed the contemporary situation as Munich 1938, himself as Winston Churchill, and arms control as appeasement. Reagan's second national security adviser, William Clark, according to Reagan aide George Shultz, "categorically opposed U.S.-Soviet contacts" of any sort.

There were, to be sure, a number of officials more inclined toward negotiation with the Soviets. Despite Alexander Haig's penchant for bombast and bombing—he once vowed to turn Cuba into "a fucking parking lot"—Reagan's first secretary of state was a pragmatist who had ably served Kissinger and supported Nixon's overtures to Russia and China. But Haig was not close to the president, unlike Weinberger or Clark, who had worked with Reagan in California. In the opening days of the administration, then, he and like-minded officials were at a distinct disadvantage vis-à-vis their more ideological colleagues.

INF and START

Reagan's first term was a battle between the administration's pragmatists and its conservatives, who mastered the disingenuous art of advocating progress while doing everything possible to undermine it. The battles within the Reagan administration often seemed more about tactics than about first principles. For example, rather than debate the merits of conservatism versus liberalism, Reagan aides might argue about whether a treaty ought to limit the number of missiles or the throw weight of those missiles. To a nonexpert, it would seem an arcane topic, but such disagreements were in fact manifestations of differing worldviews. Throw weight was the bugaboo of the Committee on the Present Danger, representing as it did the possibility that the Soviets were pursuing a war-winning capability—proof of their ideological extremism and the futility of negotiations.

The first serious challenge for the conservative contingent in the White House was the so-called Intermediate-Range Nuclear Forces, or INF, talks. In the late 1970s, the Soviets had begun to deploy a new missile, the SS-20, aimed specifically at European targets. In 1979, President Carter, meeting with the heads of Britain, France, and West Germany, had agreed to deploy intermediate-range nuclear missiles in Western Europe to offset the SS-20. Specifically, the United States would send hundreds of Pershing II ballistic missiles and nuclear-armed Tomahawk cruise missiles to West Germany and Italy. The missiles had little military value—the United States could already destroy any Soviet target it wanted to with its ICBMs, SLBMs, and bombers. Instead, they were intended to reassure the Europeans of America's commitment to their defense. Nonnuclear NATO countries like West Germany doubted that, if the Soviet Union did fire its SS-20s at European targets, the United States would respond in kind, since that would leave it open to retaliation. The Pershings helped couple European security to American security. At the same time, Carter had agreed to enter into talks with the Soviets to get rid of the SS-20s altogether, thus obviating the need for the counter-deployment.

Conservatives had no interest in the talks, but pragmatists pressured Reagan to commit to them in 1981. As Strobe Talbott recounts in his superb history of Reagan's early arms control efforts, forced to accept negotiations, conservatives did everything they could to sabotage them while appearing as reasonable as possible. This meant stalling both their more pragmatic colleagues and the Europeans—who wanted to reach a diplomatic solution before the Tomahawks and Pershings were deployed in late 1983—by counseling caution and patience and further study.

When Reagan ended the stonewalling by calling for talks to proceed before the end of the year, the Reaganauts switched tactics: They proposed positions they knew the Soviets would never accept. The most famous example was the so-called zero-option, in which Perle suggested that, if the Soviets removed their SS-20s, the United States would not deploy any intermediate-range missiles in Europe. In effect, the Soviets would have to concede something in exchange for nothing. When the State Department suggested a fallback position in the event the Soviets didn't agree to disarm unilaterally, Perle appeared before the Senate Armed

Services Committee and compared any deviation from the zero option to Chamberlain's appeasement of Hitler in 1938.

When, as expected, the Soviets rejected the zero-option, conservatives actively worked to block any compromise. Reagan had appointed Nitze to lead the INF team, a choice that on the surface seemed to be yet another sign of his antipathy toward arms control. Nitze, after all, had provided the intellectual firepower to the Committee on the Present Danger's battle against SALT II. But Nitze's ideological proclivities were complicated. While he had argued in the mid-1970s that the United States was not well enough prepared to fight a nuclear war, he had also negotiated large parts of the SALT I accords, which acknowledged that there was no way to win such a war. In fact, Nitze believed in mutual assured destruction, but unlike McNamara and others, he worried that it was a very fragile condition: If the nuclear balance was not carefully managed, one side could gain a decisive advantage. As a member of the foreign policy establishment who had effectively defected from its orthodoxy, Nitze was trusted by no one. Arms controllers still smarted from his testimony against SALT II, and conservatives suspected that at heart Nitze wanted the chance to bring about an agreement with the Soviets.

Nitze did in fact wish to broker an INF deal, and so, in mid-1982, he took matters into his own hands. He had been instructed to offer the zero-option and nothing more, but, well aware that they would never agree to such terms, he began private conversations with his counterpart, Yuli Kvitsinsky. One day, Nitze suggested that they go for a walk. On the side of a mountain in the Alps, as rain drizzled on their papers, Nitze and Kvitsinsky sat on a log and hammered out an agreement that greatly favored the American position. It would have reduced Soviet SS-20 deployments by two-thirds and allowed the Americans to deploy an equal number of Tomahawk launchers. But because each SS-20 had three warheads, and each Tomahawk launcher carried four missiles with one warhead each, the United States would actually be allowed more fire power. The deal also capped SS-20 deployments in Asia and forbade the Soviets from developing ground-launched cruise missiles. The only concession the United States had to make was to abandon deployment of the Pershings—a small sacrifice, Nitze felt, given that the cruise missiles were a more valuable addition to our arsenal.

Of course, Nitze still had to get Washington to agree to the deal, which in the end proved impossible. Perle's ideological obstructionism—concisely conveyed in his disparagement of Nitze as "an inveterate problem-solver"—reached fantastic heights. When word of the Nitze deal reached him, Perle tried to prevent the president from learning its details, even falsely asserting that the Joint Chiefs of Staff opposed it. Working with Weinberger, Perle ultimately persuaded Reagan to stick with the "bold" zero-option. As European pressure to do *something* increased (even Margaret Thatcher, a hard-line anticommunist and Reagan's staunchest ally, counseled compromise), Perle continued to dig in his heels: "We can't just do something; we've got to stand there—and stand firm." In early 1983, he told Weinberger that it would be better to deploy no missiles at all than to be forced to accept a bad deal. In other words, he argued that forgoing deployment in return for nothing was better than forgoing deployment in exchange for something. The position made no sense, but the Reagan team held firm to it, once again preventing the adoption of a viable arms control deal. In November 1983, the first Pershing II missiles arrived in Germany—and the Soviets walked out of the talks.

The negotiations on long-range, or "strategic" arms were just as fruitless. In May 1982, Reagan gave a speech at Eureka College, his alma mater, renaming the SALT talks "START." That is, instead of the Strategic Arms *Limitation* Talks, we would now have the bolder Strategic Arms *Reduction* Talks. The president's START proposal had been delayed by another battle between the pragmatists in the administration, led by Richard Burt, and the Reaganauts, led again by Richard Perle. Burt wanted to supercharge the SALT process and seek reductions in warheads and launchers, but Perle wanted to focus on throw weight. The president's proposal at Eureka was a compromise between the two—and it made no sense whatsoever.

For one thing, the proposal would have resulted in a highly destabilizing balance of forces. It called for each side to deploy no more than 850 ballistic missiles and no more than 5,000 warheads, of which no more than half could be on ICBMs. To those unfamiliar with nuclear policy, the idea of reductions sounded much better than the incredibly high "caps" on forces allowed by SALT I and II. But putting so many warheads on so few missiles meant that in a crisis each side would be tempted to launch first. As conservative nemesis Paul Warnke put it, "if the Russians accept Mr. Reagan's proposal, he'll be forced to reject it himself." But there was never any chance that the Russians would accept the proposal because it, like the INF zero-option, asked the Soviets to disarm while the United States did almost nothing. Because the Soviet nuclear force consisted largely of ICBMs, the proposal would have required the Soviets to dismantle three times as many launchers as we did. And the proposed limitations on throw weight would have forced the Soviets to reduce their arsenal by 60 percent, while leaving ours untouched.

It might have been possible to rationalize this approach as simply a maximalist opening offer from which the United States could back down as a concession. But the administration tied the hands of American negotiators. Cruise missiles such as the Tomahawk were becoming a powerful addition to our nuclear arsenal, and our technology was significantly ahead of the Soviets'. Since the Soviets regarded our cruise missiles as offsetting the advantage they had in throw weight, they would never unilaterally reduce their ICBMs if the United States did not consider cruise missile reductions. Unfortunately, Reagan signed a National Security Decision Directive that forbade American negotiators from even discussing cruise missiles until the Soviets had made concessions on throw weight—in essence, he forbade any diplomatic quid pro quo.

All of this mischief was compounded by the appointment of Edward Rowny as chief START negotiator. Rowny, a retired general, had been a foreign policy adviser to Jesse Helms and, not surprisingly, did not believe in the practice of diplomacy. He employed the technique of "telling it like it is"—or, less euphemistically, insulting one's negotiating opponents—and since he had been given a completely nonnegotiable position by the administration, he had plenty of opportunities to use it. He spent his time lambasting the Soviets for not understanding the issues at hand, emphasizing his Polish (i.e., anti-Russian) heritage, and staging walkouts over the seating arrangements. Rowny felt that he was leading a revolution in arms control with his blunt talk, even bragging about it in a memo that he dispatched to the White House, but the START talks were going nowhere.

By late 1982, the situation had become so untenable that Congress decided the Reagan administration needed adult supervision—its arms control proposal was not only nonnegotiable, it was dangerous—so it threatened to withhold funds for the MX missile. In response, Reagan appointed a blue-ribbon commission in January 1983 to review the administration's arms control policies. Headed by retired general and former Kissinger aide Brent Scowcroft, the commission sported a list of foreign policy eminences, including Henry Kissinger, James Schlesinger, and Harold Brown. In April, the commission called for a new approach to arms control, but instead of heeding its advice, the administration "compromised" by offering the Soviets *two* nonnegotiable proposals: Either accept direct limits on throw weight or accept strict limits on heavy ICBMs, which would indirectly limit throw weight. The Soviets complained that the United States was still trying to force them to disarm unilaterally: "Your idea of 'flexibility,'" fumed one Soviet negotiator, "is to give a condemned man the choice between the rope and the ax."

By August 1983, Congress was so displeased with the administration's intransigence that it brought back Scowcroft—in Talbott's words, "The Legislative Branch had, in effect, fired the Executive Branch for gross incompetence in arms control"—and asked him to craft a compromise. This he did, developing a standard measure for nuclear military might that would enable the two sides to reduce their atomic arsenals equivalently, despite their different structures. Congress was satisfied, and the Reagan administration adopted the proposal in slightly amended form, but the Russians found it unwieldy. Their reaction was probably skewed by the fact that Rowny, rather than presenting it as the compromise it was, emphasized that it would reduce throw weight. The "basic position of this Administration has not changed," Rowny declared. "Ambassador Rowny," the Soviet negotiators concluded, "is not a serious man." When a round of talks ended in December, the Soviets set no date for a return.

The conservative position had by now become far more sophisticated: By never rejecting negotiations outright, the administration could always claim that it was pursuing them with vigor, and if critics complained that its proposals were nonnegotiable, it could simply, if disingenuously, claim that it wanted to substantively reduce nuclear arsenals, not just perpetuate the status quo.

To Fight and Win a Nuclear War

The Reaganauts might well have succeeded in their aims had they not apparently been preparing to fight a nuclear war, believing that the United

States could emerge from one victorious. Reagan was a strong opponent of mutual assured destruction. Since Donald Brennan had coined the acronym "MAD," many conservatives had rejected what they considered its self-imposed vulnerability, and the 1980 Republican platform rejected the concept of deterrence through assured destruction. It did so in part because the party believed, as Reagan said, that "the Soviet Union decided some time ago that a nuclear war was possible and was winnable, and they have proceeded with an elaborate and extensive civil protection program. We did not have anything of that kind because we went along with what the policy was supposed to be"—i.e., mutual assured destruction. The implication was that we needed to develop our own defenses so that we, too, could fight—and win—a nuclear war. Serious critics of MAD did not think such a victory was possible, but rather worried that, if the Soviets *believed* they could win, they would feel politically emboldened—and that as a result we might be forced to back down in a crisis.

Alas, many Reagan officials were not such subtle thinkers. When Senator Claiborne Pell asked Eugene Rostow during his confirmation hearings if he thought the United States could survive a nuclear onslaught, Rostow optimistically noted that Japan "not only survived but flourished after the nuclear attack." Pressed as to whether we could survive a *full* nuclear strike—one involving thousands of nuclear warheads, instead of the two bombs dropped on Hiroshima and Nagasaki—Rostow observed: "The human race is very resilient. . . . Depending upon certain assumptions, some estimates predict that there would be ten million casualties on one side and one hundred million on another. But that is not the whole of the population." Amusingly—or perhaps not—that was the assessment George C. Scott's character, General Buck Turgidson, gave of a nuclear war in Stanley Kubrick's satire *Dr. Strangelove:* "I'm not saying we wouldn't get our hair mussed. But I do say, no more than ten to twenty million killed, tops, depending on the breaks."

Other members of the administration were similarly sanguine. During the 1980 campaign, for example, when journalist Robert Scheer asked soon-to-be-vice-president George H. W. Bush how a nuclear war could be won, Bush responded with specifics: "You have a survivability of command and control, survivability of industrial potential, protection of a percentage of your citizens, and you have a capability that inflicts more damage on the opposition than it can inflict upon you. That's the way you can have a winner." Richard Pipes, whom Reagan appointed to the National Security Council, maintained that, in a nuclear conflict, the "country better prepared could win and emerge a viable society" and gave a lengthy interview to the *Washington Post* in which he counseled readers to worry less about the subject—even though he said the odds of nuclear war were two in five. Colin S. Gray, a Reagan adviser to ACDA and the State Department, wrote an article arguing that "victory is possible," provided the United States was prepared to fight.* Energy Secretary James B. Edwards, whose portfolio included the nuclear weapons laboratories and production facilities, said that in an atomic exchange, "I want to come out of it number one, not number two"—the implication being that there would be a measurable difference.

To both experts and laypeople, such comments suggested either profound ignorance or unforgivable flippancy. Their concern was only heightened in May 1982, when the Pentagon's five-year procurement plan leaked to the press. The Defense Guidance document, set to be signed by Weinberger, indicated that the military wanted to be able to wage nuclear war against the Soviet Union "over a protracted period." The *New York Times* ran a story on its front page under the headline "Pentagon Draws Up First Strategy for Fighting a Long Nuclear War." According to the document, in a nuclear conflict American forces "must prevail and be able to force the Soviet Union to seek earliest termination of hostilities on terms favorable to the United States." Then, in August 1982, the *Los Angeles Times* ran a story on National Security Decision Directive Number 13 (NSDD-13), signed by Reagan in late 1981, which allegedly marked "the first reported time the U.S. government has declared that nuclear war can be won." As public concern mounted the *Washington Post* summed up the conventional wisdom: The Reagan administration "has created the impression that it is more inclined to fight than its predecessors, and that it believes a nuclear war, even possibly a protracted one, could be fought and won."

To be fair, these steps were not the revolution in nuclear doctrine that the press made them out to be. Ever since the Kennedy administration had been horrified to learn that our war plan entailed launching our entire

---

*Gray's coauthor was Keith Payne, who became Bush's deputy assistant secretary of defense for forces policy—i.e., the civilian in charge of nuclear planning.

nuclear arsenal at once, policy makers and war planners had sought better options in case deterrence failed. Robert McNamara had overseen the
development of flexible response, which would allow us to respond to
an attack with a proportionate amount of force and, in theory, prevent
escalation to an all-out war. Similarly, Nixon's nuclear doctrine, outlined
by James Schlesinger in January 1974, said that, in a nuclear conflict, the
United States would "seek early war termination on terms acceptable to the
United States and its allies, at the lowest level of conflict feasible." Likewise,
President Carter signed Presidential Directive Number 59, which read,
"We must be capable of fighting successfully so that the adversary would
not achieve his war aims" and that we must "preserve the possibility of
bargaining effectively to terminate the war on acceptable terms that are as
favorable as practical." It referred to this as a "countervailing strategy."

Reagan's advisers, then, had some justification for arguing, as they did,
that they had done little different from their predecessors. But there was a
difference: Although they may have wanted war-fighting options, Reagan's
predecessors all realized that even a modest amount of nuclear foreplay
was likely to elicit what Herman Kahn had called a "war orgasm," a danger Reagan's people didn't seem to understand. For one thing, the Defense
Guidance was disturbingly more ambitious than its predecessors, as it specifically called for the ability to wage a six-month nuclear war, with pauses
for reloading silos and firing fresh volleys of missiles. It also provided for
"a reserve of nuclear forces sufficient for trans- and post-attack protection
and coercion." In other words, it called for having enough nuclear weapons to win one war—a war involving so many weapons that we would
have to draw on "a reserve of nuclear forces"—and immediately be ready
to deter or fight another. The idea that a post–nuclear holocaust America
would use its remaining nuclear might to influence global events seemed
rather optimistic. To paraphrase Albert Einstein, if World War III were
fought with nuclear weapons, World War IV would most likely be fought
with sticks and stones.

The administration's other war preparations were just as confident—
and just as misguided. As we've seen, there are three chief methods for
limiting damage from a nuclear strike. The first is counterforce targeting,
whereby you destroy the enemy's nuclear forces. The other two are civil
defense and missile defense. As Glenn Kent's 1964 study for Robert McNamara had shown, no combination of these three strategies could protect

the United States against a determined adversary, as it was always easier to build offenses than defenses. Furthermore, even trying to protect yourself was dangerous, because it signaled that you believed a nuclear war was winnable. That, in turn, could prompt your adversary to launch first during a crisis before a counterforce strike took out part of his arsenal. The potential for destabilization is not simply theoretical. Interviews with former Soviet military officials have revealed that PD-59, intended simply to provide the United States with options during a crisis, convinced the Soviet leadership that America was preparing a preemptive strike. Conversely, as noted in chapter 3, American conservatives, hawks, and neocons likewise were alarmed by the Soviets' alleged belief that a nuclear war could be fought and won.

The Reagan administration only increased this instability by deciding to pursue both missile and civil defenses. On March 23, 1983, Reagan gave one of his most famous speeches, calling upon the scientists who gave us the atomic bomb to cleanse their sin by inventing a defense against ballistic missiles that would render nuclear weapons "impotent and obsolete." Via the Strategic Defense Initiative, or SDI, Reagan hoped to eliminate mutual assured destruction as the basis for nuclear strategy. Instead of relying on retaliation to deter an attack, we would rely on a shield to intercept and destroy Soviet nuclear warheads before they could reach the United States. Conservatives were ecstatic, seeing SDI as the ultimate refutation of mutual assured destruction and therefore of the status quo, which left us unable to seek victory over the Soviet Union. The day after Reagan's SDI speech, Goldwater sent him a one-sentence letter: "That was the best statement I have ever heard from any President." Reagan's question, "Wouldn't it be better to save lives than to avenge them?," was a seductive one, but it was also naive and dangerous. Remember, MAD was not a policy choice; it was a condition. Reagan genuinely believed he could replace it with a perfect defense, but no such thing was possible. A perfect defense had never existed in the history of warfare, and there was ample evidence to show that the Soviets could penetrate any missile defense by using metal chaff, decoys, or just a larger number of warheads. SDI would be useful, however, in dampening a retaliatory strike if we first destroyed most Soviet missiles on the ground via a preemptive counterforce strike. Although the Soviets would still be able to inflict enough damage that a first strike by the United States would be suicidal, it would be "less suicidal" to the extent that such a concept made sense, which some Reagan officials believed it did. In short, SDI was a better adjunct to a first strike than it was a stand-alone defense. That made it critically destabilizing, which is why missile defenses had been outlawed by the ABM Treaty in the first place.

Faith in the powers of civil defense, meanwhile, was embodied in Thomas K. Jones, a deputy secretary of defense in the Reagan Pentagon. Jones had been studying the topic for several years and had become enamored of Soviet plans for protecting its population. If the United States took similar steps, Jones said, it could recover from an all-out Soviet nuclear strike—a strike that would involve thousands of nuclear warheads—in a mere two to four years. All people needed to do, Jones said, was "dig a hole, cover it with a couple of doors and then throw three feet of dirt on top. It's the dirt that does it." True, urban areas would have to be evacuated so that city dwellers could find enough dirt, everyone would need to know how to make a ventilation pump, and there would be serious sanitation and supply issues. But Jones wasn't worried. "If there are enough shovels around, everybody's going to make it." When Jones's comments appeared in the *Los Angeles Times* in early 1982, the *New York Times* editorial page wondered if Jones wasn't perhaps a character from Doonesbury, rather than a Pentagon official. The Senate, less amused, subpoenaed him.

Jones could have been dismissed as a lone crank were it not for the fact that the GOP platform had called for a "civil defense which would protect the American people against nuclear war at least as well as the Soviet population is protected." In the spring of 1982, the administration asked Congress for $4.3 billion for a program that it claimed would protect 80 percent of Americans in the event of a massive Soviet nuclear strike. Louis O. Giuffrida, whom Reagan had appointed to lead the Federal Emergency Management Agency, had impressed the idea on the president. As Giuffrida said of nuclear war, "It would be a terrible mess, but it wouldn't be unmanageable." FEMA's head of civil defense, William Chipman, believed not only that many civilians would survive but that America itself would soon enough reemerge as a functioning democracy: "As I say, the ants eventually build another anthill."

Officially, the Reagan administration maintained that it was working toward peace, that its actions were simply reasonable efforts to protect the American people, and that nuclear war was a remote possibility. But its most important member was himself less than convinced; indeed, by the end of 1983 he was quite alarmed about the possibility of nuclear war. As it happened, he had good reason to be.

The Year of Fear

The conservative policies of the early Reagan years—the military buildup, the sabotage of negotiations, and the apparent preparations for fighting a nuclear war—were all grossly destabilizing, so that all that was needed was a crisis or a misunderstanding to spark a nuclear conflagration. In the fall of 1983, history was only too happy to oblige. At 3:26 A.M. Tokyo time on September 1, a Soviet Su-15 fighter jet fired two missiles at a Korean Airlines 747 passenger plane. Flight KAL007 had been en route from Alaska to Seoul when, for unknown reasons, it strayed into Soviet airspace. Lieutenant Colonel Gennadi Osipovich had scrambled his jet, intercepted the aircraft, fired warning shots at it, and, when the plane did not respond, fired two missiles at it, sending the 747 on an agonizing drop into the Sea of Japan, killing all 269 of its passengers, among whom were 63 Americans, including a U.S. congressman.

Reagan and his aides were furious. A visibly angry George Shultz, whom journalists had dubbed the Sphinx for his usual reluctance to share his thoughts or emotions, called a press conference just four hours after receiving the news. To American officials, the KAL incident was an appalling demonstration of the communists' disregard for human life. Although intercepts of Soviet radio traffic soon showed that the Soviets had mistaken the 747 for a spy plane—in fact, an American reconnaissance flight had just left the area—the Reagan administration was unswayed, its anger only intensified by Moscow's initial refusal to admit any culpability. On September 5, 1983, Reagan delivered a televised speech from the Oval Office in which he referred to the episode as a "massacre," a "crime against humanity," and "an atrocity." The following week, Shultz met with Soviet foreign minister Andrei Gromyko for what Gromyko later called the "sharpest exchange I ever had with an American Secretary of State, and I have had talks with fourteen of them." Days later, Gromyko's plane was denied permission to land in New York, where he was to attend the opening session of the United Nations General Assembly.

The Soviets—already flustered by two years of calls for them to unilaterally disarm, Reagan's "evil empire" speech, and the launch of SDI—reacted badly. The KAL incident, Soviet ambassador Anatoly Dobrynin wrote in his memoirs, "proved a catalyst for the angry trends that were already inherent in relations during the Reagan presidency." On September 29, Soviet general secretary Yuri Andropov, who had succeeded Brezhnev in November 1982, issued a public statement saying that U.S.-Soviet relations could not improve as long as Reagan was president: "If anybody ever had any illusions about the possibility of an evolution to the better in the policy of the present American administration, these illusions are completely dispelled now." Other Soviet statements began emphasizing the danger of war, and the Soviet press referred to Reagan as a "madman" and compared him to Hitler. Gromyko worried that "the world situation is now slipping toward a very dangerous precipice."

The American people, too, were growing increasingly agitated. President Carter's aborted plans for the neutron bomb and his agreement to deploy the Pershings and cruise missiles had fueled a peace movement in Europe in the late 1970s, a movement that grew exponentially during Reagan's first term and spread across the Atlantic. By the end of 1981, 76 percent of Americans believed a nuclear war would erupt within a few years. The military buildup, the anti-Soviet bombast, the lack of progress on arms control, and the administration's apparent willingness to fight a nuclear war led millions of Americans to join the nuclear freeze movement, which demanded an immediate halt to the arms race. On June 12, 1982, almost a million people marched in protest in New York City. That November, a referendum calling for the immediate halt to weapons deployments appeared on the ballot in ten states, thirty-seven cities and counties, and the District of Columbia. It passed almost everywhere.

A visceral fear of nuclear holocaust had seized the public. Jonathan Schell's call for nuclear disarmament, *The Fate of the Earth*, published in 1982, began with vivid descriptions of how nuclear war would destroy the country as we knew it—and became a bestseller. In 1983, *War Games*, starring Matthew Broderick, hit theaters. In the movie, an intelligent supercomputer takes over the North American Aerospace Defense Command (NORAD) and prepares to launch a nuclear strike on the Soviet Union; after gaming out all the possible options and responses, however, the computer decides that the exercise is pointless. In Reagan's

America, Hollywood played the role of Bernard Brodie, reminding viewers that, in the game of global thermonuclear war, "the only winning move is not to play." Later that year, one hundred million viewers tuned in to ABC's *The Day After*, a TV movie portraying the residents of Lawrence, Kansas, in the aftermath of a nuclear war. Where *War Games* could not help but be campy, *The Day After* was terrifyingly vivid and believable. By the end of 1983, 85 percent of Americans supported the nuclear freeze movement.

Publicly, the administration alternately dismissed such worries and reassured the concerned. Reagan himself, however, had watched *The Day After*, and in his memoirs he reflected that the movie left him "greatly depressed" and made him "aware of the need for the world to step back from the nuclear precipice." If it seems vaguely ridiculous for a Cold War president to reach this conclusion only after watching a made-for-TV movie, remember that Reagan biographers have long noted that his connection to film was often stronger than his connection to reality. He also became far more intellectually and emotionally engaged when presented with issues framed as personal stories, rather than as policy proposals.

Reagan's depression significantly worsened weeks later, when he was briefed for the first time on the nation's nuclear war plan. The fact that the president had put off the briefing for over two years, despite the entreaties of his advisers, was itself a sign of his discomfort with nuclear weapons. Indeed, some of his advisers doubted that Reagan would ever order a nuclear strike, even in retaliation for a Soviet attack. Meeting with the president in the Situation Room, Weinberger and General John Vessey, the Chairman of the Joint Chiefs of Staff, explained that the United States was targeting fifty thousand Soviet sites with nuclear arms. Only half of those sites were military; the rest were economic, industrial, political, and population centers. If the war plan was implemented, they informed Reagan, the Soviets would almost certainly retaliate, destroying the United States as a functioning society. Officials at the briefing said Reagan was "chastened" and grew brooding afterward. Weinberger recalled that the president found the briefing extremely disturbing. Reagan's diary entry for that day characterizes the session as a "most sobering experience," and, in his memoirs, he wrote that the exercise reminded him of *The Day After:* "In several ways, the sequence of events described in the briefings paralleled those in the ABC movie."

Then fiction threatened to become reality. As fear of a nuclear conflict was growing in Reagan's mind, it was reaching critical mass in that of his counterpart, Yuri Andropov. Before becoming the Soviet general secretary in 1982, Andropov had served as head of the Soviet intelligence service, the KGB, for fifteen years. In May 1981, Andropov told a gathering of KGB officers that the United States was actively preparing for war, and warned of "the possibility of a nuclear first strike." The top priority of the KGB and the GRU, the Soviet military intelligence service, accordingly became detecting preparations for that strike. Instructions were sent to Soviet agents in NATO capitals and Japan calling for "close observation of all political, military, and intelligence activities that might indicate preparations for mobilization." The reasoning was that, if the United States were going to launch a first strike, it would be signaled by detectable changes in communications and the like, which would give Moscow some advance warning. The program was known as VRYAN, the Russian acronym for "Surprise Nuclear Missile Attack." When Bzezhnev died and Andropov succeeded him, VRYAN was given even greater priority.

The events of 1983 seemed to confirm Andropov's paranoia. When Reagan announced the launch of SDI in March, Andropov said he was "inventing new plans on how to unleash a nuclear war in the best way, with the hope of winning it." Then came the shooting down of the KAL flight, and if that incident demonstrated to Reagan and his aides the callousness with which the Soviets regarded human life, the American response suggested to Andropov that the United States might now be laying the diplomatic groundwork for war. To Andropov, the event was a genuine tragedy, but given that U.S. military forces had been aggressively probing Soviet air defenses since 1981 (and finding significant gaps in radar coverage), how did they *expect* the Soviets to respond to another plane within Soviet airspace? On top of all this, the Americans were on the verge of deploying Pershing II ballistic missiles in Western Europe. Although the decision to do so was largely a political one, the Soviets viewed the missiles as first-strike weapons—they were highly accurate and could reach Russia in only four to six minutes, giving Moscow an inhumanly short time to respond to an attack. As the November deployment date neared, VRYAN became central to Soviet military strategy, suggesting that, if preparations for an attack were detected, the Soviets would strike preemptively.

On November 2, 1983, the United States and its NATO allies commenced a military exercise known as "Able Archer," simulating the use of nuclear weapons to test command and control procedures. NATO had conducted such exercises before, but the fall of 1983 was particularly tense—and Able Archer was far more realistic. For one thing, it involved high-ranking civilian leaders, including British prime minister Margaret Thatcher and German chancellor Helmut Kohl. (By contrast, Soviet politicians had not participated in such war games since 1972.) For another, the exercise required NATO forces to escalate through the military alert levels, up to DEFCON-1, at which point nuclear weapons would have their safeguards removed and be ready for use. Able Archer was also a very large exercise, encompassing the entirety of Western Europe, from Turkey to Scandinavia, and NATO forces seemed to be employing new techniques for relaying commands—just the sort of anomalous behavior for which agents participating in VRYAN had been told to report.

According to Oleg Gordievsky, the intelligence chief at the Soviet embassy in London at the time (and a double agent providing material to the British government), KGB officers began reporting to Moscow that NATO was preparing for an attack. The night of November 8, 1983, Moscow sent high-priority telegrams to its KGB stations in Western Europe specifically asking agents for any information on an impending surprise nuclear strike on the USSR. There was, in fact, little evidence of such an attack, but as often happens in crisis situations, errors were made, and Soviet agents reported that NATO troops were on the move. Soviet intelligence concluded that the "exercise" might in fact be a ploy to disguise preparations for nuclear war. Warsaw Pact fighter aircraft armed with nuclear weapons were placed on alert at bases in East Germany and Poland.

When Able Archer ended on November 11, so did the war scare. But as national security adviser Robert McFarlane later admitted, "The situation was very grave." Shultz called the episode a "close call"—"quite sobering." Indeed, Reagan and his aides soon realized that they had nearly started a nuclear war. In early 1984, when the CIA reported that the Soviets had truly believed that Able Archer might have been a prelude to a preemptive nuclear strike, Reagan was shocked. According to McFarlane, he felt "genuine anxiety," was rattled by the Soviets' panicky response, and later that day raised the specter of Armageddon with his advisers.

Reagan Does Arms Control

The events of the fall of 1983 had a profound impact on Ronald Reagan. The president was, and had for a long time been, a nuclear abolitionist—a fact that eluded even his most careful contemporary observers. At the 1976 Republican convention, for example, Reagan invoked the specter of a post-nuclear world. That speech offered an important clue to his convictions, as Lou Cannon has explained: "This clue did not lead us anywhere, however, because most of us in the journalistic community did not realize then that there was a mystery to solve. By 1980, Reagan was a familiar figure on the national political stage. There seemed nothing enigmatic about him."

Signs of Reagan's true leanings appeared intermittently even during his first years in office, when his anti-Sovietism seemed to be at its peak. As he rested in George Washington Hospital in 1981, recovering from surgery to remove the bullet that John Hinkley had fired into his chest, he told Terence Cardinal Cooke that God had spared his life so that he might "reduce the threat of nuclear war." The next day, Reagan drafted a letter to Brezhnev calling for "disarmament" and a "world without nuclear weapons." (His horrified advisers stripped the language out.) Reagan told aides that he saw nuclear weapons as "horrible" and "inherently evil," and twice during the first two years of his presidency he asked them to draw up plans to eliminate them all. (Believing it an irresponsible idea, they never followed up on it. "He can't have a world without nuclear weapons!" Richard Burt exclaimed at one point. "Doesn't he understand the realities?") It became clear to his aides and later to his biographers that Reagan believed literally in the end of the world as foretold in Revelations, that Armageddon would come about through nuclear war, and that it was his responsibility to stop it.

At first glance, it is difficult to reconcile Reagan the abolitionist with Reagan the militarist—the man who increased military spending, allowed his aides to put forth obviously nonnegotiable arms control proposals, rejected mutual assured destruction, and called for the buildup of strategic and civil defenses. Each of these efforts, however, can also be interpreted as a sincere, if misguided, product of Reagan's hatred of nuclear weapons. Reagan believed that the Soviets would reduce their atomic arsenal only if they were faced with the prospect of an arms race. Well before his conservative brethren, the president realized that the Soviet Union was approaching an economic crisis and would shy away from yet another round of missile buildups. At the same time, genuinely concerned about American military inferiority, he concluded, perversely, that he needed to rearm in order to disarm. As Paul Lettow has written in his book *Ronald Reagan and His Quest to Abolish Nuclear Weapons,* "Reagan emphasized time and again, that the aim of his arms build-up was to attain deep cuts in nuclear weapons; most people did not listen to what he was actually saying." Reagan's quest for ultimate abolition helps explain why he advanced the zero-option and his first START proposal: He believed he was challenging the Soviets to think differently and he didn't understand that he was effectively asking them to unilaterally disarm.

If few people heard what Reagan was saying, it was because to believe that he was sincere meant one had to accept that he was also profoundly ignorant of nuclear strategy. But, in fact, Reagan *was* profoundly ignorant of many of the details of America's nuclear armaments. He once told a group of congressmen, for example, that bombers and submarines did not carry nuclear weapons; on another occasion, he said that submarine-launched ballistic missiles could be recalled once in flight. He told Brent Scowcroft that he had not realized that the principal threat from the Soviet Union was that its gigantic ICBMs might destroy ours in a preemptive strike. Indeed, Reagan did not seem to understand that the concept of the "window of vulnerability" referred *specifically* to that threat, even though it had been the signature issue of the Committee on the Present Danger (of which Reagan was a member) and one of the principal themes of his 1980 campaign. In October 1981, when a journalist asked Reagan when the window of vulnerability would open, he responded with a non sequitur, saying that the Soviet navy was already superior to that of the United States (which wasn't even true). Reagan's initial plan for rectifying our supposed ICBM vulnerability involved putting the MX missile in Minuteman silos, and, when journalists asked why they would be any less vulnerable than the Minutemen, he confessed that he didn't know.*

---

*In order to address the potential vulnerability of our ICBMs, the Carter administration had developed a plan to shuttle 200 multiwarhead missiles among 4,600 shelters in the Nevada and Utah desert. The idea was that since the Soviets would never know which shelter was hiding the missiles, they would have to use thousands of warheads to take out a mere 200 missiles. Weinberger, who also knew little about nuclear strategy, did not like this plan because it was Carter's and so, as an interim measure, proposed deploying the MX in existing silos.

Reagan's ignorance of nuclear matters was matched only by his blindness to how his actions might be perceived by the Soviets. It had apparently not even occurred to him that adopting a war-fighting strategy, beginning a widespread civil defense program, researching a missile shield while increasing the military budget by 35 percent, starting a new bomber program, deploying a new ICBM, and deploying missiles in Europe could be construed as threatening. Like Barry Goldwater and John Ashbrook, Reagan could not believe that anyone could perceive the United States as anything but righteous. It took the events of 1983 to make him realize, as he wrote in his memoirs, that "many people at the top of the Soviet hierarchy were genuinely afraid of America and Americans" and that "many Soviet officials feared us not only as adversaries but as potential aggressors who might hurl nuclear weapons at them in a first strike."

Reagan himself was responsible for much of the tone of proposals such as SDI, but as Lou Cannon has written, "Reagan did not know enough about nuclear weapons systems to formulate a policy to accomplish his objectives. He was susceptible to manipulation by advisers who shared his militant anti-communism but not his distaste for nuclear deterrence and who wanted neither arms reduction nor arms control." That began to change when he named George Shultz secretary of state in 1982. Until that point, the administration had been dominated by Weinberger and other conservatives who did their best to sabotage arms control efforts. Shultz, by contrast, wanted to begin high-level dialogue with the Soviets, and his influence within the administration only increased when Bill Clark resigned as national security adviser in late 1983, replaced by the more pragmatic Robert McFarlane. Shultz and McFarlane told Reagan that America had built up enough strength to convince the Soviets it was serious and that it was now time to begin sincere negotiations. They were aided in their efforts by Nancy Reagan, who wanted her husband to go down in history as having reduced, not increased, the risk of nuclear war.

A charm offensive now began in earnest. In December 1983, Reagan told *Time* magazine that he would no longer refer to the Soviet Union as the "focus of evil." Indeed, he dropped what was known as the "standard threat" speech and began speaking more frequently of nuclear disarmament. On January 16, 1984, he gave a talk notably different in tone from his earlier perorations on the Soviet Union. In this, he was helped by Jack

Matlock, a career foreign service officer recently put in charge of Soviet affairs at the National Security Council, who drafted a text emphasizing diplomacy over confrontation. While Reagan made a point of asserting that he had reversed the military decline of the 1970s, the speech's real emphasis was on the need for negotiations and the possibility for compromise: "The fact that neither of us likes the other system is no reason to refuse to talk. Living in this nuclear age makes it imperative that we do talk." Matlock even suggested incorporating—and Reagan agreed to use—a quote from Kennedy's American University speech: "So let us not be blind to our differences," he said, "but let us also direct attention to our common interests and to the means by which those differences can be resolved." Such sentiments did away with the rhetoric not just of good and evil, but of us and them.

On February 23, 1984, McFarlane received a letter from the new Soviet leader, Konstantin Chernenko (Andropov had died after only fifteen months in office), who said he saw an "opportunity to put our relations on a more positive track." The following week, the National Security Council decided to renew serious dialogue with the Soviets. That September, the State Department welcomed Gromyko to the White House. The meeting broke the tensions that had built up in 1983, and within months, arms control talks had resumed—this time with a single set of discussions addressing both INF and START. When Chernenko died in March 1984, Reagan sent Vice President George H. W. Bush to the funeral with an invitation to hold a summit with the new Soviet leader, Mikhail Gorbachev.

Reagan believed strongly in the power of personal communication and negotiation. He was confident that, if given the chance, he could convince Moscow of the need to step back from the brink. In his memoirs, he wrote that the war scare of November 1983 had made him "even more anxious to get a top Soviet leader in a room alone and try to convince him we had no designs on the Soviet Union and the Russians had nothing to fear from us." His rhetoric also underwent a further shift; rather than describing the United States and the Soviet Union as in conflict, he spoke of "misunderstandings" and the peaceful intentions of the United States. In his January 16, 1984, speech, Reagan had personally inserted a section about how, if a Russian and an American couple were put together in a room—he called them Jim and Sally, and Ivan and Anya—they would not argue about the merits of their respective governments, but would relate to each other as human beings and seek out points of commonality, proving that "people don't make wars."

When Gorbachev accepted his invitation, Reagan was excited, prepping for the meeting as though it were a presidential campaign debate. (Matlock played Gorbachev.) And he did his best to make the summit, which was held in Geneva, a personal one. Although the official program of events called for only a fifteen-minute initial one-on-one meeting with Gorbachev, Reagan, without telling most of his advisers, arranged for more personal time with Gorbachev—even stoking the hearth that led the meeting to be known as the "fireside summit." Ultimately, the men talked for five hours. Although they did not resolve any strategic issues, Reagan felt they had inaugurated a "fresh start" in U.S.-Soviet relations.

Gorbachev soon realized that Reagan was a radical who genuinely wanted to rid the world of nuclear weapons, but who barely understood the debates that had been driving U.S.-Soviet nuclear relations for decades. He began playing to Reagan's eagerness, sending him a letter in January 1986 that called for the abolition of all nuclear weapons by the year 2000. He proposed first cutting strategic arsenals by 50 percent, banning weapons in outer space, and halting nuclear testing. Perhaps most remarkably, Gorbachev proposed the dismantling of all intermediate-range systems in Europe—in other words, he accepted the zero-option.*

That October, the two superpower leaders met at Hofdi House, an isolated compound outside of Reykjavik, Iceland. Following up on Gorbachev's letter, they began trading radical proposals for disarmament. Gorbachev first suggested reducing strategic arms by 50 percent, including deep cuts in Soviet ICBMs, and elimination of all INF missiles in Europe. The Americans countered that, over a period of five years, 50 percent of all strategic weapons should be destroyed and, over the subsequent five years, all remaining ballistic missiles would be dismantled—a formulation that would have allowed each side to keep many bombers and cruise missiles. Gorbachev upped this ante by proposing that *all* strategic weapons be eliminated at the end of ten years. Reagan then said it would be fine with him "if we eliminated all nuclear weapons," thereby offering to destroy tactical

---

*Of course, since the United States had now deployed 600 intermediate-range missiles in Europe, the option was no longer as one-sided as it had been when the Reagan administration first offered it in 1981.

weapons in Europe and elsewhere as well. When Gorbachev replied, "We can do that," Shultz chimed in, "Let's do it."

Ultimately, though, they came to an impasse over SDI. No responsible Soviet leader could accept significant reductions in weapons if he believed the United States was able to build a missile shield. Reagan, who was convinced that SDI would enable the United States and the Soviet Union to get rid of their nuclear weapons, "since we've proven they can be rendered obsolete," offered to share the technology with the Soviets. Gorbachev found this absurdly naive; after all, even if Reagan was sincere in his desire to share the technology with Moscow, there was no guarantee that future administrations would honor the deal. Besides which, Reagan didn't seem to realize that even a 100 percent effective SDI would not defend against cruise missiles and bombers and therefore could not end the nuclear threat. In fact, it simply would have convinced the Soviet Union that the United States sought a first-strike capability, since the Americans were so far ahead in cruise missile and Stealth bomber technology. Gorbachev did not insist on complete abandonment of SDI; he simply asked Reagan to respect the terms of the ABM Treaty while they were eliminating their missiles and confine SDI research to the laboratory. But Reagan refused, believing that such a deal would effectively kill the program.

Gorbachev replied that they would then have to "forget everything they discussed." Eduard Shevardnadze, Gorbachev's minister of foreign affairs, jumped in at this point to say that they "were so close" to making history that, "if future generations read the minutes of these meetings, and saw how close we had come but how we did not use these opportunities, they would never forgive us." Indeed, reading the minutes of that meeting twenty years later, even while knowing that the Cold War ended peacefully, it is difficult not to wonder if a deal to eliminate all U.S. and Soviet weapons might not have radically altered the course of history, whether disarmament on such a massive scale might have so strengthened the norms against nuclear weapons that the nonproliferation regime might not be as fragile as it is today. But as Shultz put it, "Reykjavik was too bold for the world." Even the pragmatists on Reagan's team were shocked that he had nearly given up the entire nuclear arsenal—and that Shultz had encouraged him to do so. American security had rested for so long on nuclear deterrence, and the warming of U.S.-Soviet relations was so new, that virtually no one could imagine denuclearization. Prime

Minister Thatcher and French president François Mitterrand were aghast, given that a nuclear-free Western Europe would have been far more vulnerable to the formidable Red Army perched on its borders. In the end, ironically, it was Reagan's utopianism, hitched as it was to a missile shield, that preserved the status quo.

Over the course of the following year, however, Gorbachev and his advisers took a closer look at the Strategic Defense Initiative and realized they had little to worry about. (Indeed, it is hard to understand why they were so concerned in the first place. Twenty years later, we still do not have a reliable defense against even a limited missile attack, let alone a space-based shield that would protect us from thousands of Soviet warheads "just as a roof protects a family from rain," as Reagan envisioned.) Still hoping to reach a deal with the president, Gorbachev delinked SDI from his offer to eliminate all intermediate-range nuclear forces. In December 1987, the American and Russian leaders met in Washington and signed the INF Treaty.

It was a historic moment: the first time that an entire class of weapons had been eradicated, the first time that the Soviet Union and the United States had agreed on verification that included on-site inspections, and the first time that the superpowers' nuclear arsenals had been reduced, even if only by 5 percent. The mood surrounding the Washington summit and the signing of the INF Treaty was nothing less than jubilant. Reagan's approval rating shot up, and among the American people, Gorbachev was more popular than Reagan. Gorby mania swept the capital, and crowds lined the route taken by his ZiL limousine to catch a glimpse of the Soviet leader. Those gathered at Connecticut Avenue and L Street in Washington on December 7 were rewarded when Gorbachev spontaneously jumped out of the limo and waded into the crowd, stopping traffic. Amid such heady progress, Reagan hoped for progress on START, but in early 1988, he announced that there was not enough time remaining in his administration to conclude a deal on strategic weapons. He was disappointed, but he had done more than any other president to end the arms race. That May, taking a victory lap, he paid a visit to the evil empire itself.

Conservative Reaction

By the end of his second term, Reagan's foreign policy had become the antithesis of everything conservatives believed. Both the means (negotiation) and the ends (coexistence and disarmament) the president was pursuing were in complete conflict with the means (confrontation) and the ends (victory over evil) dictated by the conservative worldview. As Reagan turned toward accommodation with Gorbachev, conservatives found their voice within the administration reduced to a whisper, and they resorted to increasingly desperate attempts to sabotage the arms control process.

When Reagan first began opening up to the Soviets, for example, conservatives like Jesse Helms and Richard Perle began accusing the Soviet Union of violating arms control agreements, of "noncompliance" with their treaty obligations. They hoped this charge would undercut efforts at negotiation, but because by now they had lost substantial control over the policy-making process—with Reagan taking a greater personal interest in nuclear affairs and trusting Shultz to move forward—there was little they could do. Weinberger and William J. Casey, Reagan's CIA director and an original founder of *National Review,* objected to the Geneva summit itself. On the eve of the meeting, Weinberger leaked to the press a letter he had recently sent to Reagan detailing supposed Soviet treaty violations and warning Reagan that any deal he reached with Gorbachev would imply acceptance of those infractions. It was a clumsy attempt to undermine the talks that rankled administration pragmatists, including Reagan himself, who excluded Weinberger from the Geneva delegation. But the accusation of cheating was one that conservatives would draw on time and again.

When Weinberger and Casey tried to get Shultz fired for promoting talks with the USSR, Reagan sided with his secretary of state: "George is carrying out my policy," Reagan wrote in his diary. "I'm going to meet with Cap and Bill and lay it out to them. Won't be fun, but it has to be done." Direct appeals to the president on substance floundered as well. When the president reacted excitedly to Gorbachev's January 1986 letter calling for the abolition of all nuclear weapons by 2000, Edward Rowny warned the president that the Soviets couldn't be trusted and that verifying a deal would be impossible; he begged the president not to "go soft on this." Reagan dismissed his concerns and launched into what Rowny later called a Martin Luther King–like speech: "I have a dream. I have a dream of a world without nuclear weapons. I want our children and grandchildren particularly to be free of these weapons." Perle and adviser Ken Adelman managed to scuttle the possibility of disarmament at Reykjavik

U . S . vs . THEM

by playing to Reagan's obsession with missile defense—telling him that confining SDI testing to the laboratory would kill the program (which was not true).

Conservatives, as distrustful of summits in 1987 as they had been when a young Bill Buckley protested Nikita Khrushchev's visit to the United States, looked askance at Gorbachev's visit to Washington. When the White House suggested that the Soviet leader address a joint session of Congress, Republicans rebelled—the man was a communist, after all. Then-congressman Dick Cheney, a member of the House Republican leadership, spoke for his colleagues: "Addressing a joint meeting of Congress is a high honor, one of the highest honors we can accord anyone. Given the fact of continuing Soviet aggression in Afghanistan, Soviet repression in Eastern Europe and Soviet actions in Africa and Central America, it is totally inappropriate to confer this honor upon Gorbachev. He is an adversary, not an ally."

Conservatives particularly detested the INF Treaty, which relegitimated the process of arms control. Paul Weyrich, head of the Free Congress Committee, said, "Reagan is a weakened president, weakened in spirit as well as in clout, and not in a position to make judgments about Gorbachev at this time." Buckley was enormously disappointed and led a campaign in *National Review* against the treaty's ratification—the cover read, "Reagan's Suicide Pact." In the *New York Times*, Hedrick Smith reported that, before Reagan even signed the treaty, two dozen leaders of the grassroots Right held a strategy dinner at a Washington-area Ramada Inn to discuss, as one attendant put it, "what to do about summit fever, what to do about Reagan's relationship with Gorbachev—the idea being that Reagan was appeasing liberals in Congress, appeasing the Communists, . . . putting moderates like Frank Carlucci at Defense, and cutting deals with the evil empire." Although some 80 percent of Americans supported the treaty, the Right waged a campaign against the accord that included three hundred thousand letters and a newspaper advertisement comparing 1988 to 1938 and Reagan to Neville Chamberlain. Helms and his conservative colleague Steven Symms of Idaho introduced amendments to the treaty that would have made it unacceptable to the Soviets. Helms, backed by Perle, actually suggested that the language of the treaty would have permitted the Soviets to maintain a "secret force" of SS-20s. When his amendments were defeated, Helms led a filibuster against the treaty, but it, too, failed.

Reagan fired back against his conservative opponents, saying before the Washington summit, "I think that some of the people who are objecting the most and just refusing even to accede to the idea of ever getting an understanding, whether they realize it or not, those people, basically, down in their deepest thoughts, have accepted that war is inevitable and that there must come to be a war between the two superpowers." At the end of Reagan's term, George F. Will wrote a long piece in *Newsweek:* "How wildly wrong he is about what is happening in Moscow. . . . Reagan has accelerated the moral disarmament of the West—actual disarmament will follow—by elevating wishful thinking to the status of political philosophy." The *New York Times's* William Safire mocked the president's supposed rapport with the Soviet leader: "He professed to see in Mr. Gorbachev's eyes an end to the Soviet goal of world dominance."

Conclusion

Reagan's status as a pariah of the conservative movement changed after the Berlin wall fell, the Cold War ended, and the Soviet Union broke up. Basking in the glow of American victory, conservatives decided to claim credit for the sunset of a communist nation armed with enough nuclear weapons to destroy the United States many times over. In the minds of the Reagan Victory School, as it would become known, it was Reagan's conservatism—that is, his conviction that the Cold War was a battle between good and evil, and the policies that flowed naturally from that conviction—that had forced the Soviet Union to implode.

This retroactive embrace took several forms, one being the emphasis placed on the so-called Reagan Doctrine, which ostensibly called for assisting anticommunist insurgents in reasserting control of their homelands. In October 1983, Reagan had said, "The goal of the free world must no longer be stated in the negative, that is, resistance to Soviet expansionism. The goal of the free world must instead be stated in the affirmative. We must go on the offensive with a forward strategy for freedom." Similarly, in 1983 Reagan signed National Security Decision Directive Number 75 (NSDD-75), which stipulated that the United States ought "to contain and over time reverse Soviet expansionism" and "to promote, within the narrow limits available to us, the process of change in the Soviet Union toward a more pluralistic political and economic system." In conservative hindsight, these statements described not containment—that status quo policy promulgated by George Kennan and his ilk—but *rollback*. Like Burnham and Goldwater, conservatives said, Reagan had pursued victory. And so he got it.

The only problem with this interpretation of the Reagan presidency is the lack of evidence supporting it. To be sure, Reagan fought communism on several fronts. In Afghanistan, he supplied the rebel mujahideen with $600 million and Stinger missiles to use against Soviet helicopters. When socialists deposed Prime Minister Maurice Bishop on the tiny Caribbean island of Grenada, Reagan sent 6,000 troops to crush the 800-man indigenous army and install a pro-Western government. In Poland, the Reagan administration supplied covert aid to Solidarity, the trade workers union that would ultimately oust the communist puppet government. And in Nicaragua, where the left-wing Sandinistas had deposed strongman Anastasio Somoza in 1979, Reagan provided financial and military assistance to the rebel contras. When Congress, skittish about becoming embroiled in a Central American Vietnam, banned all support for the contras, the Reagan administration illegally channeled money to them, eventually selling arms to Iran at inflated prices and funneling the profits to the Nicaraguan "freedom fighters."

But none of these examples—save perhaps the geostrategically insignificant case of Grenada—constituted "rollback." In Poland, when the Soviets ordered a military crackdown on Solidarity in 1981, the White House did little, imposing sanctions on high-tech goods but then lifting them under pressure from Western European allies. Whatever support the administration may have given the Afghan mujahideen, it can hardly be considered a triumph of *conservative* foreign policy, given that the rebels were also supported not only by the Carter administration but by the Chinese communists, who were loath to see the Soviets expand their influence farther into Central Asia. Reagan's support was itself equivocal: By 1985, he had lifted most of the sanctions that Carter had imposed on the USSR after its 1979 invasion, despite the fact that Soviet troops still occupied Afghanistan.

One likewise has to question the seriousness of rollback in Nicaragua. Reagan never considered sending American troops there, even though he said we had a moral duty and a strategic interest in preventing Soviet "subversion" in Central America, and even though conservatives were clamoring for action. (At one point, Reagan complained to his chief of staff, "Those sonsofbitches won't be happy until we have 25,000 troops in Managua, and I'm not going to do it.") At times, the Reagan administration favored a negotiated settlement rather than armed confrontation between the contras and the Sandinistas. And, of course, it was hardly in line with conservative doctrine to sell arms to Iran, which had orchestrated the kidnapping of several Americans in Beirut, in hopes that the Ayatollah Khomeini would sign off on the release of the hostages. If conservatives looked askance at negotiation with the Soviet Union, they should certainly disapprove of paying ransom to terrorists.

The fact that there was little coherence to the Reagan Doctrine stems from the fact that there never *was* an actual Reagan Doctrine. As McFarlane has said, "Doctrines are things which come from thoughtful analysis of problems, threats, possible ways of dealing with them. . . . Not one nanosecond went into any [analysis] associated with the support of pro-democracy insurgent elements through the world." The term "Reagan Doctrine" was actually coined by neoconservative columnist Charles Krauthammer in an article he wrote for *Time* magazine in April 1985. Krauthammer had been urging open support for the contras since 1983, and he seized on Reagan's declaration in his 1985 State of the Union address that "we must not break faith with those who are risking their lives on every continent from Afghanistan to Nicaragua to defy Soviet-supported aggression." Krauthammer later explained that he "hoped that a 'doctrine' enshrining the legitimacy of overthrowing nasty communist governments would obviate the need for rhetorical ruses . . . and keep the debate—and the administration—honest." In other words, he knew that the administration was not naturally inclined to such an aggressive strategy.

Indeed, Reagan's policy toward the Soviet Union was similar to that of every president since Truman. The parts of NSDD-75 that speak of reversing Soviet expansionism and promoting change within the USSR are actually remarkably similar to the language Kennan used in his famous "X Article," which stated: "The United States has it in its power to increase enormously the strains under which Soviet policy must operate, to force upon the Kremlin a far greater degree of moderation and circumspection than it has had to observe in recent years, and in this way to promote tendencies which must eventually find their outlet in either the breakup or the gradual mellowing of Soviet power." Reagan was not the first to seek "victory" in the Cold War; the goal of containment had always been to force ultimate change in the Soviet Union. Besides, far from promoting confrontation, NSDD-75 also provided that the United States seek "a stable and constructive basis for U.S.-Soviet relations." That is to say, Reagan officially hoped to achieve the very coexistence that conservatives abhorred.

In many respects, though, this argument is irrelevant. Even if Reagan did pursue rollback, the United States did not win the Cold War because Reagan shipped arms to Nicaragua. Reagan did not sweep up Moscow's proxies until the Soviet Union remained the world's only bastion of Marxism, holding the line against a surge of democracy and capitalism. Rather, the Soviet Union collapsed at the center. It caved under its own weight, in the process shedding the Eastern bloc and satellites in an attempt to reform and strengthen itself. (In fact, the Politburo had abandoned the Brezhnev Doctrine, which mandated intervention in satellite states questioning Soviet control, in 1981.)

The Soviet economy had been struggling since the late 1960s. Its rate of growth plummeted steadily from 4 percent or 5 percent in 1968 to between 0 percent and 2 percent in 1978, with total stagnation or even contraction certain by the mid-1980s. The impact on the populace was severe. Grain production, hampered by collectivist agricultural policies, had plateaued in the 1960s even as the Soviet population continued to expand by some eighty million people over the next twenty years. The USSR was thus forced to become the world's largest importer of grain. For a time, it was able to pay for this through oil exports, but when oil prices collapsed in 1985, food shortages ensued. Life expectancy dropped and infant mortality rose—the first time such a thing had happened in an industrialized country in peacetime. Amid such grim statistics, the Soviet military budget remained enormous, devouring 15 percent to 20 percent of GNP throughout the Cold War (meaning that it imposed three times the economic burden of the U.S. defense budget, on an economy that was one-sixth the size). As Reagan took office, then, the Soviet Union was in obvious need of economic reform, including military cutbacks.

Yet conservatives choose to see Reagan's hand in the Soviet economic crisis as well. Although the Soviet Union may have been under duress by the time Reagan took office, they maintain that he exacerbated this distress to the point where the Soviet Union simply surrendered. Reagan increased military spending from $185 billion to $323 billion in his first term, and the Strategic Defense Initiative threatened to send the superpowers on another exhausting leg of the nuclear arms race. Faced with this prospect, conservatives argue, the Soviets were forced to change their ways, reorienting their foreign policy, pushing arms control talks in order to reduce the burden nuclear forces put on the economy, and implementing economic reforms—all of which ended not only the Cold War but the Soviet Union itself. Whereas Carter was left playing defense, the Gipper took the ball the final ten yards against the Reds, spending them into the ground and leading the United States into the end zone.

Superficially, this is a plausible argument. Soviet economic distress was in no small part a function of military spending, which in turn was in no small part a function of Cold War competition with the United States. It therefore stands to reason that U.S. military spending helped push the Soviets toward their eventual meltdown. But that is not the same thing as saying that Reagan—or conservative foreign policy—was the decisive factor. For one thing, the military buildup for which conservatives gave Reagan credit had actually begun during the previous administration, when Jimmy Carter had increased defense spending by 6 percent from 1979 to 1980. (In fact, some of the largest recent military spending increases had been initiated by liberal presidents—Truman, at the beginning of the Cold War; Kennedy, in response to the "missile gap"; and Johnson, because of Vietnam. Military competition with the Soviets had been a forty-year-long, nonideological process.) Most important, as the Reagan White House earmarked ever more funding for the Pentagon, the Soviet Union did not respond in kind. Its defense budget remained essentially static during the 1980s. In short, the Soviet Union suffered no economic distress as a result of the Reagan buildup.*

This leaves conservatives advancing the rather more speculative case

---

*It's also worth noting that no one in the Reagan administration believed the United States could bankrupt the Soviets. Team B, for example, had insisted that the Soviet economy was actually growing and could keep funding the military with little regard for the rest of the economy: "Within what is, after all, a large and expanding GNP, . . . Soviet strategic forces have yet to reflect any constraining effect of civil economy competition, and are unlikely to do so in the foreseeable future." Conservatives are therefore retrofitting the Reagan administration—and themselves—with a degree of agency and optimism that they simply did not possess.

that the *mere prospect* of running another leg of the arms race led the Soviets to throw up their hands in despair. But that contention is wholly unconvincing, for there is much evidence to suggest that Gorbachev had been convinced of the need for fundamental economic reform well before Reagan became president. According to scholar Robert English, Gorbachev had become disillusioned with the Soviet system as early as the late 1960s, and in 1979, soon after he arrived in Moscow to serve on the Central Committee, he created a brain trust of unorthodox economists to discuss the prospects for reform. Among other things, reform meant restricting military spending—a conclusion that other Soviet leaders were reaching at the same time. Brezhnev, Andropov, and Chernenko had all sought to limit growth in the Soviet military budget. Even Soviet military officers recognized that the economy simply could not support existing commitments. It was Gorbachev, however, who took the leap, creating the conditions for economic reform and military drawdown and changing Soviet foreign policy, chiefly in its relationship with the United States. Arms control was thus both a means and an end for Gorbachev, allowing him to convince Washington that Moscow was not a threat and, ultimately, reducing military expenditures by reversing the arms race. Reagan did not convince Gorbachev that reform was necessary; the miserable state of the Soviet Union, eroded by decades of communism, did.

What role did SDI play in this drama? As a tool for nuclear war fighting, missile defense was clearly a product of conservative thinking.* More than another bomber or ICBM, SDI would have fueled the arms race because it undermined the concept of stable parity that underlay the SALT agreements. It also leveraged the growing American technological advantage over the Soviet Union, which was being left behind as the information revolution unfolded in the West. And clearly it disturbed the Soviets—at least initially. At Geneva and again at Reykjavik, Gorbachev focused on SDI, at one point insisting apropos of nothing that SDI was not threatening because the Soviet economy was quite strong—a defensiveness that suggested that he was, in fact, quite concerned.

But there is little to suggest that SDI was the straw that broke the Soviet bear's back. As General Glenn Kent had shown twenty years before Reagan

---

*Though, as we have seen, Reagan did not consider it a war-fighting tool, but naively thought it was a tool to end war.

announced the program, the Soviets did not need to compete with SDI in order to neutralize it—and they were well aware of that fact. "Our response to SDI will be effective. The United States expects us to create analogous systems, they hope to outrun us technologically," Gorbachev acknowledged. "But . . . for only 10 percent of its cost we can produce a countersystem capable of nullifying SDI." The Soviet Union actually did design and deploy just such a system: the Topol-M missile, whose 550-kiloton warhead is designed to evade defenses; 312 are in the field today.

Why, then, did Gorbachev make SDI such a sticking point in arms control negotiations, abandoning the prospect of nuclear disarmament at Reykjavik—a prospect he genuinely welcomed? Because the American pursuit of a countrywide missile defense suggested that Reagan's intentions were far from beneficent, that he was not serious about ending the arms race. Quite understandably, the Soviets considered SDI a signal—coming as it did amid a massive arms buildup, the Defense Guidance, the furor over the KAL flight shoot-down, the American deployment of Pershings in Europe, and the bowel-loosening Able Archer exercise—that the United States was preparing to fight a nuclear war. With Gorbachev's comrades in the Politburo closely monitoring his reorientation of Soviet foreign policy and his opening to the United States, Gorbachev himself was apprehensive, testing Reagan's intentions, needing to satisfy himself that the United States was not going to exploit Soviet conciliation. But when he realized that Reagan had no desire to fight a war, that his commitment to SDI was the naive product of a genuine abolitionism—and that the system was never going to work, anyway—he dropped his opposition, allowing for the signing of the INF Treaty and progress on START.

Few serious historians, including Reagan's own advisers, credit SDI with playing an important role—if any role at all—in ending the Cold War. Instead, they point to the endemic weakness of the Soviet state and in particular Gorbachev's willingness to reform. Jack Matlock has explained, "Communist rule ended in the Soviet Union not because of Western pressure or because the Cold War was over. It ended because its leader came to understand that the system under which the Soviet Union had been ruled since the Bolshevik Revolution was a barrier to its further development." William Odom, a Soviet expert and retired army general who headed the National Security Agency in Reagan's second term, also emphasizes the role of Gorbachev: "The Soviet Union was doomed to an eventual breakdown, but it could have been delayed for several years, perhaps decades. Several totalitarian systems in much worse economic shape—North Korea, Cuba, Vietnam—have outlasted the Soviet Union. Gorbachev's role, therefore, is necessary for explaining the timing and manner of the system's collapse."

None of which is to say that Reagan did not contribute significantly to the Cold War's peaceful conclusion. He was crucial—but he was crucial because he recognized Gorbachev as a reformer and adapted quickly, avidly pursuing negotiations and ratcheting down the nuclear tension that he himself had helped create. Reagan's first-term aggression only emboldened the Soviet hard-liners and brought the United States and the Soviet Union to the brink of nuclear war in late 1983. Had Reagan continued his belligerently anti-Soviet rhetoric and refused to negotiate with Gorbachev—as, say, Buckley and Perle would have done—Gorbachev would have lost his room to maneuver. Similarly, had someone less sure of himself been in the Oval Office—if, say, Reagan had not survived John Hinkley's bullet and the more cautious George Bush had taken charge—the United States might not have responded as dramatically to Gorbachev's overtures.

In mythologizing Reagan as a conservative icon—that is, in claiming that it was Reagan's Manichaeanism that won the Cold War—conservatives not only exaggerate his role in winning the Cold War, they pervert his legacy. Reagan cannot be understood without acknowledging the enormous role that his nuclear abolitionism and his willingness to negotiate played in his presidency. These are, respectively, an end and a means that conservatives found abhorrent, and yet they are the spine of Reagan's second term. While it is true that Reagan thought in terms of good and evil, that moral framework did not become a moralism for him. That is, he did not translate his worldview into policies that made accommodation with the Soviets anathema and therefore impossible. He condemned the Soviet Union as "evil," but it was his willingness to back away from that challenge—not the challenge itself—that peacefully ended the Cold War. As Lou Cannon wrote, "Reagan's vision of nuclear apocalypse and his deeply rooted conviction that the weapons that could cause this hell on earth should be abolished would ultimately prove more powerful than his anti-communism."

Alas, conservatives would quickly expunge this from their memories. At his funeral, few spoke of Reagan's opening to the Soviet Union. Instead, in its aftermath, they proposed that the Pentagon be renamed the Ronald Reagan National Defense Building. And even though the Cold War was long over, George W. Bush would eschew deterrence in favor of missile defense and nuclear war fighting, and negotiation in favor of moralistic confrontation. Having failed to learn the lessons of the Cold War, conservatives would let a new danger infect the post-9/11 world: the danger of nuclear terrorism.

PART TWO

CONSEQUENCES

Chapter Five

HIBERNATION

"ABM: RIP" READ THE MACABRE HEADING. "Edwin J. Feulner, President of The Heritage Foundation, cordially invites you to a reception." The cryptic invitation gradually got more specific: "For 30 years, the Anti-Ballistic Missile Treaty has served to bolster the policy of mutually assured destruction (MAD) and impose crippling restrictions on the nation's missile defense programs. President Bush, recognizing the inappropriateness of MAD and the policy of vulnerability to missile attack, announced on December 13, 2001, that the United States is withdrawing from the treaty." That withdrawal, spurring its very own funereal cocktail party, would take place officially six months later, on June 13, 2002.

On the evening of June 12, 2002, several hundred conservatives—senators, congressmen, generals, policy makers, and scholars—accordingly gathered in the caucus room of the Russell Senate Office Building on Capitol Hill to munch on hors d'oeuvres and raise their glasses at a "cheerful wake for a flawed treaty." The mood was, not surprisingly, buoyant, for "flawed" was really too mild a description for the loathing the assembled crowd felt for the agreement. To the right wing, the ABM Treaty had symbolized everything that was wrong with American foreign policy during the Cold War: negotiating with evil, fearing nuclear war instead of preparing to win it, and abandoning faith in American exceptionalism and divine superiority.

One of the most jubilant of the celebrants was a man unfamiliar to most Americans. John R. Bolton, undersecretary of state for arms control and international security, ranked just below Secretary of State Colin Powell and his deputy, Richard Armitage, and supervised the Bush administration's efforts to control weapons of mass destruction worldwide. Three years later, Bolton, with his distinctive shag haircut and bushy but dour mustache, would become a well-known public figure when the president nominated him to represent the United States at the United Nations—an odd choice, many thought, given that Bolton did not believe in the institution or its purpose. (Among his more memorable utterances on the subject were "There is no United Nations" and "The secretariat building in New York has 38 stories. If it lost 10 stories it wouldn't make a bit of difference.") To the president's critics, Bolton's appointment epitomized everything wrong with Bush's approach to international affairs; to the president's supporters, it symbolized everything they had come to love in Bush's first term.

Bolton has been variously described as an isolationist, a hard-liner, a neoconservative, and a unilateralist. Some of these labels are more accurate than others, but none really captures the tradition from which Bolton and many of his colleagues in the Bush administration hailed. That is, of course, conservatism.

Bolton had always been a conservative. In 1964, at the tender age of fifteen, the young subscriber to *National Review*—which would later offer him an internship—had joined the burgeoning right wing, campaigning for Barry Goldwater in his home state of Maryland. From then on, his ideological path was straight, devoid of the hairpin turns that characterized so many conservative and neoconservative careers. At the height of the Vietnam War, he attended Yale, where, like William F. Buckley, Jr., his conservatism was reinforced by close contact with liberal academe. "It was like being in enemy territory," he recalled. After law school, he convinced the Washington firm of Covington & Burling, where he was an associate, to take on the landmark campaign finance case *Buckley v. Valeo*. Bolton worked on the suit for over a year, in the process getting to know its plaintiff, Senator James L. Buckley, Bill's brother. He also became acquainted with James Baker, and when the conservative revolution elevated Ronald Reagan to the White House, Bolton was lifted along with it to positions at the Agency for International Development, the Justice Department, and the State Department.

Bolton believed in the historical precedent of American exceptionalism, which for him, as for conservatives during the 1950s and 1960s, translated into unilateralism. From Washington and Jefferson's opposition to entangling alliances, to the Monroe Doctrine, to Westward expansionism, to the Senate's rejection of the League of Nations, American foreign policy, he felt, was marked chiefly by a desire for liberty—which in international affairs meant sovereignty, the freedom from interference by other nations. As a libertarian, Bolton drew a link between an individual's right to be free of government interference at home and America's right to be free from the interference of treaties, institutions, or any other formal diplomatic arrangement abroad. "International law" was just a liberal construct to him, and vaunted symbols of "internationalism" that even conservatives supported, such as NATO, he argued, were in fact so dominated by the United States as to be unilateralist in practice. Europeans might be willing to subordinate their sovereignty to international organizations; Americans were not.

When Bush nominated Bolton to that epitome of international organizations, the United Nations, journalist Samantha Power complained that Bolton described himself as pro-American—"as if that required him to be anti-world." But Bolton's ideology *did* require him to be antiworld; American exceptionalism and, by association, American conservatism had always been oppositional. Boltonism was simply the quintessential example of the us-versus-them worldview.

In November 2000, Bolton—who had spent many of the Clinton years as a vice president at the American Enterprise Institute—got a call from Baker asking him to go to Florida, where George W. Bush and Al Gore were locked in a battle for the state's electoral votes. Baker needed Bolton, an election law expert, to help run the GOP's legal team, a task that brought him a degree of conservative celebrity when he burst into a library in Tallahassee where workers were examining ballots for hanging chads and said, "I'm with the Bush-Cheney team, and I'm here to stop the count." In a speech not long afterward, Dick Cheney joked that when he was asked what job Bolton should get in the administration, his answer was "anything he wants."

Bush appointed Bolton the nation's top arms control official, a decision every bit as perverse as making him ambassador to the United Nations, and a position in which he was able to do significantly more damage.* "He is the kind of man with whom I would want to stand at Armageddon," Jesse Helms declared at Bolton's confirmation hearing—simultaneously a perfect choice of words, given the men's Manichaeanism, and an exceptionally poor one, given the job's nuclear responsibilities. As he settled

*Interestingly, although it now had a somewhat different title (undersecretary of state for arms control and international security), this job was the same one James Buckley had held during the Reagan administration.

into his office on the sixth floor of the State Department in the spring of 2001, Bolton placed on his coffee table a memento from his days in the conservative revolution: a hand grenade mounted on a small wooden base with a plaque that read "Truest Reaganaut." He quickly went to work dismantling the structure of international arms control, beginning with the ABM Treaty.

After September 11, 2001, a myth developed—encouraged by the Bush administration—that "everything had changed." It was a useful myth, one that allowed for the Patriot Act, Guantánamo Bay, and, of course, a foreign policy that emphasized military action while eschewing diplomacy. Bush's State of the Union address in January 2002, in which he dubbed Iran, Iraq, and North Korea and their supposed terrorist allies an "axis of evil"; his commencement address at West Point in June 2002, in which he said that America would maintain "military strengths beyond challenge" and suggested that "pre-emptive" action might be needed to prevent rogue states from acquiring weapons of mass destruction; and the White House's National Security Strategy, released in September 2002, which laid out a policy of military dominance, all combined to form what would be known as the Bush Doctrine, a doctrine that abandoned deterrence and containment in favor of preventive war. Suddenly, analysts were atwitter about a "revolution" in U.S. foreign policy.

The revolution, however, had been under way for quite some time. George W. Bush and many of his aides were conservatives, and by the time they came to office, conservatism was an established fixture of American political life. True, following the end of Soviet communism, the movement did suffer from what one diplomat called "enemy deprivation syndrome." Because so much of conservatism had revolved around an apocalyptic battle against the satanic Soviet Union, what were conservatives supposed to do if there was no evil? Bush himself identified the dilemma plainly during the 2000 campaign: "When I was coming up, it was a dangerous world. And we knew exactly who the 'they' were. It was us versus them, and it was clear who 'them' was. Today we're not so sure who the 'they' are, but we know they're there." Nevertheless, the operating precept remained the same as it had been during the Cold War: The United States stood in opposition to a hostile world, even if now the nature of that hostility was not fully understood.

From this assumption flowed a unilateralism and militarism that critics found shocking in 2001. Yet for all the quailing about the historic loss of multilateralism and bipartisanship, few noticed that this was just a manifestation of the same nationalism that had guided conservatives for decades. Later, after 9/11, an absolutist moralism, focused on terrorists and rogue regimes, would be reinjected, giving conservatism a renewed vitality similar to that which had marked its birth in the 1950s. Yet the Bush administration's foreign policy—marked by a distrust of international institutions, hatred of arms control, derision of negotiation, a quest for military dominance, even a preference for nuclear war fighting—was conservative from its very inception, and it was remarkably similar to what the Right had advocated during the Cold War. In this context, the hatred of the ABM Treaty was a bridge connecting two supposedly distinct historical periods. The Bush administration represented a purer form of conservatism than has ever been seen in office—not only after 9/11, but before.

Solving for Mr. X

Before there was 9/11, there was 11/9. On November 9, 1989, Brent Scowcroft hurried into the Oval Office to tell George H. W. Bush that the Berlin Wall had fallen. The president and his national security adviser immediately turned on the television to see crowds of Berliners joyously reunited after nearly thirty years of Soviet-enforced separation. Bush had entered office wary of Reagan's speedy rapprochement with Gorbachev, and his most conservative aides—Secretary of Defense Dick Cheney, in particular—had been skeptical. The fall of the wall erased all remaining doubt. Soviet control over Eastern Europe had evaporated; soon the Soviet Union itself would cease to exist. A decades-old conflict that had several times threatened to destroy civilization had ended peacefully.

President Bush's attentions immediately turned to stabilizing the disintegration of the no-longer-evil empire, in an attempt to ensure that what could be a "crash" would instead be a "soft landing," as Secretary of State James Baker put it. Over the next three years, his administration dismantled much of the Cold War military apparatus, withdrawing most tactical nuclear weapons from abroad; negotiating a treaty capping conventional weapons deployments in Europe; completing the START I accord, which Reagan had started; and crafting a successor agreement, START II, that called for even greater cuts and restrictions, including a prohibition on land-based MIRVs. Bush was more concerned with preserving stability than with laying out a vision for a world without a Soviet Union. The closest he came to articulating a post–Cold War foreign policy doctrine was in speaking of a "new world order" when he forged an international coalition to repel Saddam Hussein from Kuwait. It was, Scowcroft later wrote, a conscious effort to set out a "precedent for the approaching post–Cold War world," in which the end of superpower conflict could allow for a much greater degree of cooperation and even collective security. But however conscious an effort, it was nonetheless a modest one: The Gulf War coalition was explained more easily in terms of national interest than in terms of supranational order, and the model it supplied would not be used again.

Of course, George Bush had never been particularly good at the "vision thing," but the problem was hardly his alone. Indeed, for the next ten years, foreign policy discussion consisted of variations on the theme "What now?" Journals like *Foreign Affairs, Foreign Policy,* and the *National Interest* went into analytic overdrive, searching for the next "Mr. X," a George Kennan-like figure who could impose order upon an inchoate world. Kennan, however, had had the benefit of a specific enemy and therefore a pressing strategic need—defense of the country. Did the United States now have such an enemy, and if so, who or what was it? Before long, even policy makers who had suffered through the Cold War's most knee-weakening moments became nostalgic for the supposed strategic clarity that only a strong, identifiable foe could provide. The future seemed so devoid of potential ideological conflict that scholar Francis Fukuyama famously argued we had reached "the end of history."

Confusion reigned with particular tyranny on the right. Anticommunism had been essential to the conservative enterprise, fusing libertarians with traditionalists after World War II and drawing in disaffected hawks and neocons in the 1970s. Within weeks of the Berlin Wall's fall, however, that fusion was replaced by fission as conservative factions broke apart, each searching for a new raison d'être. Richard Viguerie, the direct-mail baron who had been instrumental in empowering the New Right, lamented to *Newsweek,* "At the core of 75 percent of conservative thinking and action is anti-communism. You take that away and you take away the glue that has held the movement together for a generation." Three months before the 1992 election, *The Economist* surveyed the state of the move-ment that had so recently dominated America's political landscape and found that conservatives "have not the faintest idea what they agree on."

Their dilemma was deepened by the fact that, at the very moment con-servatism was deprived of communism's centripetal power, the man head-ing the Republican Party was not a conservative. Bush was a throwback to an earlier era, an Eisenhower moderate in a party now dominated by the descendants of Buckley and Goldwater. Culturally, he was precisely the sort of establishment elitist distrusted by a populist base that had increas-ingly shifted toward the South and West. Whatever his ties to Texas, the proper and patrician Bush could not escape the fact that his blood was a Yale blue. As president, he offended the Right's libertarian sensibilities with regulatory measures like the Clean Air Act and the Americans with Disabilities Act, and in 1990 he committed the mortal sin of raising taxes as part of a budget compromise with congressional Democrats.

His foreign policy, meanwhile, was implemented by a team of Kiss-inger acolytes, such as Scowcroft, who rejected the moralism of the Right in favor of steady, balance-of-power politics. Bush oversaw the reunifica-tion of Germany but stifled objection as the Chinese crushed protesters in Tiananmen Square and watched from the sidelines as Yugoslavia frac-tured into bloody fragments. When the wall fell, preserving stability, not celebrating victory, was his primary concern, a reserve that conservatives found suspicious. As historian David Halberstam noted, "The destruction of the wall represented not merely the West's triumph in a long, difficult struggle against a formidable adversary, but equally important, a triumph in their minds of good over evil, proof that we had been right and they had been wrong." Moreover, it was proof that conservatives had been right and *liberals* had been wrong. Yet at a press conference that November after-noon, the mild-mannered president would say only that he was pleased. Bush might have been Reagan's successor, but to conservatives he was clearly not Reagan's heir.

The 1992 presidential candidacy of Patrick J. Buchanan, a former Nixon speechwriter, underscored the conservative split. Most Americans—and most American politicians—were by now eager to reap a post–Cold War "peace dividend." Without the Soviet military threat, they reasoned that defense expenditures could drop, freeing money for tax cuts, deficit reduc-tion, social programs, or pet projects. Buchanan took this notion one step further, arguing that we should reduce not only our military expenditures but our foreign commitments writ large, and to that end he proposed slashing foreign aid and pulling American troops from their dozens of bases in Europe and Asia, leaving the United States to be guarded by powerful sea, air, and space forces. If Bush was a throwback to 1950s moderate Republicanism, Buchanan and his vision of Fortress America were a throwback to 1930s isolationism. He even adopted "America First" as his campaign slogan (though he sometimes amended it to "America first—and second, and third"). In response to Bush's ideological weakness, and reflecting the postcommunism confusion of the Right, *National Review* actually endorsed Buchanan in the GOP primaries, despite the fact that his protectionism and isolationism ran directly counter to the magazine's founding tenets.

In stark contrast to Buchanan and his isolationist followers were the neoconservatives, who, as the Warsaw Pact dissolved, quickly sought to redefine America's role in the world. Ben Wattenberg of the American Enterprise Institute (who had served as cochair of the Coalition for a Democratic Majority) advocated that global democratization should form the core of a post–Cold War foreign policy: "Americans have a missionary streak and democracy is our mission." Tyranny, after all, had not perished with the fall of the Soviet Union. Wattenberg wanted to "wage democracy"—and American-style democracy, at that: "American taxpayers didn't put up trillions of dollars in the Cold War to create a few more Swedens." There was a certain irony in this position, given that Jeane Kirkpatrick's signature article, "Dictatorships and Double Standards," had criticized Carter precisely for prioritizing the promotion of human rights among America's more authoritarian allies. And, to be fair, not all neocons embraced the breadth of this vision: Nathan Glazer counseled "modesty" in post–Cold War policy, while Kirkpatrick herself wrote that "with a return to normal times, we can again become a normal nation."

Most second-generation neoconservatives, however, embraced democratization as the logical ideological successor to anticommunism. A number of prominent neocons—such as Penn Kemble and Joshua Muravchik, who as young men had led the assault on Carter's arms control policies—accordingly voted for Clinton in 1992, believing him more likely to confront tyranny than the coldly realist Bush, who had left Saddam in power ("coitus interruptus," in Norman Podhoretz's description), consorted with the butchers of Tiananmen Square, and saw little need to involve the

United States in Bosnia. Among neoconservatives, in other words, even though the evil empire had been vanquished, there remained a fixation on regime, a continued insistence on seeing the world in terms of good and evil. By contrast, conservatives of a more traditional Buckley/Goldwater stripe retreated somewhat to a less moralistic and therefore less virulent oppositionalism, focused more narrowly on the defense of American interests than on the promotion of American values. Still, both schools of thought rallied around the idea of cementing America's post–Cold War dominance by seizing the opportunity created by the Soviet collapse to prevent the rise of any evil strong enough to compromise the security or moral integrity of the United States—to ensure, in other words, that victory was made permanent.

This notion took root not only in the commentariat—where, for example, Charles Krauthammer called for "universal dominion"—but in government, particularly in the Pentagon's policy planning office, headed by Paul Wolfowitz, who would become George W. Bush's deputy secretary of defense. In 1991, it began work on a now-famous study intended to spell out the rationale for U.S. military forces after the Cold War—the Pentagon's attempt to answer the same "what now?" question with which every foreign policy thinker was wrestling. The Defense Planning Guidance, as it is known, was written by Zalmay Khalilzad, who, like Wolfowitz, had been a student of Albert Wohlstetter's at the University of Chicago and who would later hold several high-level positions in the Bush 43 administration. His first draft argued that America's "first objective is to prevent the reemergence of a new rival." Hostile regional powers like Iraq should be kept weak enough that they would be unable to exercise global influence, and "advanced industrial nations" such as Japan should be dissuaded from challenging U.S. leadership, or even seriously *thinking* about challenging it. "We must maintain the mechanisms for deterring potential competitors from even aspiring to a larger regional or global role."

The policy outlined in the DPG was stunningly ambitious and, when it was leaked to the *New York Times,* generated a public uproar. So aggressive a policy hardly seemed appropriate for what many hoped would be a time of more cooperative international relations, led by the United States. Wolfowitz therefore asked one of his assistants, I. Lewis "Scooter" Libby (later Vice President Cheney's chief of staff), to redraft the document. Libby, in turn, engaged in a bit of rhetorical sleight of hand, making the document's language more diplomatic while actually strengthening its substance, further emphasizing the role that military dominance would play in dissuading potential rivals. Those who read it closely would also discover that Libby had emphasized American freedom of action, proposing that the United States act preemptively to shape "the future security environment" and do so unilaterally if "international reaction proves sluggish or inadequate."

The Defense Planning Guidance was not couched in moralistic terms— Pentagonese does not have words for loaded terms like "good" and "evil"—but in its emphasis on what was essentially permanent victory, its drafters were drawing on the same oppositionalist, us-versus-them worldview that had long characterized conservatism. If the good versus evil meme had led to an emphasis on victory during the Cold War, neo-conservatives were now looking to make victory permanent so that there would never again be a question of engaging with evil. As journalist James Mann wrote, the Defense Planning Guidance said that "America need not and should not reach an accommodation with any other country. Now, however, the United States was not combating a single, known rival, such as the Soviet Union or China. Rather, America was making sure no future adversary with whom anyone could suggest the need for détente would ever emerge." Moreover, the DPG was aimed not only at potential enemies, but also at allies such as France and Germany. Two centuries after Washington warned of European entanglements, conservatives wanted to make sure that America never had to subordinate itself to the Continent again. The dominance recommended in the DPG was merely a means to achieving ultimate liberty and sovereignty. Conservatives were thrilled. Cheney embraced the DPG, asking that the document be released under his name and telling Khalilzad, "You've discovered a new rationale for our role in the world."

When Bill Clinton was elected president in 1992, conservatives of all stripes retreated from government to the world of think tanks and op-ed pages, where the differences between neoconservatives and their more cramped brethren soon became more pronounced. In 1996, William Kristol (Irving Kristol's son) and Robert Kagan published a widely read article in *Foreign Affairs* called "Toward a Neo-Reaganite Foreign Policy," which advocated a posture of "military supremacy and moral confidence."

American foreign policy after the Cold War should be one of "benevolent hegemony," they argued, in which America should enshrine its military lead and actively promote democracy abroad. Whereas Buchanan parroted John Quincy Adams's nineteenth-century admonition against going "abroad in search of monsters to destroy," Kristol and Kagan retorted, "Why not? The alternative is to leave monsters on the loose, ravaging and pillaging to their hearts' content."

In 2000, Kristol and Kagan published *Present Dangers,* a volume of essays by prominent neoconservatives that reiterated the DPG's insistence on military dominance while also promoting a moralistic view of the world. The editors emphasized the evil of our enemies and derided the notion of "engagement," a term they placed in dismissive quotation marks, just as Goldwater had done with "negotiation." "When it comes to dealing with tyrannical regimes," they wrote, "the United States should seek not coexistence but transformation." Excepting its advocacy of democracy promotion, the package was a perfect echo of Cold War conservatism—down to the insistence that the character of regimes was more important than their nuclear capabilities. As one chapter in *Present Dangers* observed, "Advocates of the [Clinton] administration's approach to nonproliferation often fall prey to the central fallacy of arms controllers: that the weapons themselves are the problem, not the regimes that possess them."

Somewhere between neoconservative messianism and Buchananite isolationism, nationalistic conservatives were fashioning a more restrictive view of U.S. involvement abroad, redefining conservatism as "realistic"—by which they meant not Kissingerian but antiutopian. In response to Kristol and Kagan's piece on neo-Reaganism, two analysts from the conservative Heritage Foundation—citing William F. Buckley, among others—argued that a true conservative foreign policy could not operate "without limits and constraints." In the *National Interest,* John Bolton advocated "an interests-based foreign policy grounded in a concrete agenda of protecting particular peoples and territories, defending open trade and commercial relations around the world, and advancing a commonality of interests with our allies." Rather than venturing abroad in search of monsters to destroy, Bolton suggested that if a dictator should become embarrassingly monstrous, we should just quietly offer him asylum. Having spent the past forty years calling for Americans to take up arms in a global anticommunist crusade, conservatives had apparently rediscovered Edmund Burke—and were even quoting Walter Lippmann, a man who had found George Kennan's realistic writings too messianic. The heirs of Buckley had gone from Goldwater to Goldilocks—an isolationist foreign policy was too small, a neoconservative one too large, and they needed one that was just right.

Occasionally, their more restrictive definition of the national interest brought conservatives into conflict with their neoconservative brethren. In Kosovo, for example, where Slobodan Milosevic was slaughtering Muslims, neocons by and large urged intervention while conservatives balked. More often than not, however, the conservative focus on national interest did not contradict the neoconservative impulse to democratization. When Kristol and Kagan founded the Project for a New American Century in 1997 to promote the values they had outlined in their *Foreign Affairs* piece, conservatives such as Dick Cheney and Donald Rumsfeld (as well as social conservatives such as Gary Bauer and Dan Quayle and economic libertarians like Steve Forbes) signed its founding statement, which proclaimed: "American foreign and defense policy is adrift. Conservatives have criticized the incoherent policies of the Clinton Administration. They have also resisted isolationist impulses from within their own ranks. But conservatives have not confidently advanced a strategic vision of America's role in the world." Many conservatives, including Bolton, signed the group's famous 1998 open letter to President Clinton calling for the overthrow of Saddam Hussein. Conservatives and neoconservatives alike agreed on stronger support for Taiwan, stronger criticism of the United Nations, and harsher stances toward North Korea and China. They shared the goal of military dominance outlined in the 1992 Defense Planning Guidance, with some conservatives, such as Rumsfeld and Senator Malcolm Wallop, even calling for dominance in space, the final military frontier. And they all—including the isolationists—agreed on America's top security priority: national missile defense.

To both conservatives and neoconservatives, then, the emphasis in international relations—*even in a time of peace*—was on conflict, not cooperation. This instinct in turn, manifested itself in the same degree of distrust of diplomacy and international institutions that it had during the Cold War. Both supported a strong military because, in a world full of dangers against which diplomacy was useless, the military was the only way for America to defend itself. And interestingly, just as it had in the 1950s, their worldview was one that, to a large extent, could incorporate isolationists with little effort—isolationism, after all, being perhaps the quintessential us-versus-them ideology.

This oppositionalism put them in direct conflict with the foreign policy of President Clinton, who emphasized what Madeleine Albright—first his UN ambassador and then secretary of state—called "assertive multilateralism," which held that U.S. interests were protected by strengthening and acting through rule-based international bodies such as the UN. Through a web of overlapping institutions such as NATO, the Association of Southeast Asian Nations, the European Union, the International Monetary Fund, the World Bank, and others, Clinton believed that the Truman administration's success in creating a civil interstate system in the West could be extended worldwide in a way that had not been possible during the Cold War. As Strobe Talbott, Clinton's deputy secretary of state, has written, "Clinton believed . . . what we had in the wake of the cold war was a *multilateral* moment—an opportunity to shape the world through our active leadership of . . . [international] institutions."

In practice, Clinton had mixed success in capitalizing on that multilateral moment, due in no small measure to the Republican-controlled Congress. He signed the Kyoto Protocol limiting greenhouse gas emissions but could not get it ratified, and he didn't sign the treaty establishing the International Criminal Court until his last month in office, fearing the political fallout. Arms control, not always a priority during the Clinton years, made only fitful progress. For example, Clinton was able to negotiate a Comprehensive Test Ban Treaty, fulfilling the decades-old dream of outlawing nuclear testing, but he failed to secure Senate approval. He convinced Ukraine, Belarus, and Kazakhstan to surrender the nuclear weapons left on their territory after they broke away from the Soviet Union, but India and Pakistan surprised the administration with their 1998 nuclear tests. Clinton and Russian president Boris Yeltsin agreed on a framework for deep nuclear reductions in a START III treaty, but those cuts fell victim to Jesse Helms's focus on missile defense.

Significantly, though, Clinton believed that arms control was an essential part of a "new strategy of security" for a "new global era" defined by ever-tightening integration, and that reducing the danger from nuclear weapons required U.S. leadership and international cooperation. In 1995, the Clinton administration secured the indefinite extension of the Nuclear Non-Proliferation Treaty, and in 2000 agreed to thirteen specific steps to reinforce it. Speaking of transnational threats like proliferation, terrorism, and global warming, the president said, "We must avoid both the temptation to minimize these dangers and the illusion that the proper response to them is to batten down the hatches and protect America against the world. The promise of our future lies in the world. Therefore, we must work hard with the world."

The liberal embrace of a more us-*and*-them approach to international affairs in the 1990s was highlighted by the nature and tone of conservative opposition to Clinton. One of only two foreign policy issues mentioned in Newt Gingrich's Contract with America was the concern that "the administration appears to salute the day when American men and women will fight, and die, 'in the service' of the United Nations"—where all of "them" were housed. (The other issue was missile defense.) Jesse Helms, who ascended to the chairmanship of the Senate Foreign Relations Committee in 1995, not only withheld U.S. dues from the UN but railed against the International Criminal Court, the Kyoto Protocol, the Comprehensive Test Ban Treaty, and Clinton's engagement with North Korea. In 1995, Bob Dole blasted what he saw as Clintonian globaloney, writing, "The failures of Assertive Multilateralism/Enlargement lie not just in its execution or communication—they lie in its very conception. . . . U.S. sovereignty must be defended, not delegated. . . . International organizations—whether the United Nations, the World Trade Organization, or any others—will not protect American interests. Only America can do that." At the 1996 GOP convention, in his speech accepting the Republican presidential nomination, Dole even got a roar of applause for mocking UN Secretary-General Boutros Boutros-Ghali's name.

During the 2000 presidential campaign, it was difficult to place George W. Bush precisely within the conservative pantheon. To many, he sounded like his realist father, speaking about the importance of great power relations as his top foreign policy adviser, Condoleezza Rice, a Scowcroft protégée, looked on. It didn't hurt that, in May 2000, he gave a major foreign policy address flanked by Scowcroft, Kissinger, Powell, and George Shultz. At the same time, however, Bush also called for a "forward strategy for freedom" a Reagan phrase that simultaneously evoked the conservative Cold War call for a "forward strategy for America" and the more recent neoconservative advocacy of democratization—and he even ended one speech with a quote from Alexander Solzhenitsyn. At heart, Bush's worldview was bifurcated in the same way as Buckley's, Goldwater's, Kristol's, and Bolton's: When Bush looked abroad, he saw a hostile world of "terror and missiles and madmen." "The Evil Empire has passed," Bush said, "but evil remains."

From this observation he drew the same conclusions that conservatives had been drawing for the past half century. He warned of the limits of "smiles and scowls" and belittled the naïveté of treaties. As the 1992 Defense Planning Guidance had, he advocated military dominance, assuring an audience at the Citadel that he sought not only peace through strength, but "the peace of overwhelming victory," in which the United States would never again have to compromise itself through engagement with enemies. It was the epitome of the us-versus-them worldview in which military technology created a Fortress America, which was able to strike anywhere around the world without entangling itself directly in foreign affairs. That position differed sharply from the emerging liberal consensus, and, just as during the Cold War, it was reflected most prominently and most dangerously in nuclear policy.

The MADness of King George(I)

On May 1, 2001, just a few months after becoming president, Bush introduced what he called a "new strategic framework." Speaking at National Defense University, he asked the audience "to think back some thirty years to a far different time in a far different world." It was a time and a world in which we were locked in an existential battle for survival with the Soviet Union, each side armed with thousands of nuclear weapons. The guiding doctrine for those weapons, Bush said, had been mutual assured destruction, codified in the ABM Treaty, by which each side deliberately left itself vulnerable to attack. But now, he explained, we faced a different enemy: rogue states that might soon build nuclear missiles and that might not be susceptible to deterrence. This new threat required a new response—a national missile defense that could shoot down incoming ICBMs—which in turn required that we move "beyond the constraints of the 30-year-old ABM Treaty." That agreement, Bush insisted, "does not recognize the present or point us to the future. It enshrines the past."

The president was being disingenuous; his support for missile defense was not simply a function of the post–Cold War security environment. Conservatives had wanted to field missile defenses ever since the Soviet Union had developed ICBMs, subjecting the United States to the possibility of nuclear attack. But, somewhat paradoxically, following the collapse of the Soviet Union—and with it the likelihood of a missile attack—conservative calls for missile defense increased. In 1994, Republicans made deployment of a national missile defense a chief national security plank of the Contract with America.

Their new rationale for such a defense—the threat from rogues like North Korea—was rather flimsy, given that no such state actually had ICBMs and that in 1995 the U.S. intelligence community issued a National Intelligence Estimate stating that no rogue state would be able to develop a ballistic missile capable of hitting the continental United States or Canada for fifteen years. Conservatives were so angered by this reassuring finding that, in a throwback to Team B, they commissioned an outside panel to review the intelligence community's methodology and conclusions. They were even angrier when that panel, headed by Robert Gates—George H. W. Bush's CIA director—found that "the Intelligence Community has a strong case that, for sound technical reasons, the United States is unlikely to face an indigenously developed and tested intercontinental ballistic missile threat from the Third World before 2010." Moreover, Gates indicated that there had been "no breach of the integrity of the intelligence process."

Frustrated by Gates's failure to identify "politicization" in the intelligence community, conservatives in Congress commissioned yet another study, this one led by Donald Rumsfeld. Its conclusions, presented in July 1998, agreeably stated that the threat posed by emerging missile powers was in fact "broader, more mature and evolving more rapidly" than the intelligence community reported.* It warned that rogue states would be capable of inflicting "major destruction on the U.S. within about five years of a decision" to acquire long-range missiles. Ominously, the commission implied that Iran and North Korea might have already made such decisions. Much like its ideological predecessor, the Team B report, the

---

*Paul Wolfowitz was another of the commission's nine members. Steve Cambone, who became Bush's undersecretary of defense for intelligence, was the commission's staff director.

Rumsfeld report's methodology was flawed, assuming the worst about potential U.S. enemies without actual evidence to support those assumptions. According to defense analyst John Pike, "Rather than basing policy on intelligence estimates of what will probably happen politically and economically and what the bad guys really want, it's basing policy on that which is not physically impossible. This is really an extraordinary epistemological conceit, which is applied to no other realm of national policy, and if manifest in a single human being would be diagnosed as paranoid."

Nevertheless, conservatives did have a point: Rogue regimes *were* developing longer-range missiles. In August 1998, for example, North Korea had tested a Taepodong-1 missile. The test failed, but the missile had shown some technological promise—and its launch caught U.S. intelligence unaware. If the missile ever proved operational, it would be able to carry a small payload (though nothing as heavy as a nuclear warhead) to the outer reaches of Alaska. This did not exactly represent an imminent threat, as conservatives insisted, and a missile defense was not exactly ready for deployment. Still, all things being equal, a limited defense against a handful of rogue-state missiles—the plan initially called for about twenty interceptors—might be better than no defense at all.

Accordingly, the following year, Congress passed and Bill Clinton signed a one-sentence bill declaring, "It is the policy of the United States to deploy as soon as is technologically possible an effective National Missile Defense system capable of defending the territory of the United States against limited ballistic missile attack." But when asked to make an official decision to deploy the system the following year, the president declined to do so. In part, he wasn't persuaded the technology worked (the system's prototype interceptor had failed in two out of three attempts), but he was also concerned about Russia's and China's adamant opposition to U.S. withdrawal from the ABM Treaty.* While acknowledging that no other country should have a veto over our national security decisions, Clinton noted, "We can never afford to overlook the fact that the actions

*Although there was not actually a missile defense system ready at this time, in order to meet the goal it had of deploying a system by 2005, the Department of Defense believed it needed to begin building a special radar in Alaska in the summer of 2001. The "deployment decision" simply meant allowing the Pentagon to hire contractors to begin work on that site.

and reactions of others in this increasingly interdependent world do bear on our security."

Unfortunately, guided by the exact opposite worldview, Bush did overlook that fact. Although his proposed missile defense was allegedly intended to counter rogue-state threats, even a limited system could have an impact on the nuclear balance with Russia (and China). Ending the ABM Treaty would not nullify the MAD relationship we had with those countries; it would simply undermine it. The ABM Treaty recognized and formalized the U.S.-Soviet deterrent relationship, but the relationship itself was largely a function of the weapons themselves—and the United States and Russia still had thousands of nuclear weapons each. The fact that the United States and Russia were no longer enemies did matter—our nuclear relationship with the United Kingdom, for example, was not generally considered a MAD one, even though the missiles on a single British sub could wipe out most American cities—but nuclear weapons were so destructive that capabilities, much more than intentions, determined the nature of nuclear relationships. One had to be absolutely certain of another state's intentions not to be concerned about the "balance of terror," and even in the post–Cold War world, neither Washington nor Moscow felt any such certainty. And Russian military planners knew that, once the technology was mastered, a small defense could quickly become a large defense.

Conservatives, however, had always believed that MAD was a policy choice—a *liberal* policy choice—and in 2001 they continued to do so. In fact, they argued that by choosing to perpetuate MAD via the ABM Treaty, we were actually perpetuating an antagonistic relationship with Russia. Conservatives had spent the Cold War arguing that regimes, not weapons, caused conflict—that intentions were far more important than capabilities—and therefore that arms control could do nothing to stabilize the U.S.-Soviet relationship. Now, ironically, they were maintaining the opposite: that the vulnerability imposed by nuclear weapons was the chief "sticking point" in the relationship, as Secretary of Defense Donald Rumsfeld put it. Suddenly, nuclear weapons *did* generate animosity and instability. Conservatives clouded this contradiction by blaming "adversarial arms control," rather than arms per se. In other words, they argued that negotiation undermined relationships. On November 9, 2001, nine Republican senators—including conservatives Jesse Helms, Trent Lott, and Jon

Kyl—sent a letter to the president urging him to withdraw from the ABM Treaty because it had become "the most significant obstacle to improved relations between the United States and Russia."

This was simply not true. To the contrary, Russia considered the treaty a sign of stable relations. Since the end of the Cold War, Moscow had had trouble funding its military and made no secret of its interest in reducing the number of nuclear warheads it deployed from 6,000 to 1,500. But it feared doing so if the United States was going to deploy defenses or maintain a larger nuclear arsenal. Even after the Cold War the Russians wanted to maintain nuclear parity. Led by President Vladimir Putin, Russian officials repeatedly stressed the importance of the ABM Treaty in maintaining stability and preserving confidence that a smaller Russian arsenal would not be susceptible to a disarming U.S. first strike. Standing next to Bush at a July 2001 press conference in Genoa, Italy, Putin said, "As far as the ABM Treaty and the issues of offensive arms, I've already said we've come to the conclusion that [the] two of these issues have to be discussed as a set . . . one and the other are very closely tied." When Bush argued that the United States and Russia didn't need treaties because they had "a new relationship based on trust," Putin corrected him: "The world is far from having international relations that are built solely on trust, unfortunately. That's why it is so important today to rely on the existing foundation of treaties and agreements in the arms control and disarmament areas."

Bush officials, naturally, rejected Russian suspicions; Rumsfeld, for one, called them "silly." Just as Goldwater, Ashbrook, and Reagan had refused to believe that the Russians could actually fear an American first strike, so did the Bush team. Yet on January 25, 1995, the Russian military notified then-President Boris Yeltsin that it had detected a missile launch—possibly from a nuclear-armed U.S. submarine hoping to decapitate the Russian leadership. Yeltsin immediately convened an emergency teleconference of his senior defense officials to debate a nuclear counterstrike. Fortunately, two minutes before their deadline to retaliate—that is, two minutes before the suspected missile would have detonated on Russian soil—the Russians realized that the "missile" was actually a Norwegian scientific rocket. That incident helps explain Russian president Putin's objections to Bush's proposed withdrawal from the treaty as well as his refusal of multiple entreaties for "joint withdrawal." Bush spent most of 2001 trying to convince Putin otherwise, and when he was unsuccessful in doing so, Bush announced that the United States would unilaterally withdraw from the treaty.

Why would the Bush administration undermine relations with Russia in the name of improving relations with Russia? Was pursuing a defense that was still in its technological infancy worth frightening the Russians over a rogue-state threat that was likewise in its technological infancy? For conservatives, absolutely. For isolationists, missile defense renewed the dream of Fortress America, allowing us to retreat even further from crises abroad. For nationalists and moralists, missile defense was a shield against engagement and détente in the event that, say, North Korea was to develop a nuclear-armed ICBM. For neoconservatives, missile defense was a necessary adjunct to their proactive vision of changing regimes and democratizing the world. A dictator with nuclear-armed missiles could act with near impunity, deterring the United States from taking action against him. By contrast, a missile shield would empower us in a crisis. As journalist Lawrence F. Kaplan argued, "[M]issile defense is about preserving America's ability to wield power abroad. It's not about defense. It's about offense. And that's exactly why we need it." William Kristol and Robert Kagan called missile defense the "sine qua non for a strategy of American global pre-eminence." Missile defense was not simply a weapons system—it was the ultimate symbol of the us-versus-them worldview.

The MADness of King George (II)

This full-throttle approach to missile defense might not have been so provocative had the Bush administration not also taken steps to increase its freedom to act offensively—including with nuclear weapons. In announcing his new strategic framework, Bush said that following the Cold War, nuclear weapons need not play such a large role in our security. As a demonstration of their lessened importance, he indicated that he would reduce our nuclear arsenal to the smallest possible size. But even as he announced this—even, in fact, as he did reduce our nuclear arsenal—he was not only *reaffirming* but *increasing* its role in U.S. foreign policy.

In November 2001, Bush and Putin jointly announced that they would reduce their deployed strategic arsenals from 6,000 warheads to between 1,700 and 2,200 warheads. The following May, they formalized this commitment in the Moscow Treaty.* Although the Bush administration heralded the agreement as proof of the president's revised view of nuclear weapons, the agreement was not, in fact, that progressive. For example, although its reductions seemed dramatic, Presidents Bill Clinton and Boris Yeltsin had agreed to pursue similar cuts in 1997. Where Bush's treaty differed was in permitting far greater flexibility: It did not require the destruction of delivery vehicles (as START I and II had), nor did it call for exploring the destruction of warheads (as the START III framework had). This meant that either side could remove weapons from missiles and bombers, store them, and redeploy them in the future. In fact, Colin Powell acknowledged in July 2002 congressional testimony that "the treaty will allow you to have as many warheads as you want," and Bush indeed planned to keep several thousand in a reserve that would enable the United States to redeploy 2,400 warheads in less than three years. (As Bolton later wrote approvingly, the treaty "provided 'exit ramps' to allow for rapid changes.") Oddly, the treaty contained no verification procedures (it was only 500 words long), making it, in essence, a handshake agreement. And finally, in a bit of diplomatic quantum mechanics, the treaty's warhead limit was slated to take effect on the very day that it expired—December 31, 2012—meaning it would be valid for no more than twenty-four hours.

Nevertheless, Bush declared that the accord "ended a long chapter of confrontation" and "liquidate[d] the Cold War legacy of nuclear hostility between our countries." The reality was significantly more modest and, in fact, was not much different from what it had been at the Cold War's close. Under the START II accord signed by Bush père (but never ratified), the Pentagon had planned to maintain 500 Minuteman III ICBMs, 14 nuclear-armed Trident submarines, 21 B-2 bombers, and 76 B-52 bombers. Under the Moscow Treaty, U.S. forces in 2012 would comprise 450 Minuteman III ICBMs, 14 nuclear-armed Trident submarines, 21 B-2 bombers, and 56 B-52 bombers. Thus, if you were to believe George W. Bush, he was dispensing with MAD and Cold War thinking and ushering in a new era of closer U.S.-Russian relations by trimming a total of 50 missiles and 20 airplanes.

Contrary to the president's claims, the Moscow Treaty actually

---

*Formally, the agreement is known as the Strategic Offensive Reductions Treaty, or SORT, which led to some mocking about it being "sort of a treaty."

preserved a Cold War–type nuclear relationship between the United States and Russia. Because nuclear weapons are so destructive, the United States needed only a few hundred to deter a nuclear attack; the 192 warheads on a single fully loaded U.S. Trident submarine, for example, could kill fifty million people if aimed at Russian cities. The United States needed 1,700–2,200 warheads only if it was planning to wage a nuclear war with Russia and destroy its nuclear weapons on the ground—that is, to maintain a counterforce posture. Although Bush asserted that Russia was no longer an enemy, the only targets that could necessitate 1,700–2,200 U.S. warheads (let alone the redeployment of several thousand warheads in storage) were the 1,500 nuclear weapons that Russia was expected to keep. No other military contingency—even a counterforce strike against China, which has approximately 200 warheads, of which only 20 are deployed on missiles capable of reaching the United States—required more than a few hundred warheads. In short, Bush's "new strategic framework" was still designed to fight nothing less than an all-out nuclear war with Russia.

In fact, the framework actually increased the role for nuclear weapons in other potential conflicts as well. In 2000, Congress passed a law requiring that the next administration complete a review of U.S. nuclear posture—that is, the purpose and structure of our atomic arsenal. When the Bush administration took over, it did just that, and its findings—presented to Congress on December 31, 2001—declared that the post–Cold War security environment required a wholly new nuclear posture. Instead of pursuing a "threat-based approach" that tailored America's force to defeat a specific country—i.e., the Soviet Union—it proposed that the United States pursue a "capabilities-based approach" that maximized the range of tasks for which nuclear weapons could be used: "Greater flexibility is needed with respect to nuclear forces and planning than was the case during the Cold War. . . . [A]lthough the number of weapons needed to hold those assets [valued by adversaries] at risk has declined, U.S. nuclear forces still require the capability to hold at risk a wide range of target types."

The Nuclear Posture Review should have said "a wider range of target types," given its remarkable enthusiasm for the post–Cold War uses of nuclear weapons. It called for a "new triad" composed of conventional and nuclear offensive forces, missile defenses, and a revitalized infrastructure that could produce and test new nuclear weapons if necessary. The review spoke of the need to be able to target nuclear forces anywhere in the world within a few hours, and specifically mentioned North Korea, Iran, Iraq, Libya, Syria, China, and Russia. It called for the ability to strike mobile and dispersed targets and noted with concern that some seventy countries had some ten thousand underground bunkers that the existing U.S. arsenal might not be able to destroy. These hideaways necessitated new types of nuclear arms: "bunker-busting" weapons that could destroy deeply buried targets and low-yield warheads that could be used on smaller targets while killing fewer civilians—thereby disinhibiting the president from using them.

When excerpts of the classified NPR were leaked to the *Los Angeles Times,* many journalists and defense experts responded with shock, arguing that the Bush administration had blurred the bright line between conventional and nuclear weapons, making the latter more "usable." The *Boston Globe* called the posture "twisted," while the *New York Times* complained that Bush had turned the United States into a "nuclear rogue." In fairness, the NPR itself could be interpreted more generously. While it did call for the United States to be able to strike a wide variety of targets, each of the scenarios it proposed for using nuclear weapons could, in theory, have been covered by previous doctrine, as well. Although the United States had long pledged not to use nuclear weapons against nonnuclear states, all administrations had reserved the right to use nuclear weapons to preempt or respond to a nuclear attack, and both the Bush 41 and Clinton administrations had suggested that they might likewise use nuclear weapons to respond to a chemical or biological attack. Each of the states mentioned in Bush's posture review had or was thought to have a nuclear, chemical, or biological weapons program. Thus, it was possible to argue that Bush's NPR fit within existing parameters of nuclear use.

This generous interpretation of the administration's intentions was demolished in May 2005, however, when defense analyst William Arkin reported that the Bush administration had developed a program called Global Strike, formalized as Contingency Plan 8022. CONPLAN-8022 was the operational implementation of Bush's emphasis on preventive and preemptive attacks—and it included a nuclear option. Throughout 2002—in the State of the Union, his June West Point speech, the White House's National Security Strategy, and the National Security Strategy to Combat Weapons of Mass Destruction—Bush had repeatedly stressed the possibility that we would need to strike our enemies before they could hurt us. At no time had he mentioned *nuclear* preemption, but in a classified presidential directive he signed on January 10, 2003, Bush defined Global Strike as "a capability to deliver rapid, extended range, precision kinetic (*nuclear and conventional*) and non-kinetic (elements of space and information operations) effects in support of theater and national objectives." [Emphasis added.] He tasked the Global Strike mission to the U.S. Strategic Command, the military entity established specifically to oversee deployment and use of the nation's nuclear arsenal, and told it to "be ready to strike at any moment's notice in any dark corner of the world."

Global Strike was intended chiefly to expand our ability to use precision conventional weapons and information warfare to combat terrorists and rogue state threats, but, as nuclear weapons analyst Hans Kristensen has chronicled, military officers involved with the program have publicly and repeatedly referenced its nuclear component. Admiral James O. Ellis, who headed STRATCOM until July 2004, made it clear in a February 2003 speech that Global Strike included a nuclear option. That same month, General Richard Myers, then chairman of the Joint Chiefs of Staff, testified to the House Armed Services Committee: "With its global strike responsibilities, the Command will provide a core cadre to plan and execute nuclear, conventional, and information operations anywhere in the world." And, on November 18, 2005—after successfully conducting an exercise dubbed "Global Lightning," which, according to STRATCOM, served as "a bridging exercise between nuclear and non-nuclear forces"— the Pentagon announced that Global Strike had achieved initial operational capability.

In a September 2005 article in *Arms Control Today,* Kristensen revealed that in March 2005 the Joint Chiefs of Staff had published a draft document called the Doctrine for Joint Nuclear Operations, which laid out the rationale for the use of nuclear weapons. It eliminated any ambiguity about the Bush administration's willingness to employ them preventively or preemptively in situations for which our arsenal had never been conceived: regional conflicts in which the enemy had used neither nuclear weapons nor chemical or biological weapons. In fact, the doctrine stipulated that nuclear weapons could be used in a wide variety of circumstances:

• Against an adversary intending to use WMD against U.S., multinational, or allies' forces or civilian populations

- In the event of an imminent attack by biological weapons that only nuclear weapons can safely destroy
- To attack deep, hardened bunkers containing chemical or biological weapons or the command and control infrastructure required for the adversary to execute a WMD attack against the United States or its friends and allies
- To counter potentially overwhelming adversary conventional forces
- For rapid and favorable war termination on U.S. terms
- To ensure the success of U.S. and multinational operations.

The United States had long considered using nuclear weapons first in a conflict—most notably if the Red Army had attacked Western Europe, overwhelming our conventional forces. But the Cold War was over, and, rather than diminishing the role of weapons no president had ever wanted to use, the Bush administration was talking about their preemptive, preventive, or simply convenient use against much lesser threats. This was unprecedented—and went far beyond the so-called strategic ambiguity that Bush 41 and Clinton had referred to in suggesting that the United States might *respond* to a chemical or biological attack with nuclear weapons. The Bush administration was blurring, if not erasing, the line between conventional and nuclear weapons and lowering the threshold at which the nation would go nuclear, proposing an array of tactical uses for weapons that were supposed to be used only in strategic conflicts. The Bush Pentagon was effectively acknowledging that the United States might use nuclear weapons first, against a nonnuclear state, before any hostilities had taken place. In fact, the Doctrine for Joint Nuclear Operations went as far as to replace the phrase "nuclear war" with "conflict involving nuclear weapons" throughout, because "nuclear war" implied that both sides were participating, when, according to the Pentagon, most nuclear conflicts were likely to be one-sided.

This was not just abstract theorizing. In 2002, the administration asked Congress for $15 million to study development of a modified, robust nuclear earth penetrator—a weapon that could drill into the ground and destroy a deeply buried bunker. It also requested that Congress rescind a ban it had imposed on researching low-yield weapons—that is, weapons with less than five kilotons of explosive power. Legislators have yet to fund these programs, but the navy has already made changes to the Trident missile's reentry vehicle that give it far greater accuracy, making it suitable for Global Strike–type precision missions.* The Pentagon has incorporated the ability to plan and rapidly execute a range of nuclear strikes against regional actors into the same computer platform that governs the national nuclear war plan (formerly known as the Single Integrated Operational Plan, or SIOP, now known as Operational Plan, or OPLAN, 8044-2). The Nuclear Posture Review also called for building a new facility to manufacture plutonium cores for nuclear weapons, a new facility for producing tritium (the isotope that is fused in hydrogen bombs and that is used to boost the yield of fission weapons), and a new infrastructure for conducting nuclear tests—to say nothing of its call for a new ICBM by 2018, a new nuclear submarine and SLBM by 2028, and a new nuclear bomber by 2040 to replace aging delivery systems.

This emphasis on a flexible nuclear offense was not a response to the attacks of September 11. Many of these developments had been previewed in a report the National Institute for Public Policy issued in January 2001, just as the Bush administration took office. NIPP is a conservative think tank run by Keith Payne—the same Keith Payne who in 1980 coauthored the *Foreign Policy* piece "Victory Is Possible," which argued that the United States could win a full-scale nuclear war with the Soviet Union, with American casualties limited to a mere twenty million. That argument had been absurd, but the notion that the United States could gain some benefit from using nuclear weapons against regional actors—especially if they could not retaliate—was not. In 1945, we had achieved a political objective—the end of war with Japan—by dropping atomic bombs on Hiroshima and Nagasaki. MAD did not apply in such one-sided situations. Such was the case with states such as Iran, Iraq, North Korea, and others. The spread of threats from the Soviet Union to smaller actors had given the nuclear war fighters a new lease on life.

In 1999, Payne had convened two dozen conservative defense intellectuals—including several veterans of Team B and the Committee

*The navy also wants to replace the nuclear warheads on some Tridents with conventional warheads, which could be used in Global Strike missions. The Bush administration cites this as an example of how it has reduced the role of nuclear weapons, but it is also a good example of how it has blurred the line between nuclear and conventional weapons. And there is always the danger that an enemy could mistake the launch of a conventionally armed SLBM for a nuclear attack—and retaliate.

on the Present Danger—to proselytize for the continued necessity and utility of nuclear weapons. Their 2001 report argued that mutual assured destruction was no longer an appropriate framework for our nuclear arsenal given the unpredictability of the post–Cold War world. In an uncertain security environment, the report contended, the United States required the ability to build up (or scale down) its forces as necessary; the key was "adaptability." Nuclear weapons might be necessary for deterring the use of chemical, biological, or nuclear forces by either regional actors (such as Iran or North Korea) or global powers (Russia or China). Much like Bush's Doctrine on Joint Nuclear Operations, the report maintained that the United States might need nuclear weapons in a conventional conflict; and, like the NPR, it recommended "low-yield, precision-guided nuclear weapons for possible use against select hardened targets such as underground biological weapons facilities." The doctrinal basis for the document was that nuclear weapons should serve not only a deterrent function but also a counterforce function—that they could be used to achieve political and military objectives, even against nonnuclear enemies.

When Bush took office, he put Payne in charge of the Nuclear Posture Review, and when the review was completed, he appointed Payne deputy assistant secretary of defense for forces policy, a position that gave him responsibility for nuclear force planning.

In short, at a time when we ought to have been deemphasizing the role of nuclear weapons—at the exact time, in fact, that the president was saying we *were* deemphasizing their role—we were actually increasing it, all in the name of enhancing our freedom of action. The principle behind Global Strike mirrored Donald Rumsfeld's reluctance to commit a sufficient ground force to Iraq, and it echoed the conservative emphasis on air power and nuclear forces during the early years of the Cold War. Ground troops, after all, meant a greater commitment, a greater foreign entanglement. Bombers and missiles, by contrast, allowed the United States to keep its distance even while protecting its interests abroad. Global Strike represented the next—some might say the ultimate—manifestation of this principle, allowing for the possibility of purely unilateral military action. There was no need for allies and no need for nation building. Just as missile defense could protect us from having to engage the world, so Global Strike could allow the United States to dominate the world while standing utterly apart from it.

An Allergy to Treaties

The same desire for freedom of action that compelled Global Strike bred a deep antipathy to treaties. In constructing its nuclear fortress, the Bush administration naturally dismissed not only the ABM Treaty but strategic arms control generally, insisting time and time again that in the post–Cold War world, the U.S.-Russian relationship need not be so ritualized. Condoleezza Rice, portraying herself as a lapsed "high-priestess of arms control," quipped that we no longer needed to debate theological questions like "how many warheads could dance on the head of an SS-18." John Bolton asserted that there was no need for "traditional arms control negotiations with small armies of negotiators inhabiting the best hotels in Geneva for months and years at a time." In fact, it was only after continued pressure from Putin that Bush reluctantly agreed to codify each side's nuclear reductions in the Moscow Treaty—"If we need to write it down on a piece of paper," he said condescendingly, "I'll be glad to do that." Bolton considered that treaty "the end of arms control."

Bush's reluctance to make such commitments had nothing to do with his conviction that the U.S.-Russian relationship had changed for the better. It was once again simply a function of the centuries-old distaste for formal diplomatic arrangements that constrained American sovereignty. Conservatives had disliked entering into agreements during the Cold War, even when they maintained a nuclear balance that was in U.S. interests, and they disliked them now, even when the twenty-first century presented a host of challenges that were inarguably transnational. In the nationalist worldview, liberty and sovereignty were the ultimate ends; the only problem was that, just as the Soviet nuclear arsenal had rendered liberty dangerous, so, increasingly, had globalization. Our security could no longer be guaranteed through national action alone. The Bush administration consistently refused to acknowledge this fact, as when it torpedoed a deal that would have improved our ability to fight bioterrorism.

The Biological Weapons Convention, signed in 1972, outlawed the production and stockpiling of germ weapons,* but it lacked any verifi-

---

*The actual *use* of such weapons was banned by the 1925 Geneva Convention, which did not prevent many countries, including the United States, from developing stockpiles of bioweapons.

cation procedures—a lacuna that several nations exploited. In the early 1990s, the former Soviet Union admitted to having illegally maintained a large bioweapons program for the previous two decades. As more and more countries seemed poised to develop biological weapons, the parties to the treaty decided to develop an enforcement protocol.

Participants in this process knew that absolute verification—that is, determining with 100 percent certainty that no state was violating the treaty—would not be possible. For one thing, even a small arsenal of certain biological agents can be used to great effect, making a dangerous cache easy to hide. For another, some dangerous pathogens and toxins have peaceful uses, in everything from vaccines to cosmetics. (Botox, for example, is derived from the botulinum toxin, which can kill by paralyzing the respiratory muscles.)* The purpose of the protocol was therefore to make it harder, though not impossible, to cheat. To this end, the negotiators drafted a protocol to the treaty that would require nations to declare facilities that could be used to produce bioweapons (such as containment labs), to establish regular inspections of those facilities, and to allow for special investigations if a treaty violation were suspected.

In July 2001, however, the Bush administration declared that it would not support the protocol because it would not cover enough relevant facilities and could therefore not assure compliance. But this had never been the point: The drafters of the protocol were simply trying to decrease the likelihood that a state or terrorist group would acquire biological weapons by increasing the chances that they would be caught. The system would not be perfect—among other things, the negotiators had to be sensitive to the needs of pharmaceutical companies, which feared that inspectors might steal proprietary information—but it would at least serve as a useful deterrent and intelligence-gathering apparatus. It would certainly be better than nothing. In fact, a system of declarations, regular inspections, and investigations would be *much* better than nothing. Bolton, however, called the draft a "least common denominator proposal," saying, "The time for 'better than nothing' proposals is over. It is time for us to work together to address the [biological weapons] threat."

*Toxins—that is, poisons produced by living organisms—are covered by the BWC, as are viruses and bacteria. Botulinum is produced by the *Clostridium botulinum* bacterium, which can be found in soil around the world.

Given such objections, one might have expected that the administration would counterpropose a protocol that covered a greater number of facilities, so that compliance might be more verifiable. Instead, it did exactly the opposite, declaring that the "traditional arms control methods" being pursued by the negotiating group—and in fact the group itself—were useless and should be replaced by a meeting that would discuss steps that were voluntary, not legally binding. When other states angrily objected, the U.S. ambassador to the negotiations proposed postponing *all* talks for four years. Such recalcitrance was particularly unaccountable given that, amid the rancorous debate in late 2001, American citizens began receiving anthrax-laced letters in the mail. Five people died, and seventeen others were sickened, but the administration would only suggest steps that each nation could take individually and refused to hear of reviving the protocol. Said Bolton, "It's dead, dead, dead, and I don't want it coming back from the dead."

Verification had often been a stalking horse for conservative opposition to treaties, and hard-liners had used it to great effect during the Reagan administration. But paradoxically, conservatives seemed to be satisfied only when there was no verification whatsoever, as in the Moscow Treaty. For example, in July 2004, the Bush administration announced that it felt a verifiable treaty to halt the world's production of fissile material for weapons purposes—an agreement that could have capped Pakistan's nuclear arsenal, among others—was not possible and therefore should not be pursued. It is difficult to argue that, say, 90 percent verification is worse than nothing, yet that in fact is what conservatives maintain. But despite the hubbub conservatives inevitably raise about the verification gaps in every arms control treaty—the NPT, the SALT I Interim Agreement, SALT II, the INF Treaty, START I, START II—none of these treaties has put the United States at a disadvantage vis-à-vis its enemies.*

The Bush administration worked hard to kill many other international accords as well, using a variety of rationales and excuses. In March 2001, Bush forced Christine Todd Whitman, the head of the Environmental Protection Agency, to retract a statement that his administration would address global warming by limiting U.S. emissions of carbon dioxide—

---

*Conservatives certainly believe that the ABM Treaty harmed U.S. interests, but not because of verification—rather, because of the constraints that it imposed on our missile defense program.

and perhaps even ratifying the Kyoto Protocol, which required developed nations to cut their greenhouse gas emissions. Conservatives such as Bolton opposed the Kyoto Protocol not simply on policy grounds—i.e., that it was too restrictive or not restrictive enough—but on constitutional grounds. Bolton believed that American unilateralism was not simply a function of our historical distaste for engagement but of our system of government. In the case of Kyoto, the executive's right to make foreign policy was impinging upon the legislative branch's essential role in making domestic policy. Unfortunately, by this logic, the president cannot sign any international agreement that caps carbon emissions—tying our hands in the face of an existential threat.

Bolton used the same argument on the most harmless of pacts: a nonbinding "program of action" developed at a July 2001 UN conference to address the illicit trade in handguns, rifles, and assault weapons—a critical issue for war-torn developing countries. The United States has long recognized small arms as both a threat to its security and a humanitarian catastrophe, negotiating several treaties to address the problem. But faced with a proposal to discuss civilian ownership of weapons designed for military purposes and limits on arms sales to substate groups, the Bush administration balked. Even though the standards the conference proposed for civilian gun ownership were strictly voluntary and were in fact less restrictive than U.S. gun laws, Bolton objected on the grounds that the Second Amendment protects an individual's right to bear arms. In the end, the offending provisions were removed from the program of action, leaving it seriously weakened. Never mind that the program of action would not have affected a single American's right to bear arms: "From little acorns, bad treaties grow," Bolton explained.*

Conclusion

Before September 11, 2001, the Bush administration was already well on its way to enacting a conservative agenda that not only sought to render

---

*Five years earlier, conservatives had also opposed the treaty banning chemical weapons, in part because it would allegedly have violated the U.S. chemical industry's Fourth Amendment right against unlawful searches. According to Phyllis Schlafly, the "New World Order" was "closing in on American business." She failed to mention that the chemical industry supported the treaty.

our Cold War victory permanent through military dominance—thus obviating the need to ever again deal with dictators—but also by freeing us from any constraints, regardless of whether they helped or harmed our national security, in the process freeing us from the need to deal with friends and allies as well. After September 11, the administration would justify such boldness—and other drastic measures—by claiming that the terrorist attacks had changed everything. But they had really begun claiming that "everything had changed" immediately upon taking office. As Condoleezza Rice said of the post–Cold War world in July 2001, "This is a big shift to wrap one's mind around, but we cannot cling to the old order like medieval scholars clinging to a Ptolemaic system even after the Copernican revolution. We must realize that the strategic world we grew up in has been turned upside down." In truth, however, whether the Bush administration was presented with old problems, such as the Russian nuclear arsenal, or new problems, such as global warming, it simply chose old solutions. Conservatives were fixated on a nineteenth-century view of a twenty-first-century world.

Why did any of this matter? Wasn't it a good thing to be militarily dominant, to be prepared for all eventualities, even if that meant preparing a wide range of nuclear options, even preemptive ones? Not necessarily. For one thing, it wasn't at all clear that nuclear weapons were actually superior for many of the new missions for which they were being slated. For example, even an atomic warhead could penetrate only so far into the earth before it shattered, and our enemies could always just dig their bunkers deeper. For another, the Bush administration's policies effectively forced us to *react* to threats. That is, rather than proactively preventing the dangers from weapons of mass destruction, Bush officials focused largely on responding to threats that they seemed to assume were inevitable. Missile defense was the epitome of waiting until the last possible minute—almost literally—before stopping a warhead from detonating on American soil. Soon after it took office, the Bush administration renamed the White House office of nonproliferation the office of *counter*proliferation. In doing so, it no doubt intended to sound more aggressive, but nonproliferation refers to preventing the spread of WMD, whereas counterproliferation refers to rolling back proliferation that has already occurred. After September 11, the administration did become more proactive, but even military preemption—ostensibly an aggressive, forward-leaning policy—

presumed that the United States had failed to prevent a threat from emerging in the first place.

Conservatives would maintain that they were simply preparing for the worst—prudently weaving a safety net, just in case—but in an odd bit of myopia failed to understand how diplomacy could reduce the odds that the worst would happen. They contradicted themselves, seeing arms control both as a tool used only against one's enemies and as a tool that could only be used during times of stability. For example, the NIPP report confusingly argued that we didn't need arms control because the Cold War was over and at the same time insisted that we needed flexibility to deploy more weapons should a Cold War–like conflict with China or Russia restart. But of course the whole purpose of arms control was to stabilize a potential enemy's capabilities so that one did not have to worry about his intentions. Douglas Feith, an undersecretary of defense, got it precisely backward when he simplistically argued, "If we had mutual trust and real security, you wouldn't need these agreements, and if you need these agreements, then it is an illusion to say that you have mutual trust and security." The notion that mistrustful parties might need to find a way to coexist had apparently not occurred to him.

Conservatives failed to recognize that arms control was an attempt by nations to pursue the shared interest of avoiding the worst. Indeed, they failed to understand that preparing for the worst could actually increase the odds of the worst. Like their conservative forebears, who had not perceived how the Soviets could possibly feel threatened by the American buildup of nuclear forces during the Cold War, Bush officials simply dismissed the idea that a missile defense backed by improvements to our arsenal and guided by a more aggressive nuclear posture would bother anyone. To them, it was obvious that we posed no threat to Russia simply because they said we posed no threat. Our allies knew us well enough, they thought, to understand what we were doing; and it was lunacy to expect that any rogue state would alter its behavior one way or another based on our actions—rogues were rogues, after all, and did what they wanted. To be sure, withdrawal from the ABM Treaty has not prompted the renewed arms race that some liberal analysts feared. But our offensive and defensive nuclear posture *did* matter.

One study commissioned by the Pentagon found that the Bush administration's nuclear policies had increased international uncertainty about

America's intentions, lowered the threshold for nuclear use, and discouraged allies from helping us to combat nuclear proliferation. It concluded that, while the adversarial nuclear posture of the Cold War might no longer be appropriate, the "nuclear laissez-faire" of the Bush administration had allowed "the emergence of potentially damaging nuclear anxieties" in Russia and China. Both countries, it concluded, were concerned that the United States was trying to move beyond a deterrent relationship to one of nuclear primacy.

Theirs was not an irrational fear. In a provocative essay published in 2006, two American scholars argued that Russia's nuclear forces had so deteriorated in size and quality, and that America's had so qualitatively improved, that the United States was on the verge of having the ability to launch a disarming first strike—a situation that had not existed since the 1950s. If true, the deterrent relationship was already grossly unstable, and a U.S. missile defense could make it considerably worse, allowing us to mop up any Russian forces that evaded a first strike. The same point applied to China, whose arsenal consisted of only a few dozen ICBMs.

In 2007, when the Bush administration announced it would install ten missile interceptors and an advanced radar system in Eastern Europe, Russian officials warned that they would target the sites with nuclear weapons and implied that they would speed their work on new ICBMs and a new submarine-launched ballistic missile. United States claims that the interceptors were not directed at Russia did not sway them. "In questions of military-strategic stability there are . . . immutable laws, actions, counteractions, defensive, offensive systems," Russian foreign minister Sergey Lavrov explained. "These laws operate regardless of how somebody would like to see this or that situation. The military has its own duty, to figure out threats and take countermeasures." Putin stated that U.S. missile defense plans were "destroying the strategic equilibrium in the world. In order to restore that balance without setting up a missile defense system we will have to create a system to overcome missile defense, and this is what we are doing now." The Kremlin announced it would stop observing the limits on conventional arms in Europe that George H. W. Bush had negotiated, and that it might also withdraw from the Intermediate-Range Nuclear Forces Treaty, which Reagan had signed.

The irony—only one of many in Bush's nuclear policy—was that the existing U.S. missile defenses hardly inspired confidence. In December

2002, Bush ordered the deployment of an initial, rudimentary system by the fall of 2004, which was of course a presidential election year. Perhaps the announcement would have appeared less politically motivated if the proposed system had not failed an intercept test the previous week. Nonetheless, although the administration did not conduct a single intercept test for the following two years, it deployed six interceptors in Alaska and one in California by the end of 2004. Any existing confidence in the system quickly evaporated when testing resumed in December 2004. In that test, and one in February 2005, the interceptors failed to even launch. In a simple test the following year, the system did intercept a target, but the Government Accountability Office reported that it "has not completed sufficient flight testing to provide a high level of confidence that [it] can reliably intercept ICBMs." Nevertheless, the administration deployed another dozen interceptors and expanded its sights to Europe.

But the greatest danger of a conservative foreign policy in the post–Cold War world would not come into relief until after September 11, when the transnational nature of the threats America faced would become immediately apparent, and yet conservatives would react in the nationalistic way they always had. In the summer of 2000, the drafters of the Republican platform had inserted in their manifesto a reference to conservatism's demigod, Winston Churchill. "The era of procrastination, of half-measures, of soothing and baffling expedients, of delays, is coming to a close," Churchill had intoned prophetically in 1936. "In its place we are entering a period of consequences." It was a more apt quote than the GOP writers could have imagined. For half a century, conservatives had been insisting that ideas had consequences, and in that they were correct. Conservatism had been struggling throughout that period to take control of American politics. Now a man who believed their ideology more fully than even Ronald Reagan had was president. During the first months of his administration, Bush's conservatism was evident, but when heated with the rhetoric of absolutist moralism—of good versus evil—it would take on a more messianic aggressiveness. Looking back on the terrorist attacks, foreign policy thinker Robert Kagan wrote, "America did not change on September 11, it only became more itself." The same could be said of conservatism, and the consequences for America, and the world, would be profound.

Chapter Six

APOTHEOSIS

For all of the dark mystery that surrounds nuclear weapons, an atomic bomb is a fairly simple device that leverages a quirk of nature. Among the various elements, plutonium and a specific form of uranium, known as U-235, have a particularly unstable atomic structure. That is, their nuclei, composed of protons and neutrons, are likely to split apart if they collide with a free-flying neutron. When this happens, the atom fissions, producing two smaller atoms and several more free neutrons that fly off on their own. The total mass of these offspring is less than that of the parent atom, and even though the difference is minute, the amount of energy released is, proportionally, enormous, dictated by Einstein's famous equation $E = mc^2$, where E is the energy released, m is the difference in mass, and c is the speed of light.

Even in dense metals like uranium and plutonium, however, there is an enormous amount of space between atoms. In such an empty area, an errant neutron is unlikely to collide with anything. A nuclear weapon is essentially a device for increasing the odds that peripatetic neutrons run into their neighbors. It can do this simply by gathering together enough plutonium or highly enriched uranium (HEU) that a neutron is given a target-rich environment. Or, it can take a smaller amount of material and suddenly compress it, so that the material becomes denser and the space between atoms is dramatically reduced. In either case, the result is the same. Each fission event causes two or more other atoms to fission, which in turn cause another two to fission, and so on. The chain reaction develops exponentially and with great speed. Within milliseconds, a tremendous amount of energy is released.

Like the workings of an atomic bomb, the immediate effects of a nuclear explosion are readily predictable. If a ten-kiloton weapon—that is, a relatively small bomb, and one within the technical abilities of a terrorist group—was to explode in downtown Washington, this is what would happen. As the weapon's core went critical, it would release so much energy that the point of detonation would be heated to one hundred million degrees centigrade—about ten times hotter than the surface of the sun, vaporizing all nearby matter. Quickly, a fireball would expand to four football fields in diameter, emitting a pulse of heat that would cause all combustible material within two-thirds of a mile to burst into flame, burning and blinding people caught in the open.

At almost the same moment, the heat from the explosion would super-heat the nearby gases, causing them to rapidly expand in a sphere that moved away from ground zero at supersonic speeds. As they did so, the surrounding air would be compressed into a fast-moving, high-pressure front. The speed and pressure of the wave—combined with the hurricane-force winds left in its wake—would crumple houses and blow down buildings for half a mile in every direction. Every building within forty square miles would be damaged. People outside would be tossed about, their eardrums and lungs ruptured as air forced itself into every bodily cavity. Collapsing structures and falling debris would crush those not cut to shreds by hundreds of thousands of shards of flying glass. Fires would rage everywhere, ignited by the intense heat of the explosion and fed by ruptured gas lines and newly created mounds of kindling.

For the first minute after the explosion, intense radiation in the form of gamma rays and neutrons would fly from ground zero, ravaging all living tissue it encountered. It would be followed by fallout—radioactive particles generated by the explosion as well as bits of irradiated dirt and debris that had been swept into the air by the fireball and had drifted with the wind, gradually falling back to earth. On an average day in Washington, a narrow plume of fallout would be carried at least one hundred miles to the northeast, contaminating a finger of land that reached across the Chesapeake Bay.

And then the chaos would begin.

After the explosion, hundreds of thousands—perhaps millions—of people would try to flee the area. Many, if not most, would be hampered by damaged roads and fallen bridges, power outages, and traffic accidents caused by panic. The government has made little effort to instruct people on what to do in the wake of a nuclear attack, and those trying to get news or instructions would likely find that the circuitry in their radios, televisions, and phones had been fried by the electromagnetic pulse produced by the explosion. Fire-fighters, police, and paramedics trying to help the injured, put out fires, and restore order would encounter the same obstacles. All would be trapped out-doors as lethal radiation—strongest in the three hours after the blast—began to rain down on them.

Those who made it out of the area would find little relief. Area hospi-tals would be inundated by victims not only of trauma, but of the signature scars of nuclear weapons: burns and radiation poisoning. Severe burns are one of the most life-threatening and care-intensive injuries a person can sustain, but there are only 1,500 burn beds in the entire country—just a handful in each state—and, at any given moment, most of them are already occupied. Victims of radiation sickness would be accompanied by hun-dreds of thousands of "worried well" who feared they had been poisoned. Few drugs are available for the treatment of radiation poisoning—and those are in short supply. If a ten-kiloton weapon exploded in downtown Washington, more than two hundred thousand people would die. Another ninety thousand would be sick or injured.

Bedlam would not so much ripple across the country as it would simul-taneously erupt in cities across America because there would be little rea-son to believe that there was only one bomb. Just as on the morning of September 11, it would take hours to sort rumor from fact, to determine what had actually happened, and to ascertain how serious the threat of further attack was. In the meantime, major cities would likely empty as fearful residents fled conspicuous targets such as New York, Chicago, Los Angeles, and San Francisco. Besides the sheer social displacement—there would be nowhere for this many people to go—the economy would come to a halt. The government would likely compound this problem by shut-ting down ports and air traffic to minimize the risk of another detonation. One government study estimates that an attack on New York City could cost $12.4 trillion—nearly the entire gross domestic product of the entire country for one year. The country would enter a period devoted solely to reconstruction.

Besides the death, disease, and economic deprivation that would fol-low a nuclear explosion, the most lasting consequences could well be political. In the wake of the September 11 attacks, which killed three thousand people, the United States has taken extraordinary measures to defend itself. The Bush administration has suspended the writ of habeas corpus in certain cases; it has built a prison in Guantánamo Bay specifically so that the facility would be beyond the reach of the law; it has set up black facilities around the world to secretly hold and interrogate suspected terrorists; and it has authorized warrantless wiretapping of U.S. citizens. Imagine the reaction to an attack that was one hundred times worse. We would no longer debate whether water boarding was appropriate. A strike on Washington that killed most members of the three branches of government and their staffs could well plunge the country into anarchy.

The National Planning Scenarios—a document compiled by the Homeland Security Council to help local, state, and federal authorities respond to attacks by weapons of mass destruction—have framed the existential character of such an event with a degree of emotion unusual for a technical government report: "The personal loss of loved ones would be immeasurable. The health consequences to the population directly impacted would be severe. The physical damage to the community would be extreme. The costs of the decontamination and rebuilding would be staggering. But these losses do not begin to address the true implications of this type of an incident[.] The detonation of an IND [improvised nuclear device] in a U.S. city would forever change the American psyche, as well as its politics and worldview."

Admittedly, these are predictions. But there is one certainty: No other attack could do as much damage. Chemical and biological weapons are often grouped with nuclear weapons under the umbrella term "weapons of mass destruction," or WMD, but it is a seriously misleading phrase. Chemical weapons are extremely difficult to use, even in a sophisticated terrorist attack. The most successful, coordinated use of nerve agents in skyscrapers, or the explosion of a chlorine gas storage facility upwind of an urban area, might kill between six thousand and eighteen thousand people. A biological weapon could be far more deadly, but effective bioweapons are also much harder to construct. And in the years since September 11, we have developed an effective way to contain the most dangerous agent, smallpox, through mass vaccinations. The anthrax attacks, however frightening, killed or sickened very few people. The odds of a cataclysmic bioattack seem very low.

While odds of a nuclear attack are likewise low, they are simply not low enough. Experts have put the odds between 1 percent and 50 percent over the next decade. Matthew Bunn, a respected Harvard researcher, constructed a mathematical model for estimating the threat and concluded that, in any given year, the odds of a nuclear attack are about one in thirty. That might not sound particularly alarming, but if there's a 3 percent chance of an attack in any given year, the odds of an attack sometime in the next ten years are 29 percent. Or, as Bunn once put it, "I believe it's likely enough that it significantly reduces the life expectancy of everyone who lives and works in downtown Washington, D.C., or New York." Certainly, there is no lack of terrorist motivation. George Tenet, the former director of central intelligence, has written that al Qaeda wants to launch a nuclear attack and even tried to buy Russian nuclear devices on the black market in 2002 and 2003.

There is only one conclusion to be drawn from these data: The war on terrorism, whatever else it is, must first and foremost be a war on nuclear terrorism. Conservatives agree. As Jonah Goldberg, *National Review*'s editor-at-large, observed, "If you didn't have nuclear weapons, it would be sort of silly for America to see the war on terror as an existential battle."

The average citizen listening to the president and his aides after September 11 would have assumed they understood that. George W. Bush, who had already been speaking about the dangers posed by rogue states with weapons of mass destruction, now warned of the horrifying possibility that rogue states might help terrorists acquire those weapons. In the run-up to the Iraq war, administration officials focused specifically on the prospect of nuclear terrorism, warning that we must preempt the threat before it became imminent—we must not let the "smoking gun become a mushroom cloud." In 2004, Bush stated that the greatest threat facing the United States was a terrorist armed with a nuclear weapon.

But if the Bush administration had been most concerned about the atomic threat, it would not have invaded Iraq. In late 2002, before the war, we knew that North Korea and Iran had far more advanced nuclear programs than Saddam did, even if our most damning intelligence about his alleged atomic efforts had been true. Anyone reading the papers would have known this. In December, North Korea announced it was restarting its nuclear facilities, which had been frozen under a 1994 deal with President Clinton, and the next month a *Time* magazine cover with the headline "THE BIGGER THREAT?" featured an illustration of dictator Kim Jong Il surrounded by missiles. In February 2003, international inspectors entered a nuclear facility in Iran and were shocked to find a partial cascade of centrifuges for enriching uranium. (Low-enriched uranium is used as nuclear reactor fuel, but as the enrichment level increases so does the material's potential for use in a nuclear bomb.*) Yet despite the fact that North Korea was one of the world's leading weapons proliferators, and Iran, a revolutionary Islamist regime, was the world's leading sponsor of terrorism—and both, of course, were avowed enemies of the United States—the president chose to focus on Iraq.

If, in 2000, Bush had not been certain who the "them" in the us-versus-them formula was, 9/11 should have provided the answer: Al Qaeda was post–Cold War enemy number one. For conservatives, the attacks resurrected the good-versus-evil framework that they had venerated during the Cold War—but the evil was not limited to al Qaeda. Rather, on September 11, evil lit up around the world like stains under a black light. Having readopted this moralistic view of the world, conservatives naturally embraced its ramifications again as well. Even as their priority should have been nuclear terrorism, Bush officials focused instead on the alleged threat posed by evil regimes. Then, rather than focusing on those with nuclear programs, an effort that would at least have helped prevent nuclear terrorism, they targeted the one enemy that could be dispatched with the greatest degree of moral clarity. Why would they prioritize the abstract defeat of evil over a concrete existential threat? Because they always had. And so the threat would get worse.

The Return of Good and Evil

Although Bush entered the presidency as a conservative, there had been questions about his ideological bona fides during the campaign. He had spoken of an ideologically suspect "compassionate conservatism"; and

---

*Natural uranium contains only a small amount of the U-235 isotope—it is principally comprised of U-238. Enrichment is the process of generating a higher concentration of U-235. Anything below 20 percent U-235 is considered low-enriched uranium; anything over 20 percent is considered highly enriched uranium; and above 90 percent is weapons grade.

several of his closest advisers, such as Karen Hughes and Andy Card, were moderate Republicans, not movement conservatives.

But when the *Washington Post* surveyed presidential appointments two months after Bush's inauguration, it found an administration dominated by conservatives—conservatives who had grown up during the Goldwater years, had joined the movement and taken up mid-level positions under Reagan, and were now seasoned enough to run the government. Intellectuals from the Cato Institute, the American Enterprise Institute, and the Heritage Foundation were inundated with opportunities—and several of them, such as John Bolton and Labor Secretary Elaine Chao, were given high-level jobs. Staffers from *National Review* and William Kristol's conservative *Weekly Standard* joined the White House as speechwriters. While there were several moderates in the Cabinet—Colin Powell at State, Paul O'Neill at Treasury, and Christine Todd Whitman at the Environmental Protection Agency—only Powell would retain any influence beyond 2001; O'Neill and Whitman would be forced out in 2003. Not long after Bush took office, Heritage Foundation founder and New Right guru Paul Weyrich gleefully announced, "This administration is shaping up to be the best"—by which he meant better even than Reagan's.

The Reagan comparison was apt on several levels. Both men, for example, were highly instinctive, placing a great premium on personal interactions. Both were more easily swayed by narrative and anecdote than by argument and evidence. Both men were Westerners with an individualistic, frontier mentality. If Bush's Texas ranch, purchased during the 2000 campaign, seemed a pretense to many—"all hat and no cattle," in one memorable formulation—it was nevertheless clear that Bush felt more at ease in Midland than in Cambridge or New Haven. What Bush remembered of his time at Yale in the late 1960s was not the political controversies that roiled campus—controversies that animated contemporaries like John Kerry and John Bolton—but the intellectual condescension of the students and faculty. (As a freshman, Bush had approached the eminent liberal chaplain William Sloane Coffin and mentioned his father's recent defeat in a brutal Senate race. Coffin had replied, "Oh, yes, I know your father. Frankly, he was beaten by a better man.") As Bush would later explain to a journalist: "What angered me was the way such people at Yale felt so intellectually superior and so righteous." Such elitism would be strictly forbidden at the Bush White House, where degrees from the University of Michigan or Texas A&M were welcomed, while Ivy League pedigrees aroused suspicion. Culturally, then, Bush was more like Reagan than like his own father, who was a card-carrying member of the Eastern establishment.

Bush's economic policies were similar to Reagan's as well, though with a less ideological basis. Both men were supply-siders, passing dramatic tax cuts during their first year in office, and both were foes of government regulation, pleasing their libertarian constituents. But whereas Reagan, a charter subscriber to *National Review,* justified his economic leanings in terms of William F. Buckley, Jr.'s high-minded philosophy, Bush's policies derived primarily from personal experiences in Texas and in business, where wealthy men complained to him about the stifling effect of taxes and regulation. Reagan had made a political career out of expressing Goldwater's ideas more eloquently than the man himself could; Bush only read *The Conscience of a Conservative* after his father told him to. And whereas Reagan claimed in his first inaugural address that "in this present crisis, government is not the solution to our problem; government is the problem," Bush believed that "we have a responsibility that when somebody hurts, government has to move."

In foreign policy terms, however, Bush was far more conservative than Reagan. Although Reagan had spoken in terms of good and evil, he had not followed that worldview to its logical end, dismissing the notion of nuclear war fighting and ultimately negotiating with the Soviet Union. By contrast, even before 9/11, Bush had embraced the utility of nuclear weapons and had shied away from negotiation. It was not until the terrorist attacks, however, that the extent of his ideological devotion became clear. The September 11 attacks reinserted the good-versus-evil trope into U.S. foreign policy, allowing conservatives—and George W. Bush in particular—to reach their true potential.

Bush's life can be divided, without too much oversimplification, at about his fortieth birthday. He had been only an average student at Yale and avoided service in Vietnam by serving in a relaxed unit of the Texas Air National Guard. By his twenties, he had developed a drinking problem. During a few eventful months beginning in late 1972, Bush trashed a rented house in a drunken frenzy, urinated on a parked car during an election night celebration, and challenged his father to a fistfight ("mano-a-mano"). Four years later, he was arrested for driving under the influence near the family home in Kennebunkport, Maine. Nevertheless, during these years, he managed to get his MBA from Harvard, and in 1977 he founded an oil company called Arbusto. That same year, he began to campaign for an open congressional seat. But he lost that race, and despite the good health of the Texas oil industry, Arbusto was plagued by dry wells. Eventually, Bush merged his failing company with one owned by some friends, which in turn failed during a slump in oil prices and was purchased by Harken Energy in a stock swap.

Throughout this period, Bush's failures propelled him laterally—his last name did not allow him to fall too far. The congressional race had given him some recognition in Texas, and of course his father had been elected vice president in 1980 (after which Bush had opportunistically changed "Arbusto" to the more clearly eponymous "Bush Exploration"). The high points of these years were his marriage to Laura and the birth of his twin daughters, Jenna and Barbara, in 1981. But even his relationship with his wife was marred by what is often called Bush's "boorishness"— that is, obnoxious behavior encouraged by liberal doses of beer and bourbon. Bush insists that he was not an alcoholic, but clearly, his drinking was problematic, and he realized that he needed to quit.

The strength to get sober came from God—more specifically, from the relationship with God that Bush developed through a Bible study group in Midland that his close friend (and future commerce secretary) Don Evans recommended to him. In his 1999 autobiography, Bush writes that his path to Christ began with a conversation he had with the Reverend Billy Graham in 1985 at his family's compound in Kennebunkport. ("Over the course of that weekend, Reverend Graham planted a mustard seed in my soul, a seed that grew over the next year.") His spiritual cultivation, however, seems to have come from the Midland group, where Bush immersed himself in biblical parables. Bush's religiosity was based not on an intellectual theology, but on the personal relationship he felt he had developed with Jesus. With that relationship came a strong sense of right and wrong, a duality that would remain with Bush and decisively inform his view of the world. As Evans said, Bush's newfound faith gave him "a very clear sense of what is good and what is evil."

In 1986, a reborn Bush quit drinking, and his life rapidly improved. In 1987, he moved to D.C. to work on his father's presidential campaign, becoming the family enforcer and the link between Bush 41 and the evangelical movement. Two years later he organized the purchase of the

Texas Rangers baseball team, eventually selling his share, initially worth $600,000, for $15 million. In 1994, he defeated the popular Ann Richards to become governor of Texas. Four years later, he won reelection in a landslide victory, and shortly thereafter told friends that God had called him to run for president.

The mid-1980s therefore marked a dramatic turning point for Bush on several different axes. His adult life could be divided into alcoholism and sobriety, doubt and religious rebirth, professional mediocrity and phenomenal success. These pivots were simply the knuckles of a single hinge. As Bush told one audience, "I would not be president today if I hadn't stopped drinking seventeen years ago. And I could only do that with the grace of God." Bush's life could be cast in binary terms: before and after. As it had been for Bush personally, so it was for the Bush presidency after September 11, when, he said, "a great cause became clear." The life of the nation, too, was divided into before and after.

Although Bush was hardly as thoughtful as William F. Buckley or Whittaker Chambers, his religiosity continued to inform his politics and in particular his foreign policy. If Bush's economic outlook was more corporatist than libertarian, his foreign policy, in which moralism and nationalism fused seamlessly, was a purely conservative one. In the aftermath of the attacks, Bush pronounced the war on terrorism "a monumental struggle of good versus evil." Speaking at the National Cathedral on September 14, 2001, the president laid out the challenge: "Just three days removed from these events, Americans do not yet have the distance of history. But our responsibility to history is already clear: to answer these attacks and rid the world of evil."

This was, to say the least, an ambitious goal, but it was one from which Bush never backed away. His speeches and press conferences and statements over the subsequent months are rife with references to "evil," "evildoers," and even "the evil one"—a reference to Osama bin Laden. It quickly became clear that casting the war on terrorism as a moral struggle was not simply a rhetorical device but the literal way in which the president viewed the conflict. In his January 2002 State of the Union address, he upped the ante, calling Iran, Iraq, and North Korea an "axis of evil"—a phrase speechwriters chose to appeal to the president's fundamentalism. In February 2002, the president said, "I don't believe there's many shades of gray in this war. You're either with us or against us; you're either evil or you're good." In his speech at West Point on June 1, 2002, he said, "Moral truth is the same in every culture, in every time, and in every place. . . . We are in a conflict between good and evil, and America will call evil by its name."

Initially, the incessant use of such language drew some smirks, mocked as the simplistic moral code of a cowboy. American liberals, Europeans, and not a few Muslims worried that the president was a captive of the Religious Right, bound to a Christianist agenda—his foreign policy a "crusade," as Bush himself once unfortunately termed it. Yet although Bush's worldview was undoubtedly informed by his religiosity, it was less significant as a function of his faith than as a further expression of the binary, exceptionalist foreign policy of modern conservatism.

After all, the "good" in the good-versus-evil formula is not defined in traditional moral terms but in terms of whatever is good for American interests, which since the seventeenth century has often been considered synonymous with God's will. Conversely, "evil" is defined not according to some standard of biblical morality but according to what is bad for the United States. A good-versus-evil worldview is moralist; it is not necessarily moral. And that moralism need not be linked to religion. Thus Dick Cheney, who is not a particularly religious man, characterized the war on terrorism as "a struggle against evil" and praised Bush for his "moral clarity." Condoleezza Rice, whose foreign policy had been nurtured by realists like Brent Scowcroft and Bush 41, said, "We can never let the intricacies of cloistered [academic] debate—with its many hues of gray and nuance—obscure the need to speak and act with moral clarity. . . . We must recognize that truly evil regimes will never be reformed. And we must recognize that such regimes must be confronted, not coddled. Nations must decide which side they are on in the fault line that divides civilization from terror."

The conservative movement embraced this Manichaeanism. Rich Lowry, Buckley's successor as editor of *National Review,* wrote approvingly that Bush "seems instinctively to understand evil" and observed that Bush saw the war on terrorism in spiritual terms—it was his "most important faith-based initiative." This was the conservatism of the 1950s, before America had fully realized how constrained the United States was by the presence of another nuclear-armed superpower. Indeed, the similarities to the Cold War vision of the world were striking. Charles Krauthammer said that after September 11, the Bush administration immediately fathomed "that the successor to the great ideological wars of the 20th century had presented itself to us—that just as communism was the successor to fascism . . . the war on terrorism was now the successor to those great ideological struggles." Bush himself repeatedly compared terrorists to communists, saying that "the terrorists are successors to the murderous ideologies of the twentieth century," and adding that "we are the heirs of the tradition of liberty."

Some on the right even felt that the term "war on terror" didn't convey the necessary seriousness. James Woolsey and Norman Podhoretz insisted on referring to it as "World War IV"—much as James Burnham had insisted on regarding the Cold War as the "Third World War"—as did Reagan's former speechwriter Peggy Noonan, who called New York firefighters the "first and still greatest warriors of World War IV." A controversy actually broke out in *National Review* when Newt Gingrich labeled the war on terrorism "World War III"; Mark Steyn wrote that the difference is "not just semantic: It gets to the heart of how we see the struggle."

Bush acknowledged that this was not a traditional war—that it would be a long struggle without clear interim victories. (He once even said of the war, "I don't think you can win it.") At the same time, anyone who attempted to argue that "war on terror" was a poor frame of reference was accused of lacking backbone and moral clarity. During the 2004 campaign, John Kerry suggested that the threat of terrorism could be reduced to the point where it was just a nuisance. Bush replied, "I know that some people question if America is really in a war at all. . . . After the chaos and carnage of September the eleventh, it is not enough to serve our enemies with legal papers." Cheney likewise warned, "We'll fall back into the pre-9/11 mind-set, if you will, that in fact these terrorist attacks are just criminal acts, and that we're not really at war." In 2007, as some of the Democratic candidates for president edged away from this concept, conservatives responded with derision. Much as they had during the Cold War, conservatives in the war on terrorism insisted that victory was simply a matter of will.

Of course, in some respects a good-versus-evil framework was an apt one for the post-9/11 world and, in Afghanistan, the conservative impulse meshed perfectly with our actual strategic needs. If the unprovoked murder of three thousand people was not evil, then the word had little meaning. Not only did the United States need to uproot a vast base for terrorism that sought to murder millions of Americans; it also had to strike back after such a massive attack to demonstrate its power and deter, if not terrorists themselves, at least states from aiding terrorists. And it had an unquestionable right to punish the perpetrators of a great crime.

But the interests of the United States soon diverged from the imperatives of conservatism. Just as it had during the Cold War, the binary view of the world had numerous ramifications for policy—ramifications that Cheney succinctly explained: "We cannot deal with terror. [The war on terrorism] will not end in a treaty. There will be no peaceful coexistence, no negotiations, no summit, no joint communiqué with the terrorists. The struggle can end only with their complete and permanent destruction and in victory for the United States and the cause of freedom."

That approach might have been feasible if the war on terrorism had been confined to merely fighting terrorists. After all, few Americans had any desire to negotiate with al Qaeda or to see President Bush sit down with Osama bin Laden in Geneva. But in January 2002, Bush expanded the scope of the war on terrorism to include Iran, Iraq, and North Korea—the axis of evil. Five months later, John Bolton added Libya, Syria, and Cuba to that list. Apparently, even though the September 11 attacks had supposedly changed everything, the war on terrorism would be waged according to the Manichaean worldview conservatives had embraced in the 1950s. And the ramifications would be the same. Coexistence, containment, and negotiation constituted appeasement; the only way to deal with evil was to confront it, to roll it back, to end it. Conservatives happily reembraced this "moral clarity" because they were convinced that it had been responsible for winning the Cold War. As Bush explained, "President Reagan went to Berlin. He was clear in his statement. He said, 'tear down the wall,' and two years later the wall fell." As we have seen, however, during the Cold War, such moralism and oppositionalism had blurred the nature of the conflict and led the United States and the Soviet Union to the brink of a nuclear confrontation. In the post-9/11 world, conservatism would once again blur the nature of the threat we faced and once again increase our vulnerability to nuclear disaster.

Cooperative Threat Reduction

One reassuring fact about nuclear terrorism is that it is preventable. The fissile material—highly enriched uranium or plutonium—that is required for a nuclear weapon is difficult to make. No terrorist group could enrich uranium or reprocess plutonium on its own, meaning that if it wanted to build an atomic bomb it would need either to steal or buy fissile material from a nuclear power. Which is why after 9/11, nuclear experts had one priority: to undertake a massive effort to clean up loose nuclear material around the world, particularly in Russia, where in 2001 more than six hundred tons of fissile material lay guarded in some instances by only the flimsiest of measures. Conditions in the more than forty other countries with weapons-usable materials were just as insufficient and sometimes worse.

We know that terrorists are eager to exploit these security loopholes and gain possession of nuclear material. Osama bin Laden described obtaining nuclear weapons as a "religious duty," and al Qaeda operatives met with senior Pakistani nuclear officials in August 2001. Russian officials have acknowledged that terrorists have scouted nuclear warhead facilities in their country. All told, there have been two dozen known trafficking incidents involving fissile material since 1992. Fortunately, the quantities of materials taken were quite small and not sufficient to build weapons. But our luck may someday run out, particularly if steps aren't taken to secure the "more than two hundred addresses" where Harvard's Graham Allison calculates nuclear bombs or materials are present.

Well before the attacks on the World Trade Center and Pentagon, just as the Bush administration took office, a blue-ribbon bipartisan commission headed by Lloyd Cutler and Howard Baker recommended that the United States significantly boost funding devoted to addressing this problem in Russia, lest it become a "virtual 'Home Depot'" for terrorists seeking nuclear weapons. The shelves were certainly stocked: Russia housed the equivalent of eighty thousand nuclear weapons. "Imagine if such material were successfully stolen and sold to a terrorist like Osama bin Laden," the commission warned. The United States had, in fact, been trying to secure these stockpiles since the end of the Cold War, under an effort conceived by senators Sam Nunn and Richard Lugar, and though the Clinton administration had spent approximately $1 billion annually

on such programs, Baker and Cotler recommended that that figure be tri-
pled. Terrorist acquisition of Russian weapons-usable material, the commission concluded, represented "the most urgent unmet national security
threat to the United States today."

Unfortunately, the Bush administration disagreed with that assessment. Some of the relevant programs—collectively known as cooperative
threat reduction efforts—were run by the Pentagon, and Donald Rumsfeld
had absolutely no interest in them. Cooperative threat reduction, as the
name suggests, hardly suits the conservative us-versus-them framework.
Paying our former enemy to secure its own weapons so that we will not be
threatened by them does not constitute a clear, military, zero-sum situation. Indeed, some in the administration shared the view of the effort's
congressional opponents, led by California Republican Duncan Hunter,
who believed the programs actually undermined U.S. security. The United
States was not only funding work that the Russians should pay for themselves, critics charged, but it also enabled the Kremlin to spend more on
developing new weapons for the Russian military. Moreover, they quib-
bled that certain items and facilities paid for by the United States could be
used by Russia not only to secure and dispose of older weapons but also
to preserve and enhance operational military capabilities. And in some
cases, the money was simply wasted on projects in which Moscow simply
had no interest.

Such skepticism clearly influenced the administration's initial budget
proposals, which cut Energy Department programs dedicated to threat
reduction by $100 million to $775 million, and equivalent Pentagon projects by $40 million, to $403 million. (By contrast, the administration
requested nearly a $4 *billion* boost in missile defense funding, for a total
of $8.3 billion. Rather than focusing on making it harder for terrorists to
acquire nuclear weapons, the administration was devoting its resources
to building defenses against what an intelligence community assessment had determined would be the least likely means by which a nuclear
attack would be carried out against the United States.) Still, threat reduction funding may have been given a reprieve, since one National Security
Council staffer conducting a formal review of the effort actually suggested that most of the programs be cut. Why his advice was not followed
is uncertain, but perhaps it reflected a desire by the White House to avoid

controversy, especially given that during the presidential campaign Bush had promised he would "ask the Congress to increase substantially our assistance to dismantle as many of Russia's weapons as possible, as quickly as possible."

Then came 9/11, and in its immediate aftermath the administration requested $20 billion in emergency funding for homeland security. Not a dollar of it was allotted to security upgrades for loose Russian nuclear material, even though the danger had certainly been brought to the president's attention. According to a report in the *Washington Post,* dozens of intelligence analysts had convened shortly after Bush's inaugural to ask where al Qaeda might be able to obtain a nuclear weapon. According to Richard Clarke, who, as the administration's head of counterterrorism, organized the conference, the analysts concluded that it would be most likely to exploit weaknesses in the control of the former Soviet nuclear arsenal. A subsequent National Intelligence Estimate came to a similar conclusion. "[T]he former Soviet Union, Pakistan—those were the highest risks," said Richard A. Falkenrath, a former Bush homeland security official.

Nevertheless, the Bush administration not only declined to increase funding but left the pre-9/11 cuts to cooperative threat reduction programs in its 2002 budget. Only after Congress and concerned nongovernmental organizations objected was the funding restored. For the next several years, the administration did nothing to ramp up the programs. Each year, Congress would push for a bit more funding, and although the administration would accede, the White House provided no leadership. Advocates for stronger threat reduction efforts—noting that such efforts were split among the Defense, State, and Energy departments—suggested that the president appoint a "czar" with access to the Oval Office, who could cut through the bureaucracy that often surrounded these programs and make certain the president could push them forward. But although the president has appointed czars for food safety, cybersecurity, manufacturing, AIDS, bird flu, and the Afghanistan and Iraq wars, he never agreed to coordinate threat reduction efforts from the White House.

At times, the lack of U.S. government attention to this problem has become embarrassing. When the United States wanted to spirit away enough material for two nuclear bombs from the Vinca Institute in Serbia in August 2002, a private organization footed much of the bill. Established in January 2001 by media mogul Ted Turner and Sam Nunn, the Nuclear Threat Initiative provided $5 million to help facilitate the operation, doubling the State Department's contribution of $2.5 million. At least the State Department was involved; Spencer Abraham, then head of the Energy Department, which ran programs to secure bomb material worldwide, reportedly learned of the Vinca success from newspaper accounts.

Even when the Bush administration looked as if it were taking action, it was often doing less than met the eye. For example, at a G8 summit in June 2002, the Bush administration announced the "Global Partnership Against the Spread of Weapons and Materials of Mass Destruction," under which participating nations committed to spending $20 billion on threat reduction over the next ten years, with the United States providing half of that sum. This sounded impressive but in fact only committed the Bush administration to existing funding levels—about $1 billion a year—for the next ten years. Similarly, in May 2004 the administration announced with great fanfare its "Global Threat Reduction Initiative"—a program that essentially merged previously separate efforts to retrieve U.S.-origin nuclear material from abroad, to convert reactors worldwide to run on less dangerous forms of nuclear fuel, and to help return Soviet-origin nuclear materials to Russia. To be fair, the administration ratcheted up funding for these efforts and added an initiative to identify any previously overlooked sources of nuclear or radiological materials, but benchmarks for achieving the goals extended into the next decade. When criticized for not spending more money and acting more rapidly, Bush officials insisted the slow pace was dictated more by the state of the technology and of cooperation with other states than by finances. In 2004, the administration also succeeded in winning unanimous adoption of Security Council Resolution 1540, which mandated that governments institute "appropriate effective" physical security measures and controls on their nuclear (as well as biological and chemical) materials. Unfortunately, the resolution did not define "appropriate effective," making it difficult to assess whether countries were fulfilling their obligations. That year, six hundred tons of fissile material remained unsecured at Russian sites; less material had been secured in the two years after the 9/11 attacks than in the two years before.

At times, the Bush administration has rejected the idea that such material poses a threat. As John Bolton told the *Post:* "I don't believe that at this point, or for some number of years, there's been a significant risk of a Russian nuclear weapon getting into terrorist hands. I say that in part because of all the money we've spent . . . but also because the Russians themselves are completely aware that the most likely consequence of losing control of one of their own nuclear weapons is that it will be used in Russia." This assessment flew in the face of all available evidence regarding what had and had not been accomplished in Russia. While there are no longer huge holes in security fences as there once were, only 54 percent of former Soviet facilities containing nuclear material had had security upgrades completed by the fall of 2005. Russia's stockpile of highly enriched uranium has only been reduced by 18 percent, while its stores of plutonium remain at previous levels. The United States also still has no idea how many Russian tactical nuclear weapons exist, where they are stored, or how well they are guarded. These are the weapons that nuclear experts calculate terrorists would most likely steal because their smaller size makes them easier to transport and conceal.

The Bush administration has occasionally also appeared to deliberately frustrate some threat reduction efforts. In 2002, it refused to certify that Russia was in compliance with international accords banning chemical and biological weapons, thereby blocking any new funding for threat reduction activities by the State and Defense departments. Although the Clinton administration had similar concerns about Russian activities in these areas, it chose not to block threat reduction funding because it believed Moscow was generally interested in abiding by its arms control commitments. The Bush administration (namely Bolton) also insisted on taking a tough line in negotiations with Russia on liability provisions for a 2000 agreement that committed Russia and the United States to dispose of thirty-four metric tons of plutonium apiece. Bush officials sought to absolve the U.S. government, firms, and individuals working in Russia on the project of any liability for accidents or even sabotage. The issue was not resolved until September 2006.

Why have Bush officials cared so little about loose nuclear material?

One explanation, according to Harvard researcher Matthew Bunn, is that the administration has been more focused on regimes than on weapons. Of the president's many speeches about weapons of mass destruction, Bunn observes, only one has mentioned Nunn-Lugar programs; the rest concern the nexus between regimes and terrorists. Because Russia is no longer considered an evil regime—indeed, the Bush administration has tried assiduously to fit Moscow into its "new strategic framework"—Bush officials saw little reason to focus our efforts there. As Bush told an audience in Pennsylvania during the 2004 campaign, "[W]e had to take a hard look at every place where terrorists might get those weapons and one regime stood out: the dictatorship of Saddam Hussein." Yet as nuclear expert Graham Allison has maintained, if a nuclear weapon had exploded in an American city before the Iraq war, Saddam Hussein's Iraq would not have even been among the top ten suspects. Rather, Russia and Pakistan would have topped the list, followed by states such as Ukraine and Ghana, which have highly enriched uranium in Soviet-era research reactors.

Eventually—perhaps because John Kerry made it such an issue in the 2004 campaign—the Bush administration took a few important steps to secure loose fissile material. In February 2005, for example, Bush and Putin announced that they would work to speed threat reduction efforts, and the day before the 2006 G8 summit in St. Petersburg, they announced the Global Initiative to Combat Nuclear Terrorism, which encourages nations to secure their nuclear material.

Nevertheless, in June 2005, former senator Sam Nunn said, "In measuring the adequacy of our response to today's nuclear threats—on a scale from one to ten, I would give us about a three, with the summit between Presidents Bush and Putin moving us closer to a four." In December 2005, when the 9/11 Commission issued its final report card on progress made in meeting its recommendations, it gave nonproliferation efforts a pathetic "D," a grade based entirely on the failure to move quickly enough to secure material in the former USSR. The president needed to declare this a priority, to "ride herd on the bureaucracy," the commissioners said. "The Commission called for 'a maximum effort' against this threat. Given the potential for catastrophic destruction, our current efforts fall far short of what we need to do." But there was little chance it would be otherwise. The administration was focused on other things. The weapons had never been the problem.

Iraq: Not a Nuclear Threat

In his January 2002 State of the Union address, President Bush redefined the post-9/11 threat that America faced. In the immediate aftermath of the attacks, he had directed his anger at terrorists and the states that support them, thus justifying the invasion of Afghanistan, whose ruling Taliban regime refused to root out the al Qaeda presence in its country. Now, however, Bush singled out the rogue regimes of Iran, Iraq, and North Korea, which he said were pursuing chemical, biological, and nuclear weapons: "States like these, and their terrorist allies, constitute an axis of evil, arming to threaten the peace of the world. By seeking weapons of mass destruction, these regimes pose a grave and growing danger. They could provide these arms to terrorists, giving them the means to match their hatred. They could attack our allies or attempt to blackmail the United States."

Later, this formulation would be criticized for conflating the terrorist and rogue state threats, which it did. None of these nations, for example, was thought to have particularly strong al Qaeda connections or presences; and at one point Bush seemed argue that the 9/11 attacks proved the need for his national missile defense system, even though no terrorist group could ever acquire an ICBM. But if the administration had focused on *nuclear* terrorism, then Bush's formulation would have been a useful construct. Aside from Russia and Pakistan—which, as friends, could be dealt with in a less confrontational fashion—Iran, Iraq, and North Korea were potential sources of fissile material for terrorists. Besides which, even if they didn't aid terrorists in making a nuclear weapon, the idea of Kim Jong Il, the Ayatollah Khomenei, or Saddam Hussein achieving a nuclear capability was, in and of itself, disturbing. It wasn't remarkable, then, that the president had singled out these three states. What was remarkable was that, among them, he would single out Iraq for invasion in March 2003, because by the fall of 2002 it was clear that Iraq presented the least serious nuclear threat of the three.

In the mid-1970s, the shah of Iran had declared that he wanted to initiate an atomic energy program and soon signed a deal with the German engineering firm Siemens to build a nuclear reactor in the Gulfside city of Bushehr. In 1979, however, the shah was ousted in the Iranian revolution, and the theocrats who seized power shunned scientific cooperation with the West, stymieing the country's technological development. What's more, the Ayatollah Khomenei considered nuclear weapons evil. The nuclear program stopped, only to be revived in the mid-1980s during the Iran-Iraq war, when it became clear that Iraq was pursuing nuclear weapons—an effort that was itself a response to Iran's earlier nuclear program—and when Saddam Hussein began using chemical weapons against Iranian troops.

Iran's resuscitated nuclear program, however, did not stop when the war did. Nor was it halted after U.S. and coalition forces decisively ousted Saddam's forces from Kuwait in 1991. By that time, the Iranian program had gathered its own momentum and would proceed, albeit fitfully, for the next decade. Iran's progress was speeded by China, which secretly provided it with nearly two tons of uranium ore, and by Russia, which in 1995 agreed to recommence the work on the Bushehr reactor that the Germans had abandoned after the revolution. The United States tried to discourage the Chinese and Russian assistance, but had limited success. But even more dangerous help was coming from a network of suppliers affiliated with A. Q. Khan, the so-called father of the Pakistani nuclear program, who in the 1990s arranged for Iran to purchase designs and parts for centrifuges that would enable it to enrich uranium. United States and British intelligence had been aware that Iran had been constructing secret facilities—and they were worried that Iran was pursuing nuclear weapons—but their information was limited. So they had waited.

Then, in August of 2002, just as the Bush administration was ramping up its case for war with Iraq, an Iranian opposition group publicly alleged that Iran had a secret program to enrich uranium. Early the following year, Iran's president announced that the country was seeking to master the nuclear fuel cycle, meaning it would learn to mine uranium, convert it into a form that could be used in centrifuges, enrich it, fashion it into fuel rods for reactors, and ultimately reprocess spent fuel. The same technology would enable it to make nuclear weapons. That was a far more dangerous prospect than the reactor Russia was building in Bushehr, which would be subject to IAEA safeguards and whose fuel would be supplied by Russia, so that none could be diverted to make weapons.

In February 2003, Iran finally allowed a team of IAEA inspectors to visit a deeply buried facility in the town of Natanz, which was surrounded by antiaircraft batteries. The Iranians had once claimed the facility was an agricultural research center, but now they were eager to show off their progress. Inside, the inspectors were shocked to find a pilot cascade of 160 operating centrifuges, with room for hundreds more. Especially alarming was the fact that the Iranians announced they were building a commercial plant with room for 50,000 centrifuges—capable of enriching enough uranium for twenty to thirty weapons each year.

The situation was even more disturbing in North Korea, which had also been pursuing a nuclear program for quite some time. In the 1980s, it had built a small nuclear reactor in Yongbyon with Soviet assistance, as well as a plant for reprocessing the spent fuel from the reactor into plutonium. By the early 1990s, concern had grown that Pyongyang was trying to build a plutonium bomb, and in 1993 North Korea, which was a party to the Nuclear Nonproliferation Treaty, refused to grant IAEA inspectors access to two suspicious sites. A standoff, crisis, and very nearly war ensued, as North Korea announced its attention to withdraw from the NPT. In 1994, after long negotiations—and an intervention by former president and unofficial envoy Jimmy Carter—the United States and North Korea signed the Agreed Framework. Under that deal, North Korea was to freeze all activity at Yongbyon and submit it to international inspection; in return, the United States would build it two proliferation-resistant nuclear reactors and supply it with heavy fuel oil while they were being constructed. The only problem was that U.S. intelligence estimated that, before the Yongbyon reactor was closed, it might have produced enough plutonium for one or two weapons for which they could not account.

Then in mid-2002—again, just as the Bush administration was beginning to make its case for war against Iraq—U.S. intelligence discovered that North Korea had been importing materials to start a uranium-enrichment program. This violated North Korea's obligations and indicated that it was likely still pursuing nuclear weapons. When the United States confronted Pyongyang, the North Koreans apparently admitted having an HEU program, expelled weapons inspectors from the country, withdrew from the Nuclear Nonproliferation Treaty, threatened to extract the plutonium from spent fuel it had been storing since 1994, and warned it would restart the Yongbyon reactor—a step that would enable it to produce about one weapon's worth of plutonium every year. Although it was not clear how far along the uranium-enrichment program was—a question that remains controversial—there was no doubt by early 2003 that North Korea could rapidly reprocess its spent fuel either to make nuclear weapons or to sell on the black market.

By contrast, the Iraqi nuclear program seemed to be nonexistent—it certainly was not as advanced as either its Iranian or North Korean counterparts. Although Saddam did have a substantial nuclear program at the end of the Gulf War, inspectors from the International Atomic Energy Agency had dismantled it and kept Iraq's atomic facilities under monitored lockdown. In the late 1990s, the Iraqi leader became increasingly obstructionist, and in November 1998 the inspectors left. United States and British planes subsequently bombed Iraqi weapons sites in retribution for his failure to cooperate. From that point until late 2002, Saddam did not allow further intrusive inspections. He did, however, permit small teams from the IAEA to monitor previously mined stores of uranium to ensure that they were not being used or diverted.

The departure of the inspectors, who provided a valuable on-the-ground source of information, was a great loss for U.S. intelligence, which was subsequently forced to rely more heavily on satellite data and such. Even so, American analysts were not particularly concerned about an Iraqi nuclear program. From 1998 to March 2002, every unclassified intelligence assessment released by the United States government indicated essentially that Iraq was probably continuing "low-level, theoretical research and development"—meaning that it might have been considering a nuclear program, but that it was taking few, if any, steps to reconstitute one. On February 7, 2001, when Director of Central Intelligence George Tenet presented his unclassified annual Worldwide Threat Briefing—which details concerns about all rogue states, as well as potential proliferators such as Pakistan, Russia, and China—he did not even *mention* a potential Iraqi nuclear program.

All that changed the following year, after Bush began to focus on Iraq. In his March 2002 Worldwide Threat Briefing, Tenet said: "We believe Saddam never abandoned his nuclear weapons program." Another CIA report said that "most analysts assess Iraq is reconstituting its weapons program." On August 26, Cheney announced, "[W]e now know that Saddam has resumed his efforts to acquire nuclear weapons." In his October 7 speech laying out the case against Iraq, Bush described the threat from Saddam as "unique." Using potent imagery, high-level officials such as Condoleezza Rice repeatedly claimed that, whatever the evidence or lack thereof, "we don't want the smoking gun to be a mushroom cloud." Shortly thereafter, the intelligence community released an unclassified National Intelligence Estimate, which concluded that Iraq "remains intent on acquiring" nuclear weapons, and that it could produce one between 2007 and 2009. These new estimates were dramatically more threatening than the old, even though there was little new evidence to support the change—and the evidence that did exist was highly questionable.

For example, in July 2001, a shipment of aluminum tubes was intercepted en route to Iraq. One CIA analyst—whom the *Washington Post* called "Joe"—strongly believed that Iraq intended to use the tubes as rotors in centrifuges for enriching uranium, and the Bush administration seized on that interpretation as evidence of a revived nuclear program. Although there was significant doubt among government experts as to the purpose of the tubes, in early September 2002 Bush officials leaked news of the intercepted shipment to the *New York Times,* which reported, "More than a decade after Saddam Hussein agreed to give up weapons of mass destruction, Iraq has stepped up its quest for nuclear weapons and has embarked on a worldwide hunt for materials to make an atomic bomb, Bush administration officials said today." That same morning, Cheney, Powell, Rice, and Rumsfeld appeared on the Sunday morning political talk shows to tout the news of the tubes as evidence of a reconstituted nuclear program. Bush himself cited the tubes in a September 12 address to the United Nations calling for Iraq's disarmament.

The only problem was that the government's centrifuge experts at the Department of Energy disagreed with Joe's analysis, arguing instead that the tubes were intended for artillery rockets. The intelligence community retained doubts as well, and expressed those doubts in a classified estimate of the Iraqi threat that it prepared for Congress. However, the declassified version, released on October 1, simply cited, without qualification, the tubes as evidence that Saddam "remains intent on acquiring nuclear weapons." When Senator Bob Graham—a skeptical Democrat on the Intelligence Committee who had seen the classified version—pressured the

CIA to make its qualms public, George Tenet's office released only some caveats, saying the White House had ordered him not to release more. The administration had already made up its mind. As Cheney asserted, "We do know, with absolute certainty, that he is using his procurement system to acquire the equipment he needs in order to enrich uranium to build a nuclear weapon."

Then, in January 2003, the administration introduced its second major piece of evidence. In early 2002, Cheney had received intelligence via Italy that Saddam was seeking to acquire yellowcake uranium from Niger. (Yellowcake is processed uranium ore, which must be converted to uranium hexafluoride, gasified, and enriched using centrifuges before it can be used in weapons.) The Office of the Vice President asked the CIA for more information, so the Agency sent former ambassador Joe Wilson to Niger to investigate. Wilson reported that, given the strict control over Niger's uranium mines, it was highly unlikely, if not impossible, that five hundred tons could have been diverted to Iraq. Nevertheless, the story persisted within the Bush administration and found its way into the president's January 2003 State of the Union address, in which Bush stated, "The British government has learned that Saddam Hussein recently sought significant quantities of uranium from Africa."

In November 2002, UN and IAEA inspectors were readmitted to Iraq and found no sign of a nuclear weapons program. Each piece of the administration's case soon began to crumble under their inspection. For example, the National Intelligence Estimate had cited activity at Saddam's former nuclear facilities as evidence of a renewed program. When the IAEA team visited the sites, it found no signs of nuclear activity. Jacques Baute, the head of the IAEA's inspections in Iraq, specifically investigated the twin pillars of the administration's case—the tubes and the uranium—and quickly determined that they were both false. In a few hours' research on the Internet, he determined that the documents purporting to record the uranium sale were obvious forgeries. (They used the wrong letterhead and gave the wrong date for Niger's constitution, and the foreign minister who supposedly signed one of the documents hadn't held that post for years.) A team of five centrifuge experts assured Baute that the tubes were for rockets. Baute informed the Bush administration of his conclusions and asked if there was additional material that supported its case, but the Americans and the British refused to turn over any further evidence. On

March 7, 2003, in his final report before the United States invaded, IAEA chief Mohamed ElBaradei said, "After three months of intrusive inspections, we have to date found no evidence or plausible indication of the revival of a nuclear weapons programme in Iraq."

The Bush administration, which had demeaned United Nations weapons inspections from the outset, rejected these findings. Conservatives did not trust the institution any more than they had in the 1960s, often using the same pejoratives they had used decades earlier. For example, Victor Davis Hanson, a conservative military historian admired by both Bush and Cheney, wrote that the United Nations was guided by "utopian socialism." Only pressure from Colin Powell in September 2002 had convinced Bush that the international community would be more likely to support military action if we first tried to peacefully disarm Iraq. Cheney had retorted that "a return of inspectors would provide no assurance whatsoever of [Saddam's] compliance with U.N. resolutions. On the contrary, there is a great danger that it would provide false comfort that Saddam was somehow 'back in his box.'" The conservative press, meanwhile, simply mocked inspections. George F. Will compared the congressmen who were calling for unfettered inspections to "Lord Haw Haw," a British citizen who had broadcast propaganda for Hitler, and labeled Kofi Annan Saddam's servant—likening him to Neville Chamberlain. Rich Lowry wrote in *National Review* that "the 'international community,' and many Democrats in Congress, want a return of weapons inspectors to Iraq, which is like insisting that we return to searching for needles in haystacks owned by a farmer who hates us and will do anything to obstruct our work. . . . [O]nly one new inspection process makes sense: Remove Saddam first, inspect later." Frequently, Bush officials and their conservative supporters misleadingly argued that the IAEA had given Iraq a clean bill of health just before the 1991 Gulf War, after which we learned that Saddam had been shockingly close to being able to build a bomb. Of course, the IAEA's work before the war had been limited to sites that Iraq allowed it to see, whereas from 1991 through 1998, and in 2002 and 2003, its access was nearly unlimited. In fact, the Iraq Survey Group, the team of American inspectors tasked after the invasion with ferreting out Iraq's alleged weapons of mass destruction, found that the only reason that Saddam admitted having a nuclear program in 1991 was that "aggressive UN inspections left him no choice," thus demonstrating their utility.

In sum, in the fall of 2002, the Bush administration had an ill-defined picture of a suspected program based on four-year-old data that were soon undermined by facts yielded by expert, on-the-ground inspectors. The bits of new "evidence" it had were, at best, highly disputed if not obviously wrong—and the administration knew so before it went to war. Even if one chooses to blame the administration's failures entirely on the intelligence community, the UN inspections still should have served as a circuit breaker, stopping the rush to war. There was no empirical reason to believe that Saddam had a nuclear program. Meanwhile, North Korea, a known weapons proliferator, had a nuclear program that could produce plutonium for weapons within months, and Iran, whose terrorist ties were more extensive than Iraq's, was openly trying to enrich uranium. Even knowing what we knew then, it was clear that Iraq was the member of the axis of evil that posed the least threat to the United States.

Metaphysician, Heal Thyself

But that assumes, of course, that the Bush administration could be convinced by evidence. Its distrust of the IAEA inspectors, though certainly a reflection of conservative antipathy for the United Nations, was also a function of a much broader and much deeper distrust of experts. At both an intellectual and a cultural level, conservatives have never trusted experts, with their dry data and lack of moral understanding. Social scientists, in their view, were like physicians who saw a human being as merely a collection of tissue and bone, whereas conservatives and neoconservatives were metaphysicians who valued the soul. The establishment elite at the State Department and the Central Intelligence Agency had been suspect for decades. UN experts were doubly cursed, as both scientists and representatives of world government. Just as the Bush administration represented the apotheosis of modern conservatism's nationalist and moralist attitudes, so, too, did it epitomize conservatism's rejection of empiricism. This manifested itself clearly not only in its convictions regarding Iraq's nuclear ambitions but also in its prewar insistence that Saddam Hussein had close ties to al Qaeda.

From nearly the moment the Twin Towers fell the administration was convinced that Saddam Hussein bore some responsibility for the tragedy.

Bush cornered Richard Clarke shortly after the attacks and asked him to look into a connection, and he announced at a September 17, 2001, meeting of the National Security Council: "I believe Iraq was involved, but I'm not going to strike them now. I don't have the evidence at this point." Just hours after the attack, Rumsfeld raised the possibility of strikes on Iraq, as did Paul Wolfowitz. The administration obviously wanted there to be a connection. The only problem was, there wasn't one.

In April 2001, during a high-level interagency meeting on terrorism, Clarke argued that the administration needed to focus on Osama bin Laden. Wolfowitz was visibly annoyed by the suggestion, complaining, "I just don't understand why we are beginning by talking about this one man bin Laden," whom he referred to as the "little terrorist in Afghanistan." When Clarke replied that he was the head of a network called al Qaeda that "alone poses an immediate and serious threat to the United States," Wolfowitz disagreed. "Well, there are others that do as well, at least as much. Iraqi terrorism for example." In fact, Iraq had committed no known terrorist attack against the United States since 1993, when Saddam tried to have former president George H. W. Bush killed. But Wolfowitz persisted in arguing—in what was essentially a conspiracy theory—that Saddam had been responsible for the 1993 bombing of the World Trade Center—a belief that was not supported by evidence. (Wolfowitz would later send former CIA director and fellow neoconservative James Woolsey on a mission to try to confirm this theory. He came up with nothing.)

In October 2001, just weeks after the attacks, conservatives in the Pentagon began searching for evidence to establish a link between Iraq and al Qaeda. To this end, they established an office under the purview of Douglas Feith, the undersecretary of defense for policy, to provide an alternative analysis of the available intelligence. Feith was a lawyer who had studied under Richard Pipes as an undergraduate at Harvard, bonding with him over a common desire to destroy the Soviet Union. He had then served in the Reagan administration as Richard Perle's counsel and as a deputy assistant secretary of defense. He emerged from the Cold War a member of the Reagan Victory School: "The so-called realist school said that the Soviet Union would never collapse, and that efforts to make it collapse are running the risk of instability. The Reagan, neocon view was considered lunacy. I pride myself that I was on the right side of that debate. The intellectual class was on the wrong side." This was a gross mischaracterization of the debates and their outcome—the very premise of containment, the theory of "the so-called realist school," was that the Soviet Union would ultimately collapse—but what is notable in Feith's remark is that he blames the entire "intellectual class" for subscribing to this belief.

That was the same new class critique that had underlain the Team B exercise in 1976, and, in fact, Feith and his colleagues explicitly saw their efforts as a reincarnation of that effort. In a memo dated November 26, 2001, Feith's subordinate, Assistant Secretary of Defense Peter Rodman, asked Deputy Secretary of Defense Paul Wolfowitz to "[o]btain approval of creation of a Team B," which "[t]hrough independent analysis and evaluation . . . would determine what is known about al-Qaida's worldwide terror network, its suppliers, and relationship to states and other international terrorist organizations." Wolfowitz was more than happy to approve this effort. Whereas most analysts now regard Team B as a methodologically flawed exercise that produced erroneous conclusions, Wolfowitz believed the effort had proven the limits of CIA analysis. In a 1994 paper, he argued that the Agency's methodology "allows [analysts] to conceal ignorance of facts, policy bias or any number of things that may lie behind the personal opinions that are presented as sanctified intelligence estimates."

One of the original members of this Iraq campaign was David Wurmser, a neoconservative who had long advocated Saddam's overthrow and had been working for John Bolton at the Department of State. Later, the intelligence effort run out of Feith's office would be taken over by Abram Shulsky, who (like Wolfowitz) had been a student of Leo Strauss's at the University of Chicago. In 1999, Shulsky and fellow Strauss protégé Gary Schmitt wrote an essay in which they used Strauss's maxims to critique American intelligence methods. Its conclusions reflected the Team B critique: The failure of U.S. intelligence to understand the fundamentally evil nature of rogue regimes led it to underestimate the capacity for deception. Using the social science methods of Sherman Kent, American analysts tended to impute American-like motives to their subjects—to "mirror-image"—when in fact tyrannies behaved completely differently.

Admittedly, the CIA had failed to uncover that Iraq had an advanced nuclear weapons program before the Gulf War. It had failed to predict the Indian nuclear tests in 1998. And, of course, though it had increasingly warned of al Qaeda activity, it had failed to stop the 9/11 plot. Now, as the

CIA and the rest of the intelligence community dismissed the notion of a collaborative link between Iraq and al Qaeda, there were certainly reasons to challenge its conclusions. But Feith's office went far beyond skepticism. Instead of sharply questioning the premises behind the intelligence and ensuring that faulty assumptions did not guide analysis, Feith's team simply adopted faulty assumptions of its own. Whereas the CIA did its best to be objective, Feith abandoned the notion of objectivity all together. And as had been the case with Team B, the result was flawed analysis.

The chief product of Feith's work was a briefing titled "Assessing the Relationship Between Iraq and al Qaida." It opened with a critique of the intelligence community's methodology. The CIA and other agencies, it charged, applied too rigorous a standard for evaluating whether a claim was in fact supported by the available evidence. The briefing went on to make the case for what it called a "mature, symbiotic" relationship between Saddam and the terrorist organization, citing "more than a decade of numerous contacts" between Saddam and al Qaeda and "multiple areas of cooperation," including "possible Iraqi coordination with al Qaida specifically related to 9/11." The intelligence community had found just the opposite. And when an analyst from the Defense Intelligence Agency went over the Feith material, he found significant methodological flaws. Eventually, the Pentagon's inspector general investigated the appropriateness of Feith's techniques. Feith maintains that he should have been allowed to question the findings of the intelligence community, which is absolutely true. But as the Pentagon inspector general's report points out, there is a process for that very purpose: "The first and preferred method for incorporating an alternative analysis is through the standard process of coordination. Analysts are expected to marshal their facts, build coherent arguments, and defend those arguments while coordinating with other experts across the Intelligence Community. In the vast majority of cases, analytic judgments either stand or fall on the merits of their evidentiary base, intrinsic logic, and quality. In those rare instances where analysts build a strong case, but cannot achieve consensus support for their analysis, an alternative judgment is justified."

Nevertheless, Feith's briefing was presented to Rumsfeld; to Tenet and the head of DIA; to Stephen Hadley, the deputy national security adviser; and to Scooter Libby, Cheney's chief of staff and national security adviser. Like Wolfowitz, Cheney strongly distrusted the CIA, having been the secretary of defense when the agency failed to track Saddam's nuclear program before the Gulf War. That distrust festered throughout the 1990s and apparently peaked after the September 11 attacks. As one former colleague of those in Cheney's office told journalists Franklin Foer and Spencer Ackerman, "They so believed that the CIA were wrong, they were like, 'We want to *show* these fuckers that they are wrong.'"

The disregard for the truth was not just a predilection of the administration's neoconservatives. The icon of epistemological obfuscation was Donald Rumsfeld, who, like John Bolton, had little interest in promoting democracy in the Middle East. At press briefings in the run-up to the war, when asked about the failure of UN weapons inspectors to find evidence of Iraqi WMD programs, Rumsfeld repeatedly reminded journalists that "the absence of evidence is not evidence of absence." Strictly speaking, this was a reasonable assertion, but Rumsfeld failed to acknowledge that it was absence of evidence for an extremely important proposition: namely, that Saddam presented a grave and growing threat to the United States. Worse, he and Feith seemed to believe that "absence of evidence" could be construed as evidence for their own beliefs. That is, if you are convinced that Saddam is evil and deceptive, then a lack of evidence can be interpreted as proof of his deception and therefore his evil. In science, a theory is a proposition whose veracity can be tested; it is essential that a theory be falsifiable. If it is not, then it is not a theory, but a faith-based assertion—or, as a popular quip went, a Feith-based one.

The Real Reason

In addition to its inflated claims about Iraq's nuclear program and its ties to al Qaeda, the Bush administration incessantly used the term "weapons of mass destruction" to the point where it became firmly implanted in the public consciousness. But biological and chemical weapons did not constitute an existential threat—and Iran and North Korea were thought to have active biological and chemical weapons programs as well.* Obviously,

---

*According to intelligence community estimates in late 2002—that is, during the run-up to the Iraq war—Iran had a biological weapons program as well as a stockpile of "blister, blood, choking agents and probably nerve agents and the bombs and artillery shells to deliver them." North Korea was thought to have a "sizeable stockpile" of "nerve, blister, choking and blood agents" and the weapons to deliver them, as well as an active

then, the administration was deliberately trying to make Iraq appear singularly threatening. But why?

One answer consistent with conservatives' priorities was that they considered Iraq uniquely evil. Certainly Bush called Saddam evil and spent a great deal of time focusing on his character and intentions, as opposed to his capabilities. He often noted that Saddam supported anti-Israel terrorism, had tried to assassinate former president Bush, and had openly praised the 9/11 attacks. He had invaded two of his neighbors in the past two decades. He had used chemical weapons not only against Iran in the 1980s, but against the Kurds within his own borders. As Bush said to the United Nations in September 2002, "Tens of thousands of political opponents and ordinary citizens have been subjected to arbitrary arrest and imprisonment, summary execution, and torture by beating and burning, electric shock, starvation, mutilation, and rape. Wives are tortured in front of their husbands, children in the presence of their parents—and all of these horrors concealed from the world by the apparatus of a totalitarian state."

But Iran and North Korea were hardly beacons of humanitarianism. Besides the nuclear, chemical, and biological weapons programs both countries maintained, the State Department considered Iran the world's chief "sponsor of terrorism," and North Korea was one of the world's most promiscuous proliferators of missile technology. Both countries were also grossly illiberal. North Korea was in the throes of a bizarre cult of personality, led by the son of the country's founder. Deviants from Kim Jong Il's totalitarian *juche* philosophy can be sent, along with three generations of their families, to North Korea's vast network of gulags, where they are used as slave labor and become severely malnourished, to the point of eating bark, rats, and snakes—a diet shared by much of the population during the 1990s, when Kim's economic policies left as many as 62 percent of North Koreans chronically underfed and killed between five hundred thousand and three million people. Meanwhile, up to a quarter of

---

biological weapons program. And while Iraq had only short-range Scud missiles, Iran had tested the medium-range Shahab-3 and was working on a longer-range version, the Shahab-4. North Korea had an advanced ballistic missile program that had launched the Taepodong-1 in August 1998, fueling conservative calls for missile defense.

the country's GDP goes to maintain its 1.2 million-man army, the world's fourth largest.

Even if one wanted to launch a strike specifically against a Middle Eastern nation because, as Thomas Friedman put it, "a terrorism bubble had built up over there—a bubble that posed a real threat to the open societies of the West and needed to be punctured," theocratic Iran might have made a more justifiable target than the secular government of Iraq. Although Iran is nominally a democracy, it is ruled by an unelected cadre of theocrats, and repression is a common feature of political life. Reform-minded intellectuals, democracy activists, university students, and journalists can be arrested, imprisoned, and tortured. Like Iraq, Iran used chemical weapons during their war in the 1980s, and it also relied on "human waves" to clear minefields for Iranian troops.

For conservatives, however, Iraq's evil was not simply a function of its moral horrors; it was a function of the moral compromise it had forced on America as a result of our efforts to contain it over the previous decade. Rather than decisively dealing with Saddam in 1991, we had boxed him in. But the box was riddled with holes. The northern and southern portions of the country were no-fly zones, patrolled by American fighters, but Saddam routinely took shots at them. Legally, Saddam was bound by United Nations resolutions to disarm, but he had not cooperated with inspectors since 1998. Economically, Iraq remained under sanctions that allowed it to sell nothing but oil and import nothing but food and medical supplies, but oil smuggling was netting Saddam billions. Although our policy toward North Korea and Iran was essentially one of containment as well, neither of those cases was nearly as messy. Iraq was a reminder of the moral equivocation, and the lack of psychological satisfaction, that containment—a strategy that conservatives had detested since George Kennan had written the "X" article half a century earlier—offered.

Conservatives had openly advocated Saddam's ouster in the late 1990s, through the Project for a New American Century's open letter to President Clinton and through their support for the Iraqi National Congress, an exile group. Their anti-Saddam campaign began early in the Bush administration—two weeks after taking office, Cheney released $98 million for the INC that Congress had appropriated under the Iraq Liberation Act, but that had been held up by the State Department, which questioned the group's efficacy. The overthrow of Saddam was also the topic of the first meeting of Bush's National Security Council.

September 11 gave conservatives the justification they needed to overtly abandon containment. At West Point, Bush explained: "For much of the last century, America's defense relied on the Cold War doctrines of deterrence and containment. In some cases, those strategies still apply. But new threats also require new thinking. Deterrence—the promise of massive retaliation against nations—means nothing against shadowy terrorist networks with no nation or citizens to defend. Containment is not possible when unbalanced dictators with weapons of mass destruction can deliver those weapons on missiles or secretly provide them to terrorist allies." Cheney used almost identical language: "As we face this prospect, old doctrines of security do not apply. In the days of the Cold War, we were able to manage the threat with strategies of deterrence and containment. But it's a lot tougher to deter enemies who have no country to defend. And containment is not possible when dictators obtain weapons of mass destruction and are prepared to share them with terrorists who intend to inflict catastrophic losses on the United States."

This tack was very similar to their earlier argument that mutual assured destruction did not apply in the post–Cold War world. (Though oddly, Bush was now insisting that the September 11 attacks had invalidated deterrence.) Bush, Cheney, and others failed to acknowledge that—just as they had never believed in mutual assured destruction—they had never believed in containment either. (And just as they did not actually abandon mutual assured destruction vis-à-vis Russia, they would not actually abandon containment via-à-vis Iran, North Korea, and other countries.) But Iraq gave them a chance to test a post-9/11 version of rollback. At West Point, Bush warned, "The war on terror will not be won on the defensive. We must take the battle to the enemy, disrupt his plans, and confront the worst threats before they emerge." The National Security Strategy emphasized the role that preemption would play in a post-9/11 world: "In an age where the enemies of civilization openly and actively seek the world's most destructive technologies, the United States cannot remain idle while dangers gather."

What truly made Iraq unique, then, was not only that it epitomized the failure of containment, but also that it offered the possibility of redemption through military rollback—a morally pure solution to an ugly problem. It allowed us to go on the offense rather than simply

managing a problem. It eliminated the root evil, rather than demanding some sort of coexistence with it. In some ways, then, the preferred
means of policy dictated the preferred ends of policy. If Iraq did not fit
the precepts of conservatism any more closely, it better fit the ramifications of those precepts. In short, Iraq was the most invadable member of
the axis of evil.

For one thing, it offered a far better legal case for war. Although the
Bush administration did not really care about such niceties, a "legitimate"
casus belli could attract allies, placate the American public, and ease postwar operations. Iraq had clearly violated multiple UN resolutions and as
a result was under almost full international sanctions, allowed to sell oil
only to purchase food and medical supplies. By contrast, many countries
traded with Iran, and its nuclear activity, though clandestine, did not necessarily violate its commitment under the Nonproliferation Treaty. North
Korea was more economically isolated and had actually pulled out of the
treaty, but clearly diplomacy needed to be attempted before its neighbors
would back war. (In fact, China would probably never support war, having
no desire to see U.S. troops along its border guarding a unified democratic
Korea. China had also signed a treaty in 1961 stating that it would defend
North Korea in the event of an attack.) A war against Iraq, as Bush pointed
out, could be cast as a war of enforcement, backing up the will of the international community.

Militarily, North Korea and Iran defied easy solutions. North Korea could
respond to any attack by raining three hundred thousand shells and rockets
per hour down on Seoul, South Korea's capital and one of the world's largest
cities. Those shells and rockets might well be armed with chemical weapons
(including VX, sarin, and mustard gas) or biological weapons (including
anthrax, botulism, cholera, hemorrhagic fever, plague, smallpox, typhoid,
and yellow fever). Pentagon officials estimate that the ensuing conflict
across the entire peninsula would produce at least three hundred thousand American and South Korean military casualties—to say nothing
of civilian deaths and injuries. Ultimately, we would win, but the collapse
of the North Korean regime would unleash a flow of refugees that would
destabilize China and South Korea, which would also have to absorb the
economic cost of reunification.

Military options for Iran were similarly limited. Iran's nuclear facilities
are numerous, dispersed, and in some cases located in major population

centers or deep underground. As Natanz and Arak have shown, Iran is capable of hiding nuclear facilities—even large ones. Although a strike would certainly delay Iran's nuclear program, it would probably not stop it, just as Israel's strike on the Osiraq reactor in 1981 did not stop Iraq's. In fact, air strikes would probably radicalize the Iranian public, shore up support for the regime, and reinforce the desire for nuclear weapons. And in response to the strike, Iran would attempt to raise oil prices; attack our forces in Afghanistan and Iraq; retaliate via terrorists against Israel, U.S. bases and embassies worldwide, and perhaps even the continental United States; and stir up Islamist and Shiite violence against our allies in Saudi Arabia and the Gulf.

Invasion was an even less feasible option. Iran has twice as many people as Iraq, and it's four times as large. The country is massive and mountainous, hindering the movement of U.S. troops and supply lines and providing endless opportunities for effective guerrilla warfare by Iranian paramilitaries. Besides which, in 2003, Iran's government was far better perceived worldwide than Saddam's regime, and at the time, it contained a substantial contingent of reformers. It is not clear what allies, if any, would join the United States in such an invasion—a major problem when the United States would need to position massive numbers of troops in advance.

By contrast, Iraq was a U.S. war planner's dream. Trained for generations to defeat a massive Soviet armor invasion of Eastern Europe, U.S. forces would be right at home demolishing a set-piece army on flat terrain. A decade of sanctions and no-fly zones had weakened Iraq's military, while American armed forces had steadily improved. Defeating the regime in Iraq was such a sure thing that Paul Wolfowitz fretted after 9/11 that we should invade Iraq instead of Afghanistan because *Afghanistan* might become a quagmire. Former Reagan official Ken Adelman's infamous assertion that invading Iraq and toppling Saddam Hussein would be "a cakewalk" was true—at least in the narrowest sense—and the administration knew it. After the Gulf War, it was easy for it to convince itself that the only thing standing between us and regime change was our own lack of will. As one senior administration official acknowledged to a reporter in 2004 when asked why the administration was insisting on a *diplomatic* solution to the North Korean crisis: "I admit there appears to be more than a little irony here. But Iraq was a different problem, in a different place, and we had viable military options."

Conclusion

Solace was scarce amid the immediate shock and violation of September 11, 2001. Soon we would marvel at the courage of those who had acted to save others during the confusion, the chaos, the sheer incomprehension of the day's events. Later, reassured by our own resilience, we would relax a little, recognizing that the nation had survived this calamity and that American life would go on. But while the dust of the Twin Towers was still billowing over lower Manhattan and the Pentagon still burned, we had only the cold comfort of knowing that the attack could have been worse, much worse. Osama bin Laden has called for the deaths of four million Americans. Al Qaeda has tried to acquire nuclear weapons. After 9/11, the Bush administration should have focused the entire resources of the government, the military, and the citizenry on securing every last bit of fissile material on the planet. Instead, it invaded Iraq.

The costs of the Iraq war have, of course, been enormous. By the end of 2007, 3,880 American troops had been killed and 28,000 had been wounded—many of them losing eyes or limbs, many suffering significant brain damage. An untold number of Iraqi civilians have been killed—the estimates range from 78,000 to an unimaginable 650,000. Security collapsed immediately after the invasion because the United States invaded with too few troops to secure the peace. It ignored the advice of the United Nations, which had developed significant expertise in nation building during the 1990s. It ignored the recommendations of the CIA, which emphasized the importance of immediate postattack stability and warned that occupation would make Iraq a magnet for extremists. And it ignored the findings of the State Department, which had compiled a thirteen-volume report that presciently laid out many of the consequences of invasion.

But conservatives did not trust so-called experts at places like the UN, the CIA, and State. Besides which, neoconservatives believed that the United States would not need to build democracy in Iraq, but simply unshackle it. In 2005, two years after the invasion, with Iraq edging ever closer to civil war, Feith mused about a paradox. It was possible, he said, to be an expert on a region or a culture, but to nevertheless fail to devise the appropriate strategy for interacting with it. Far wiser than such misguided experts was the president, who had "more insight, because of his knowledge of human beings and his sense of history, about the motive force, the craving for freedom." When journalist Jeffrey Goldberg pointed out to Feith that American troops had not been greeted with flowers, as many in the administration had predicted, Feith replied that Iraqis had simply been afraid of die-hard Saddam supporters. "But," he said, "they had flowers in their minds."

Rumsfeld had also dismissed the counsel of the experts around him, including army Chief of Staff General Eric Shinseki, who warned that it would take hundreds of thousands of troops to pacify Iraq, and postconflict experts, who noted that we would need between three hundred thousand and five hundred thousand troops, based on the troop-to-population ratios used to stabilize Bosnia and Kosovo. Conservatives, however, had no desire to undertake a nation-building enterprise that would entangle the United States in the affairs of a foreign people. Rumsfeld, who would later dismantle the army's Peacekeeping Institute, warned in February 2003 of the "dangerous dependency" created by nation building. Bolton agreed, saying of Iraq: "My thought was—and this is exaggerating—we hand 'em a copy of the Federalist Papers, say good luck, and then we're out of there." The so-called Rumsfeld Doctrine, which envisioned lighter and more mobile forces, was intended to enable the military not only to deploy to a crisis quickly, but also to return home with greater speed as well. It is one of the Iraq war's festering ironies that the Bush administration went to war to replace the moral ugliness of containment with the purity of victory, only to be stuck in the ugliest of quagmires.

These costs would have been justified had they enabled us to secure a dangerous nuclear program. But they did not, nor were they intended to. Had they been, it is unlikely that our invading forces would have allowed the looting of Iraq's most sensitive atomic facilities. Take, for example, the Tuwaitha complex—a sprawling site that was once the main hub of Iraq's secret nuclear program, including the Osiraq reactor. Tuwaitha contained the only known nuclear material in Iraq as of 2002: two tons of low enriched uranium, five hundred tons of natural uranium, and other radioactive materials suitable for use in a dirty bomb—all under IAEA lockdown since the 1990s. Yet the Department of Defense gave American troops no guidance on securing loose radiological materials until four months after the invasion, forcing ground commanders to make ad hoc decisions. Tuwaitha was a low enough priority that looters from a nearby village managed to break in, steal hundreds of barrels of yellowcake and other radioactive materials, empty them out, and use them for weeks to bathe, cook, and hold drinking water.

We eventually learned, via the Iraq Survey Group, what the IAEA had found before the war began: "Iraq did not possess a nuclear device, nor had it tried to reconstitute a capability to produce nuclear weapons after 1991." Had preventing a nuclear 9/11 been the president's priority, this ought to have been devastating news. Instead, the president continued to maintain that he had done the right thing, even telling ABC's Diane Sawyer that there was no difference between Saddam's actually having weapons of mass destruction and there being a possibility that he might try to acquire them at some point in the future. Bolton concurred, insisting that, knowing everything we know now, overthrowing Saddam was unquestionably the right thing to do because his nuclear scientists might have reconstituted a weapons program at some point. He was a potential threat, and as neoconservative Richard Perle and David Frum asked, how imminent did the threat have to be for us to take it seriously? The answer, of course, is that it had to be *more imminent than the other threats we faced.*

Indeed, the opportunity cost of the war has been perhaps even more significant than its direct costs. Afghanistan, for example, received but a fraction of the attention that it required after the fall of the Taliban. But it is the reduction in our leverage for dealing with Iran and North Korea that has been the most dramatic ramification of the Iraq campaign. The threat of force played a key role in resolving the last North Korean nuclear crisis in 1994. As negotiations bogged down, the Pentagon strengthened its forces in South Korea. President Clinton prepared to deploy fifty thousand troops to the region, and he considered an air strike on the Yongbyon facilities. That buildup encouraged the North to compromise. Robert Gallucci, the lead U.S. negotiator, believes the threat of force was "essential" to ending the standoff. "[The North Koreans] started looking at this, I'm pretty sure, and didn't like what they saw—and they shouldn't have, because we were actually doing things that would help us be in a better position to launch a strike."

By contrast, in the fall of 2002, the Bush administration was so fixated on going to war with Iraq that it sought to downplay the North Korean nuclear program (the president called Pyongyang's uranium efforts "a bit of troubling news") and barely discussed the Iranian one. One of the most curious side effects of minimizing the seriousness of the North

Korean situation was that the proudly hawkish Bush administration suddenly began to sound rather dovish. Just days after the uranium program became public, the president reassured Pyongyang that "the United States has no intention of invading North Korea"—a move that Gallucci called "plain dumb." But according to Bush, "This is not a military showdown; this is a diplomatic showdown."

That approach obviated any chance of coercive diplomacy—the iron-fist-velvet-glove approach that Clinton had used in North Korea and that the Bush administration itself had successfully used in Iraq: By shipping more than a hundred thousand troops to the region, Bush had forced Saddam to readmit weapons inspectors. (It is yet another irony of the Iraq war that before it was a military disaster it was a diplomatic success.) The problem was that the administration didn't believe in diplomacy. After 9/11, logic dictated that the United States do everything it could to protect itself from nuclear attack. Instead, in the thrall of a conservatism reinvigorated by a moralistic outlook on the world, the Bush administration focused on evil regimes. It prioritized those regimes not according to the threat they presented, but according to the moral cleanliness with which they could be dispatched. Iran and North Korea could not be dispatched easily, and so the threats they posed would be left to fester.

Chapter Seven

CATASTROPHE

ON A COLD DAY in February 2001, an air force colonel named Steve Hadley set up a telephone line in the private residence of the White House so that George W. Bush could call his counterpart in South Korea. It was one of a series of phone calls that the newly inaugurated president was making to reach out to American allies around the world, letting them know that whatever the change in Washington's leadership, their friendship remained important to the United States. As Bush began speaking with Kim Dae-jung, Charles L. "Jack" Pritchard, a sandy-haired, goateed former army officer, watched quietly. Pritchard had spent most of his career in the military, serving as the U.S. attaché in Tokyo and eventually becoming President Clinton's director of Asian affairs. Bush had kept him on staff as a Korea adviser, and Pritchard had written talking points for the president to use during his discussion, among them the importance of cooperating in their dealings with North Korea. But when Kim Dae-jung began to explain to Bush the necessity of engaging Pyongyang, the president—sitting, ironically, in the Treaty Room of the White House—departed from the script. Turning to Pritchard, he cupped his hand over the mouthpiece and said, "Who is this guy? I can't believe how naive he is!"

Thus began President Bush's involvement with Korea. "Moral clarity," he would later say, required that we not "gloss over the brutality of tyrants," and while he didn't know much about North Korea, he did know that it was run by a brutal tyrant. "I loathe Kim Jong Il!" Bush shouted at journalist Bob Woodward in August 2002. "I've got a visceral reaction to this guy, because he is starving his people. And I have seen intelligence of these prison camps—they're huge—that he uses to break up families, and to torture people." (A few years later, he met a man who had been imprisoned in a North Korean gulag and invited him to the White House to discuss his memoir, *The Aquariums of Pyongyang*.) He would not change his opinion of Kim Jong Il, Bush promised, "until he proves to the world that he's got a good heart." That was a tall order, so for the first crucial years of the Bush presidency, the United States avoided contact with the North.

Bush's approach contrasted sharply with the pragmatism of his predecessor. Though the Clinton team bore few illusions about the true nature of the North Korean leadership, it had nevertheless met with its representatives dozens of times and had managed to persuade the North to shut down its plutonium production in 1994 via the Agreed Framework, effectively capping its suspected nuclear arsenal. Four years later, after North Korea tested a long-range missile, Clinton wondered if that engagement had been a mistake and asked his former secretary of defense, William J. Perry, to review U.S. policy toward the nation. Perry concluded that the United States should try to negotiate an end to North Korea's nuclear and missile programs. Beginning in 1999, talks in Pyongyang, culminating in an October 2000 visit by Secretary of State Madeleine Albright, led to a moratorium on missile testing by the North and came "tantalizingly close," in the words of one American negotiator, to a formal deal under which North Korea would have stopped all missile testing and exports. Clinton himself hoped to visit the North Korean capital to sign a missile treaty, but progress stalled and time ran out on his presidency.

That had suited conservatives, who worried that Clinton, desperate for a last-minute deal to buff the postimpeachment tarnish off his presidency, would have given the North Koreans whatever they wanted. Conservatives had disparaged the Agreed Framework, for while pragmatists saw the deal as a modest price to reduce the nuclear threat to the United States—certainly less than the cost of war—conservatives lamented that a communist dictator had been allowed to blackmail the United States of America. Senator John McCain claimed that, in propping up a tyrannical regime, we were abandoning the moral clarity that had won the Cold War—we had returned instead to "appeasement." The Bush team often contrasted itself with the Clinton negotiators; conservatives, John Bolton said, would never be seen "dancing in Pyongyang" like Albright.

For this reason, Bush's North Korea policy was often dismissed as "ABC"—that is, "Anything but Clinton." But his objections to engagement ran deeper. The Bush administration, as the apotheosis of conservatism, hewed strictly to a moral absolutism. The entire purpose of pursuing military dominance—as per the National Security Strategy, missile defense, and Global Strike—was to obviate the need for détente with dictators. North Korea did not lend itself to a simple military solution, as Iraq would, but just as during the Cold War, conservatives rejected coexistence on principle. Summing up the implications of that worldview, Dick Cheney once gave what could be the administration's motto: "We don't negotiate with evil; we defeat it."

As a result, when, in October 2002, the Bush administration confronted North Korea over its apparent uranium-enrichment program—and when the Agreed Framework subsequently collapsed—it was left with few courses of action. Unable to confront the North militarily, and unwilling to bargain with it diplomatically, it was forced to resort to a policy that one official called "no carrot, no stick and no talk." The results were catastrophic. By the end of 2006, North Korea had produced enough plutonium for up to ten nuclear weapons and had even tested one. Similarly, confronted with a secret Iranian uranium-enrichment program, the United States refused to parley with Tehran, despite repeated pleas by the IAEA and members of the European Union. Instead, Bush officials pursued regime change, a long-term strategy that allowed Iran to proceed with its nuclear plans. Often frustrated by their failures, their inability to rid the world of evil, Bush officials assuaged their moral sensibilities by "calling evil by its name." Conservatives, who were fond of deriding treaties as mere pieces of paper, had actually opted for an even less forceful alternative: taunting.

Bush conservatives could justify this absurdity to themselves only because, like their Cold War equivalents, they did not regard nuclear weapons themselves as the greatest threat to the United States; evil regimes posed the true danger. North Korea was a criminal state, conservatives would remind critics calling for engagement. Nuclear weapons were merely pieces in the game we played against those regimes. (After meeting with Bush, one Seoul-based human rights organizer said, "I felt that he agreed with me in that the human rights issue was more important than the nuclear issue.") So it was that, even as it argued that North Korea and Iran should not be allowed to have uranium-enrichment capabilities, the administration prepared to sell nuclear technology to India, a state that had never signed the Nuclear Nonproliferation Treaty and was therefore not entitled to such assistance under international norms or U.S. law. More significantly, India was involved in a simmering arms competition with Pakistan, a state whose nuclear arsenal was rendered terrifying by its pockets of radical Islamism and the instability of the government itself. Providing India with nuclear technology—even for civilian use—would free resources that it could use to build its arsenal, which would prompt a similar buildup in Pakistan. But India, conservatives insisted, was a friend, and a strong India could serve as a counterweight to that old conservative hobgoblin, China. And because the Bush administration also considered Pakistan a friend, it continued to funnel tens of millions of dollars to Islamabad even after its top nuclear scientist, A. Q. Khan, was found to have been running a worldwide network of nuclear proliferators—and even after Pakistan refused to let American intelligence interview him.

All of which meant that midway through Bush's second term, North Korea was reprocessing plutonium; Iran was enriching uranium; India was eagerly awaiting an infusion of nuclear technology that could spur proliferation in South Asia; and A. Q. Khan was resting quietly under house arrest far from inconvenient questions. Which is not to say the Bush administration had no successes in halting proliferation. It did. Its successes just happened to come on those rare occasions when it abandoned everything conservatives believed in.

North Korea

Satellite photos of Earth at night reveal a black planet dotted by specks of light. The glow from cities and towns paints the coasts of Europe and blankets the United States. Africa, which remains largely undeveloped, is dark. In Asia, Japan is brightly lit; the east coast of China is booming; South Korea is radiant and, like other islands, clearly outlined. Except, of course, that South Korea is not an island. It takes a moment to realize that the dark space that separates it from the northeastern tip of China is North Korea, marked by a single dim pinprick of light: the capital city of Pyongyang.

North Korea is a dark land—literally. Power for its twenty-three million impoverished citizens is often cut off completely, with an exception made for party cadres who live in the capital. The Democratic People's

Republic of Korea, as it is officially (and euphemistically) known, is the last Stalinist regime on Earth, and in its darkness, George W. Bush saw the perfect metaphor, speaking of "the light and opportunity that comes with freedom, and the dark that comes with a regime that is oppressive." Donald Rumsfeld actually kept a copy of the satellite picture in his office. ("Except for my wife and family, that is my favorite photo," he said.) It was not surprising, then, that when South Korean president Kim Dae-jung came to Washington in March 2001, just a few weeks after his first conversation with Bush, his attempts to bring "sunshine" to the North would be met with great skepticism.

Initially, it had appeared that the Bush administration would follow up on the Clinton administration's promising but unrealized missile deal. Although the Bush team was clearly wary of the North, its more pragmatic members saw value in engagement. Richard Armitage, Colin Powell's deputy at the State Department, had published a paper in 1999 that called for a comprehensive approach that would address U.S. security concerns while offering Pyongyang the possibility of normalized relations. Because Bush himself had said that a ballistic missile attack was the greatest threat the United States faced (hence his emphasis on missile defense), it only made sense to try to eliminate a leading threat at its source. So, as President Kim arrived in Washington on March 6, 2001, Powell, who had been briefed on the missile talks by Albright and her staff, told reporters, "We do plan to engage with North Korea to pick up where President Clinton and his administration left off. Some promising elements were left on the table."

Powell, however, had spoken too soon. Conservatives had long wanted to kill the Agreed Framework, not negotiate a follow-on accord, and there were many who were willing to fight Powell on the issue. At the Department of Defense these included Donald Rumsfeld, Paul Wolfowitz, Douglas Feith, and J. D. Crouch, an assistant secretary who had long opposed arms control efforts. At the State Department John Bolton fought his more diplomacy-minded colleagues and apprised administration conservatives of the department's efforts to engage. The National Security Council's nonproliferation director, Robert G. Joseph, who had contributed to the National Institute for Public Policy's 2001 nuclear posture review, also opposed dealing with the North. He was backed in the White House by Dick Cheney and a number of vice-presidential aides. Condoleezza Rice herself was on record as opposing the Agreed Framework. Throughout

2001 and 2002, these conservatives battled the more pragmatic members of the Bush team, sabotaging their efforts at every turn. The result was an erratic policy whose ultimate direction few could fathom.

On March 7, the day after Powell had told the press Bush would talk with the North about its missiles, he was forced to retract his statement. Stepping into the hallway outside the Oval Office, where Bush was meeting with Kim, he told reporters, "There was some suggestion that imminent negotiations are about to begin—that is not the case." Powell later admitted, "I got a little far forward on my skis." Shortly thereafter, Bush invited reporters into the Oval Office and told them that he would not continue the Clinton policy. As Kim looked on, distraught, the president said that he had "some skepticism about the leader of North Korea" and that he wasn't sure the United States should trust him: "We're not certain as to whether or not [the North Koreans] are keeping all terms of all agreements." Instead, the administration announced that it would conduct a policy review.

Although the State Department participated in the review, Robert Joseph dominated it, according to Pritchard. The result was a bizarre hybrid policy that called for talks while simultaneously setting conditions to which the North Koreans were not likely to agree, much like the zero option Richard Perle had proposed during Reagan's first term. For example, while the Clinton administration had focused on nuclear and missile issues—issues that were the most important to us and that Pyongyang was willing to discuss—the Bush team also insisted that North Korea adopt "a less threatening conventional military posture," even though the commanders of U.S. forces in South Korea felt the deterrent balance on the peninsula was stable. Ominously, the review also called for "improved implementation" of the Agreed Framework, suggesting that the United States was going to ask North Korea for further concessions without offering any of its own, as well as 100 percent verification of any missile deal—an impossible metric. The review also seemed to back away from Clinton's promise that the United States harbored no "hostile intent" toward the North. Bush did promise that he would reward North Korea if it responded "affirmatively" to his "comprehensive approach," but North Korea rejected the linkage of conventional forces to the agreement as an attempt to unilaterally disarm it.

The president himself seemed to remain of two minds on the subject.

In his January 2002 State of the Union address, he labeled North Korea part of the axis of evil, calling it "a regime arming with missiles and weapons of mass destruction, while starving its citizens." But the following month, during a visit to South Korea, he called for talks with the North and promised that the United States had no intention of attacking it—a fear that had surfaced a few weeks earlier after the press reported that the Bush administration's Nuclear Posture Review called for preparations to use nuclear weapons against the North. Unfortunately, in a question and answer session with reporters, the president also called the North Korean government a "despotic regime" and repeated the line about starving its people. In April 2002, Jack Pritchard was able to convince the North that the White House, despite its rhetoric, was serious about talks. But just as the North Koreans agreed to meet, Bush backed away, announcing that, instead of the 2001 policy review ideas, he wanted to pursue a "bold approach" that dealt with all outstanding issues, including human rights, without protracted negotiations.

Whether the president was serious remains unclear, but the question soon became moot. In the fall of 2002, a new National Intelligence Estimate reported that North Korea had been importing equipment to enrich uranium. United States intelligence had suspected since the Clinton administration that North Korea might be attempting uranium enrichment, but the evidence was now far stronger: The North Koreans were cheating on their promise not to pursue nuclear weapons.*

Immediately, the administration split into two camps. Both regarded the uranium program as a serious problem, but whereas the pragmatists thought it was a problem that could be solved (not least because the program seemed to be in its infancy), Bolton, Feith, and Joseph saw an opportunity to put an end to the Agreed Framework once and for all. In early October 2002, James Kelly, the assistant secretary of state for East Asian affairs, flew to Pyongyang for the first official U.S.-North Korea talks of the Bush administration. He confronted the North Koreans with the NIE's

---

*The uranium-enrichment program did not necessarily violate the Agreed Framework itself, under which North Korea had promised to freeze its *plutonium* facilities. However, North Korea had agreed to the "denuclearization of the peninsula" in a 1992 agreement with South Korea (a treaty referenced in the Agreed Framework), and at the very least the NPT required Pyongyang to notify the IAEA of any enrichment activity. Thus, North Korea was violating the spirit and the letter of several accords.

findings, and the talks soon ended. Kelly and his entourage reported that their North Korean interlocutors had admitted to the existence of the uranium program—a charge the North Koreans later denied.

On October 27, the state-run Korean Central News Agency said that if the United States was willing to conclude a peace treaty with North Korea, North Korea "will be ready to clear the U.S. of its security concerns." But Bush was not interested in a peace agreement, notwithstanding his repeated assurances that he had no intention of attacking the North. In November, Kim Jong Il sent the president a letter saying, "If the United States recognizes our sovereignty and assures non-aggression, it is our view that we should be able to find a way to resolve the nuclear issue in compliance with the demands of a new century." Despite the direct appeal, Bush still refused to respond. Instead, to punish the North for its uranium program, the administration cut off the monthly shipments of heavy fuel oil that it was providing under the terms of the Agreed Framework.

The situation quickly deteriorated. In response to the cessation of fuel shipments, the North declared the Agreed Framework dead. On December 12, Pyongyang said that it would restart its nuclear facilities, and on New Year's Eve it expelled IAEA inspectors who had been monitoring the reactor, cooling pond, and reprocessing facility at Yongbyon since 1994. On January 10, 2003, North Korea announced that it was withdrawing from the Nuclear Nonproliferation Treaty, effective the next day. Around the same time, it began unloading spent fuel rods from the cooling pond.

By early 2003, the situation with North Korea had become a full-blown crisis, but President Bush, focused on Iraq, refused to label it as such. The danger was that if the North Koreans reprocessed those rods into plutonium, they would have enough fissile material for another six to eight nuclear weapons. (It was believed that they might already have one or two.) Even worse was the fact that while IAEA inspectors had been able to keep an eye on the material, with them gone, we would not know where any reprocessed rods were stored. Any chance to forcibly destroy them—through air strikes, say—had disappeared. When confronted with a similar situation in 1994, the Clinton administration had declared the reprocessing of plutonium a "red line," beyond which the United States would use military action. But President Bush would not establish any red lines; in fact, he went out of his way to state that he had no intention of attacking the North, insisting repeatedly that the solution to the

North Korean nuclear crisis was diplomatic, not military. There was only one problem: Despite its feints in 2001 and 2002, the Bush administration did not actually want to talk to Kim Jong Il. As the crisis mounted, Bush officials remained firm that there would be no "quid pro quo," no trading carrots for compliance.

The result was that for nineteen months, the situation was stalemated. For three months after the North admitted to the uranium program, the Bush administration simply refused to communicate with Pyongyang. In January 2003, the White House finally said it would be willing to talk, but not negotiate, with the North about how it could "meet its obligations to the international community." The Bush administration would, in other words, be willing to tell North Korea that it had transgressed, but it would not bargain. The North insisted that the crisis could be resolved through bilateral negotiations, but Bush would not consider one-on-one talks. When Armitage deviated from this line during testimony he gave to Congress on February 4—"Of course we're going to have direct talks with the North Koreans." It was just a question of when and how, he said.—Bush became furious and banned his staff from discussing the possibility of bilateral talks in public.

The administration insisted that it was declining a tête-à-tête with the North Koreans because that had been the Clinton approach to negotiating the Agreed Framework, and the Agreed Framework had clearly failed. (In truth, the United States had negotiated the Agreed Framework in close cooperation with South Korea and Japan, and the Framework had succeeded in stopping North Korea's plutonium program, which is what it had been intended to do.) But the administration's disinclination to engage in bilateral talks seemed more morally than tactically motivated. Conservatives within the administration had realized that, while they could not stop any and all talks with the North, they could prevent bilateral talks and, just as important, they could restrict the latitude given to American negotiators—again, much as Perle had done during the Reagan administration—so that little or no progress would be made.

By April, in an odd outsourcing of U.S. foreign policy, the Bush administration finally agreed to meet with the North if the Chinese chaperoned the gathering. But when American negotiators sat down with their North Korean counterparts in Beijing that month, they would state only that an improved relationship between the two countries might be possible, but

CATASTROPHE

241

that North Korea had to denuclearize first—and they were under strict instructions not to talk to the North Koreans directly. To no one's surprise, the North Koreans walked out.

Soon Russia, Japan, and South Korea agreed to join the negotiations, and when the first round of the so-called six-party talks convened in August 2003, the United States moderated its position. While it now agreed to meet with the North Koreans bilaterally—for thirty minutes—it still refused to make any concessions until North Korea had completely, irreversibly, and verifiably dismantled its nuclear program. Increasingly, despite the fact that it was North Korea that had triggered the crisis with its apparent violation of the Agreed Framework, U.S. intransigence was seen by other parties at the meeting as the cause for its escalation. Explained one high-level Chinese diplomat, "The American policy towards DPRK—this is the main problem we are facing." When the Chinese tried to negotiate a joint statement to demonstrate some progress from the talks, they found the United States unwilling even to agree to Pyongyang's insistence that U.S.–North Korea relations be based on "the intention to coexist." On December 12, Cheney rejected a draft of the joint statement, explaining, "I have been charged by the president with making sure that none of the tyrannies in the world are negotiated with."

Instead of coexistence, most Bush administration officials hoped for a policy of "strangulation" leading to "regime change." Both Rumsfeld and Cheney suggested that economic pressure might force Kim's downfall. As one Bush official told the *New York Times* in 2003, "If we could have containment that's tailored to the conditions of North Korea and not continue to throw it lifelines like we have in the past, I think it goes away." Wolfowitz argued that the regime was "teetering on the edge of economic collapse," and Bolton maintained that regime change was the "ultimate objective." Aaron Friedberg, Cheney's deputy national security adviser, nicely summed up the administration's priorities when he stated that the most dire ramification of a failed six-party process was that Kim would remain in power, apparently not realizing that the six-party process was not designed to oust Kim—and could in fact only succeed in stopping the North's nuclear program if the regime was assured of its survival.

Just as it had been during the Cold War, the evil of the regime was more important for conservatives than mitigating the danger posed by its nuclear weapons. The problem with regime change in Korea, however, was that it was a long-term solution to a short-term problem. In fact, the North Korean leadership was remarkably secure. Despite the fact that millions of people had starved because Kim Jong Il had diverted an obscene portion of his nation's income to weaponry, there was little sign that his grip on power was weakening, and there was no popular resistance to speak of. The only chance for regime change was a wholesale collapse of the country, and neither the Chinese nor the South Koreans particularly wanted that to occur; it was they, after all, who would have to deal with the resulting influx of millions of refugees. By contrast, the nuclear threat was rapidly increasing. In the spring of 2003, the North Koreans removed the eight thousand spent fuel rods from the cooling pond at Yongbyon and began extracting plutonium from them.

By September 2003, with no progress on negotiations, the North Koreans apparently began preparing a nuclear test. The administration had little choice but to act as though nothing was wrong. When questioned, Powell was blasé: "If they test, we'll take note of their test. . . . The president has already accepted the possibility that they might test. And we will say, 'Gee, that was interesting.'" Bush seemed sanguine about an increasingly aggressive and atomic Pyongyang. When a reporter asked him if he was concerned about the possibility that North Korea might have six to eight nuclear weapons, the president simply turned up his palms and shrugged. Later, trying to downplay the fact that the Bush administration had allowed North Korea to quadruple its nuclear arsenal, Bolton said, "This is quibbling, to say they had two plutonium-based weapons and now they have seven. The uranium enrichment capability gives them the ability to produce an unlimited number." In fact it was not quibbling. Having an extra half dozen weapons gave North Korea the freedom to use a few—or even sell a few—and still maintain an arsenal. The uranium program, by contrast, was years away from producing any fissile material.

The Bush administration's nonchalance was shocking—particularly given that it had just invaded another country on the basis of its suspected nuclear program. When confronted with the fact that it was doing almost nothing while a rogue nation churned out A-bombs, the administration would point to the May 2003 Proliferation Security Initiative, a loose affiliation of nations it had established to coordinate efforts to interdict shipments of unconventional weapons and related materials. PSI was a sound idea, but it did not give states any powers they did not already have (several countries had performed interdictions in the past), nor did it obligate its members to do anything specific. The voluntary enforcement of already existing laws does not exactly constitute a robust counterproliferation policy. PSI not only did nothing to stop North Korea from continuing to manufacture nuclear material, but the initiative could not even guarantee that it could prevent such material from being shipped abroad. It takes only a grapefruit-size ball of plutonium to make a bomb, and neither China nor South Korea had agreed to participate in the program.

In 2004, calls for bilateral talks grew stronger. The North Koreans themselves insisted that this was the only way to deal with the problem, but despite the increasing size of their nuclear arsenal and the utter lack of progress otherwise, the Bush administration continued to insist on the six-party format. Increasingly, it cited the importance of China, an odd strategic decision that raised Beijing's status in the region while lowering Washington's. Finally, in June 2004, under pressure from its allies—and from John Kerry's presidential campaign—it made North Korea an offer in which Russia, South Korea, China, and Japan would resume fuel oil shipments to the North if it provided an accounting of all its nuclear facilities, after which the United States would consider drafting security assurances and would discuss lifting sanctions and addressing the North's energy needs. By that time, however, the North Koreans had apparently decided to see how the presidential election turned out.

Bush's second term did not begin auspiciously. Although the president appointed Christopher Hill—a career foreign service officer who had helped Richard Holbrooke hammer out the Dayton Peace Accords—as his chief North Korea negotiator, suggesting a shift toward diplomacy, he and Rice continued to rail about the evil of Kim Jong Il. In January 2005, at Senate hearings to confirm her appointment as secretary of state, Rice listed North Korea as one of the world's six "outposts of tyranny." On April 28, while Hill was abroad on one of his first official trips as Bush's Asian envoy, the president undermined him by going out of his way to insult the North Korean leader: "Kim Jong Il is a dangerous person," he said at one press conference, apropos of nothing. "He's a man who starves his people. He's got huge concentration camps. And . . . there is concern about his capacity to deliver a nuclear weapon. We don't know if he can or not, but I think it's best, when you're dealing with a tyrant like Kim Jong Il, to assume he can." (The president would later consider it a concession when he referred to him as "Mr. Kim" instead of "the tyrant.")

Hill nevertheless made progress—but only by evading the administration's mandate against bilateral engagement. Rice was well aware that the North Koreans wanted to sit down individually with the Americans but was adamant that bilateral talks take place only as a quid pro quo for some sort of North Korean concession. Perversely, the Bush administration was offering negotiations in exchange for changed behavior, rather than using negotiations to change behavior; they had reversed the standard cause and effect of diplomacy. Hill, however, managed to get the North Koreans to come back to the six-party talks by arranging a dinner in Beijing between him and his counterpart, hosted by the Chinese. When the Chinese hosts mysteriously failed to show up, Hill went ahead with the dinner, and the North Koreans, satisfied with this de facto bilateral sit-down, announced that they would return to negotiations. But as Hill extended his negotiating authority to its limit, nearing a deal with the North, conservatives were again plotting to scuttle negotiations.

On September 19, 2005, the six-party talks reached a breakthrough, with all countries committing to "the verifiable denuclearization of the Korean Peninsula in a peaceful manner." The chief sticking point had been North Korea's insistence that it was entitled to receive light-water reactors in return for disarming, which had been one of the provisions of the 1994 Agreed Framework. When the United States was understandably reluctant to accept this, the Chinese brokered a compromise statement, which observed that North Korea "stated that it has the right to peaceful uses of nuclear energy" and that the "other parties expressed their respect" and would discuss the reactor request "at an appropriate time." However, the following day the White House forced Hill to read a hard-line statement written by administration conservatives defining the "appropriate time" for discussion as being after North Korea had disarmed. Meanwhile, the Treasury Department announced that it was imposing sanctions on Banco Delta Asia, a Macau-based financial institution, for allegedly laundering North Korean funds. Upset by the U.S. statement and the sanctions, the North Koreans refused to talk to the United States for the next fifteen months.*

---

*The Treasury Department announced the new sanctions on September 15, 2005, in the Federal Register. However, the North Korean leadership—along with most Americans—did not realize this had been done until several days later.

By 2006, Congress was so frustrated that, in a move reminiscent of its 1983 call for adult supervision of Reagan's arms control policies, it demanded that the Bush administration appoint a North Korea policy coordinator to "provide policy direction for negotiations with North Korea relating to nuclear weapons, ballistic missiles, and other security matters" and to "provide leadership for United States participation in Six Party Talks on the denuclearization of the Korean peninsula." The White House ignored it.

Iran

The Bush administration's approach to Iran followed a similar pattern. The United States and Iran had not had diplomatic relations since the 1979 hostage crisis, during which revolutionary forces had held 52 Americans for 444 days. The episode had demoralized America, effectively ended the Carter presidency, and led the United States to supply arms to Iraq, which would invade Iran in 1980. In the intervening quarter century, little had improved. For years, U.S. intelligence had suspected that Iran was pursuing a nuclear weapons program, but it had lacked hard evidence. In late 2002 and early 2003, however, following the discovery of nuclear facilities in Natanz and Arak, it was clear that Iran had been deceiving the international community for nearly two decades, illegally hiding its efforts from the IAEA. Iran claimed that it only wanted to produce nuclear fuel for power reactors, as it was entitled to under the Nonproliferation Treaty, but its secrecy—combined with the fact that its abundant oil and gas reserves made nuclear power seem an economically questionable source of energy—left few analysts convinced.

In late 2001, the United States and Iran had briefly cooperated. Iran had immediately expressed its condolences after the September 11 attacks, and as the United States invaded Afghanistan, Tehran offered its support, agreeing to assist search-and-rescue missions should American pilots be shot down, providing information on the Taliban and introductions to the Northern Alliance, and even detaining Afghan warlord Gulbuddin Hekmatyar in Tehran. This assistance was born less of altruism than of Iran's long-standing conflict with the Taliban, but it was useful nonetheless. At the Bonn Conference, held in the winter of 2001 to establish postwar Afghanistan's government, Iran provided what Western diplomats later called crucial support, convincing the Northern Alliance to share power with other Afghan political factions. Colin Powell met briefly with the Iranian foreign minister at the UN General Assembly in November 2001. And the U.S. and Iranian navies even began cooperating to intercept Iraqi oil being smuggled out of the Persian Gulf. It seemed increasingly possible that the relationship could be normalized—the Iranians specifically said that they were willing to talk unconditionally, with the hope of reversing a quarter century of hostility— so in late 2001, under the direction of Richard Haass, the State Department's policy planning staff began formulating a plan to engage Iran.

Conservatives, however, were not interested in engaging Iran; on the contrary, they had wanted to overthrow its government for years. In 1995, for example, then–Speaker of the House Newt Gingrich sought $18 million to fund regime change in Iran. After September 11, a small number of conservatives believed that Bush should invade Iran before Iraq. For example, Michael Ledeen, a fellow at the American Enterprise Institute and a frequent contributor to *National Review,* wrote, "We should liberate Iran first—now. . . . Faster please, opportunity is knocking at our door." Eliot Cohen—a prominent neoconservative thinker who would later join the Bush administration—observed, "The overthrow of the first theocratic revolutionary Muslim state [Iran] and its replacement by a moderate or secular government would be no less important a victory in this war than the annihilation of bin Laden." Within the Bush administration, just as on North Korea policy, officials who wanted to engage Tehran, such as Powell and Haass, were outnumbered by conservatives—at the Pentagon, the National Security Council, the vice president's office, and John Bolton's office at the State Department—who wanted regime change and who undermined efforts of their more pragmatic colleagues. In late 2001, for example, Flynt Leverett, a Middle East expert on Bush's National Security Council, drafted a National Security Presidential Directive that would have allowed for engagement with Iran. But the Pentagon and the Office of the Vice President had Douglas Feith draft an opposing directive, resulting in bureaucratic stalemate and thus no engagement.

Proengagement forces within the administration faced a severe setback on January 3, 2002, when the Israeli military interdicted a shipment of weapons on the *Karine A,* apparently supplied by Iran and destined for the Palestinian territories via Hezbollah. Three and a half weeks later, in his State of the Union address, President Bush effectively shut the door on negotiations by naming Iran, along with Iraq and North Korea, as part of the "axis of evil." Given Iran's recent cooperation on Afghanistan, the insult came as a shock to Tehran, but as Bush later explained, when Bob Woodward asked him about Iran's inclusion in the speech: "It is very important for the American president at this point in history to speak very clearly about the evils the world faces. . . . I believe the United States is *the* beacon for freedom in the world. And I believe we have a responsibility to promote freedom that is as solemn as the responsibility is to protecting the American people, because the two go hand-in-hand."

The Bush administration soon began speaking more openly of spurring Iranian regime change using internal pressure. As Rumsfeld said: "[T]he thought that [the Iranian people] should be under the thumb of the extremists that govern that country is just a crime. . . . I think that it is not beyond the possibility that the Iranian people could throw off that regime." It simultaneously made it clear that it was against any sort of rapprochement: In April 2002, Rice observed, "The problem with Iran is that its policies unfortunately belie the notion that engagement with it has helped." In July, President Bush issued a strong statement of support for prodemocracy, antiregime forces in Iran—the first time the White House had publicly done so—leading then-president Mohammed Khatami to denounce him as a "war-monger." So later that year, when news of Iran's secret uranium-enrichment activities began to emerge, the Bush team had no interest in negotiating a halt to them. On October 30, 2002, Mohamed ElBaradei met with President Bush in the Oval Office and told him that the Iranians wanted to meet with the Americans to discuss their nuclear program. ElBaradei offered to help set up talks and even to keep them low profile, but Bush brushed him off. His goal, as he would later tell British prime minister Tony Blair, was to "free Iran."

A more shocking refusal to engage came the following spring. On May 4, 2003, just twenty-two days after the fall of Baghdad, Tim Guldimann, the Swiss ambassador to Tehran, faxed the State Department a two-page document labeled "Roadmap." Because the United States does not have formal diplomatic relations with Iran, Guldimann has sometimes served as a conduit for important communications. The Roadmap was precisely that—a proposal from the Iranian government outlining the terms of a possible "grand bargain" under which Iran would fully cooperate with the IAEA concerning its nuclear program, forsake its support for terrorism, and recognize Israel's right to exist. In return, it sought the normalization of relations, including a promise that the United States would not attempt regime change. Guldimann reported that he had spoken at length with Sadegh Kharazi, Iran's ambassador to France, who ascertained that the proposal had been vetted by his uncle, Foreign Minister Kamal Kharazi; by President Khatami; and by his father-in-law, Iran's supreme religious leader, Ayatollah Ali Khamenei.

It was a remarkable offer, but the administration wanted no part of it. In fact, after discussions between Bush, Cheney, Rumsfeld, and Powell, the White House had the State Department reprimand Guldimann, informing him that he had exceeded his mandate, and filed a complaint with the Swiss government. As Bolton later explained to the *Washington Post*, "We're not interested in any grand bargain." In mid-2003, conservatives were confident that they did not need to negotiate with Iran. Having invaded Iraq and captured Baghdad in only twenty days, the U.S. military seemed unstoppable. American power in the region was at a high, while Iran's seemed to be waning. Oil prices were falling, and domestic unrest was roiling Tehran. Bush conservatives thought that the regime was about to collapse—and they were looking to give it a push.

That same month, via a secret diplomatic channel in Geneva, Iran offered to trade information on al Qaeda terrorists that it had captured for information on representatives of an anti-Iranian terrorist group, the Mujahedin-e-Khalq, that U.S. forces had captured in Iraq. The White House again refused, with Rumsfeld and Cheney arguing that the MEK, which they hoped would overthrow the Iranian regime, was not actually a terrorist organization, even though the State Department officially considered it one. Feith went so far as to send two of his subordinates to Rome to meet with members of the MEK and an intermediary, Manucher Ghorbanifar, the notorious arms dealer who served as a middle man in the Iran-contra affair.* In essence, Bush conservatives hoped to use the

---

*One of the subordinates was Larry Franklin, who was later charged with inappropriately sharing a classified policy document on Iran with the American Israel Public Affairs Committee, a right-wing, pro-Israel lobbying group based in Washington. Franklin was convicted and sentenced to twelve and a half years in prison.

MEK as a vanguard for regime change, much as they had planned to use Ahmed Chalabi and the Iraqi National Congress in Iraq. (The fact that that scheme had not worked either before or after the U.S. invasion did not appear to faze them.) It was a moral as well as a tactical calculation; according to Leverett, after September 11, White House officials, fielding offers of assistance from countries like Iran and Syria, had decided that while they would accept help, they would not offer anything in return and would not try to build nascent cooperation into a more formal relationship.

Then, on May 12, 2003, all hopes for engagement were scuttled when terrorists assaulted several foreign-worker compounds in Riyadh, Saudi Arabia, killing thirty-five. Despite a lack of evidence, Rumsfeld and Cheney claimed that Iran had been involved through its alleged support for al Qaeda. Bush shut down the Geneva channel. As of the summer of 2003, we were not talking with Iran at all.

Bush explained to Tony Blair that there could be could be no quid pro quo on the nuclear issue: "There has to be no ambiguity, and no rewards unless there is complete dismantlement." Instead, the United States wanted to immediately refer Iran to the UN Security Council for sanctions. In the interim, Iran's attempts to enrich uranium continued unimpeded—until the Europeans stepped in. In the fall of 2003, France, Germany, and the United Kingdom convinced Iran to suspend its enrichment activities, cooperate with the IAEA, and permit intrusive inspections. Rather than welcome this progress, the United States continued to push to have Iran referred to the Security Council for violating its safeguard agreements. Bolton and other conservatives mocked efforts at engagement. "How many IAEA meetings does it take to screw in a lightbulb?" he quipped.

In January 2004, ElBaradei met with Colin Powell, again asking the United States to take a serious role in negotiations, but Powell demurred. The IAEA and the Europeans believed that U.S. participation in the talks was essential, in part because Iran wanted assurances that the United States would not attack it and in part because Iran knew the Europeans would require American approval to make good on any incentives they offered, such as accession to the World Trade Organization. At one point during the negotiations, as British diplomat John Sawers was trying to convince the Iranian delegation to abandon uranium conversion, a senior Iranian diplomat told him: "Look, John, that's what we are saving up for

negotiating with the Americans. We can't spend all our possible concessions in negotiating with you. We'll have nothing left." As the Europeans
struggled—at one point winning more specific concessions, only to have the
Iranians balk in their implementation—the Bush administration just watched
from the sidelines. As it had outsourced a large portion of North Korea policy
to China, so it was "leaving the driving to the EU," as Bolton later wrote.

If the administration's approach had been part of an effort to encourage Iranian compliance with negotiations, it might have made some
sense—part of a good cop–bad cop strategy designed to elicit maximum
conciliation from Tehran. But the Bush team had no intention of becoming involved with the negotiations. Asked at a London seminar what he
thought of the EU's carrot-and-stick approach to the Iranian nuclear program, Bolton said, "I don't do carrots." The problem was that the administration didn't really do sticks, either. Although the Bush administration
repeatedly made it clear that "all options were on the table," it never explicitly threatened military action or established red lines beyond which it
would force Iran to pay some explicit price. Absent coercion or diplomacy,
the Bush administration's strategy was essentially one of hope—hope that
the Iranian regime would collapse, yielding morally pure victory. Unfortunately, just as with North Korea, dramatic change was unlikely; not only
was the regime relatively stable, but Iranian reformers appeared committed to the nuclear program as well.

It was not until its second term that the Bush administration agreed to
support the EU's diplomatic efforts with Iran. But throughout 2005, it still
refused to actually participate in the negotiations, even in a multilateral
setting. In fact, despite its professed backing, it was not clear that the Bush
administration really wanted a diplomatic resolution. In January, when
Senator Joseph Biden asked Condoleezza Rice whether she would accept a
verifiable deal that got rid of Iran's nuclear and ballistic missile programs,
she demurred: "Oh, I think we would have to say that the relationship
with Iran has more components than the nuclear side." What components
could possibly be more important than nuclear weapons issues? According
to Rice, human rights—that is, the moral character of the Iranian regime.
The administration's problem was still the regime, not the weapons.

Unfortunately, the regime was only gaining strength, and by 2005 it
had become all too clear that the United States was tied down in Iraq. The
country was on the verge of civil war and the U.S. military was strain-

ing to keep enough troops and matériel in theater. Meanwhile, oil prices had surged, strengthening Tehran's grip on the country. Finally, in June, radical hard-liner Mahmoud Ahmadinejad defeated pragmatist Akbar Hashemi Rafsanjani, becoming president of Iran that August—the same month Iran resumed uranium conversion and talks with the Europeans broke down.

Libya

Even as it failed with Iran and North Korea, the administration scored one stand-out success: On December 19, 2003, the Libyan government announced that, after negotiations with the United States and the United Kingdom, it was giving up its unconventional weapons and ballistic missile programs. Thousands of centrifuge components were loaded onto ships and taken from Tripoli to the Oak Ridge National Laboratory in Tennessee. It was subsequently determined that the Libyan nuclear program had made little progress—it had enriched no uranium, and it was not clear that Libyan scientists had the technical know-how to erect and run a centrifuge cascade—but the accomplishment was significant nevertheless. In a war on terrorism that had few public successes, it was gratifying to see Libya's nuclear equipment stored in a U.S. warehouse and feel that the world had become a bit safer.

The Bush administration seized on Libya's denuclearization as proof that its approach to nonproliferation and to rogue states—indeed, its entire worldview—was correct. It reasoned that, because Libyan leader Muammar Qaddafi had approached the United States to discuss his weapons programs immediately before the American invasion of Iraq, he had been "scared straight." This was a useful, if wishful, interpretation. By December 2003, it had become clear that, even if there were illicit arms programs in Iraq, they were not nearly as threatening as the administration had insisted they were. If, however, the war had intimidated Libya into disarming, Bush would have a retroactive justification for an invasion whose original rationale had become increasingly dubious. Just as important, the Libya case seemed to prove that conservatives could solve rogue state problems in a morally pure but nonmilitary way—that they did not have to settle for containment or for the distasteful quid pro quo that had characterized deals like Clinton's 1994 Agreed Framework with North Korea. They could simply demand disarmament.

The only problem with this interpretation of events was that it was not true. The United States had had a tempestuous relationship with Qaddafi ever since he seized control of the country in 1969. It had been friendly with the Libyan monarchy he deposed—there was even an American base outside Tripoli—and Qaddafi's radical foreign policy, which relied on terrorism as a tool of statecraft, forced a sharp break. In the 1980s, the Reagan administration increasingly tightened economic sanctions and fought military skirmishes with Libyan forces, trying not only to stop the regime's support for terrorism but to hasten its collapse. That did not happen; indeed, Reagan's 1986 air strikes on Tripoli—launched in retaliation for the Libyan-backed terrorist bombing of a West Berlin nightclub that killed two U.S. soldiers—apparently strengthened Qaddafi's grip on power. But after two Libyan intelligence agents were indicted for the bombing of Pan Am flight 103 over Lockerbie, Scotland (which had killed 270 people, including 189 Americans), President George H. W. Bush won multilateral support for tougher international sanctions that effectively cut Libya off from the rest of the world. The United Nations hoped to compel Libya to turn over the agents it believed responsible for the bombing and to compensate the families of the victims.

By the late 1990s, the situation was stalemated. Libya refused to let the bombing suspects be tried in the United States or the United Kingdom, and no one would lift sanctions until the suspects faced a court and the victims' families were paid. The Clinton and Blair administrations accordingly proposed a compromise that allowed for the suspects to be tried in the Netherlands. Qaddafi agreed, on the condition that the trial not be used to delegitimize his rule. To reassure him, UN Secretary-General Kofi Annan sent him a letter pledging that the trial would focus only on the two Libyan officials involved and would not attempt to "undermine" his regime. In 1999, the U.S. and British governments began negotiations with the Libyans, with the aim of normalizing relations and lifting all remaining sanctions. After years of sanctions, the Libyans were eager for a deal. According to Martin Indyk, Clinton's lead negotiator, "Libya's representatives were ready to put everything on the table."

When the Bush administration entered office, it was startled to discover how far negotiations toward normalization had progressed and did not pursue them until after the September 11 attacks, when Qaddafi expressed sympathy and offered to help the United States any way he could, including fingering possible suspects. The first Bush administration meeting with the Libyans, conducted by Assistant Secretary of State William Burns, was held on October 3, 2001. In August 2002, Qaddafi approached the British and offered to discuss his WMD programs. Blair agreed to the proposal and mentioned it to Bush in September when the two met at Camp David. Bush approved the idea, and Blair wrote to Qaddafi in October 2002 suggesting that a dialogue begin in which abandonment of WMD programs could lead to normalization of relations with the United States.

Libya did not respond until March 2003, when it was clear that U.S. and British military might was going to be unleashed against Iraq. While Bush saw Libya's response as proof that his Iraq strategy was a "game changer," Cheney was still leery of setting a precedent: "You don't want to reward bad behavior," he warned. A decision was made to go forward with the talks but to keep John Bolton and conservatives at the Pentagon in the dark so that administration conservatives could not sabotage a potential deal. The CIA and its British counterpart, MI6, spearheaded the secret negotiations. While acknowledging that they had a chemical weapons program, the Libyans initially denied having a nuclear program, and it was only after German and Italian authorities helped interdict a shipment of centrifuge components bound for Libya aboard the *BBC China* in October that the Libyans conceded its existence.*

Things moved quickly from there, and when Libya announced it was abandoning its WMD programs, the Bush team credited its muscular foreign policy. Cheney said, "President Bush does not deal in empty threats

---

*Conservatives say the Proliferation Security Initiative—a Bush administration initiative—was crucial in solving the Libyan problem. But for one thing, PSI is a fairly nonideological program (though it has the characteristic Bush refusal to make its arrangement legally binding); it thus says nothing about the utility of conservatism in nonproliferation. More important, PSI was not responsible for the *BBC China* interception. Although many officials, including Rice and Bolton, have claimed otherwise, the fact is that other governments were involved in the interdiction, and then–Assistant Secretary of State John Wolf told the magazine *Arms Control Today* that it was not a PSI operation but the result of other ongoing activities.

and half measures, and his determination has sent a clear message. Just
five days after Saddam was captured, the government of Libya agreed to
abandon its nuclear weapons program and turn the materials over to the
United States." In fact, the Bush administration claimed that the Libyans had essentially surrendered and that there had been no negotiation
involved. As one Bush administration conservative told the *Washington
Post,* "It's 'engagement' like we engaged the Japanese on the deck of the
Missouri in Tokyo Bay in 1945. The only engagement with Libya was the
terms of its surrender." A top Bush arms control official contended that no
rewards were offered or promises made, insisting that Washington pledged
"only that Libya's good faith, if shown, would be reciprocated."

But several factors belie the contention that Libya suddenly capitulated
with no negotiations or assurances. For one thing, Libya had been trying to
work its way back into the international community's good graces for some
time—hence its eager participation in the negotiations over the Lockerbie
bombing. In fact, Libya had even offered to put its chemical weapons program on the table in the 1990s, but the Clinton team had demurred, deciding
to save weapons issues for a later stage in the negotiations. In 1999, Qaddafi
had also expelled Abu Nidal's terrorist group from Libya and pledged his support for Clinton's efforts in the Israel-Palestinian peace process—a dramatic
shift from his stance in the 1970s and 1980s. Moreover, back-and-forth negotiation had clearly been involved. According to Flynt Leverett, who worked
on Bush's Libya policy, there was an "explicit quid pro quo" providing that,
if Libya accepted responsibility for the Lockerbie bombing and paid off the
families, UN sanctions would be lifted. That sort of reciprocity underlay the
weapons negotiations as well; according to Leverett the quid pro quo in this
instance was that U.S. sanctions would be dropped in exchange for Libya's
disarmament. Qaddafi's son Saif has said that the United States and Britain
also promised his father they would not try to oust him.

The evidence indicates that Qaddafi had been rethinking his nuclear
program and hoping to improve relations with the international community long before the Iraq war. Even if the war was a significant factor in
forcing Libyan denuclearization, it does not validate either the war itself
or the president's "strategy" for dealing with nuclear proliferation more
generally. It is silly to invade one country that does not have a nuclear program to demonstrate to another nation what you might do to it if it doesn't
behave. Wars are expensive and bloody things; they are not signals to be

sent lightly. If Libya was a more serious problem than Iraq, then we should have invaded Libya.

But the key point is that, whatever the role of force in making Libya give up its WMD ambitions, it was *only after guarantees against regime change and for a quid pro quo that the deal worked*. In fact, the British felt the deal was jeopardized when John Bolton—who had written that Clinton's 1999 pledge not to undermine Qaddafi was "appeasement"—wanted to push Libya harder, believing the goal of U.S. policy should be regime change. Fortunately, according to *Newsweek*, high-level British officials intervened, asking the State Department to ensure that Bolton was removed from the decision-making process and reassuring Muammar Qaddafi that policy change, not regime change, was the goal.* Left unchecked, the administration's ideological impulses would have scuttled the negotiations. In other words, for its Libya policy to bear fruit, the administration had to give up its notion that dealing with an evil regime was anathema; it had to accept coexistence even though Qaddafi continued to violate human rights. Libya is thus the exception that proves the rule.

India

The Bush administration's rollback of Libya's nuclear program was offset by its encouragement of India's. On July 18, 2005—reversing nearly three decades of U.S. policy—President Bush announced that his administration would "work to achieve full civil nuclear energy cooperation with India." The two governments completed negotiations on a deal by which the United States would provide India with nuclear fuel, reactor technology, and dual-use goods (items with both civilian and military applications) that had previously been off limits to the world's largest democracy because of its unsanctioned nuclear weapons program.

After India had refused to sign the Nuclear Nonproliferation Treaty in 1968, calling it discriminatory, it continued its program of nuclear research,

---

*Bolton gives a somewhat different version of the episode: "What had happened, though—at the time of the *BBC China* seizure—was I said, 'Let's make it [the seizure] public. This is a great example of PSI at work.' And the British at that time feared that if we made that public, it would queer the negotiations with Libya. Which, frankly, at that time was fine with me because I wanted regime change. So that's where the dispute was."

using a reactor it had purchased from Canada and U.S.-supplied heavy water (a hydrogen isotope used to control nuclear reactions)—both of which had been supplied on the explicit condition that they be used only for peaceful purposes. Also, in 1974, it had exploded a not-so-peaceful nuclear device. Washington, angered by India's deception, soon passed laws to ensure that U.S. atomic technology would never again be abused in such a fashion. It also established an international cartel, called the Nuclear Suppliers Group, to encourage other states to similarly restrict their exports. These steps did not stop the Indian program, however, and in 1998, it conducted a series of nuclear tests, violating the norm against proliferation that the NPT had established, as well as a norm against nuclear testing recently codified in the 1996 Comprehensive Test Ban Treaty. The United States sanctioned India and backed a UN resolution demanding that it abandon its nuclear program.

Given that context, it was shocking that the Bush administration would renew Indian access to nuclear technology. Not only would the deal argu-ably violate U.S. commitments under the NPT, but it would also require changing U.S. laws and Nuclear Suppliers Group restrictions that the United States had written specifically to constrain India's atomic activi-ties. While it is true that the Bush administration was not proposing to aid India's nuclear *weapons* program, the proposed deal could not help but have that effect. Almost three decades as a nuclear pariah, during which it had been cut off from foreign suppliers, had taken a toll on India's nuclear activities. Most important, India had a limited supply of uranium, which had constrained both its civilian and its nuclear programs. Foreign nuclear trade would free domestic uranium to be used solely for its weapons pro-gram, potentially enabling New Delhi to more than double its annual pro-duction of nuclear warheads. And if India built more nuclear weapons, it was likely that its chief enemy, Pakistan—nuclear-armed, jihadist-riddled, and politically unstable—would do the same.

Encouraging Pakistan to expand its nuclear program is serious busi-ness, given that experts consider it one of the most likely sources for ter-rorists to acquire fissile material. But Nicholas Burns, undersecretary of state for political affairs, explained to the Senate that the administration wanted to "transform relations with India . . . founded upon a strategic vision that transcends even today's most pressing security concerns." In other words, anyone worried about the proliferation impact of the deal was missing the forest for the trees. India, after all, was the world's largest democracy, with a growing and rapidly modernizing economy. Like the United States, it feared Islamic radicalism, in India's case because of its experience fighting jihadists in Kashmir. Rumsfeld and others also saw U.S.-India ties as a way to constrain China, long a strategic rival of both countries. The alliance, Bush officials said, was a natural one.

What they never explained, however, was why, if India naturally shared our interests, we had to bribe it to cooperate with us. Moreover, if we were to go to war tomorrow with China over, say, Taiwan, what benefit would accrue from an alliance with India (an alliance, by the way, that this deal does not formally establish)? Perhaps thirty years from now, a strengthened and allied India could be a valuable counterweight to Chinese power (assuming that India remains an ally and China remains a rival), but how does that long-term potential benefit outweigh the short-term cost to the nonproliferation regime?

Such questions don't seem to bother most Bush officials. Robert D. Blackwill, once Bush's ambassador to India and a chief architect of the deal, wrote that the administration decided to "stop hectoring India about its nuclear weapons" and that he took it upon himself to tune out the "nagging nannies" in the State Department who were concerned about nonproliferation.* Proliferation among friends had never bothered conservatives, which was why they had opposed the Nonproliferation Treaty in the first place—because it prevented us from giving nuclear weapons to West Germany. Now the Bush administration was declaring that the deal was a reward for India's good global citizenship. "We treat India, a democratic, peaceful friend, differently than we treat Iran and North Korea, and we're happy to say that," Burns explained. "If that's a system of double standards, we're very proud to establish that double standard on behalf of a democratic friend." *National Review* agreed, calling the deal a "diplomatic triumph" and arguing that critics needed to learn to discriminate between friendly nations and enemies. Prominent neoconservative Robert Kagan acknowledged that the nuclear deal "no doubt" had damaged the nuclear nonproliferation regime, but he argued that supporting nonproliferation at the expense of a friend's interests "would be a terrible bargain."

---

*Interestingly, in this case John Bolton and his successor, Robert Joseph, were among the "nagging nannies" at the State Department, arguing for a deal that more tightly restricted India's use of U.S. technology.

Many Bush officials actually maintained that the deal would prevent the further spread of nuclear weapons, in that it would allow India to join the nonproliferation "mainstream" and thus make its nuclear sector more transparent. They cited a series of measures to which India had agreed: pursuing negotiations on a fissile material cutoff treaty, securing nuclear materials, bolstering nuclear export controls, and maintaining a nuclear test moratorium. The problem here was that India was already taking these steps. The only new pledges New Delhi made in the deal were to officially separate its nuclear complex into military and civilian sectors and to grant international inspectors greater access to the latter. In fact, the purpose of such inspections is to prevent a country from channeling nuclear materials from a legal civilian program to an illegal military one; they serve little purpose if a military program is already operating in parallel, manufacturing nuclear bombs without restriction. (Recognizing this, one of the deal's architects argued that we might as well simply let the Indian military use U.S. nuclear technology.)

Ultimately, the administration was arguing that we should cooperate with India both because it had been a responsible global citizen and because we could then better constrain its behavior. In fact, despite its protestations to the contrary (backed by the Bush administration), India did have a worrisome nonproliferation record. The Bush administration itself had, as of 2007, imposed sanctions on nine different Indian entities for proliferation, mostly for transactions with Iran, of all places. India likewise did not seem particularly keen on enforcing the broader nonproliferation regime or aiding American efforts to constrain Iran's nuclear program. While Indian officials have indicated that they oppose an Iranian nuclear weapon, they have been reluctant to do anything about it. After a September 2005 IAEA vote, India stated that it did not see Iran as "non-compliant" and did not "agree that the current situation could constitute a threat to international peace and security." The following May, India backed Iran's "inalienable right" to nuclear technology.

The danger of the India deal, however, was not so much that U.S. technology might make its way to Iran, but rather that our perceived hypocrisy might damage other nonproliferation efforts. While the United States might declare India good and Iran bad, not all nations—some of which we might need to pressure Tehran—make such a clear distinction. Similarly, if proliferation was sometimes acceptable, then how would we prevent another nuclear-supplier state such as China or Russia from aiding a state that we deemed unstable or adversarial? Finally, the deal signaled to states with whom we were friendly that we might not frown upon their developing a nuclear program, even though in fact we had many nonnuclear friends (such as Egypt and Saudi Arabia) that we would not want to begin enriching uranium, not to mention many nuclear-capable friends (such as Japan and Taiwan) that we would not want developing atomic bombs. To many conservatives, this did not a pose a dilemma. Charles Krauthammer and David Frum, for example, both supported giving Japan nuclear weapons technology to increase pressure on North Korea. But such "acceptable" proliferation had already produced unacceptable results—most notably in allowing Pakistan's nuclear weapons program to take root in the first place.

Pakistan's nuclear program stemmed from its insecurity about India's greater military power—an anxiety that only became more pronounced after India conducted its nuclear test in 1974. Aiming to right the balance, an ambitious Pakistani scientist named Abdul Qadeer Khan, who had been working in Europe, returned to Pakistan the following year with centrifuge blueprints and other data, including contact information for various nuclear technology suppliers, which he had stolen from his Dutch employer, the nuclear company Urenco. Over the course of years, Khan slowly built a network of foreign suppliers and helped assemble Pakistan's nuclear complex. The United States knew of his efforts but hesitated to intervene because, wedged between the Soviet Union and China, Pakistan was a valuable outpost from which to monitor the twin engines of global communism. Following the 1979 Soviet invasion of Afghanistan, neighboring Pakistan became all the more geostrategically critical, as it was perfectly situated to help the United States funnel weapons and aid to Afghan fighters. In a memorandum to President Carter shortly after the Soviet invasion, national security adviser Zbigniew Brzezinski recommended that the United States send Pakistan more arms, noting that, regrettably, "our security policy toward Pakistan cannot be dictated by our nonproliferation policy."

The Reagan and George H. W. Bush administrations agreed, ignoring the activities of Khan and his fellow bomb builders. In a commendation letter for one CIA officer operating in Pakistan, the U.S. ambassador in 1983 wrote, "His collection efforts on the Pakistani effort to develop nuclear weapons is amazingly successful and disturbing. I would sleep better if he and his people did not find out so much about what is really going on in secret and contrary to President Zia's assurances to us." Only after the Soviet withdrawal from Afghanistan lessened Pakistan's strategic value to the United States did Bush stop ignoring Khan's activities. In 1990, he declared that he could no longer certify that Pakistan did not have a nuclear device (as required by U.S. law) and congressionally mandated sanctions came into force. But by that time, there was no turning back for Khan and Pakistan. In May 1998, when India conducted a series of nuclear explosions, Pakistan responded with its own nuclear blasts, and Khan's stature as a national hero was guaranteed.

Unfortunately, Khan had played a seminal role not only in Pakistan's nuclear program, but in those of several other countries. At some point in the 1980s, Khan had shifted his network from purchasing to retail. Khan-connected individuals and firms stretched from the United Kingdom south to South Africa east to Malaysia and west to Italy, Spain, Switzerland, and Germany, with an outpost in the United Arab Emirates. Other countries linked to Khan and his associates included Chad, Egypt, Mali, Nigeria, Niger, Saudi Arabia, and Sudan; his known customers included Iran, Libya, and North Korea. It was Khan's network that supplied the centrifuges found spinning in Iran, the transfers that led the Bush administration to confront North Korea, and the centrifuge components intercepted en route to Libya.

Clearly, the failure to stop the Khan network earlier is not exclusively a conservative oversight. Nor is "acceptable" proliferation solely a conservative sin. As noted in chapter 3, the United States had helped Britain with its nuclear program in the 1950s and 1960s, acceded to France's, and turned a blind eye to Israel's. In the post-9/11 world, however, the stupidity of this policy should have been evident. Yet when the Bush administration confronted Musharraf after Libya's exposure proved the extent of Khan's responsibility for proliferation, the Pakistani president merely placed Khan under house arrest—and he has only let foreign governments and IAEA investigators question Khan through Pakistani intermediaries. The Bush administration not only acceded to this decision but continued to funnel billions of dollars in aid to the Musharraf regime, dubbing Pakistan a "major non-NATO ally" despite fears that Khan's network continues to operate independently of its central node.

Conclusion

During its confrontation with the Bush administration, North Korea reprocessed enough plutonium for between eight and ten nuclear weapons, and in October 2006, it conducted its first nuclear test. The extent of its uranium-enrichment program remains unknown. Iran has enriched uranium to 4 percent U-235 in its pilot facility and continues construction on a larger commercial facility that will hold thousands of centrifuges. Although in December 2007 the U.S. intelligence community released a National Intelligence Estimate indicating that Iran had stopped developing nuclear warheads in 2003—predictably prompting conservatives to call for a Team B to determine why the CIA had gone soft on Iran—it also judged that Iran was continuing to expand its capacity to enrich uranium, meaning that it continues to cultivate material and expertise that could enable it to resume a weapons program in the future.

United States policy could have produced different outcomes. In February 2007, the Bush administration reversed course and held direct talks with North Korea and promised to release funds impounded by Banco Delta Asia, enabling Chris Hill to finalize a deal on North Korea's denuclearization. Under the terms of the agreement, the United States will provide heavy fuel oil as the North shuts down its Yongbyon reactor and allows IAEA inspectors back into the country. The two nations will then pursue a series of reciprocal steps leading to the full disclosure of Pyongyang's nuclear programs and normalization of relations with the United States. In sum, it is a deal remarkably like the Clinton administration's Agreed Framework, with the big difference being that now the North has significantly more plutonium for which we have to account—and should the deal fall through, it will be in a much stronger position than in 2002. The North Korean regime seems no weaker for the years of antagonistic treatment by Bush conservatives.

The government in Tehran, meanwhile, is clearly stronger in absolute and relative terms than it was five years ago. Oil prices are soaring, a crackdown on dissidents has shored up the regime's authority, and the country's standing in the region has been dramatically improved by the fall of the Taliban, the chaos in Iraq, and Israel's failed war against Lebanon (and the incorporation of Hezbollah into the Lebanese government). The Bush administration has tried to change policy—so far to no avail. On May 31,

2006, Rice announced that the United States would join talks with Iran if it first suspended uranium enrichment. (While there is a case to be made for that conditional approach—after all, Tehran had previously agreed to suspend enrichment while conducting talks with the Europeans—Rice again seems to have confused diplomatic means with diplomatic ends. Making the goal of negotiations a precondition for negotiations is non-sensical.) Iran has yet to respond, but the fact that it halted its arms program in 2003 seems to indicate that it is a rational actor whose choices can be influenced, rather than an evil regime hell-bent on an atomic arsenal. There is no guarantee that responding to Iran's "grand bargain" road map five years ago would have succeeded, but it seems clear that the Bush administration missed a remarkable opportunity.

Chapter Eight

FUTURE

LAUNCHING HIS SECOND TERM with a rhetorical offensive, President Bush outlined a vision of widespread democratization in his inaugural address on January 20, 2005: "The survival of liberty in our land," he said, "increasingly depends on the success of liberty in other lands. The best hope for peace in our world is the expansion of freedom in all the world. America's vital interests and our deepest beliefs are now one."

A few conservatives looked askance at such Wilsonian rhetoric—and not a few liberals complained that Bush had stolen their issue—but it was a heady time. Ten days after the president spoke, Iraqis held free elections for the first time since 1954, and the purple ink used to mark the fingers of those who voted quickly became a symbol of freedom and American beneficence. Only a few days earlier, Palestinians had held their first presidential contest in nearly a decade, electing moderate Mahmoud Abbas. Then, in February, former Lebanese prime minister Rafik Hariri was assassinated, sparking a wave of popular protests against the Syrian forces that had occupied the country since 1976 and were presumed to be behind the attack. At the culmination of the so-called Cedar Revolution, Syria announced that it would withdraw its troops—a remarkable development that was accompanied by news that Egyptian president Hosni Mubarak would allow candidates to challenge him in that fall's election. Amid such democratic drama, even Iraq war skeptics began wondering if President Bush had been onto something. Might the toppling of Saddam actually have transformed the political dynamic of the Middle East?

Unfortunately, enthusiasm soon faltered as democracy failed to yield liberalism. In Iraq, a parliament elected largely on the basis of religion and ethnicity soon deadlocked along religious and ethnic lines. In Palestine, parliamentary elections held in January 2006 brought the terrorist organization Hamas to power. The Egyptian elections Mubarak had offered proved farcical, and he was reelected with 88 percent of the vote. To cap things off, Iranians elected the populist—and virulently anti-Western—Mahmoud

Ahmadinejad to the presidency. The notion that our vital interests and our deepest beliefs were now one seemed questionable at best.

Throughout 2005, President Bush clung to the notion that freedom was the ultimate solution to terrorism, but, while it might have been the ultimate solution, it very clearly was not the immediate one. On July 7, for example, terrorists set off four bombs in London's transit system, killing fifty-two people; the perpetrators were all Britons—residents of one of the world's oldest and most stable democracies. At best, democratization was a long-term process, one that would do little to stem the immediate threat from terrorism, including nuclear terrorism. At worst, it was simply a cynical ploy by the president to avoid dealing with regimes he found unpleasant. Whichever it was, the problem of terrorism was growing worse. As researchers Peter Bergen and Paul Cruickshank concluded in 2007, the Iraq war had led to a 600 percent increase in the average number of annual jihadist terrorist incidents. Even excluding attacks in Iraq and Afghanistan, there had still been a 35 percent increase in terrorism worldwide.

Then, in the latter half of 2005, the Bush administration suffered a bewildering array of setbacks. In late August, Hurricane Katrina struck New Orleans—a tragedy from which Bush seemed aloof and to which federal response was woefully inadequate. Critics, and a number of supporters, began to wonder if Bush had the competence to govern, and the notion that the administration was run by ideological hacks gained currency when the president nominated the embarrassingly unqualified Harriet Miers to replace Sandra Day O'Connor on the Supreme Court. Then the scandals began. Tom DeLay, the ruthlessly effective House majority leader, was indicted on charges of conspiring to violate campaign finance laws. Subsequently, two of his aides were convicted in a widespread lobbying scandal, and DeLay himself resigned in mid-2006. Then, in September 2006, Republican representative Mark Foley was accused of improper contact with underage boys. In late October, Vice President Cheney's chief of staff, Scooter Libby, was indicted on obstruction of justice and perjury charges.

In the 2006 elections, Democrats won back control of both the House and the Senate, a feat that had seemed impossible only a few years earlier. By mid-2007, the president's poll numbers were lower than Richard Nixon's during Watergate. The *Washington Post* called his fall "the most drastic political collapse in a generation."

Driving Bush's crash was the increasing chaos in Iraq. The question of whether the invasion had been wise had, by the middle of the president's second term, faded into the background as critics and supporters alike searched for a way to stanch the bleeding, restore some semblance of order to the country, and extract the United States from a war whose length had exceeded that of American involvement in World War II. In the face of such obvious catastrophe—and the results of the 2006 elections, which were widely seen as a rejection of the administration's Iraq policy—the White House proved remarkably reluctant to change course. In 2005 and 2006, the administration asserted repeatedly that the United States must not "cut and run." Nevertheless, in December 2006, the Iraq Study Group—a blue-ribbon commission led by Bush family consigliere James Baker—called for a strategic shift that, among other things, would bring Iran and Syria into a regional process to stabilize Iraq. Many interpreted the report as a face-saving way for Bush to recast his policies, but the president and his supporters dismissed the report's calls for engagement. Instead, Bush opted to take the advice of an American Enterprise Institute report called "Choosing Victory" and increased the number of troops in Baghdad.

Despite his intransigence on Iraq, Bush's foreign policy began perceptibly to change. The president still saw the war on terrorism as a Manichaean struggle—even inviting prominent historians and philosophers to the White House to discuss the nature of evil—but the conservative cadre of advisers that had once surrounded him was dispersing. In June 2005, Paul Wolfowitz left the Pentagon to head the World Bank; two years later, he was forced to resign after giving his girlfriend, a bank employee, a substantial pay raise. Douglas Feith left the Pentagon in the summer of 2005 as well. A year later, after the midterm elections, Bush forced out the enormously unpopular Donald Rumsfeld and replaced him with the more pragmatic Robert Gates.* John Bolton, whose influence had declined when he left Washington for the United Nations, also retired at the end of 2006; it was clear that he could not win confirmation from a Democratic Senate. In January 2007, Robert Joseph, a former National Security Council staff

---

*Interestingly, the commission on ballistic missiles that Rumsfeld had led in 1998 was appointed not only because conservatives saw the 1995 NIE as too dovish, but also because their first attempt to undermine the report via a Team B had largely reaffirmed the NIE's conclusions. That first Team B had been led by Gates.

member who had taken over for Bolton as the State Department's chief arms control official, quit. And Vice President Cheney's national security team was shaken by the trial and ultimate conviction of Scooter Libby.

One of the first signs that these developments were presaging a shift in policy was the September 2005 agreement with North Korea, hampered though it was by the statement subsequently forced on negotiator Christopher Hill, and the investigation of Banco Delta Asia. Then, in May 2006, Condoleezza Rice announced that if Iran suspended uranium enrichment, the United States would join the European Union in talks about its nuclear program. Iran did not agree to that proposition, but in March 2007, U.S. and Iranian diplomats met face-to-face to discuss how to stabilize the situation in Iraq—a major step for an administration that had shunned engagement. At about the same time, the Bush administration approved a deal with North Korea to shut its nuclear facilities, a deal remarkably similar to Clinton's 1994 Agreed Framework.

This metamorphosis was in some ways similar to that of the latter Reagan administration, and it, too, sparked anger from conservatives, who felt betrayed. Elliott Abrams, a deputy national security adviser, sent angry e-mails to colleagues in February 2007 demanding to know why the president had agreed to remove North Korea from the list of state sponsors of terrorism. Bolton, now out of government and free to speak his mind, lambasted the administration for unfreezing the Banco Delta Asia funds and providing fuel oil if North Korea would shutter its nuclear program: "This obvious quid pro quo is not only embarrassing, it sets a dangerous precedent for other regimes that would blackmail the U.S." Bolton remained insistent on regime change, as did his successor, who actually quit because he could not countenance the North Korea agreement.

Their outrage—particularly about the willingness to engage Iran— was shared by the conservative commentariat. As one AEI scholar put it, "I don't have a friend in the administration, on Capitol Hill or any part of the conservative foreign policy establishment who is not beside themselves with fury at the administration." Newt Gingrich raised the inevitable charge of appeasement, and Richard Perle asked, "How is it that Bush, who vowed that on his watch 'the worst weapons will not fall into the worst hands,' has chosen to beat such an ignominious retreat?" In *Commentary,* Norman Podhoretz wondered, "Is the Bush doctrine dead?" while the

Wall Street Journal worried that Condoleezza Rice was leading President Bush to ruin. Conservatives even turned on one another, with nationalists assailing their more neoconservative brethren for their utopian dream of democratizing the Middle East. Meanwhile, neoconservatives blamed the incompetence of the administration for the Iraq morass.

None of them questioned the tenets of conservatism itself. None of them concluded that the fundamental flaw in policy was the division of the world into good and evil, us and them. In fact, when the GOP candidates lined up for the presidential race in 2007, they reaffirmed the planks of conservative foreign policy. John McCain, Mitt Romney, and Rudy Giuliani all disparaged the United Nations, with Romney calling it an "extraordinary failure." Taking a page from Reagan's 1976 playbook, when as governor of California he had made opposition to the Panama Canal treaties a badge of patriotism, they played upon nationalist sentiment by opposing the Law of the Sea Treaty—a commonsense agreement, supported by everyone from the Sierra Club to the U.S. Navy, that defined national responsibilities governing use of an international resource, the oceans. (Channeling Bolton, Giuliani explained, "I cannot support the creation of yet another unaccountable international bureaucracy that might infringe on American sovereignty and curtail America's freedoms.")

Each of them hastened to assume Reagan's legacy, even as they misconstrued it, unanimously rejecting negotiations with Iran while advocating preemptive tactical nuclear strikes. Romney waxed apocalyptic in one us-versus-them campaign ad, warning: "It's this century's nightmare—jihadism. Violent, radical Islamic fundamentalism. Their goal is to unite the world under a single jihadist caliphate. To do that, they must collapse freedom-loving nations, like us." McCain agreed, having proclaimed at the 2004 GOP convention, "It's a big thing, this war. It's a fight between a just regard for human dignity and a malevolent force that defiles an honorable religion by disputing God's love for every soul on earth. It's a fight between right and wrong, good and evil." In an essay for *Foreign Affairs,* Giuliani genuflected before every conservative cliché of the previous fifty years, writing of a war against evil, the danger of appeasement, and the need for victory.

Some of this rhetoric was merely that: run-of-the-mill pandering to the base during primary season (even George H. W. Bush had run as a

conservative in 1988); after all, it was the Republican base—the 30 percent of the electorate that supported Bush into his final year—that would
decide the nominee. And although Manichaeanism may fail strategi-
cally abroad, it succeeds politically at home; the American people may be
almost finished with the Bush presidency, but they are not nearly finished
with conservatism. Which is a big problem. If America is going to defend
itself, it is going to have to beat its addiction to simplistic worldviews—to
fight nuclear terrorism pragmatically and cooperatively. "Us versus them"
must become "us and them."

Why We Cling to Good and Evil

When humans are afraid, they have an odd tendency to do things that
make them feel safer while actually increasing the danger they face. For
example, a driver might purchase a sport utility vehicle because its greater
height and weight and its dominating appearance make him feel more
secure, even though studies have shown that SUVs are significantly less
safe than minivans. Some consumer preferences are particularly paradoxical. A cultural anthropologist hired by Chrysler to help design the
PT Cruiser found that big windows made car buyers feel vulnerable, so
Chrysler shrunk its rear window. That reduced visibility and therefore
made the car more dangerous to drive, but it did make drivers feel more
secure. As journalist Malcolm Gladwell observed, "That's the puzzle of
what has happened to the automobile world: feeling safe has become more
important than actually being safe."

A similar dynamic is at work in American foreign policy. In chapter 1,
I argued that when conservatives propound an us-versus-them, good-
versus-evil worldview, they are tapping into a venerable tradition in
American political culture—a tradition of exceptionalism, through which
Americans see their country as unique and even divinely ordained. But
they are also drawing upon something much deeper: an innate tribalism
that has been reinforced through millennia of evolution.

This natural tendency, and the impact it has on our political behavior, has been demonstrated in extensive psychological testing. In 1973,
Ernest Becker published a book called *The Denial of Death,* which began
with the simple premise that while, like other animals, humans are
imbued with a biological urge to survive, we, unlike other animals, are

also imbued with the understanding that we will die. Becker posited that the tension between the genetic desire to live forever and the knowledge that we will not do so fosters terror—terror that we assuage by constructing worldviews in which our lives are given meaning beyond the purely corporeal. Religious faith is one obvious strategy, but the worldviews that Becker described did not have to promise literal immortality to be soothing; they could also provide symbolic immortality, such as the patriotic belief that, as Americans, we are part of a great democratic experiment that affords us tremendous liberty and that will continue on long after we have died.

In subsequent decades, psychologists have tested Becker's hypotheses, which are collectively known as terror management theory. They have confirmed that thinking about death increases our anxiety on a subconscious level (though, interestingly, it has no effect on our conscious mood); they have confirmed that worldviews do in fact reduce anxiety about death, as Becker theorized; and they have demonstrated that, when thoughts of death are intensified, we hew more closely to worldviews—whether religious, ethnic, or nationalist—that diminish our anxiety. For example, when asked to consider their own mortality, a group of American college students became far less tolerant of anyone who criticized the United States.

This phenomenon has significant political ramifications. In one study, subjects were asked to answer two death-related questions regularly used in terror management tests and then asked to read speeches by three candidates in a hypothetical gubernatorial race.* The "charismatic candidate" stressed a grand vision and group identity with statements like "You are part of a special state and a special nation." The "relationship candidate" emphasized communication and mutual respect, saying, "I inform everyone of all new programs or policies and am open for suggestions." The third, a "task-oriented candidate," emphasized his ability to effectively solve problems: "I do not promise to change the world; the goals set out before us are realistic yet challenging." Control subjects who were not asked to consider their mortality strongly preferred the

---

*The questions were "Please briefly describe the emotions that the thought of your own death arouses in you" and "Jot down, as specifically as you can, what you think will happen to you as you physically die and once you are physically dead."

relationship candidate to the charismatic candidate, while subjects who had been asked to think about death showed a sharp increase in preference for the charismatic candidate. (Support for the task-oriented candidate was about the same in both groups.)

Researchers concluded that, in times of stress, voters will flock to a leader who helps them forget their own mortality by convincing them that they are part of something greater than themselves. Or, as another study put it, "[R]esearch has shown that ideologies depicting one's group as special and uniquely valuable are especially effective for terror management purposes." What's more, a good-versus-evil worldview turns out to be a particularly effective version of an us-versus-them worldview. Studies have shown that "worldviews that depict one's group as engaged in a heroic struggle against evil may be particularly effective for enhancing the meaningfulness of one's worldview and the value of one's group and therefore especially useful for warding off death-related fear. Thus, when death thought accessibility is heightened, leaders who help people feel good about themselves by portraying their groups as undertaking a righteous mission to obliterate evil might be particularly alluring."

This insight helps explain George W. Bush's reelection. His 2004 campaign emphasized national security issues, and though he had had a few successes, such as Libya's denuclearization, he had also given voters many reasons to doubt his leadership. By then, the rationale for the Iraq war had utterly collapsed, while both Afghanistan and Iraq seemed to be slipping into anarchy. The North Korean and Iranian nuclear programs did not generate the headlines that Iraq did, but John Kerry took pains to point out the administration's failures there—as he did its inexplicable failure to secure loose nuclear material in the former Soviet Union. In the summer of 2004, the 9/11 Commission's final report concluded that the Bush administration had not done nearly enough to prevent the terrorist attacks. And a week before the election, Osama bin Laden appeared in a videotaped message to the American people—a blunt reminder that after three years of "war," Bush had failed to capture the most wanted terrorist in the world.

Yet Bush prevailed, winning the election by some three million votes, and polling data revealed that he had won not in spite of security issues, but because of them. Political psychologists have found that invoking the September 11 attacks has the same effect on subjects as asking them the death-related questions traditionally used in terror management studies. They also discovered that evoking thoughts of 9/11 dramatically increased support for President Bush and his foreign policy. In one experiment conducted before the 2004 election, a control group of college students preferred John Kerry by a four-to-one margin. But students asked to contemplate their own mortality preferred Bush by a margin of two to one—a startling 400 percent shift. By stressing American exceptionalism and a good-versus-evil view of the war on terror, Bush apparently served a terror-management function: "From this perspective," one study noted, "President Bush's appeal may lie in his image as a protective shield against death, armed with high-tech weaponry, patriotic rhetoric, and the resolute invocation of doing God's will to 'rid the world of evil.'"

Conservatism, in other words, although it has a clear intellectual pedigree, operates on a deep psychological level as well. The psychological dynamic that these studies establish helps explain behavior that is empirically irrational. Whether Saddam Hussein posed the greatest threat to the United States at the time of the Iraq invasion was far less important than the destruction of an identifiable evil. Focusing on the technocratic work of securing Russia's loose nuclear material was less of a psychological priority because it did not fit into a Beckerite worldview of America engaged in a grand struggle for liberty and against evil. Negotiation with states like Iran and North Korea, however practical for preventing proliferation, became far less urgent than taking a strong stand. Denouncing those nations as evil, even if it did nothing to allay the actual threat they presented, alleviated anxiety. For some, conservatism doesn't necessarily need to make sense. Walter Russell Mead has written of the emotional attachment to an us-versus-them, good-versus-evil worldview among a group of Americans he calls Jacksonians, after the Indian-fighting frontier president: "Jacksonian realism is based on the very sharp distinction in popular feeling between the inside of the folk community and the dark world without. Jacksonian patriotism is an emotion, like love of one's family, not a doctrine."

This psychological dynamic also helps explain how conservatism can foment domestic political ugliness. Just as an us-versus-them dichotomy has marked conservatives' attitudes toward the rest of the world, so, too, has it often affected their treatment of liberal and moderate dissenters, in what scholar Anatol Lieven has called the "antithesis" of the American creed. Conservatives not only see America as called to a special mission in the world, but see themselves as called to a special mission at home, protecting the creed from its detractors. It is the inversion of American exceptionalism.

Of course, conservative criticism of those who disagree with exceptionalist or conservative premises is a perfectly acceptable form of discourse—and can be a necessary corrective. For example, whatever the merits of the Vietnam War, conservatives during the late 1960s were right to object to the New Left's veneration of Ho Chi Minh and Mao Tse-tung. Similarly, conservatives were justified in their wariness of communists in government during the 1940s and 1950s for the simple reason that there *were* communists in many positions spying for the Soviets. When conservatives forwarded this argument evenhandedly—that is, while relying upon actual evidence—they were providing a valuable service. But because of its potent psychological component, conservative righteousness and judiciousness can easily shade into self-righteousness and demagoguery, as when Joe McCarthy parlayed concern with espionage into national paranoia. Although on an intellectual level, Americans may recognize that political dissent is valuable, on an emotional level it undermines their worldview, and conservatives can thus equate dissent with treason.

This despicable phenomenon manifested during the 2002 election in ads that were taken out against Bush critic Max Cleland comparing the Georgia senator (and triple-amputee Vietnam war hero) with Osama bin Laden. It was also the dynamic behind the campaign of the Swift Boat Veterans for Truth, which argued that John Kerry's antiwar activities after his service in Vietnam had been un-American. It was reflected in the conservative suggestion that those who opposed the Bush administration's policies were providing aid and comfort to terrorists. And it was reflected in the right-wing notion, perpetuated by William Kristol's *Weekly Standard* and others, that the United States had failed to stabilize Iraq because liberals had stabbed the U.S. military in the back. Their loss of nerve had fatally undermined the hard work of American troops. Recall that the surge strategy promoted by the American Enterprise Institute was titled "Choosing Victory," implying both that the only possible outcomes in Iraq were victory or defeat and that it was entirely within our power to decide which happened.

On Leadership

Fear, then, promotes conservative foreign policies, which in turn decrease American security. A politician wishing to break this cycle cannot simply emphasize the horrible possibility of nuclear terrorism—and the Bush administration's failures to rein it in—because he would, perversely, encourage a more conservative vote. Social research has shown that the way to circumvent this problem is to offer a vision of meeting a great challenge—of surmounting the threats that we face while also advancing some common good—in other words, a vision of leadership, which, fortunately, is precisely what the nonproliferation regime needs.

One of the paradoxes of American conservatism is that for all the emphasis it places on exceptionalism, it rejects the notion of U.S. leadership. Bush, like all presidents, speaks about America guiding the world, but leadership is in large part the art of persuading or coercing others to do your will. By that definition, the Bush administration has not only failed at leadership against proliferation, it has often dismissed the very concept.

In the beginning, American exceptionalism had at its core a conviction that the United States was to serve as an example to other states. What the United States did, in other words, mattered to other countries, even if it did not directly intervene in their affairs. Its actions at home would themselves exude a force outward, beyond the new republic's physical reach. American ideals would act at a distance and, in so doing, create new norms of governance—standards of right and wrong to guide conduct within and among nations.

Norms are, empirically, far squishier things than interests and power. The sources and effects of their power are difficult to quantify, in no small part because they are constructed of our *perceptions* of reality, rather than of reality itself. Consider, for example, the norm against using nuclear weapons—a norm so strong that it is sometimes called a taboo. Although it was never in our interest to employ nuclear weapons against the Soviet Union because we would have been destroyed in a retaliatory strike, other factors prevented us from resorting to their use during the Cold War. How else can we explain rejecting a nuclear option in Korea or Vietnam, both drawn-out wars during which the United States suffered heavy casualties—and, in the case of Vietnam, during which the United

States showed little hesitation in bombing civilian population centers? Likewise, the nonproliferation of nuclear weapons relies heavily on a norm against their spread.

When it was opened for signature in 1968, the Nuclear Nonproliferation Treaty relied heavily on appeals to national interest. Given that the treaty allows 5 states to legally possess nuclear weapons, while prohibiting the other 183 from ever developing them, why did dozens of states agree to the two-tiered, discriminatory system—a system of nuclear apartheid, as India put it? Because it made sense for them to do so.

Nuclear weapons programs are expensive and, though they have great deterrent value, also come with great risk. Although Bush's 2002 National Security Strategy referred to the Cold War as a time of stability in which we faced a "status-quo, risk-averse adversary," the truth is that the Cold War was a period of tremendous anxiety. Though the prospect of mutual assured destruction was stabilizing, nightmare moments like the Cuban missile crisis and the Able Archer exercise, as well as various accidents and miscommunications that occurred, could have led to the total destruction of both nations, if not most of human civilization. In some respects, the decision to acquire nuclear weapons is another version of the prisoner's dilemma faced by the superpowers in deciding whether to cooperatively regulate their atomic arsenals. The safest course of action for two rivals is for neither to build nuclear weapons; if you suspect, however, that your rival is going to build them, then you had better do the same, lest you be left vulnerable. When both states make this calculation, nuclear programs and a potential arms race ensue, leaving both at risk. The NPT afforded a way out of this dilemma, whereby rivals could each be assured that the other was not building the bomb.

The treaty offered an additional inducement, as well: It promoted the sharing of nuclear technology for peaceful purposes, in particular nuclear energy, which at the time was thought to offer developing states a relatively quick path from poverty to prosperity. Finally, the treaty called upon the nuclear-armed states to take steps toward nuclear disarmament, meaning that it held out the promise that the two-tiered system would eventually become a one-tiered system.

In all of these ways, the treaty appealed to its signatories' interests. And over the past forty years, the nuclear-armed states have reinforced this dynamic. For example, the United States has offered many of its allies "positive security assurances," promising not only to defend them if they are attacked, but to defend them with nuclear weapons if necessary. This "nuclear umbrella" or "extended deterrent" allows nations like Japan to reap the security benefits of a nuclear arsenal without developing one of its own. The United States has also extended "negative security assurances" to states that do not have nuclear weapons, promising never to use nuclear weapons against them unless they attack America or its allies in concert with a state that does have nuclear weapons.*

But just as significant, the NPT operated on a normative level. That is, it not only played to the interests of nonnuclear states, it actually altered what those states believed their interests were. Take, for example, the case of Ukraine, which became a nuclear-armed state in 1991 after the breakup of the Soviet Union left it with both its sovereignty and an arsenal of atomic bombs. There were many reasons for Ukraine to retain its arsenal, not the least of which was Russia's historic expansionism, and post–Cold War Russia, however weakened, still bristled with thousands of nuclear armaments. But the norm against proliferation that had developed over the past thirty years changed its calculus. As scholar Scott Sagan has written, "Without the NPT, a policy of keeping a nuclear arsenal would have placed Ukraine in the category of France and China"—that is, states with great-power status. "[I]nstead, it placed Ukraine in the company of dissenters like India and Pakistan and pariahs like Iraq and North Korea." In other words, the treaty had lowered the prestige associated with acquiring nuclear weapons—had in fact redefined such behavior as deviant. And in a sort of positive feedback loop, this normative effect not only changed the way Ukraine perceived its national interests; it changed the nature of those interests as well, making it easier, for example, for the United States to coordinate economic inducements in exchange for Ukrainian accession to the treaty (and to threaten economic punishment if it did not accede).

The norm against nonproliferation has been reinforced in many ways. The NPT remains its most important component, but over the years, other

*As explained in chapter 5, the Bush 41 and Clinton administrations modified this assurance to allow for the possibility of nuclear retaliation in the event that a state attacked the United States or its allies with biological or chemical weapons. The Bush 43 administration has, in effect, done away with negative security assurances altogether.

formal and informal obligations have strengthened it. For example, the NPT requires that states declare their nuclear facilities and submit them to inspection by the International Atomic Energy Agency. When, after the Gulf War, NPT states realized that this system was not sufficient to thwart the ambitions of determined cheaters like Iraq, it adopted a more stringent set of guidelines under an agreement known as the Additional Protocol. The system of inspections, the IAEA itself, and the Additional Protocol have all become part of an evolving nonproliferation regime that also includes nuclear weapon–free zones, export controls, and the Comprehensive Test Ban Treaty.

The nonproliferation regime has affected the behavior of many states that have considered, but ultimately given up, nuclear programs—states like Taiwan, Brazil, Argentina, and South Korea. In fact, more states have given up nuclear weapons programs since the NPT was signed than have started them. These norms serve as a cushion at times when it seems that going nuclear might be in a state's self-interest, as, for example, it did for Asian countries in the wake of North Korea's 2006 nuclear test. And as the world's most powerful state—as well as a nuclear-armed power— the United States plays a key role in strengthening the nonproliferation regime.

Although it pays lip service to the NPT as a valuable treaty, the Bush administration dismisses the notion that U.S. behavior can reinforce norms that ultimately enhance our security. Indeed, conservatives often ridicule the very notion of international norms. In the 2000 *Foreign Affairs* article that served as candidate Bush's foreign policy manifesto, Condoleezza Rice derided "norms" and the "international community" as "illusory" concepts. This theme runs throughout conservative thought and applies particularly to nuclear strategy, where the high stakes force many minds toward the comfort of quantifiable metrics, like throw weight. Not believing in norms, conservatives necessarily conclude that there is no point in tailoring U.S. behavior to them. Instead, they seem to have concluded that there is little we can do to either strengthen or undermine such norms, and even if we could, it wouldn't matter. The administration contends that states are going to act in accordance with their own national interests. On one level this is certainly true: States do act so as to further their goals. But the administration ignores the fact that norms can affect what nations *perceive* those interests to be, as was the case with Ukraine and others.

Nonnuclear states consider adherence to the Comprehensive Test Ban Treaty a sign of the nuclear powers' commitment to eventual disarmament, and when the United States failed to ratify it, other states began to rethink their commitment to the NPT. According to IAEA head Mohamed ElBaradei, "The Senate vote against the ban on nuclear tests was a devastating blow to our efforts to gain acceptance of more intrusive inspections of nuclear facilities around the world." In 2000, at the conference to review implementation of the NPT that is held every five years, states unanimously agreed the CTBT should be brought into force, as one of "13 Steps" to strengthen the nonproliferation regime. The Bush administration rejected that idea as soon as it took office, eager to preserve its ability to test nuclear weapons, and it subsequently distanced itself from the "13 Steps," claiming they were commitments of another era and therefore no longer relevant.

But its lack of action on the test ban treaty is less significant than the steps the administration has taken to increase the prominence of nuclear weapons. The Nuclear Posture Review, the Doctrine on Joint Nuclear Operations, and the plans for Global Strike have all suggested that the Bush administration has lowered the threshold for nuclear use. Even if one argues, as some Bush officials do, that these are just plans, just documents, just theorizing, it is hard to ignore the administration's interest in new and modified nuclear warheads—low-yield weapons and bunker-busting atomic bombs—that serve less a strategic deterrent function than a tactical military one. All of which meant that at the 2005 NPT Review Conference, the United States was the target of considerable ire—an irony, given that the assembled states were faced with two members (Iran and North Korea) that were violating either the spirit or the letter of the treaty.

Whereas most nations sent their foreign ministers as emissaries to the conference—and whereas the United States would therefore have been expected to send Condoleezza Rice—the Bush administration sent Stephen Rademaker, an assistant secretary of state, three tiers lower in rank. (By contrast, the Clinton administration had sent Vice President Al Gore and Secretary of State Madeleine Albright to the 1995 and 2000 NPT review conferences, respectively.) In and of itself, Rademaker's presence was a signal that the Bush administration did not take the conference particularly seriously. He was, however, suitably conservative for the administration's purposes. His first job after graduating from the University of Virginia Law School had been at Covington & Burling, the same firm at which Bolton had started his career and at which he worked in the mid-1980s. In 1985, Rademaker got a job as a law clerk to James Buckley, for whom Bolton had written legal briefs and whom President Reagan had just appointed to a federal judgeship. Rademaker spent most of the 1990s on Capitol Hill as counsel to the House International Relations Committee, and when George W. Bush was elected president, Rademaker asked Bolton for a job.

Rademaker planned to use the conference as an opportunity to put additional pressure on Iran and North Korea. When he arrived, however, he found some of the other participants just as agitated about U.S. behavior—particularly its backsliding on the 13 Steps—as they were about Iranian and North Korean intransigence. The New Agenda Coalition—comprising Brazil, Egypt, Ireland, Mexico, South Africa, Sweden, and New Zealand (all nations friendly to the United States)—highlighted "the troubling development that some nuclear-weapon states are researching or even planning to develop new or significantly modify existing warheads. These actions have the potential to create the conditions for a new nuclear arms race." Close U.S. allies even joined the fray. Japan politely called upon all nuclear-armed states to take "further steps towards nuclear disarmament," while Canadian ambassador Paul Meyer pointedly took the Bush administration to task: "If governments simply ignore or discard commitments whenever they prove inconvenient, we will never be able to build an edifice of international cooperation and confidence in the security realm." In an angry op-ed titled "America's Broken Nuclear Promises Endanger Us All," former British foreign minister Robin Cook blasted the administration for its belief that "obligations under the nonproliferation treaty are mandatory for other nations and voluntary on the U.S."

Conservatives are flabbergasted by what they consider this "blame America first" mentality. The United States has, after all, gone a long way toward reducing the number of nuclear weapons in its arsenal. Even the Bush administration, which has little use for arms control and places a premium on military force, including nuclear force, has reduced the number of nuclear weapons it deploys. While the United States should get credit for such actions, because of its prominence, it unfortunately will always serve as an easy target for states looking to distract attention from their own lack of seriousness about proliferation. As Rademaker has complained, "The critics . . . will not be satisfied if the U.S. reduces [its arsenal] by 99%. So long as there is one nuclear weapon remaining in the U.S. inventory, they will point to this as a root cause of nuclear proliferation."

Conservatives not only deny that they have acted contrary to the spirit of the NPT, they petulantly reject the notion that the United States has a responsibility to take the lead on nuclear issues. Worse, they fatalistically insist that nothing we do will impact the behavior of rogue states, such as North Korea, that threaten the nonproliferation regime and the United States. Superficially, they have a point. It is difficult to imagine Mahmoud Ahmadinejad picking up a newspaper, learning that the United States has ratified the CTBT, and abandoning his nuclear program. But the international regime comprises not just the United States and a particular adversary, but an entire system of 183 nations that foreswore nuclear weapons with the understanding that they would become a less salient feature of international politics. Even if states recognized that the NPT's disarmament provisions were utopian, they had a right to believe that the role of nuclear weapons would decrease.

The Bush administration has taken the opposite approach, and in doing so has reduced the leverage the United States has with nonnuclear nations that normally could be counted on to pressure outliers like Iran and North Korea. A 2006 survey of international perspectives on U.S. nuclear policy and posture underscores this contention. In a study conducted for the U.S. Defense Threat Reduction Agency, researchers found that close American allies wanted U.S. policy makers to understand that "a greater U.S. readiness to engage on nuclear disarmament issues would pay off in increased support from other third parties in pursuing U.S. nonproliferation objectives." Another study, conducted for Sandia National Laboratories—an American nuclear research facility—found that while states are unlikely to develop nuclear weapons because of our nuclear posture, an aggressive posture hurts our diplomatic nonproliferation efforts because we are seen as hypocritical when promoting the NPT.

The United States could lead the NPT states if it wished to, but not only do conservatives fail to see how diplomacy can constrain our enemies, they fail to see how it can motivate our friends. Many of our friends

and allies—as well as dozens of other nonnuclear states—attach significant importance to nonproliferation norms. We could gain their
allegiance by taking steps that satisfied them and therefore improved
our security, both by enhancing norms from which we generally benefit
and by encouraging them to directly pressure noncompliers. Instead, we
eschew the give-and-take of diplomacy altogether. As Rademaker said a
few weeks before the conference, "We are not approaching this review
conference from the cynical perspective of, we are going to toss a few
crumbs to the rest of the world, and, by doing that, try to buy goodwill
or bribe countries into agreeing to the agenda that we think they should
focus on rather than some other agenda." In other words, the administration was not going to engage in diplomacy even if it would encourage
other states to see things our way—which only meant that it was quite
certain they never would.

NEXT

How do we fix this problem? Nonproliferation experts like to say that
there is no magic solution to the dangers posed by nuclear weapons. And
insofar as they are referring to a programmatic solution, they are correct.
The bewildering array of arms control measures is a testament both to
the complexity of the problem and to the political tendency toward incre-
mental change. True, there have been paradigm-shifting agreements,
like the ABM Treaty and the NPT, but even those have been fraught with
controversy and backsliding. What the world has managed to achieve is a
web of agreements, institutions, and norms that have tried to limit nuclear
weapons and prevent their spread.

   This web has been constructed despite the best efforts of conservatives,
whose binary ideology has led to some of the worst policy suggestions and
decisions made since the end of World War II. From Barry Goldwater's
opposition to the NPT to the belief of Reagan officials that it was possible
to win a nuclear war with the Soviets, to the Bush administration's decision
to invade Iraq, conservatism has had—and continues to have—disastrous
ramifications. In the last seven years, the Bush administration has failed
to quickly secure loose nuclear material around the globe, has ignored
North Korea's breakout from the NPT until that country had reprocessed
enough plutonium for ten nuclear weapons and actually tested one, and

has refused to parley with Iran until a lunatic president convinced the population of its "right" to enrich uranium. Remarkably, during this same period, the Bush administration managed to convince much of the world that *the United States* was the problem because it sought new nuclear weapons that would be more "usable" in battle. The administration's successes have occurred either because ideology was not a factor (as in the unmasking of the A. Q. Khan network) or because it was explicitly subverted (as in the denuclearization of Libya).

All of which does in fact suggest a simple solution: Stop seeing the world in terms of us versus them, good versus evil, with the attendant view that we must eschew coexistence, containment, and negotiation. This approach does not work, in large part because it does not reflect reality: The United States cannot stand apart from the world in the twenty-first century, if it ever could. This does not mean that treaties are always good or that multilateral solutions are always best. Nor does it mean, as some have alleged, that the United States is the world's chief proliferation problem—we should not blame America first. But we should change America first, because however conservatives have abused the idea, America *is* exceptional. Only it can lead the international coalition necessary to eliminate the threat from nuclear terrorism.

If the United States wants to head the charge against nuclear proliferation, however, it will need to rebuild its damaged credibility, restoring faith globally that Washington values the nonproliferation regime. We could start by ratifying the CTBT and recommitting ourselves to a verifiable fissile material cutoff treaty. We could reduce ambiguity about when and against whom we would use nuclear weapons, reaffirming the fact that our arsenal is intended for nuclear deterrence only. We could appoint a high-level commission to examine what verification provisions and security guarantees would be necessary to achieve the NPT's ultimate goal of nuclear disarmament. (Even if the commission concluded that the conditions for disarmament remain distant, we would have demonstrated that we have not forsaken the NPT's call for a world free of nuclear weapons.) On nonnuclear matters, we could regain considerable international prestige simply by closing the prison at Guantánamo Bay, reaffirming our obligation to the Geneva Conventions, and effectively pursuing the creation of a Palestinian state. Many of these actions could be taken quickly and unilaterally, and the resulting momentum could be used to pursue the most pressing nonproliferation need: securing or destroying every last kilogram of highly enriched uranium or plutonium around the world. Call the process kinetic diplomacy, using the goodwill generated by initial accomplishments to propel others.

Ultimately, however, we will run up against what has become the biggest conceptual challenge to the nonproliferation regime, a challenge highlighted by the case of Iran: The NPT allows countries to pursue nuclear programs for peaceful purposes, but those very same programs can also be used for martial ones. An ostensible energy program can thus be a precursor to a weapons program, as it was in North Korea, or the pretext for one, as it apparently was (and may still be) in Iran. The problem is not confined to rogue states. With Iran insisting on its right to enrich uranium, neighboring states like Egypt and Saudi Arabia are suggesting that they, too, ought to expand their nuclear programs—perhaps hedging against the possibility of a Persian A-bomb. Even if neither Iran nor its Arab neighbors builds nuclear weapons, the sheer amount of fissile material that would have been produced in states run by or permeated with Islamic militants would present a frightening new danger.

Compounding the impetus of the Iranian program, several factors are increasing global interest in nuclear power. For one thing, the demand for energy is, unsurprisingly, projected to grow dramatically in the coming decades, and concerns about energy security (because of volatility in the Middle East, unrest in Nigeria, disruptions from Mexico to Alaska, and the like) are encouraging nations to reexamine domestically available fuels. For many years, the cost of nuclear power was considerably higher than that from oil and gas, so few countries wanted to build (and fuel) reactors. However, as oil and gas prices have risen, nuclear power has become cheaper in relative terms—even as technological advances have lowered its absolute cost. Moreover, as combating global warming has become a priority, countries have begun eyeing nuclear plants, which do not emit carbon, as an environmentally friendly solution to their energy needs. Take all these factors together, and there is much talk of a potential "nuclear renaissance."

Many experts doubt nuclear power will ever be cheap enough to spark such a spontaneous renaissance—the cost of building new plants is substantial—but the IAEA does consider that "the civilian nuclear industry appears to be poised for worldwide expansion." And countries need only *believe* there may be a renaissance for the dangers of such an expansion to accrue: They may develop the technology to enrich uranium or to reprocess spent uranium fuel to extract plutonium, speculating that such a capability will enable them to be suppliers, rather than consumers, of energy. The resulting spread of nuclear know-how—specifically, the enrichment and reprocessing technology that can be used to fuel weapons as well as power reactors—would be an unmitigated security disaster. Already, several countries—including Brazil, Argentina, South Africa, and Australia—have announced their intention to pursue commercial uranium enrichment.

Policy makers across the ideological spectrum recognize the threat this situation poses and have offered possible solutions. In February 2004, President Bush called on nuclear supplier states not to sell enrichment or reprocessing technology to states that do not already possess it; at the same time he offered a reliable supply of nuclear fuel to those states that agreed to forgo such technology. (Countries that buy their nuclear fuel abroad have long feared that providers could arbitrarily cut off fuel supplies for political reasons, a fear that may motivate some to develop indigenous enrichment or reprocessing capabilities.) Two years later, Bush proposed the Global Nuclear Energy Partnership, or GNEP, a plan to encourage the ostensibly safe, cheap, and efficient expansion of nuclear power by reprocessing spent fuel, burning it in new types of advanced reactors, and recycling the spent fuel to minimize the amount of waste generated. (Currently in the United States, uranium fuel is run through a reactor only once, after which the radioactive by-product must be disposed of.) The administration believes that GNEP will permit—and even encourage—a nuclear renaissance that limits proliferation risks by discouraging states without enrichment or reprocessing technology from developing it; instead, current supplier states would offer a range of nuclear fuel services to states that have only reactors.

Bush's plan is ambitious, but seriously flawed. For one thing, it contains a fundamental contradiction: While attempting to discourage the spread of dangerous technology, GNEP itself relies on the revival and spread of just such a technology in the form of spent-fuel reprocessing. The United States issued a moratorium on reprocessing thirty years ago and has discouraged other states from reprocessing because the resulting plutonium can be used in weapons. For another thing, according to a study commissioned by the Department of Energy, the technology to be used in the new reprocessing facilities and reactors remains unproven at a commercial scale; the Congressional Budget Office has also determined that the energy produced by GNEP facilities would be more expensive than that produced via the existing nuclear fuel cycle, in which fuel is burned only once. In addition, Bush's proposals would perpetuate the two-tier nuclear system that is the source of much of the nonproliferation regime's current trouble. That is, while the NPT divides those that have nuclear weapons from those that do not, Bush's proposal would also divide those that can produce nuclear fuel from those that have to buy it. Although some states would welcome GNEP's guaranteed fuel supply, others would balk at this new nuclear "apartheid." Worse, in September 2007 the administration announced that, despite Bush's call to halt the spread of enrichment and reprocessing technology, participation in GNEP would not require any such commitment. "We're not asking countries to sign a statement that they will never enrich or never reprocess," Assistant Secretary of Energy Dennis Spurgeon explained.

For his part, ElBaradei has called for a five-year moratorium on construction of new facilities for uranium enrichment and plutonium separation, during which he hopes to pursue a more permanent resolution of the challenges posed by the nuclear fuel cycle. At the moment, the IAEA is focused on assuring a steady supply of nuclear fuel through market mechanisms, backup commitments from enrichment-capable states, and a "last resort" fuel bank run by the IAEA that would allay consumer fears of capricious supply cutoffs. The IAEA has also floated the idea of establishing multilateral nuclear facilities that would, in theory, provide a stable supply of fuel because they would be controlled by multiple states and therefore less subject to the political whims of one. However, even if that more ambitious plan proved successful, participation would be voluntary, not required. And therein lies the fundamental problem. Article IV of the NPT, which the IAEA helps implement, acknowledges the right of states to peaceful nuclear technology. Given its institutional mandate, the IAEA cannot therefore deny—or even propose denying—elements of the fuel cycle to states that want it. Which is why, in discussing the idea of a fuel bank in September 2006, ElBaradei hastened to explain, "It is not asking any State to give up its rights under NPT." Thus, the IAEA is constitutionally incapable of asking nations to forgo enrichment and reprocessing while the Bush administration is apparently unwilling to do so—and even if it was willing, its call would be interpreted as exacerbating nuclear apartheid.

One solution—albeit an extremely ambitious one—would be to level the playing field by requiring *all* states to forgo uranium enrichment and reprocessing. That is, ownership and operation of existing facilities—whether held by private, quasi-private, or government entities—would be transferred either to the IAEA or to a new institution created for the purpose, and the facilities themselves would be granted extraterritorial status, like the UN headquarters in New York. A moratorium would be placed on new reprocessing facilities, and any new enrichment plants that were built to meet growing fuel demand would likewise be internationally controlled. Nuclear-weapon states (both those inside and outside the NPT) would have to relinquish their ability to produce fissile material for weapons. States that did not already have enrichment and reprocessing technology would be forbidden from developing it, but no such state would have to worry about a disruption in fuel supply because the IAEA, or its successor, would have no incentive to discriminate in its sale of nuclear fuel, unless a state was somehow not complying with its nonproliferation obligations.

This proposal echoes one presented at the dawn of the nuclear age. In 1946, drawing on recommendations prepared by physicist Robert Oppenheimer, who had led America's wartime effort to develop the atomic bomb, Undersecretary of State Dean Acheson and David Lilienthal, chairman of the Tennessee Valley Authority, presented President Truman with a plan to internationalize much of the nuclear fuel cycle. Oppenheimer had immediately recognized the impossibility of separating the atom's peaceful uses from its military ones, so he proposed placing control of all uranium enrichment and reprocessing under an Atomic Development Authority. It was a grand plan that appealed not only to idealists, but also to pragmatists who understood the breadth of the challenges posed by the atomic age. Acheson, for one, called the final report a "brilliant and profound document." Indeed, the horrors of the bomb had convinced many that greater international cooperation, through bodies like the UN, was essential if mankind was to survive; and some, including Oppenheimer, even spoke of subordinating national sovereignty to the laws of a world government. The Acheson-Lilienthal report certainly did not propose that, but as Oppenheimer explained, "It proposes that *in the field* of atomic energy there be set up a world government. That *in this field* there be a renunciation of sovereignty. . . . That in this field there be international law."

The Acheson-Lilienthal proposal foundered because the onset of the

Cold War rendered such dramatic coordination between the United States and the Soviet Union impossible. Ceding national control over a nascent technology while on the verge of global conflict was simply not feasible. Today, however, such antagonism does not exist; whatever mistrust remains between Washington and Moscow pales in comparison with that of the late 1940s. Our experience with institutions like the United Nations may have left only few utopians dreaming of world government in the near future (and only a few radicals and conspiracy theorists truly fearing it), but there is also less geopolitical imperative to preserve sovereign control of atomic energy. The field of nuclear power offers a chance to transcend us-versus-them politics to the great benefit of U.S. security.

Of course, a proposal to internationalize the fuel cycle would encounter substantial hurdles. States that do not currently have uranium-enrichment or reprocessing technology would be denied it, discouraging those who believe that providing enrichment services will be profitable during a coming nuclear renaissance. Internationalization would also perpetuate a continued, albeit greatly lessened, sense of nuclear apartheid: States would be giving up their rights under Article IV of the NPT in addition to having given up any claim to nuclear weapons. Persuading states to join the regime would therefore require significant incentives. Based on the regular complaints of nonnuclear-weapon states, further progress toward nuclear disarmament would likely be one of the most effective inducements; those nations being asked to make further sacrifices will understandably want assurance that the nuclear-weapon states are fulfilling their existing commitments.* As an added carrot, however, enrichment-capable countries—particularly those countries, like the United States, with the

---

*The goal of nuclear disarmament has become a topic for mainstream discussion since the publication of an op-ed by George Shultz, Henry Kissinger, William J. Perry, and Sam Nunn, calling for a world free of nuclear weapons. Others have long argued that a commitment to disarmament is a prerequisite for successful nonproliferation efforts. As ElBaradei noted during the 2005 NPT review conference, "As long as some countries place strategic reliance on nuclear weapons as a deterrent, other countries will emulate them. We cannot delude ourselves into thinking otherwise." A 2006 commission headed by former Iraq weapons inspector Hans Blix similarly noted, "So long as any state has such weapons, especially nuclear arms, others will want them." In 2004, a high-level international panel that included former Bush 41 national security adviser Brent Scowcroft warned that "lacklustre disarmament by the nuclear-weapon states weakens the diplomatic force of the non-proliferation regime and thus its ability to constrain proliferation."

most to fear from nuclear proliferation—could offer not simply to share nuclear technology, but actually to construct proliferation-resistant nuclear reactors for states that legally forswear enrichment capabilities, in a kind of global Agreed Framework. Call it the Nuclear Exchange Treaty, or NEXT.

For enrichment-capable countries, too, the plan would pose challenges. What would it take, for example, to buy out the private elements of existing uranium-enrichment companies?* In the United States, any whiff of "nationalization"—let alone internationalization—would be likely to provoke industrial and ideological opposition. But the enrichment industry is small: There is only a single uranium-enrichment facility currently operating in the United States, and it is leased from the U.S. government by the United States Enrichment Corporation, a private company with a market capitalization of less than $1 billion. Internationalizing a venture that size seems a small price to pay for strengthening the nonproliferation regime. Indeed, *globally,* the enrichment industry yields only $5 billion in revenue a year. Even if there were a dramatic growth in the demand for low-enriched uranium, the industry will not be lucrative enough for Australia or any other country to justifiably block a renewal of the nonproliferation regime. Besides which, the nuclear industry as a whole would benefit tremendously from NEXT, given that it would promote the construction of dozens of new reactors worldwide; in the United States, an industry that has been moribund would suddenly spring to life. True, paying for those reactors would pose a great expense for enrichment-capable governments, but the cost would be well worth it. Reactors that discourage proliferation are far cheaper than wars to roll it back.

Indeed, the benefits of such an arrangement would be significant. First, placing all existing enrichment facilities under international control would prevent the production of any new highly enriched uranium and would prevent states that do not already have such technology from developing it. Second, the United States would have taken an enormous step toward redressing the inequities in the NPT and would therefore make it far more attractive for countries to stay within the regime and far easier

---

*There are four main uranium-enrichment companies or consortia: the United States Enrichment Corporation; Russia's Minatom; Eurodif, a joint venture among Belgium, France, Italy, and Spain; and Urenco, a joint venture among companies in Germany, the Netherlands, and the UK. China and Japan also operate commercial enrichment facilities.

for us to bring pressure to bear on countries outside of it. Even if a number of hard cases refused to join the new regime, the norm NEXT established would continue to increase pressure on them—there would be less and less justification for Iran, for example, to have a national enrichment program as other states internationalized theirs. NEXT might also provide a way to bring outlier states like India, Israel, and Pakistan within a non-proliferation framework: After all, such a treaty need not acknowledge the legitimacy of their nuclear weapons, but it would prevent them from making more; and their participation would further enhance the norm against proliferation, which has suffered from their violations. Third, although nuclear energy cannot solve the problem of climate change, it can significantly reduce carbon emissions, especially in the developing world, where countries are likely to first turn to cheap but dirty technologies like coal. (Princeton professors Stephen Pacala and Robert Socolow have estimated that tripling the output of nuclear plants could reduce carbon emissions by twenty-five billion tons over fifty years, or one-seventh of the amount they believe necessary to stabilize the climate.)

Internationalizing the fuel cycle is admittedly a Herculean diplomatic challenge—a task perhaps facilitated, but not made easy, by the end of the Cold War. Nevertheless, it is a valuable goal; and simply establishing it as such would open the door to study, interim steps, and perhaps ultimate fruition. At the very least, promoting the safe distribution of clean energy while reducing the danger from weapons-grade material would establish the United States as a leader in efforts against proliferation and global warming. And the prestige and credibility accorded an America that had taken a bold lead on not one but two issues of existential importance would be priceless.

U.S. and Them

Richard Weaver was right about one thing: Ideas do have consequences. Modern American conservatism has slowly, but ultimately with great force, molded modern American foreign and defense policy—particularly the way the United States manages its own nuclear arsenal and reacts to those of other nations. But if this book has demonstrated that ideas matter, it has also argued that they should matter less—that national security policy should not flow from ideology. Just as you do not choose a doctor for his worldview, the United States should not choose a president for his convictions about the nature of good and evil. It should, rather, elect a president on the basis of his commitment to evaluating dangers, testing responses, and getting things done—for his commitment, in essence, to empiricism, pragmatism, and leadership. In an age of nuclear terror, we need more physicians and fewer metaphysicians; in an emergency room, priests are good for only one thing.

Conservatives are right: There is evil in the world—and there always will be. All we can do is to identify the threat it poses to the United States and to minimize it. Rejecting the goal of victory in a war between good and evil—indeed rejecting the very concept of such a war—is not immoral or even amoral. One can accept that Saddam Hussein was evil without believing that the only way to deal with him was to invade Iraq. One can find Kim Jong Il loathsome and still understand that the interests of North Korea and the United States overlap sufficiently to seek an agreement that dismantles his plutonium-producing facilities. One can be perfectly aware that Mahmoud Ahmadinejad is a mad fundamentalist and still think it wise to talk directly with the Iranian government. After all, there is nothing moral about leaving the American people vulnerable to nuclear threats.

When the national interest is cast in ideological rather than empirical terms, it is usually miscast—broadened, amplified, and distorted. When conservatives define defense of the country as a "war on terror," they make terrorism—a tactic with myriad forms and practitioners—the enemy instead of the September 11 attackers and their sponsors. When they define the national interest as the victory of democracy over Islamic jihadism, they elevate the threat we face to one of civilizational struggle—and ironically make victory impossible. When they define regimes that seek weapons of mass destruction as the chief threat rather than nuclear weapons themselves, they diminish our ability to stop proliferation and put us at risk. Defining America's enemy as "evil" renders the threats we face abstract and therefore unsolvable; moral clarity becomes obfuscating.

By contrast, prioritizing existential threats yields a far more practical—and optimistic—game plan. The prospect of nuclear terrorism may be horrifying, but it is a problem with clearer parameters than terrorism writ large—let alone jihadism or evil. The fight against nuclear terrorism even provides a goal toward which we can quantifiably measure progress: the elimination of weapons-usable fissile material. And it offers us the opportunity to assume a mantle of global leadership that will not only strengthen American security but also enhance American influence around the world.

Americans cannot remain committed to a nationalistic foreign policy when the chief threats we face are transnational in nature. The United States survived the fragile infancy that necessitated an us-versus-them ideology, maturing into the world's preeminent state; and yet conservatives have clung dogmatically to the view that to become entangled with other states would grievously undermine our security. They have hewed to an eighteenth-century view of our role in the world and the dangers we face from it, when our role in the world and the dangers of the twenty-first century are well beyond what the founding fathers could ever have imagined.

This is not to say that norms, institutions, and treaties are always the best guarantors of U.S. security. That is an ideological conviction itself. The threat of force is an integral component of American foreign policy, and sometimes we may need to exercise it, even unilaterally. But the chief national security challenge facing the United States is not one of willpower in Iraq, treachery at the United Nations, or moral clarity in Iran. It is the need to reaffirm the nonproliferation regime, strengthen that regime through our own actions, and lead others in forging a new compact that will stymie states like Iran and confound would-be nuclear terrorists.

Conservatism, unfortunately, is not an ideology of leadership; it is an ideology of dominance or isolation. The conservative belief that our actions occur in a vacuum and that we cannot affect the interests or perceived interests of others is not only solipsistic, it is defeatist. And this is the fundamental problem with the conservative approach to nonproliferation: It fails to see a true leadership role for the United States, believing the United States should be apart *from* the world, rather than a part *of* it. The United States must take a hard look at its own nuclear policies as it rallies others to roll back the spread of atomic technology. After all, the war on terrorism will not be won with nuclear weapons, but it could well be lost with them.

ACKNOWLEDGMENTS

It gives me great joy to write these acknowledgments—not only because it means that I have nearly finished *U.S. vs. Them*, but because it gives me tremendous pleasure to finally repay, if only in a small way, all the people who helped me to do so.

First, I must thank my colleagues at *The New Republic*, especially Franklin Foer, whose own writing on conservatism helped inspire chapter 3 and who gave me time—and then more time—to pursue this project during a dramatic year in which the magazine was both sold and redesigned. He is a fantastic editor, and it is a pleasure to work for him. Christopher Orr helped make this book possible by offering his considerable talents at *TNR* while I was on leave, and my fellow editors, Katherine Marsh and Richard Just, graciously shouldered extra responsibilities during my absence with the great skill that comes so naturally to both. Peter Beinart read the entire manuscript and gave me rigorous comments with his customary incisiveness, and he kindly helped at the last minute with a particularly nettlesome section. Leon Wieseltier, who provided valuable guidance throughout the publication process, also read the whole book, lending the perspicacity and wisdom one would expect from one of America's great intellectuals. I feel truly privileged to have such brilliant and generous colleagues.

Indeed, it has been a pleasure to call *The New Republic* home for the past five years—an opportunity for which I am grateful to Martin Peretz. *TNR* gave me the chance to first explore conservatism's effect on nonproliferation policy in a longish piece I wrote two and a half years ago, as well as in several other articles and editorials, some of which I've borrowed from in *U.S. Vs. Them*. At *TNR*, I also want to thank Ben Crair, Dayo Olopade, Josh Patashnik, Brad Plumer, and especially Eve Fairbanks, who all, with good humor and great diligence, fact-checked and helped footnote the manuscript. Thanks also to Chloe Schama, who kept me supplied with the latest foreign policy literature as I wrote.

I owe a special debt to John B. Judis, who is not only a fellow *TNR* staffer but was also a neighbor at the Carnegie Endowment for International Peace, where he helped secure me a berth as a visiting scholar. The influence that John's writing has had on me—particularly his magisterial biography of William F. Buckley, Jr.—can be seen on many of these pages. John has made a tremendous contribution to our understanding of the country's intellectual evolution, and as I wrote *U.S. Vs. Them,* I benefited enormously from his comments, criticism, and conversation.

The Carnegie Endowment provided me a wonderful home for a year—a writer really could not ask for more—and I would like to thank Jessica Mathews, Paul Balaran, and particularly George Perkovich, who heads the endowment's nonproliferation project. I am extraordinarily grateful for their hospitality and encouragement. Joshua Kurlantzick, another member of *TNR*-at-Carnegie, also helped in bringing me to the endowment, and I have long benefited from his insights on international affairs. Sharon Squassoni was kind enough to read the entire manuscript, providing particularly useful criticism of chapter 8. Deepti Choubey also read the book and gave me astute comments. Karim Sadjadpour helped answer my Iran questions. Kathleen Higgs, who was the endowment's librarian during my research, as well as Chris Henley and Allison McCoy patiently and capably fielded dozens of requests. Caterina Dutto and Amy Reed provided research assistance at the beginning of the project. Thanks also to Peter Reid, Veronika Arrington, Lynne Sport, and Cindy Wynn.

I would also like to thank Daniel Byman at the Center for Peace and Security Studies, who generously made me a visiting researcher, thus giving me access to Georgetown University's libraries and faculty. I am very grateful to Elizabeth A. Stanley for putting me in touch with Dan.

Two foundations enabled me to extend my research by furnishing grants. I would like to thank the Ploughshares Fund, especially Paul Carroll, and the Educational Foundation of America, especially Christian Ettinger. Their assistance was enormously helpful to this project, and I am deeply appreciative of it.

In addition to my colleagues at *TNR* and Carnegie, several others offered exceptionally valuable guidance. Douglas McGray provided sage advice from the original proposal through to the jacket copy; Andrew Butters provided an important assist at a crucial moment; and Noam Scheiber and Amy Sullivan helpfully shared their literary wisdom. Derek Chollet has been unfailingly supportive on many occasions, and he furnished particular insight on the Clinton years. Spurgeon Keeny, to whom I will always be grateful for taking a big chance on a young editor nine years ago, provided incisive comments on my original *TNR* piece about conservatism and nonproliferation. Steve Fetter graciously lent a hand on chapters 2 and 6. Hans Kristensen, who has performed a great service by demystifying the Bush administration's nuclear policies, reviewed chapter 5. Spencer Ackerman, who has been one of the most prescient writers on the Iraq war, read chapter 6 and provided invaluable ideas on structure, argument, and evidence. Paul Kerr, an expert on Iran, North Korea, and many other subjects, helped with chapter 7. Scott Sagan, one of nonproliferation's wisest voices, and Jeffrey Lewis, one of its most refreshing, helped me greatly with chapter 8. Lawrence Scheinman generously gave me the benefit of his decades of experience with the nuclear fuel cycle.

Thanks also to Peter Bergen, Kai Bird, John Bolton, Linton Brooks, Matthew Bunn, Lou Cannon, Stephen F. Cohen, E. J. Dionne, Charles Ferguson, Beth Fischer, Raymond Garthoff, Laura Holgate, David Holloway, Richard Ned Lebow, James Mann, Jack Matlock, Jack Mendelsohn, John Newhouse, Don Oberdorfer, George Packer, James T. Patterson, Rick Perlstein, Paul Pillar, Pavel Podvig, John Prados, Jack Pritchard, Stephen Rademaker, Richard Rhodes, Michael Schiffer, George Shultz, Leon Sigal, Sarah Snyder, Baker Spring, Andrew Sullivan, Strobe Talbott, Sean Wilentz, and Robert Wright.

I very much appreciate the assistance of several institutions that opened their archives to me: the John M. Ashbrook Center for Public Affairs at Ashland University, the Rauner Special Collections Library at Dartmouth College, the American Security Council, and the Arizona Historical Foundation.

I want to extend a special thanks to Wade Boese, one of the country's sharpest defense analysts, who not only read the entire manuscript—parts of it several times—but also provided detailed comments, in-depth research, and close guidance on many sections. It was a privilege to work with Wade at the Arms Control Association; I am honored to call him a friend; and this book is far better for his influence.

I owe a great debt to Gail Ross, as well as to Howard Yoon, for helping cultivate the germ of an idea until it became a book. Thanks also to Kara Baskin for her help with the proposal. At Viking, I would like to thank my editor, Rick Kot, for his commitment to this book and the great care that he showed the manuscript; I feel fortunate to have had his guidance. I'd also like to thank Laura Tisdel for gracefully guiding me and the book through the many stages of editing and production.

There are several people without whom I can sincerely say that *U.S. Vs. Them* would not have been finished. Victoria C. Rowan—writer, editor, and coach extraordinaire—rescued this project when it was going off the rails and set me on a course to completion. I am eternally grateful for her help.

Barron YoungSmith, a fellow alumnus of *The Brown Journal of World Affairs,* spent a year conducting research for this book, often making keen observations that sharpened its argument. Throughout, he was diligent, indefatigable, and unflappably cheerful even in the face of my frequently preposterous requests. It's been a true pleasure to work with him, and I look forward to his career as a writer and editor.

My parents, to whom this book is dedicated, have been a constant source of support in my various journalistic endeavors. From their willingness to ply me with books at a young age, to their enthusiasm for the *Journal,* to their happy sufferance of a career focused on the most ghastly of subjects, they have given me nothing but love and encouragement. I could not have done any of this without them. Stephen, too, has consistently backed me; I am always touched (and not a little surprised) by the faith he has in his brother.

Finally, my warmest thank-you goes to Sacha Zimmerman, who was a font of strength from the inception to the completion of this project, even though it took far more time, patience, and sheer will than either of us expected. Sacha never doubted that I could write this book, but in truth I was able to do so only because I could return home to her every night. The high point of this past year—indeed of all my past years—was her promise that she would always be there. I have never been happier.

J. Peter Scoblic
January 9, 2008
Washington, D.C.

NOTES

Chapter One: WORLDVIEW

PAGE

3 *On the evening of September 17:* John B. Judis, *William F. Buckley, Jr.: Patron Saint of the Conservatives* (New York: Simon & Schuster, 1988), 175. Peter Kihss, "2,500 Anti-Communists Rally; Mayor and President Scored," *New York Times,* September 18, 1959, 18. "Music Notes," *New York Times,* September 18, 1959, 26.

3 *presidential commission:* "Deterrence and Survival in the Nuclear Age," Security Resources Panel of the Science Advisory Committee (also known as the Gaither Committee), Washington, D.C, November 7, 1957.

3 *"We are certainly":* As cited in Stephen E. Ambrose and Douglas E. Brinkley, *Rise to Globalism: American Foreign Policy Since 1938,* 8th rev. ed. (New York: Penguin Books, 1997), 163.

4 *When he took the stage:* William F. Buckley, "The Damage We Have Done to Ourselves," speech, as reprinted in *National Review,* September 26, 1959, 349–51.

5 *"[I]f National Review":* George H. Nash, *The Conservative Intellectual Movement in America, since 1945* (New York: Basic Books, 1976), 140.

5 *"[A]ll great Biblical stories":* George F. Will, *National Review,* December 31, 1980, 164.

5 *"I think eventually the pundits":* As cited in Judis, *William F. Buckley, Jr.,* 13.

6 *threatened to dye the East River:* Ibid., 175.

7 *"unless it is so bad":* As cited in Arthur M. Schlesinger, Jr., *Crisis of the Old Order, 1919–1933* (Boston: Houghton Mifflin, 1957), 173.

8 *"[T]his new world has been":* Thomas Paine, *Common Sense* (London: Penguin Classics, 1986).

10 *a sort of compromise neoisolationism:* Selig Adler, *The Isolationist Impulse: Its Twentieth Century Reaction* (New York: Free Press, 1957).

10 *"there is no commitment":* Warren G. Harding, "President's Speech to the Senate Submitting Treaties," as reprinted in the *New York Times,* February 11, 1922, 2.

11 *"We would be worse off":* James T. Patterson, *Mr. Republican: A Biography of Robert A. Taft* (Boston: Houghton Mifflin, 1972).

11 *"We have tossed":* Adler, *The Isolationist Impulse.*

11 *"In the United States":* Lionel Trilling, *The Moral Obligation to Be Intelligent: Selected Essays,* Leon Wieseltier, ed. (New York: Farrar, Strauss & Giroux, 2000).

12 *Eisenhower . . . called people:* John Micklethwait and Adrian Wooldridge, *The Right Nation: Conservative Power in America* (New York: Penguin Books, 2005), 41–42.

12 *"You remind me of":* As cited in Lee Edwards, *The Conservative Revolution: The Movement That Remade America* (New York: Simon & Schuster, 1999), 10.

12 *Eisenhower offered to stay out:* Lewis L. Gould, *Grand Old Party: A History of the Republicans* (New York: Random House, 2003), 327.

13 *"anti-Christ"* and *"You'd find us in every corner"*: Judis, *William F. Buckley, Jr.*, 27, 34.

14 *In practice, this meant:* Ibid., 97.

14 *Invited by the Yale administration* and subsequent quotes: Ibid., 77.

14 *Hayek's ideas:* Nash, *The Conservative Intellectual Movement in America, Since 1945*, 4–7.

15 *"religion [began] to assume":* Richard M. Weaver, *Ideas Have Consequences* (Chicago: University of Chicago Press, 1948), 5–6.

16 *"[W]hat has really made possible":* As cited in Nash, *The Conservative Intellectual Movement in America, Since 1945*, 37.

16 *"Political problems, at bottom":* Russell Kirk, *The Conservative Mind: From Burke to Eliot* (Washington, D.C.: Regnery Publishing, 1986), 8.

16 *Hayek delivered a paper:* Henry Regnery, "The Making of the Conservative Mind," introduction to Kirk, *The Conservative Mind*, ix–x.

17 *"dishonest in its use of facts":* McGeorge Bundy, "The Attack on Yale," *Atlantic Monthly*, November 1951, 50.

17 *But Buckley was keen:* Judis, *William F. Buckley, Jr.*, 112.

17 *"What is needed":* Ibid., 124.

17 *the magazine published its "credenda":* "The Magazine's Credenda," *National Review*, November 19, 1955, 6.

18 *"I myself believe":* William F. Buckley, Jr., *God and Man at Yale: The Superstitions of Academic Freedom* (Chicago: Henry Regnery, 1951), xvii.

19 *"To advocate isolationism today":* William Henry Chamberlin writing in *National Review*, as cited in Sara Diamond, *Roads to Dominion: Right-Wing Movements* (New York: Guilford Press, 1995), 33.

19 *"Here has our God":* As cited in Walter A. McDougall, *Promised Land, Crusader State: The American Encounter with the World Since 1776* (Boston: Houghton Mifflin, 1997), 17.

19 *"Americans were a chosen people":* Ibid. 18.

20 *The mission of the colonists:* John B. Judis, *The Folly of Empire: What George W. Bush Could Learn from Theodore Roosevelt and Woodrow Wilson* (New York: Scribner, 2004), Chapter One.

20 *"The Christian eschaton":* L. Brent Bozell, "To Magnify the West," *National Review*, April 24, 1962, 285. In a reprint of a speech given at Madison Square Garden, New York City, on March 7, 1962. Philosopher Eric Voegelin wrote that communism was an attempt to "immanetize the eschaton," to bring about heaven on earth.

20 *"irrevocably at war"* and *"satanic":* "The Magazine's Credenda," *National Review*, November 19, 1955, 6.

20 *"The belief in virtue":* As cited in Godfrey Hodgson, *The World Turned Right Side Up: A History of the Conservative Ascendancy in America* (Boston: Houghton Mifflin, 1996), 89.

21 *"fons et origo":* Gregory L. Schneider, ed., *Conservatism in America Since 1930: A Reader* (New York: New York University Press, 2003), 92.

21 *"Effective anti-Communism":* Frank S. Meyer, "The Relativist 'Re-evaluates' Evil," *National Review*, May 4, 1957, 429.

21 *a Soviet spy once:* Sam Tannenhaus, *Whittaker Chambers: A Biography* (New York: Random House, 1997), 82.

21 *Chambers was summoned:* Ibid., 79–80.

21 "This is evil, absolute evil" and "In this organic hush": Whittaker Chambers, Witness (New York: Random House, 1952), 80.

22 beg Chambers to join: Judis, William F. Buckley, Jr., 165–69.

22 "turning point in history" and "two irreconcilable faiths": Ibid., 7, 4.

22 "decided for generations" and "irreconcilable opposites": Ibid., 7, 16.

22 "not merely to arms but to Armageddon": Tannenhaus, Whittaker Chambers, 462.

22 "within twenty or thirty years": As cited in John B. Judis, Grand Illusion: Critics and
Champions of the American Century (New York: Farrar, Straus & Giroux, 1992).

23 "perfect vehicle" and "[W]e have here": George F. Kennan, "The Long Telegram,"
February 22, 1946. Available at http://www.gwu.edu/~nsarchiv/coldwar/
documents/episode-1/kennan.htm.

23 "Soviet pressure": "X" [George F. Kennan], "The Sources of Soviet Conduct," Foreign Affairs, July 1947.

23 "totalitarian regimes" and "it must be the policy": President Harry S. Truman,
"Address Before a Joint Session of Congress," Washington, D.C, March 12, 1947.

23 "animated by a new": National Security Council Paper, NSC-68, "United States
Objectives and Programs for National Security," April 7, 1950.

24 "I can state": Walter Isaacson and Evan Thomas, The Wise Men: Six Friends and
the World They Made (New York: Simon & Schuster, 1997), 338.

24 shave off his bristly guardsman's mustache: W. Averell Harriman as cited in Isaacson and Thomas, The Wise Men, 547.

24 "clearer than truth" and "crusade against ideology": Isaacson and Thomas, The
Wise Men, 398, 400.

25 "Mr. President, the only way": James Chace, Acheson: The Secretary of State
Who Created the American World (Cambridge: Harvard University Press, 1999),
166.

25 "Is this speech saleable?" and "I believe it should be": Isaacson and Thomas, The
Wise Men, 397–98.

25 "too much rhetoric": David McCullough, Truman (New York: Simon & Schuster,
1992), 649.

25 "to bludgeon the mass mind": Isaacson and Thomas, The Wise Men, 500.

26 "ordinary economic relations" and "If the Devil himself": Chace, Acheson, 218, 224.

26 "Tell him two things" and "He has a strange idea": Isaacson and Thomas, The Wise
Men, 522–23.

27 "doom Red China": Michael W. Miles, The Odyssey of the American Right (New
York: Oxford University Press, 1980), 168.

27 "into communist and 'free-world' components": George F. Kennan, Memoirs,
1925–1956 (Boston: Little, Brown, 1967), 323.

28 "fig leaf": George F. Kennan, "The Long Telegram."

28 "It is a matter of indifference": George F. Kennan, "Russia—Seven Years Later,"
September 1944. As reprinted in Kennan, Memoirs: 1925–1956. Kennan
would later say that it was a more accurate reflection of his thinking than the X
article.

28 "the only reaction of the men": "X" [George F. Kennan], "The Sources of Soviet
Conduct."

28 "[t]here is no reason, in theory" and "rival not a partner": Isaacson and Thomas,
The Wise Men, 374.

28 "[E]vil is not something": Chambers, Witness, 798.

28 *"We consider 'coexistence'"*: "The Magazine's Credenda," *National Review*, November 19, 1955, 6.

29 *"For the millions of slaves"*: Peter Viereck, *Shame and Glory of the Intellectuals* (New Brunswick, NJ: Transaction Books, 2007), 162–64.

29 *took a turn toward the paranoid:* Judis, *Grand Illusion*, 146–47.

29 *"You can get along"*: James Burnham, *Struggle for the World* (New York: John Day, 1946), 160.

29 *"the Third World War had begun"*: Ibid. See also Judis, *Grand Illusion*, 148.

29 *"has read an unusual amount"*: Burnham, *Struggle for the World*, 43.

30 *"heads we tie"*: James Burnham, "The Answer to Sputniks," *National Review*, December 14, 1957, 543.

30 *"It is hard . . . to see"*: James Burnham, *Containment or Liberation?* (New York: John Day, 1953), 48.

30 *"Yalta strategy"*: James Burnham, *Suicide of the West* (New York: John Day, 1964), 261.

30 *"mild initiative"* and *"freedom for all the peoples"*: Burnham, *Containment or Liberation?*, 120, 221.

31 *Buckley loved Burnham's work:* Judis, *William F. Buckley, Jr.*, 82, 123.

31 *"Soviet Communism starts"*: As cited in Townsend Hoopes, *The Devil and John Foster Dulles* (New York: Little Brown, 1973), 83.

31 *"We are not working"* and *"There is a moral"*: John Foster Dulles, "A Policy of Boldness," *Life*, May 19, 1952.

32 *"repudiate all"* and *"[W]e shall again"*: Republican Party platform of 1952 as viewed on www.presidency.ucsb.edu/showplatforms.php?platindex=r1952 as viewed on January 23, 2008.

32 *"Solarium Exercise"*: Anatol Lieven and John Hulsman, *Ethical Realism: A Vision for America's Role in the World* (New York: Pantheon Books, 2006), 24.

32 *"deficient understanding"*: William F. Buckley, Jr., "The Tranquil World of Dwight D. Eisenhower," *National Review*, January 18, 1958, 57–58.

32 *"that the new Eisenhower"*: Brent Bozell, "National Trends," *National Review*, December 31, 1955.

33 *"step by step"*: Frank S. Meyer, "Dilemmas of Foreign Policy," *National Review*, March 29, 1958, 304.

33 *"tranquil world"*: William F. Buckley, Jr., "The Tranquil World of Dwight D. Eisenhower," 57.

33 *"imperialist disintegration"*: John Chamberlain, ed., *National Review Reader* (New York: Bookmailer, 1957), 147.

34 *"barbarous practice"* and *"Any gangster's rule"*: James Burnham, "Summit This Summer?," *National Review*, March 22, 1958, 274.

34 *"summit meeting"*: See, for example, Frank S. Meyer, "The Concept of Fortress America," *National Review*, April 26, 1958, 400.

35 *"Today, you hear much talk"*: As cited in James Chace, "Wise After All," *American Prospect*, June 2004, 31.

35 *"it is essential"*: National Security Council, NSC-68.

35 *"silly"* and *"syndrome"*: Burnham, *Suicide of the West*, 282, 41.

35 *"forward strategy for America"*: Robert Strausz-Hupé, William R. Kintner, and Stefan T. Possony, *A Forward Strategy for America* (New York: Harper, 1961).

35 *"anti-ideological tendency"*: Burnham, *Containment or Liberation?*, 203.

Chapter Two: CANDIDATES

37 *McGeorge Bundy:* McGeorge Bundy recounts the events of that evening and his decision-making process in "Memorandum for the President, March 4, 1963," reprinted in McGeorge Bundy, *Danger and Survival* (New York: Random House, 1988), 684.

38 *"They've got enough":* John Newhouse, *War and Peace in the Nuclear Age* (New York: Knopf, 1989), 172.

38 *Joint Chiefs of Staff demanded:* Bruce J. Allyn, James G. Blight, and David A. Welch, *Cuba on the Brink: Castro, the Missile Crisis, and the Soviet Collapse* (New York: Pantheon, 1993) 383. Graham Allison and Philip Zelikow, *Essence of Decision: Explaining the Cuban Missile Crisis* (New York: Little Brown, 1971), 140–41.

38 *U-2 strayed into Soviet airspace:* Allyn, Blight, and Welch, *Cuba on the Brink,* 383.

38 *U.S. spy in Moscow telephoned:* Newhouse, *War and Peace in the Nuclear Age,* 174. Tim Weiner, "The Spy Who Loved Us," *Washington Monthly,* May 1992.

38 *"Should war indeed break out":* Newhouse, *War and Peace in the Nuclear Age,* 177.

39 *Kennedy himself estimated the chances:* Theodore C. Sorensen, *Kennedy* (New York: Harper & Row, 1965), 705.

39 *he recalled his traveling wife and children:* Thomas Reeves, *A Question of Character: A Life of John F. Kennedy* (New York: Free Press, 1991), 376.

39 *Billy Graham preached:* "The Most Dangerous Days," *New York Times,* October 15, 1992.

39 *"We locked Castro's Communism":* Humberto Fontana, "President Bush, I'm Glad You're No JFK," *Human Events online,* October 19, 2006.

39 *"surrender to blackmail":* Reeves, *A Question of Character,* 276.

39 *standard conservative take:* For example, James Burnham, like Barry Goldwater, was bitter about the peaceful outcome of the Cuban missile crisis because "the communist regime was left undisturbed" even though Cuba was "being transformed into a fortress at the same time that it was serving as the dynamic base for continental subversion." See James Burnham, *Suicide of the West,* 274.

39 *"man's political freedom is illusory":* Barry Goldwater, *The Conscience of a Conservative* (Princeton, NJ: Princeton University Press, 2007), 4.

39 *"revealed truths":* Ibid., xxiv.

39 *ghostwrote Goldwater's right-wing manifesto:* Rick Perlstein, *Before the Storm: Barry Goldwater and the Unmaking of the American Consensus* (New York: Hill and Wang, 2002), 52–53.

40 *"Communist War"—not the "Cold War":* Barry Goldwater, *Why Not Victory?* (New York: McGraw-Hill, 1962), 36.

41 *"We are at war"* and *"I doubt if any":* Ibid., 172, 150.

41 *"daring to win"* and *"central political fact of our time":* Ibid.

41, 42, 42 *"negotiation," "moral support,"* and *"A craven fear":* Goldwater, *The Conscience of a Conservative,* 95, 103, 83.

42 *"we have only two choices":* John F. Kennedy, University of Washington Speech, Seattle, Washington, November 16, 1961.

43 *"national interest is more powerful":* John F. Kennedy, speech, Mormon Tabernacle, Salt Lake City, Utah, September 26, 1963.

43 *"We must recognize":* As cited in Julius Duscha, "Kennedy Raps Goldwater Views," *Washington Post-Times Herald,* September 27, 1963, A–1.

43 *"we shall never negotiate out of fear":* John F. Kennedy, address, UN General Assembly, New York City, September 25, 1961.

43 *Kennedy's chief arms control goal:* For Kennedy's reasons in support of a test ban, see Seaborg, *Kennedy, Khrushchev, and the Test Ban* (Berkeley, CA: University of California Press, 1981), 32–33 and 193–94.

43 *The human cost of testing:* Robert A. Divine, *Blowing on the Wind: The Nuclear Test Ban Debate, 1954–1960* (New York: Oxford University Press, 1978), 4–17.

44 *Kennedy flew by helicopter:* Glenn T. Seaborg, *Kennedy, Khrushchev, and the Test Ban* 30–48.

44 *"If it means political suicide":* As cited in Perlstein, *Before the Storm,* 232.

44, 45 *He then tried to scuttle* and *In truth, nuclear scientists:* Seaborg, *Kennedy, Khrushchev, and the Test Ban,* 281, 288.

45 *"When you stop to think":* As cited in Walter Isaacson and Evan Thomas, *The Wise Men* (New York: Simon & Schuster, 1986), 631–32.

45 *later said that on-site inspections:* Seaborg, *Kennedy, Khrushchev, and the Test Ban,* 142, 242.

45 *"why bother to 'negotiate' about it?":* Goldwater, *The Conscience of a Conservative,* 98.

45 *"cute," "bewildering,"* and *"They are masters":* Goldwater, *Why Not Victory?,* 99, 116–17.

46 *"I do not subscribe":* Ibid., 119.

46 *significance of nuclear weapons:* This section owes a heavy debt to Fred Kaplan, *The Wizards of Armageddon* (Stanford, CA: Stanford University Press, 1991) and to Lawrence Freedman, *The Evolution of Nuclear Strategy* (New York: Palgrave Macmillan, 3d ed., 2003).

46 *Bernard Brodie:* The Brodie biographical information and August 7, 1945, anecdote are from Kaplan, *The Wizards of Armageddon,* 9–23.

47 *military superiority no longer mattered:* Bernard Brodie, "War in the Atomic Age," as cited in Bernard Brodie, ed., *The Absolute Weapon* (New York: Harcourt Brace, 1946), 47–49.

47 *"Thus far the chief purpose":* Bernard Brodie, "Implications for Military Policy," in Brodie, ed., *The Absolute Weapon,* 76.

47 *"national objectives in war":* Bernard Brodie, "Nuclear Weapons: Strategic or Tactical?," *Foreign Affairs,* January 1954, 227.

48 *"depend primarily":* As cited in Lawrence Freedman, *The Evolution of Nuclear Strategy* (New York: Palgrave Macmillan, 2003), 81.

48 *Plan 1-A:* Kaplan, *The Wizards of Armageddon,* 271.

48 *kill a nation:* Gerard J. DeGroot, *The Bomb: A Life* (Cambridge: Harvard University Press, 2005), 153.

48 *"Mr. Secretary, I hope":* As cited in Kaplan, *The Wizards of Armageddon,* 271–72.

48 *McNamara, a whiz kid:* Ibid., 248–57.

49 *"war orgasm":* Ibid., 223.

49 *Brodie likened the SIOP:* DeGroot, *The Bomb: A Life,* 207.

50 *Kahn, for example, in a dark tome:* Herman Kahn, *On Thermonuclear War* (Princeton, NJ: Princeton University Press, 1960).

50 *"Our damage limiting problem":* As cited in Bundy, *Danger and Survival,* 547.

51 *A thorough Pentagon study: Damage Limiting: A Rationale for the Allocation of*

Resources by the U.S. and the U.S.S.R., January 21, 1964, as cited in Kaplan, *The Wizards of Armageddon,* 315–27.

52 *what if one side thought:* For more on how perceptions can exacerbate uncertainty, see Thomas C. Schelling, *The Strategy of Conflict* (Cambridge: Harvard University Press, 1960), 207–29.

54 *"The essential feature of arms control":* Thomas C. Schelling and Morton H. Halperin, *Strategy and Arms Control* (Washington, D.C.: Pergamon-Brasseys, 1975), 2.

55 *the new conservative internationalism:* On this point, see E. J. Dionne, Jr., *Why Americans Hate Politics* (New York: Simon & Schuster, 1991), 164.

56 *"No superstition has more effectively":* "The Magazine's Credenda," *National Review,* 1955, 6.

56 *"the organization could handicap":* See, for example, James Burnham, "Ideology and Common Sense," *National Review,* October 8, 1960, 208.

56 *"You and I, dear reader":* J. D. Futch, "Whose Opinion Is World Opinion?," *National Review,* October 23, 1962, 316.

57 *"designed to control":* Goldwater, *Why Not Victory?,* 107.

57 *Goldwater had particular scorn:* Ibid., 109.

57 *concepts on which:* See, for example, As *National Review*'s editors explained, "The fundamental reason for the monstrosity of the UN as a political organization lies in the fact that a fraud—or, more gently, an illusion—is embodied in its essence: the illusion that there exists a consensus of some significant sort among all nations of the world leading them to seek peace, justice, freedom, well-being and what not, and serving as a trustworthy foundation for an international law. The truth is otherwise." Editorial, "What About UN Bonds?," *National Review,* January 30, 1962, 49.

57 *"must avoid complete reliance":* Goldwater, *Why Not Victory?,* 130.

58 *China was the ultimate rogue state:* Francis J. Gavin, "Blasts from the Past," *International Security,* Winter 2004/2005.

58 *"If the worst came to the worst":* As cited in ibid.

58 *the committee concluded:* "A Report to the President by the Committee on Nuclear Proliferation," *Foreign Relations of the United States: 1964–1968,* Volume XI, *Arms Control and Disarmament,* January 21, 1965.

59 *"to pursue negotiations":* Treaty on the Non-Proliferation of Nuclear Weapons, Article VI, signed July 1, 1968.

59 *Goldwater worried:* "Senate Again Rejects Atom Treaty Change," *Washington Post,* March 13, 1969, A10.

59 *"the Treaty may make us":* "The Week," *National Review,* March 25, 1969.

59 *"nothing in the treaty":* Memorandum by J. Terry Emerson, Goldwater's foreign policy adviser, December 12, 1968, via the Arizona Historical Foundation.

60 *"New nuclear capabilities":* "A Report to the President by the Committee on Nuclear Proliferation," *Foreign Relations of the United States: 1964–1968,* Volume XI, *Arms Control and Disarmament,* January 21, 1965.

60 *"implausible that additional":* Roswell L. Gilpatric, Minutes of discussion of the Committee on nonproliferation, *Foreign Relations of the United States: 1964–1968,* Volume XI, *Arms Control and Disarmament,* January 8, 1965.

60 *one committee member noted:* John J. McCloy, ibid.

60 *editors said it was his finest:* "William Henry Chamberlin, RIP," *National Review,* October 7, 1969, 1000.

60 *"United States ratification"*: William Henry Chamberlin, "The Great Nonproliferation Hoax," *National Review,* March 11, 1969, 229.

60 *"option to establish"*: "Senate Again Rejects Atom Treaty Change," *Washington
Post,* March 13, 1969, A10.

62 *"Moral claims involve"*: Henry Kissinger, *A World Restored: Metternich, Castlereagh
and the Problems of Peace, 1812–22* (Boston: Houghton Mifflin, 1957), 317.

62 *"a struggle between good and evil"*: Kissinger, *Years of Renewal: The Concluding
Volume of His Memoirs* (New York: Simon & Schuster, 1999), 97.

62 *"seek a more productive"*: As cited in Walter Isaacson, *Kissinger: A Biography* (New
York: Simon & Schuster, 1992), 659–60.

62 *Coexistence was an "imperative"*: As cited in Raymond L. Garthoff, *Détente and
Confrontation: American-Soviet Relations from Nixon to Reagan* (Washington,
D.C.: Brookings Institution Press, 1994), 605, footnote 24.

63 *"the destructiveness of modern weapons"*: Henry A. Kissinger, *Nuclear Weapons
and Foreign Policy* (New York: W. W. Norton, 1969), 107–11.

63 *Kissinger soon changed his mind*: Henry Kissinger, *The Necessity for Choice* (New
York: Harper & Brothers, 1960), 75–94. See also Isaacson, *Kissinger,* 88–89 and
105–7.

64 *"major effect of the ABM Treaty"*: Richard Nixon, *RN: The Memoirs of Richard
Nixon,* Volume II (New York: Warner Books, 1978), 99.

65 *"fundamental premise of détente"*: John Lewis Gaddis, *The Cold War: A New History* (New York: Penguin Press, 2007), 187.

65 *"It is not the case"*: James Burnham, "Détente (Deletions)," *National Review,*
August 2, 1974, 857.

65 *"Manhattan Twelve"*: John B. Judis, *William F. Buckley, Jr.: Patron Saint of the Conservatives* (New York: Simon & Schuster, 1988), 329–30. Charles A. Moser, *Promise
and Hope: The Ashbrook Presidential Campaign of 1972* (Washington, D.C.: Free
Congress Foundation, 1985), 3.

65 *Ashbrook had little recognition*: "A Small Paul Revere," *Time,* December 20, 1971.

65 *Ashbrook had helped launch*: J. William Middendorf II, *A Glorious Disaster: Barry
Goldwater's Presidential Campaign and the Origins of the Conservative Movement*
(Cambridge: Basic Books, 2006), 12.

65 *He was a founder*: William Rusher, "John Ashbrook, RIP," *National Review,* May
14, 1982, 532. Robert Sherrill, "Why John Ashbrook Is Running for President of
the United States," *Saturday Review,* June 3, 1972, 18.

65 *a leader of the Committee*: Robert Sherrill, "Why John Ashbrook Is Running for
President of the United States."

65 *He considered détente an illusion*: 1972 John Ashbrook for President campaign
brochure.

65 *"apostasy"*: December 15, 1971, statement by John Ashbrook to the House of Representatives, as reproduced in *Human Events,* January 8, 1972, 8–9.

65 *denounced the president's summit*: Ibid.

66 *A poll of the thirty-one thousand members*: Robert Sherrill, "Why John Ashbrook
Is Running for President of the United States."

66 *refused to participate*: "Goldwater Asks Support for Nixon Policies," *Washington
Post*/UPI, September 3, 1971, A-13.

66 *"somehow cut a deal"*: John Ashbrook, statement to the House of Representatives,
December 15, 1971, *Human Events,* January 8, 1972, 9.

66 *"close to clinical lunacy"*: Ibid.

66 *"When a strong man"*: John Ashbrook, statement to the House of Representatives, February 1, 1972, Congressional Record, 2055.

66 *the Kennedy and Johnson administrations*: Natural Resources Defense Council, "NRDC: Nuclear Data—Table of U.S. Strategic Offensive Force Loadings, 1945–2002." Available at http://www.nrdc.org/nuclear/nudb/datab1.asp.

67 *"Everyone knows"*: Ibid.

67 *"The concept of mutual assured destruction"* and subsequent quotes: Donald G. Brennan, "When the SALT Hit the Fan," *National Review*, June 23, 1972, 685–92.

67 *Phyllis Schlafly* and subsequent quotes: Donald Critchlow, *Phyllis Schlafly and Grassroots Conservatism: A Woman's Crusade* (Princeton, NJ: Princeton University Press, 2005).

68 *"when the cause for arms is removed"*: Goldwater, *Why Not Victory?*, 120.

68 *"the United States can agree"*: Anthony H. Harrigan, "Three Concessions We Shouldn't Make," *National Review*, December 30, 1969, 1312.

68 *"The total history of man"*: John Ashbrook, statement to the House of Representatives, June 29, 1972, Congressional Record, 23462.

68 *"I repeat: The nature of the regime"*: James Burnham, "SALT on Whose Tail?," *National Review*, July 21, 1972, 788.

70 *"principles are in the ascendancy"*: Ronald Reagan, speech, Ashbrook Memorial Fundraising Dinner, Ashland, Ohio, May 9, 1983.

70 *White House officials*: See, for example, Bernard Gwertzman, "Accord Expected to Offset Missile Totals and Power," *New York Times*, May 24, 1972, 1.

70 *The only explanation*: Spencer Rich, "Nixon Meets Hill Leaders on Arms Pact," *Washington Post*, June 3, 1972, A-1.

71 *"Our real preference"*: Richard Perle, transcript of an interview for the CNN Cold War series *Freeze*, March 30, 1997.

Chapter Three: MOVEMENT

72 *On November 12, 1979*: "Peace Through Strength Week" promotional, educational, and welcoming materials from the Coalition for Peace Through Strength, November 1979, attained via the American Security Council, Washington, D.C.

72 *American Security Council*: Jerry W. Sanders, *Peddlers of Crisis: The Committee on the Present Danger and the Politics of Containment* (Cambridge: South End Press, 1983), 211, 225. See also the above materials from the American Security Council.

72 *"symbol of phased surrender"*: Pamphlet, "SALT II Locks U.S. into Posture of Military Inferiority: Highlights of a Comprehensive Report Prepared by the Coalition for Peace Through Strength," Coalition for Peace Through Strength via the American Security Council.

73 The SALT Syndrome: Coalition for Peace Through Strength video, *The SALT Syndrome*, 1980 via the American Security Council.

73 *Ultimately, it was shown*: American Security Council, "Project Survival: An Urgent Television Campaign for the Defense of America, a Prospectus," June 1, 1980.

73 *outspending protreaty forces*: Sanders, *Peddlers of Crisis*, 265.

74 *60 percent to 70 percent*: Ibid., 194.

74 *"Diogenes couldn't find"*: "Détente v. Détente," *National Review*, July 12, 1974, B97.

76 *Jesse Helms:* Jesse Helms, *Here's Where I Stand: A Memoir* (New York: Random House, 2005), 83. Ernest B. Ferguson, *Hard Right: The Rise of Jesse Helms* (New York: W. W. Norton, 1986), 113–14.

76 *"showing a flair":* George F. Will, "Solzhenitsyn and the President," *Washington Post,* July 11, 1975.

77 *"the betrayal of Eastern Europe"* and *"an amicable agreement":* As cited in Walter Isaacson, *Kissinger: A Biography* (New York: Simon & Schuster, 1992), 658.

77 *"one of the great moral heroes"* and *"the American seal of approval":* As cited in ibid., 664–65.

78 *was persuaded not to challenge:* James Mann, *Rise of the Vulcans: The History of Bush's War Cabinet* (New York: Portfolio, 2004), 65, 72–73.

78 *Ford, however, knew:* John Newhouse, *War and Peace in the Nuclear Age* (New York: Alfred Knopf, 1989), 249–50. As William G. Hyland told journalist John Newhouse, the political demand from Jackson and his supporters led to a suboptimal agreement: "The main requirement was that [the president] emerge with an arms control agreement that was 'equal,' interpreted to mean equality in every category of weapons. This rather simple-minded view of what was at stake badly limited Ford's maneuvering room. In the end he succeeded in reaching an agreement that was, in fact, equal in all respects. But in doing so a greater opportunity was missed, the chance to bargain for limits on those Soviet weapons that concerned us most."

79 *Senator James L. Buckley:* As cited in Daniel Oliver, "At Home," *National Review,* December 20, 1974, B182.

79 *"the agreement recognizes":* James Burnham, "Some Missiles Are More Equal . . . ," *National Review,* December 20, 1974, 1453.

79 *"the major drawback":* As cited in "Reagan at the Start," *National Review,* December 19, 1975, 1468.

79 *Schlesinger put a different spin on it:* Fred Kaplan, *The Wizards of Armageddon* (Stanford, CA: Stanford University Press, 1991), 373.

79 *"military superiority":* Sanders, *Peddlers of Crisis,* 202.

79 *Schlesinger worried:* See, for example, "Détente: H.K. v. J.S.," *Time,* November 17, 1975.

80 *Schlesinger told Nixon:* Richard Nixon, *RN: The Memoirs of Richard Nixon,* vol. II (New York: Warner Books, 1978), 606–7.

80 *wrote Senator Scoop Jackson* and *encouraged Ford:* Garthoff, *Détente and Confrontation,* 460, 496.

80 *"the truth about our military status":* Ronald Reagan, as cited in Gerald R. Ford, *A Time to Heal: The Autobiography of Gerald R. Ford* (New York: Harper & Row, 1979), 346.

80 *tried to sabotage:* Strobe Talbott, *The Master of the Game: Paul Nitze and the Nuclear Peace* (New York: Knopf, 1988), 86–87.

80 *Rumsfeld cabled Kissinger:* Jason Vest, "Darth Rumsfeld," *American Prospect,* February 26, 2001.

80 *forcing Kissinger to abandon:* Newhouse, *War and Peace in the Nuclear Age,* 260–61.

80 *"The attitude in the Defense Department":* Ford, *A Time to Heal,* 357.

81 *"there is every prospect"* and subsequent quotes: Paul H. Nitze, "Assuring Strategic Stability in an Era of Détente," *Foreign Affairs,* January 1976, 207.

83 *"Wouldn't it be nice"*: As cited in John Newhouse, *War and Peace*, 241.

83 *the cafeteria alcoves*: Kristol and others discuss this period in Joseph Dorman, *Arguing the World: New York Intellectuals in Their Own Words* (Chicago: University of Chicago Press, 2001). See also Francis Fukuyama, *America at the Crossroads: Democracy, Power, and the American Legacy* (New Haven, CT: Yale University Press, 2006), 14–17.

84 *"hard anti-communism"*: Norman Podhoretz, *Making It* (New York: Random House, 1967), 290–291.

84 *The New Left riled*: E. J. Dionne, Jr., *Why Americans Hate Politics* (New York: Simon & Schuster, 1991), 46–47.

84 *Tom Hayden*: Dorman, *Arguing the World*, 141.

85 *McGeorge Bundy*: McGeorge Bundy, "The End of Either/Or," *Foreign Affairs*, January 1967.

85 *neoconservatives were convinced*: John Ehrman, *The Rise of Neoconservatism: Intellectuals and Foreign Affairs 1945–1994* (New Haven, CT: Yale University Press, 1995), 47–49.

86 *procedural changes took the power*: Dionne, *Why Americans Hate Politics*, 120.

86 *neoconservatives formed*: Ehrman, *The Rise of Neoconservatism*, 60.

86 *The CDM argued*: Coalition for a Democratic Majority task force on foreign policy, "The Quest for Détente," Summer 1974.

87 *"As they did in the Truman years"*: Coalition for a Democratic Majority task force on foreign policy, "For an Adequate Defense," November 19, 1975.

87 *"Come on in"*: "Come on in, the water's fine," *National Review*, March 9, 1971.

88 *"[W]e insist"*: As cited in Franklin Foer, "The Closing of the Presidential Mind," *New Republic*, July 26, 2004.

88 *"The profound crisis of our era"*: "The Magazine's Credenda," *National Review*, November 19, 1955, 6.

89 *"[W]e certainly do have it in our power"*: Irving Kristol, "A Foolish American Ism—Utopianism," *New York Times Magazine*, November 14, 1971, 103.

89 *"of political philosophy"*: As cited in Adam Wolfson, "About the Public Interest," *Public Interest*, Spring 2005.

89 *"political problems"*: Russell Kirk, *The Conservative Mind*, 7th rev. ed. (Washington, D.C.: Regnery, 1986), 8.

90 *"scientific approaches"*: George H. Nash, *The Conservative Intellectual Movement in America Since 1945* (New York: Basic Books, 1976), 55.

90 *David T. Bazelon published*: David T. Bazelon, "The New Class," *Commentary*, August 1966.

90 *neoconservatives employed his analysis*: See, for example, B. Bruce-Briggs, *The New Class?* (New Brunswick, NJ: Center for Policy Research, 1979).

90 *"It is the self-imposed assignment"*: Dionne, *Why Americans Hate Politics*, 65.

90 *Much of this animus was initially*: John B. Judis, *The Paradox of American Democracy* (New York: Routledge, 2001), 118.

91 *"anti-capitalist aspirations of the left"*: Ibid.

91 *"The simple truth"*: Dionne, *Why Americans Hate Politics*, 63.

91 *"When business finds"*: Robert L. Bartley, "Business and the New Class," in B. Bruce-Biggs, ed., *The New Class?*, 64–65.

91 *Brookings Institution had been established*: Judis, *The Paradox of American Democracy*, 122.

91 *"We're not here"*: Ibid., 127.

92 *two articles for* Foreign Policy: Albert Wohlstetter, "Is There a Strategic Arms Race?," *Foreign Policy,* Summer 1974. Albert Wohlstetter, "Rivals, but No 'Race,'" *Foreign Policy,* Fall 1974.

92 *arguing against a straw man:* Morton H. Halperin and Jeremy J. Stone, "Is There a Strategic Arms Race? (II): Comments," *Foreign Policy,* Fall 1974, 88–92.

92 *The recent miscalculation* and *CIA predictions:* John Prados, *The Soviet Estimate: U.S. Intelligence Analysis and Soviet Strategic Forces* (Princeton, NJ: Princeton University Press, 1986), 198. In a review of its track record conducted in January 1976, a study commissioned by the Agency found that while the CIA had indeed underestimated the number of new Soviet ICBMs, it had successfully predicted the deployment of new types of weapons, which was more important. The report acknowledged that the CIA had underestimated advances in throw weight, but at the same time the Soviets had not achieved the accuracy to target our Minuteman silos as early as thought. In sum, the CIA had overestimated some things, underestimated others, and gotten quite a few right. Anne Hessing Cahn, *Killing Détente: The Right Attacks the CIA* (University Park, PA: Pennsylvania State University Press, 1998), 129.

92 *holding pen for prominent conservatives:* Cahn, *Killing Détente,* 104–5.

93 *"destroying this invasive evil":* Sam Tanenhaus, "The Hard-Liner," *Boston Globe,* November 2, 2003.

94 *"There is no point":* Sanders, *Peddlers of Crisis,* 199.

94 *"consistently wrong":* Cahn, *Killing Détente,* 154.

94 *"We are in the midst":* Sanders, *Peddlers of Crisis,* 198.

94 *American intelligence revised:* Prados, *The Soviet Estimate,* 186, 192.

94 *"in the mid-1960s":* Cahn, *Killing Détente,* 108.

94 *Team B scoffed* and subsequent quotes: Report of Team B, "Intelligence Community Experiment in Competitive Analysis: Soviet Strategic Objectives, an Alternative View," December 1976.

95 *"I am unaware":* Sanders, *Peddlers of Crisis,* 201.

95 *"overall strategic superiority":* Ibid.

95 *"The question was":* Ibid.

96 *"zero-sum discussion":* Cahn, *killing Détente,* 158.

96 *"[N]umerous sources":* As cited in Sanders, *Peddlers of Crisis,* 200.

96 *"high-ranking officials":* David Binder, "New CIA Estimate Finds Soviets Seek Superiority in Arms," *New York Times,* December 26, 1976.

96 *"probably striving for":* "National Intelligence Estimate: Soviet Forces for Intercontinental Conflict Through the Mid-1980s," NIE: 11-3/8-75, November 17, 1975.

96 *General Keegan claimed:* Cahn, *Killing Détente,* 167.

97 *growth in Soviet military spending:* Noel E. Firth and James H. Noren, *Soviet Defense Spending: A History of CIA Estimates, 1950–1990* (College Station, TX: Texas A&M University Press, 1998), Chapter Five.

97 *Team B was not the first:* In 1957, for example, the blue-ribbon Gaither Committee warned ominously that, by 1959, the Soviets might be able to launch a disarming first strike against U.S. nuclear forces using ICBMs—and suggested that it might well do so once it had the ability. During the 1960 election, Kennedy exploited the fear engendered by this report to warn of an alleged "missile gap," which turned out to be fictitious.

97 *According to John Prados:* Author telephone interview with John Prados, December 12, 2006.

98 *"[T]he failure of the profession":* Richard Pipes, "Russia's Chance," *Commentary,* March 1992, 33.

99 *the Committee on the Present Danger believed:* For a collection of the CPD's policy papers and statements, see Charles Tyroler II, ed., *Alerting America: The Papers of the Committee on the Present Danger* (Washington, D.C.: Pergamon-Brasseys, 1984), 13.

99 *"The Soviet military build-up":* Committee on the Present Danger, "What Is the Soviet Union Up To?" as reprinted in Tyroler, *Alerting America,* April, 7, 1977, 13.

100 *the United States went:* Talbott, *Master of the Game,* 143ff.

100 *"'enough' may not be enough":* Tyroler, "What Is the Soviet Union Up To?" *Alerting America,* 14–15.

100 *"The early 1980's threaten":* Committee on the Present Danger, "Is America Becoming Number 2? Current Trends in the U.S.-Soviet Military Balance," October 5, 1978, cited in Sanders, *Peddlers of Crisis,* 255.

101 *Paul Warnke Unites the Right:* This section owes a heavy debt to Jerry Sanders's excellent book *Peddlers of Crisis.*

101 *"We face a single military threat":* Paul C. Warnke, "Apes on a Treadmill," *Foreign Policy,* Spring 1975, 12–29.

101 *"unilateral abandonment by the U.S.":* As cited in Sanders, *Peddlers of Crisis,* 204.

102 *The Emergency Coalition:* Ibid., 208–9.

102 *"public anger over busing":* As cited in Dionne, *Why Americans Hate Politics,* 230.

103 *"Most of the 'New Conservatives'":* John B. Judis, *William F. Buckley, Jr.: Patron Saint of the Conservatives* (New York: Simon & Schuster, 1988), 379.

103 *"I have simply nothing to say":* Ibid.

103 *"they take a religious view":* As cited in Dionne, *Why Americans Hate Politics,* 233.

103 *The canal controversy:* Sanders, *Peddlers of Crisis,* 265.

103 *"absolutely asinine"* and *"screwball, arbitrary and fictitious":* Talbott, *Master of the Game.*

103 *in collusion with "the World Peace Council":* As cited in Sanders, *Peddlers of Crisis,* 207.

104 *"the two Macs":* John Micklethwait and Adrian Wooldridge, *The Right Nation: Conservative Power in America* (New York: Penguin Books, 2005), 82.

104 *"a peculiar, almost venomous intensity":* Anthony Lewis, "The Brooding Hawks," *New York Times,* February 20, 1977.

105 *"Stunned speechless":* As cited in Newhouse, *War and Peace in the Nuclear Age,* 294.

105 *"So that we could both have gotten credit":* Ibid., 304.

106 *"appeasement in its purest form":* Coalition for Peace Through Strength video, *The SALT Syndrome,* 1980, via the American Security Council.

106 *"Our nation's situation":* As cited in Mann, *Rise of the Vulcans,* 102–3.

106 *"is not to wage a nuclear war":* Tyroler, *Alerting America.*

107 *if two thousand one-megaton warheads:* Office of Technology Assessment, "The Effects of Nuclear War," May 1979, Chapter 4, Case 3, 81.

107 *"The idea that":* As cited in Robert Scheer, *With Enough Shovels: Reagan, Bush, and Nuclear War* (New York: Random House, 1982), 74.

107 *an Arms Control and Disarmament Agency study:* Spurgeon M. Keeny, Jr., and Wolfgang K. H. Panofsky, "MAD Versus NUTS: Can Doctrine or Weaponry

Remedy the Mutual Hostage Relationship of the Superpowers?" *Foreign Affairs,* Winter 1981/1982, 295.

108 *"What fire power":* James Burnham, *Containment or Liberation? An Inquiry into the Aims of United States Foreign Policy* (New York: John Day, 1952), 179.

108 *"The basic question":* James Burnham, "The Third World War," *National Review,* March 21, 1956, 19.

108 *"A responsible objective":* Paul H. Nitze, "Assuring Strategic Stability in an Era of Détente," *Foreign Affairs,* January 1976, 222.

109 *From 1989 to 1994:* A summary of the so-called Hines report is presented in John A. Battilega, "Soviet Views of Nuclear Warfare: The Post-Cold War Interviews," Henry D. Sokolski, ed., *Getting MAD: Nuclear Mutual Assured Destruction, Its Origins and Practice* (Carlisle, PA: Strategic Studies Institute, 2004).

111 *PD-59:* On PD-59, see William E. Odom, "The Origins and Design of Presidential Decision-59: A Memoir," Henry D. Sokolski, ed., *Getting MAD: Nuclear Mutual Assured Destruction, Its Origins and Practice* (Carlisle, PA: Strategic Studies Institute, 2004).

111 *Harold Brown:* As cited in Kaplan, *The Wizards of Armageddon,* 385–86.

111 *"Especially now":* President Jimmy Carter, State of the Union Address, January 1980.

Chapter Four: PRESIDENT

112 *The National Cathedral:* David von Drehle, "Reagan Hailed as Leader for the Ages," *Washington Post,* June 11, 2004.

112 *"one of ours":* "Reagan for Today," *National Review,* June 28, 2004.

112 *"'Cross of Gold' speech":* Frances FitzGerald, *Way Out There in the Blue: Reagan, Star Wars and the End of the Cold War* (New York: Simon & Schuster, 2000), 59.

113 *"government does nothing as well"* and subseqeuent quotes: Ronald Reagan, "A Time for Choosing," speech, televised October 27, 1964.

113 *"favorite magazine":* Ronald Reagan, speech at the Madison Hotel, Washington, D.C., *National Review* reception, February 21, 1983.

113 *Podhoretz liked to brag:* John Micklethwait and Adrian Wooldridge, *The Right Nation: Conservative Power in America,* 92.

113 *"found a home":* As cited on medaloffreedom.com/henryjackson on December 15, 2007.

113 *"shining city on a hill":* Ronald Reagan, farewell address, Washington, D.C., January 11, 1989.

113 *"rendezvous with destiny":* Ronald Reagan, "A Time for Choosing."

114 *"It took approximxately":* George F. Will, "For Senator Barry Goldwater," *National Review 25th Anniversary,* December 31, 1980, 1645.

114 *"More than any other influence":* Dick Cheney, as cited in "Cheney Delivers Eulogy at Reagan's State Funeral," Washington, D.C., June 10, 2004.

114 *"Ronald Reagan believed":* George W. Bush, speech, Washington, D.C., June 11, 2004.

115 *Cannon describes it:* Lou Cannon, *President Reagan: The Role of a Lifetime* (New York: Simon & Schuster, 1991), 306.

116 *Addressing West Point's graduating class:* Ronald Reagan, "Address at Commencement Exercises at the United States Military Academy," West Point, New York, May 27, 1981.

116 *University of Notre Dame:* Ronald Reagan, "Address at Commencement Exercises at the University of Notre Dame," South Bend, Indiana, May 17, 1981.

116 *"the march of freedom"* and subsequent quotes: Ronald Reagan, "Address to Members of the British Parliament," London, England, June 8, 1982.

117 *"evil empire" speech:* Ronald Reagan, "Remarks at the Annual Convention of the National Association of Evangelicals," Orlando, Florida, March 8, 1982.

117 *Buckley protégé:* Cannon, *President Reagan*, 273–74.

117 *"We must never forget"* and subsequent quotes: Ronald Reagan, "Remarks at the Annual Convention of the National Association of Evangelicals."

117 *"take us with a phone call":* Robert Scheer, *With Enough Shovels: Reagan, Bush, and Nuclear War*, 66.

117 *"Look at the difference":* Lettow, *Ronald Reagan and His Quest to Abolish Nuclear Weapons*, 49.

117 *"halt the decline":* Ronald Reagan, "Remarks and a Question-and-Answer Session with Reporters on the Announcement of the United States Strategic Weapons Program," Washington, D.C., October 2, 1981.

117 *"strategic superiority":* As cited in Lawrence S. Wittner, *Toward Nuclear Abolition: History of the World Nuclear Disarmament Movement* (Stanford, CA: Stanford University Press, 2003), 112.

117 *"I look forward":* Ibid., 116.

118 *largest peacetime military buildup:* Ed Magnuson, "A Bonanza for Defense," *Time*, March 16, 1981.

118 *He authorized the deployment:* See, for example, Daryl Kimball, "Looking Back: The Nuclear Arms Control Legacy of Ronald Reagan," *Arms Control Today*, July 2004.

118 *"fatally flawed":* Jacob V. Lamar, "SALT II Is Finito," *Time*, June 9, 1986.

118 *In a September 1979:* as cited in Wittner, *Toward Nuclear Abolition*, 112.

118 *"Diplomacy and treaties":* Lawrence W. Beilenson, *The Treaty Trap* (Washington, D.C.: Public Affairs, 1969).

118 *"the best book written":* Beth A. Fischer, *The Reagan Reversal: Foreign Policy and the End of the Cold War* (Columbia, MO: University of Missouri, 1997), 105.

119 *told the Senate Foreign Relations Committee:* Wittner, *Toward Nuclear Abolition*, 118.

119 *"Arms control thinking":* Ibid.

119 *"favor to the Russians":* Scheer, *With Enough Shovels*, 94–95.

119 *"Arms control has developed":* Richard Burt, "The Relevance of Arms Control in the 1980s," *Daedalus*, Winter 1981, 159–77.

119 *a frustrated Henry Kissinger:* Talbott, *Deadly Gambits*, 16.

119 *Austrian State Treaty of 1955:* Talbott, *Master of the Game*, 262.

120 *"does violence":* Talbott, *Deadly Gambits*, 348.

120 *"The sense that we":* Wittner, *Toward Nuclear Abolition*, 117.

120 *"categorically opposed":* George P. Shultz, *Turmoil and Triumph: Diplomacy, Power, and the Victory of the American Ideal* (New York: Scribner, 1993), 275.

120 *"a fucking parking lot":* Mann, *Rise of the Vulcans*, 114–15.

121 *pragmatists pressured Reagan:* Ibid., 45–46. Talbott, *Master of the Game*, 163–64, and *Deadly Gambits*, 45–46.

121 *conservatives did:* Talbott, *Deadly Gambits*, 176–79.

121 *Perle appeared:* Talbott, *Master of the Game*, 171.

122 *Nitze's ideological proclivities:* Ibid., 107–8.

122 *Nitze was trusted:* Ibid., 168.

122 *took matters into:* Ibid., 170–76.

123 *"an inveterate problem-solver":* Strobe Talbott, "Arms and the Man," *Time,* December 21, 1987.

123 *even falsely asserting:* Talbott, *Master of the Game,* 176–77.

123 *Perle ultimately persuaded:* Fitzgerald, *Way Out There in the Blue,* 178.

123 *even Margaret Thatcher:* Talbott, *Deadly Gambits,* 173.

123 *"We can't just do something":* Talbott, *Master of the Game,* 178.

123 *In May 1982:* Ronald Reagan, "Address at Commencement Exercises," Eureka College, Eureka, Illinois, May 9, 1982.

123 *The president's START proposal:* Fitzgerald, *Way Out There in the Blue,* 182–85.

123 *"if the Russians accept":* Ibid., 184–85.

124 *"telling it like it is"* and subsequent examples: Talbott, *Deadly Gambits,* 278–85.

124 *Congress decided:* Ibid., 302.

125 *the administration "compromised":* Ibid., 302.

125 *"Your idea of 'flexibility'":* Ibid., 313.

125 *"The Legislative Branch":* Ibid., 340.

125 *The "basic position"* and *"Ambassador Rowny":* Ibid., 341–42.

126 *"the Soviet Union decided":* Scheer, *With Enough Shovels,* 31.

126 *"not only survived"* and *"The human race":* Ibid., 87–88.

126 *"I'm not saying":* Dr. Strangelove, or How I Learned to Stop Worrying and Love the Bomb, 1964.

126 *"You have a survivability":* Scheer, *With Enough Shovels,* 29.

127 *"country better prepared":* Wittner, *Toward Nuclear Abolition,* 119.

127 *he said the odds:* Charles Fenyvesi, "The Man Not Worried by the Bomb," *Washington Post,* April 11, 1982.

127 *"victory is possible":* Colin S. Gray and Keith Payne, "Victory Is Possible," *Foreign Policy,* Summer 1980.

127 *"I want to come out of it":* Scheer, *With Enough Shovels,* 53.

127 *"over a protracted period,"* *"Pentagon Draws Up,"* and *"must prevail":* Richard Halloran, "Pentagon Draws Up First Strategy for Fighting a Long Nuclear War," *New York Times,* May 30, 1982.

127 *"the first reported time":* Michael Getler, "Administration's Nuclear War Policy Stance Still Murky," *Washington Post,* November 10, 1982.

128 *"seek early war termination":* "National Security Decision Memorandum 242," January 17, 1974, as viewed on Nixon.archives.gov/virtuallibrary/documents/nsdm/nsdm_242.pdf on December 15, 2007.

128 *"We must be capable"* and *"preserve the possibility":* Presidential Directive/NSC-59, July 25, 1980, as viewed on jimmycarterlibrary.org/documents.pddirectives/pres directive.phtml on December 15, 2007.

128 *"a reserve of nuclear forces":* Fitzgerald, *Way Out There in the Blue,* 187.

129 *Interviews with former Soviet:* John Battilega, "Soviet Views of Nuclear Warfare: The Post-Cold War Interviews," as in Henry D. Sokolski, ed., *Getting MAD: Nuclear Mutual Assured Destruction, Its Origins and Practice* (Carlisle, PA: Strategic Studies Institute, 2004), 157.

129 *"impotent and obsolete":* Ronald Reagan, Address to the Nation on National Security, March 23, 1983.

129 *"That was the best statement"*: Lettow, *Ronald Reagan and His Quest to Abolish Nuclear Weapons*, 114.

130 *Thomas K. Jones:* Scheer, *With Enough Shovels*, 18–26.

130 *"dig a hole"* and *"If there are enough shovels"*: "The Dirt on T. K. Jones," *New York Times*, March 19, 1982.

130 *"civil defense"*: on www.presidency.ucsb.edu/showplatforms.php?platrider=r1980 as viewed on January 23, 2008. Republican Party platform of 1980, Detroit, Michigan, July 15, 1980.

130 *"It would be a terrible mess"* and *"As I say, the ants"*: Scheer, *With Enough Shovels*, 108, 3.

131 *Flight KAL007* and *Reagan and his aides:* Don Oberdorfer, *The Turn: From the Cold War to a New Era* (New York: Poseidon Press, 1991), 50–55.

131 *"massacre," "crime against humanity,"* and *"an atrocity"*: Ronald Reagan, as cited in Oberdorfer, *The Turn*, 59.

131 *"sharpest exchange"*: Robert M. Gates, *From the Shadows: The Ultimate Insider's Story of Five Presidents and How They Won the Cold War* (New York: Simon & Schuster, 2006), 269.

131 *Gromyko's plane:* Oberdorfer, *The Turn*, 61.

132 *"proved a catalyst"*: Anatoly Dobrynin, *In Confidence: Moscow's Ambassador to America's Six Cold War Presidents* (New York: Random House, 1995), 537.

132 *"If anybody ever had any illusions"*: Ibid., 512.

132 *"madman"* and *"the world situation"*: Oberdorfer, *The Turn*, 65, 61.

132 *76 percent of Americans:* Daryl Kimball, "Looking Back: The Nuclear Arms Control Legacy of Ronald Reagan," *Arms Control Today*, July 2004.

132 *On June 12, 1982:* "Randall Forsberg, Leader of Nuclear Freeze Movement, Dies," Associated Press, November 1, 2007.

132 *That November:* Wittner, *Toward Nuclear Abolition*, 176–77.

133 *"the only winning move"*: *WarGames*, 1983.

133 *one hundred million viewers:* Fischer, *The Reagan Reversal*, 115.

133 *85 percent of Americans:* Wittner, *Toward Nuclear Abolition*, 187–88.

133 *"greatly depressed"* and *"aware of the need"*: Ronald Reagan, *An American Life* (New York: Simon & Schuster, 1980), 585.

133 *he was briefed:* Fischer, *The Reagan Reversal*, 120–21.

133 *Indeed, some of his advisers:* Lettow, *Ronald Reagan and His Quest to Abolish Nuclear Weapons*, 35.

133 *Meeting with the president:* Fischer, *The Reagan Reversal*, 120.

133 *"chastened"*: Ibid., 121.

133 *"most sobering experience"* and *"In several ways,"*: Reagan, *An American Life*, 585.

134 *"the possibility of a nuclear first strike"*: Fischer, *The Reagan Reversal*, 126–27.

134 *"close observation"*: Gates, *From the Shadows*, 270.

134 *The program:* Peter Pry, *War Scare: Russia and America on the Nuclear Brink* (Westport, CT: Praeger, 1999), 10.

134 *VRYAN was given:* Gates, *From the Shadows*, 271: Dobrynin, *In Confidence*, 523.

134 *"inventing new plans"*: Benjamin B. Fischer, "A Cold War Conundrum: The 1983 Soviet War Scare," CIA report, 1997. Available at www.milnet.com/cia/conundrum/source.htm.

134 *U.S. military forces:* Benjamin B. Fischer, ibid.

134 *VRYAN became central:* Dana Allin, *Cold War Illusions: America, Europe and Soviet Power 1969–1989* (New York: Palgrave Macmillan, 1994), as cited in Fisher, "A Cold War Conundrum."

135 *had not participated in:* Battilega, "Soviet Views of Nuclear Warfare," as in Henry D. Sokolski, ed., *Getting MAD,* 158.

135 *the exercise required NATO forces:* Pry, *War Scare,* 39.

135 *employing new techniques:* Fischer, *The Reagan Reversal,* 128.

135 *KGB officers:* Oberdorfer, *The Turn,* 66.

135 *Soviet intelligence:* John Lewis Gaddis, *Strategies of Containment: A Critical Appraisal of American National Security Policy During the Cold War* (New York: Oxford University Press, 2005), 360.

135 *Warsaw Pact:* Oberdorfer, *The Turn,* 65–66.

135 *"The situation was very grave":* Fischer, *The Reagan Reversal,* 122.

135 *"close call"* and *"quite sobering":* Another interview with George P. Shultz, September 2007.

135 *"genuine anxiety":* Ibid., 134.

136 *"This clue":* Cannon, *President Reagan,* 295.

136 *"reduce the threat"* and subsequent quotes: Lettow, *Ronald Reagan and His Quest to Abolish Nuclear Weapons,* 50–51.

136 *His horrified advisers:* Cannon, *President Reagan,* 301.

136 *"horrible"* and *"inherently evil":* Lettow, *Ronald Reagan and His Quest to Abolish Nuclear Weapons,* 60–61.

136 *"He can't have a world":* Ibid., 61.

137 *"Reagan emphasized":* Ibid., ix.

137 *He once told a group:* Cannon, *President Reagan,* 291

137 *he said that submarine-launched:* Fitzgerald, *Way Out There in the Blue,* 150.

137 *did not seem to understand:* Ibid., 194.

137 *when a journalist asked Reagan:* Ronald Reagan, "Remarks and a Question-and-Answer Session with Reporters on the Announcement of the U.S. Strategic Weapons Program," Washington, D.C., October 2, 1981.

137 *did not like this plan:* Cannon, *President Reagan,* 165–71.

138 *"many people at the top"* and *"many Soviet officials":* Reagan, *An American Life,* 585–88.

138 *"Reagan did not know enough":* Cannon, *President Reagan,* 291.

138 *Shultz and McFarlane told Reagan:* Lettow, *Ronald Reagan and His Quest to Abolish Nuclear Weapons,* 136–37.

138 *Nancy Reagan:* John Newhouse, *War and Peace in the Nuclear Age,* 373.

138 *Soviet Union as the "focus of evil":* George J. Church, "Men of the Year: Reagan and Andropov," *Time,* January 1, 1984.

138 *"standard threat" speech:* Fitzgerald, *Way Out There in the Blue,* 235.

139 *"The fact that neither of us":* Ronald Reagan, Address to the Nation and Other Countries on U.S.-Soviet Relations, Washington, D.C., January 16, 1984.

139 *Matlock even suggested:* Jack F. Matlock, Jr., *Reagan and Gorbachev: How the Cold War Ended* (New York: Random House, 2004), 82.

139 *"So let us not be blind":* Ronald Reagan, Address to the Nation and Other Countries on U.S.-Soviet Relations, Washington, D.C., January 16, 1984.

139 *"opportunity to put our relations":* Garthoff, *The Great Transition,* 147–48.

139 *The following week:* Ibid., 88.

139 *"even more anxious":* Reagan, *An American Life,* 588–89.
139 *"misunderstandings":* Garthoff, *The Great Transition,* 235.
140 *"fresh start":* Ibid., 247.
140, 141, 141 *"if we eliminated," "We can do that,"* and *"since we've proven":* Lettow, *Ronald Reagan and His Quest to Abolish Nuclear Weapons,* 225.
141 *"forget everything they discussed"* and subsequent quotes: Ibid., 225.
141 *"Reykjavik was too bold":* Newhouse, *War and Peace in the Nuclear Age,* 398.
142 *"just as a roof":* Cannon, *President Reagan,* 683.
142 *Gorby mania:* Don Oberdorfer and Lou Cannon, "Summit Declared a 'Success,'" *Washington Post,* December 11, 1987.
143 *Weinberger leaked:* Garthoff, *The Great Transition,* 237.
143 *"George is carrying out my policy":* As cited in Gaddis, *Strategies of Containment,* 361.
143 *"go soft on this"* and *"I have a dream":* Lettow, *Ronald Reagan and His Quest to Abolish Nuclear Weapons,* 191, 196.
144 *When the White House suggested:* Matlock, *Reagan and Gorbachev,* 272.
144 *"Addressing a joint meeting":* Lou Cannon, "Soviet Hill Speech Blocked; White House Denies Making Invitation," *Washington Post,* November 21, 1987.
144 *"Reagan is a weakened president":* Fitzgerald, *Way Out There in the Blue,* 439.
144 *the cover read,* "Reagan's Suicide Pact": *National Review,* May 22, 1987.
144 *"what to do about summit fever":* Hedrick Smith, "The Right Against Reagan," *New York Times Magazine,* January 17, 1988.
144 *the Right waged a campaign:* Ibid.
144 *"secret force":* Cannon, *President Reagan,* 781.
145 *"I think":* Ronald Reagan, as cited in Matlock, *Reagan and Gorbachev,* 271–72.
145 *"How wildly wrong"* and *"He professed to see":* As cited in Fitzgerald, *Way Out There in the Blue,* 467.
145 *"The goal of the free world":* Ronald Reagan, Remarks at a Dinner Marking the Tenth Anniversary of the Heritage Foundation, Washington, D.C., October 3, 1983.
145–46 *"to contain and over time.":* National Security Decision Directive-75, January 17, 1983.
147 *"subversion"* and *"Those sonsofbitches":* Cannon, *President Reagan,* 366.
147 *the Reagan administration favored:* Ibid., 374–75.
147 *"Doctrines are things":* Cannon, *President Reagan,* 372.
147 *The term "Reagan Doctrine":* As cited in Cannon, *President Reagan,* 369.
147 *"The United States has it in its power":* "X" [George F. Kennan], "The Sources of Soviet Conduct," *Foreign Affairs,* 1947.
148 *"a stable and constructive":* National Security Decision Directive-75, January 17, 1983.
148 *The Soviet economy:* Stephen Brooks and William Wohlforth, "Power, Globalization, and the End of the Cold War," *International Security,* Winter 2000.
148 *Grain production:* Yegor Gaidar, "The Soviet Collapse: Grain and Oil," American Enterprise Institute, April 2007, 2.
148 *oil prices collapsed in 1985:* Ibid., 5–6.
148 *devouring 15 percent to 20 percent:* Noel E. Firth and James H. Noren, *Soviet Defense Spending: A History of CIA Estimates 1950–1990* (College Station, TX: Texas A&M University Press, 1998), 129.

148 *meaning that it imposed three times:* Gaddis, *The Cold War,* 213.

149 *Its defense budget remained:* Fitzgerald, *Way Out There in the Blue,* 474–75.

150 *Gorbachev had become:* Robert D. English, *Russia and the Idea of the West: Gorbachev, Intellectuals, and the End of the Cold War* (New York: Columbia University Press, 2000), 182–83.

150 *a conclusion that other Soviet leaders:* Stephen Brooks and William Wohlforth, "Power, Globalization, and the End of the Cold War," *International Security,* Winter 2000.

150 *Brezhnev, Andropov, and Chernenko:* William E. Odom, *The Collapse of the Soviet Military* (New Haven, CT: Yale University Press, 1998), 225.

150 *Even Soviet military officers:* Firth and Noren, *Soviet Defense Spending,* 122–25.

150 *Gorbachev focused on SDI:* Lettow, *Ronald Reagan and His Quest to Abolish Nuclear Weapons,* 171–72.

151 *"Our response to SDI":* Ibid.

151 *The Soviet Union actually did design:* Ibid.

151 *"Communist rule ended in the Soviet Union":* Matlock, *Reagan and Gorbachev,* 317.

151 *"The Soviet union was doomed":* Odom, *The Collapse of the Soviet Military,* 393–94.

152 *"Reagan's vision of nuclear":* Cannon, *President Reagan,* 292.

Chapter Five: HIBERNATION

157 *On the evening of June 12, 2002:* The description of the event comes from the Heritage Foundations 2002 annual report, "Our Business Is Solutions," 38. Author interview with Baker Spring, F. M. Kirby Research Fellow in National Security Policy, The Heritage Foundation, July 2007.

158 *"There is no United Nations":* As cited in, "Questioning Mr. Bolton," *New York Times,* April 13, 2005.

158 *"The secretariat building":* As cited in Bill Nichols, "Bush Selects Bolton as U.N. Ambassador," *USA Today,* March 7, 2005.

158 *Bolton had always been a conservative:* Author interview with John Bolton, Washington, D.C., June 28, 2007. John R. Bolton, curriculum vitae, as viewed on http://www.aei.org/docLib/20070124_BoltonlongCV.pdf on March 30, 2007. John R. Bolton, *Surrender Is Not an Option: Defending America at the United Nations* (New York: Simon & Schuster, 2007), 1–17.

158 *Bolton believed:* John R. Bolton, "Unilateralism Is Not Isolationism," Gwyn Prins, ed., *Understanding Unilateralism in American Foreign Relations* (London: Royal Institute of International Affairs, 2000). Bolton, *Surrender Is Not an Option,* 7, 76, 441.

159 *"as if that required":* Samantha Power, "Boltonism," *New Yorker,* March 21, 2005, 23.

159 *got a call from Baker:* Bolton, *Surrender Is Not an Option,* 3.

159 *"I'm with the Bush-Cheney team":* Scott Shane, "Never Shy, Bolton Brings a Zeal to the Table," *New York Times,* May 1, 2005.

159 *In a speech not long afterward:* Bolton, *Surrender Is Not an Option,* 48.

159 *"He is the kind of man":* Paul Richter, "Bolton Known to Some as the Un-Diplomat: The U.N. Ambassador Nominee Speaks His Mind Freely," *Los Angeles Times,* March 8, 2005.

160 *"revolution"*: See, for example, Ivo H. Daalder and James M. Lindsay, *America Unbound: The Bush Revolution in Foreign Policy* (Washington, D.C.: Brookings Institution Press, 2003), 1.

160 *"enemy deprivation syndrome"*: Ambassador Charles Freeman, as cited in Robert Dreyfuss, "Vice Squad," *American Prospect*, May 2006, 30.

160 *"When I was coming up"*: George W. Bush campaign remarks, January 21, 2000.

161 *On November 9, 1989*: George H. W. Bush and Brent Scowcroft, *A World Transformed* (New York: Knopf, 1988), 148.

161 *"crash" would instead*: As cited in David Halberstam, *War in a Time of Peace: Bush, Clinton, and the Generals* (New York: The Amateurs, Inc., 2002), 73.

162 *"precedent for the approaching"*: George H. W. Bush and Brent Scowcroft, *A World Transformed*, 400.

162 *"the end of history"*: Francis Fukuyama, "The End of History?," *National Interest*, Summer 1989.

162 *"At the core of 75 percent"*: As cited in Eloise Salholz, with Howard Fineman and Patrick Rogers, "A Distant Thunder on the Right," *Newsweek*, December 18, 1989, 25.

163 conservatives *"have not the faintest idea"*: "Emperor of Emptiness," *Economist*, July 25, 1992, 32.

163 *"The destruction of the wall"*: Halberstam, *War in a Time of Peace*, 10.

164 *National Review actually endorsed*: "Four More Years?," *National Review*, February 17, 1992, 12.

164 *"Americans have a missionary streak"*: As cited in John B. Judis, "The Conservative Crack-Up," *American Prospect*, November 30, 2002.

164 *"wage democracy"*: Ben Wattenberg, "Neo-Manifest Destinarianism," Owen Harries, ed., *America's Purpose* (Oakland, CA: ICS Press, 1991), 108.

164 *"Dictatorships and Double Standards"*: Jeane Kirkpatrick, "Dictatorships and Double Standards," *Commentary*, November 1979.

164 *Nathan Glazer counseled*: Nathan Glazer, "A Time for Modesty," in Owen Harries, ed., *America's Purpose*, 133–41.

164 *"with a return to normal times"*: Jeane Kirkpatrick, "A Normal Country in a Normal Time," *National Interest*, Fall 1990, 44.

164 *"coitus interruptus"*: Norman Podhoretz, "Life of the Party," *National Review*, September 13, 1999.

165 *"universal dominion"*: Charles Krauthammer, "Universal Dominion: Toward a Unipolar World," *National Interest*, Winter 1989/1990.

165 *His first draft*: "Excerpts from Pentagon Plan: 'Prevent the Emergence of a New Rival,'" *New York Times*, March 8, 1992, 14.

166 shape *"the future security"* and *"international reaction"*: Mann, *Rise of the Vulcans*, 213.

166 *"America need not"*: Ibid., 200.

166 *"You've discovered"*: Ibid., 211.

166 *"Toward a Neo-Reaganite Foreign Policy"*: William Kristol and Robert Kagan, "Toward a Neo-Reaganite Foreign Policy," *Foreign Affairs*, July/August 1996.

167 *"engagement"*: William Kristol and Robert Kagan, "National Interest and Global Responsibility," Robert Kagan and William Kristol, eds., *Present Dangers: Crisis and Opportunity in American Foreign and Defense Policy* (San Francisco: Encounter Books, 2000), 7.

167 *"When it comes to dealing":* Ibid., 20.

167 *"Advocates of the [Clinton] administration's":* William Schneider, "Weapons Proliferation and Missile Defense: The Strategic Case," *Present Dangers,* 270.

167 *In response to:* Kim R. Holmes and John Hillen, "Misreading Reagan's Legacy," *Foreign Affairs,* September/October 1996.

167 *"an interests-based foreign policy":* John R. Bolton, "The Prudent Irishman: Edmund Burke's Realism," *National Interest,* Winter 1997/98.

167 *Rather than venturing abroad:* John R. Bolton, "Bring Back the Laxalt Doctrine," *Policy Review,* August/September 1990.

168 *were even quoting Walter Lippmann:* Kim R. Holmes and John Hillen, "Misreading Reagan's Legacy."

168 *founding statement:* Project for a New American Century, Statement of Principles, June 3, 1997, viewed on www.newamericancentury.org/statementofprinciples .htm on November 25, 2007.

168 *famous 1998 open letter:* Project for a New American Century, Letter to President Clinton on Iraq, January 26, 1998, viewed on www.newamericancentury.org/ iraqclintonletter.htm on November 25, 2007.

169 *"Clinton believed":* Strobe Talbott, *The Great Experiment: The Story of Ancient Empires, Modern States, and the Quest for a Global Nation* (New York: Simon & Schuster, 2008), 331.

169 *"new strategy of security":* Bill Clinton, "Remarks by the President to the 52nd Session of the United Nations General Assembly," New York City, September 22, 1997.

170 *"We must avoid both":* Bill Clinton, "Remarks by the President on Foreign Policy," San Francisco, February 26, 1999.

170 *"The failures of Assertive Multilateralism":* Bob Dole, "Shaping America's Global Future," *Foreign Policy,* Spring 1995, 29.

170 *"forward strategy for freedom":* George W. Bush, "A Distinctly American Internationalism," speech, Ronald Reagan Presidential Library, Simi Valley, California, November 19, 1999.

171 *Alexander Solzhenitsyn:* Ibid.

171 *"terror and missiles"* and *"The Evil Empire":* George W. Bush, "A Period of Consequences," speech, Charleston, South Carolina, September 23, 1999.

171 *limits of "smiles and scowls":* George W. Bush, "A Distinctly American Internationalism."

171 *missile defense:* David Simon, "Chronology of National Missile Defense Programs," Council on Foreign Relations, June 1, 2002, as viewed on www.cfr.org/ publication/10443 on December 3, 2007.

172 *National Intelligence Estimate:* "Emerging Missile Threats to North America During the Next 15 Years," NIE 95-19, which found that "no country, other than the major declared nuclear powers, will develop or otherwise acquire a ballistic missile in the next 15 years that could threaten the contiguous 48 states or Canada," November 1995, as viewed on http://www.fas.org/spp/starwars/offdocs/nie9519 .htm on December 13, 2007.

172 *"the Intelligence Community has a strong case":* Robert M. Gates, et al., "Independent Panel Review, 'Emerging Missile Threats to North America During the Next 15 Years,'" NIE 95-19, December 1996, as viewed on http://www.fas.org/irp/ threat/missile/oca961908.htm on December 13, 2007.

172 *Its conclusions:* "Executive Summary of the Report of the Commission to Assess

the Ballistic Missile Threat to the United States," July 15, 1998, as viewed on http://www.fas.org/irp/threat/bm-threat.htm on December 13, 2007.

173 *According to defense analyst John Pike:* As quoted in Jason Vest, "Darth Rumsfeld," *American Prospect,* February 26, 2001.

173 *Congress passed and Bill Clinton signed:* National Missile Defense Act of 1999 (Public Law 106-38), passed into law July 22, 1999.

173 *"We can never afford":* Bill Clinton, speech, Washington, D.C., September 1, 2000.

174 *"sticking point":* Donald Rumsfeld, Remarks at a Pentagon News Conference, Arlington, Virginia, December 13, 2001.

174 *"adversarial arms control":* Douglas J. Feith, testimony before the Senate Armed Services Committee, Washington, D.C., February 14, 2002.

174 *nine Republican senators:* Wade Boese, "No Bush-Putin Agreement on ABM Treaty, Missile Defenses," *Arms Control Today,* December 2001.

175 *"As far as the ABM Treaty":* Vladimir Putin, statement at the G8 meeting, Genoa, Italy, July 22, 2001.

175 *"a new relationship"* and *"The world is far":* Philipp C. Bleek, "Bush, Putin Pledge Nuclear Cuts; Implementation Unclear," *Arms Control Today,* December 2001.

175 *"silly":* Donald Rumsfeld, Remarks, Pentagon Press Conference, The Pentagon, Arlington, Virginia, October 21, 2001.

175 *on January 25, 1995:* Thomas Graham, Jr., "Space Weapons and the Risk of Accidental Nuclear War," *Arms Control Today,* December 2005.

176 *As journalist Lawrence F. Kaplan argued:* Lawrence F. Kaplan, "Offensive Line," *New Republic,* March 12, 2001, 20.

176 *"sine qua non":* Kristol and Kagan, "National Interest and Global Responsibility," *Present Dangers,* 17.

176 *In announcing:* George W. Bush, speech at the National Defense University, May 1, 2001.

177 *"the treaty will allow":* Colin Powell, testimony before the Senate Foreign Relations Committee, Washington, D.C., July 9, 2002.

177 *Bush indeed planned:* J. Peter Scoblic, "Think Anew About U.S. Nukes," *Christian Science Monitor,* March 19, 2002.

177 *"provided 'exit ramps'":* John R. Bolton, *Surrender Is Not an Option,* 75.

177 *"ended a long chapter":* George W. Bush, "Remarks at the Signing of the Moscow Treaty," Moscow, Russia, May 24, 2002.

177 *Under the START II accord:* Bradley Graham, *Hit to Kill: The New Battle over Shielding America from Missile Attack* (New York: Public Affairs, 2001), 254.

177 *Under the Moscow Treaty:* U.S. State Department, 2007 Annual Implementation Report to Congress on the Moscow Treaty, as viewed on www.state.gov/t/vci/rls/rpt/88187.htm on December 16, 2007.

178 *No other military contingency:* J. Peter Scoblic, "Think Anew About U.S. Nukes."

178 *"threat-based approach," "capabilities-based approach,"* and *"Greater flexibility":* "Nuclear Posture Review," Department of Defense, December 31, 2001, 7.

179 *leaked to the* Los Angeles Times: Paul Richter, "U.S. Works Up Plan for Using Nuclear Arms," *Los Angeles Times,* March 9, 2002, A1.

179 *"twisted":* Editorial, "A Twisted Posture," *Boston Globe,* March 12, 2002.

179 *"nuclear rogue":* Editorial, "America as Nuclear Rogue," *New York Times,* March 12, 2002.

179 *William Arkin reported:* William Arkin, "Not Just a Last Resort?," *Washington Post,* May 15, 2005, B1.

180 *"a capability to deliver":* Ibid.

180 *Global Strike was intended:* William Arkin, "Not Just a Last Resort?"

180 *Admiral James O. Ellis:* Admiral James O. Ellis, speech at the Air Force Association National Symposium, Orlando, Florida, February 13, 2003, as cited in Hans M. Kristensen, "Global Strike: A Chronology of the Pentagon's New Offensive Strike Plan," report from the Federation of American Scientists, March 15, 2006, 87–89.

180 *"With its global strike responsibilities":* General Richard Myers, testimony before the House Armed Services Committee, Washington, D.C., February 5, 2003, as cited in Kristensen, "Global Strike," 90.

180 *the Pentagon announced:* Kristensen, "Global Strike," 18.

180 *Kristensen revealed:* Hans M. Kristensen, "The Role of U.S. Nuclear Weapons: New Doctrine Falls Short of Bush Pledge," *Arms Control Today,* September 2005.

180 *the doctrine stipulated:* "Doctrine for Joint Nuclear Operations: Final Coordination (2)," Joint Publication 3-12, March 15, 2005, Chapter III, 1(d)(1).

181 *replace the phrase "nuclear war":* Hans M. Kristensen, "The Role of U.S. Nuclear Weapons: New Doctrine Falls Short of Bush Pledge."

181 *This was not just:* Hans M. Kristensen, "U.S. Strategic War Planning After 9/11," *Nonproliferation Review,* July 2007, 381–83.

182 *The Pentagon has incorporated:* Hans M. Kristensen, "White House Guidance Led to New Nuclear Strike Plans Against Proliferators, Document Shows," November 5, 2007, available at http://www.fas.org/blog/ssp/2007/11/white house_guidance_led_to_ne.php.

182 *"Victory Is Possible":* Colin S. Gray and Keith Payne, "Victory Is Possible," *Foreign Policy,* Summer 1980.

183 *Their 2001 report:* "Rationale and Requirements for U.S. Nuclear Forces and Arms Control," National Institute for Public Policy, January 2001. For Payne's motivations, see Keith B. Payne, "Nuclear Weapons, Theirs and Ours," National Institute for Public Policy, May 7, 1999.

184 *"high-priestess of arms control":* See, for example, Ann McFeatters, "Rice Is Holding Her Own in Bush Boys' Club," *Chicago Sun-Times,* July 16, 2000.

184 *"how many warheads":* See, for example, Condoleezza Rice, remarks at a White House press briefing, Washington, D.C., July 13, 2001.

184 *no need for "traditional arms control":* John R. Bolton, testimony before the Senate Foreign Relations Committee, Washington, D.C., July 24, 2001.

184 *"If we need to write it down":* Philipp C. Bleek, "Bush, Putin Pledge Nuclear Cuts; Implementation Unclear," *Arms Control Today,* December 2001.

184 *"the end of arms control":* Bolton, *Surrender Is Not an Option,* 82.

185 *"least common denominator proposal":* John R. Bolton, "The U.S. Position on the Biological Weapons Convention: Combating the BW Threat," speech, Tokyo, Japan, August 26, 2002.

186 *"traditional arms control methods":* "The Arms Control Philosophy and Accomplishments of the Bush Administration," Bureau of Arms Control, State Department, Washington, D.C., February 11, 2005.

186 *"It's dead, dead, dead":* Carla Anne Robbins, "State Department's Arms Chief Leads Charge Against Treaties," *Wall Street Journal,* July 19, 2002.

186 *the Bush administration announced:* Wade Boese, "Bush Shifts Fissile Material Ban Policy," *Arms Control Today,* September 2004.

187 *July 2001 UN conference:* Rebecca Whitehair, "UN Small Arms Conference Approves Modest Plan," *Arms Control Today,* September 2001. Rachel Stohl, "United States Weakens Outcome of UN Small Arms and Light Weapons Conference," *Arms Control Today,* September 2001.

187 *"From little acorns":* John Bolton, press conference on the UN Conference on Illicit Trade in Small Arms and Light Weapons in All Its Aspects, New York City, July 9, 2001.

188 *"This is a big shift":* Condoleezza Rice, "Remarks by Condoleezza Rice, Assistant to the President for National Security Affairs, at the National Press Club Newsmaker Luncheon," Washington, D.C., July 12, 2001.

188 *even an atomic warhead:* Charles L. Glaser and Steve Fetter, "Nuclear Counterproliferation vs. Nonproliferation: Assessing the Nuclear Posture Review's New Nuclear Missions," *International Security,* Fall 2005.

189 *the NIPP report:* "Rationale and Requirements for U.S. Nuclear Forces and Arms Control," National Institute for Public Policy, January 2001, as viewed on http:// www.nipp.org/Adobe/volume%201%20complete.pdf on December 13, 2007.

189 *"If we had mutual trust":* As cited in Jeffrey Goldberg, "A Little Learning," *New Yorker,* May 9, 2005, 36.

189 *withdrawal from the ABM Treaty:* See, for example, Wade Boese, "Missile Defense Post-ABM: No System, No Arms Race," *Arms Control Today,* June 2003. See also Wade Boese, "News Analysis: Missile Defense Five Years after the ABM Treaty," *Arms Control Today,* June 2007.

189 *One study commissioned:* Lewis A. Dunn, Gregory Giles, Jeffrey Larsen, and Thomas Skypek, "Foreign Perspectives on U.S. Nuclear Policy and Posture," Science Applications International Corporation report, Defense Threat Reduction Agency, December 4, 2006.

190 *In a provocative essay:* Keir A. Lieber and Daryl G. Press, "The Rise of U.S. Nuclear Primacy," *Foreign Affairs,* March/April 2006. For a more in-depth look at this issue, see Keir A. Lieber and Daryl G. Press, "The End of MAD? The Nuclear Dimension of U.S. Primacy," *International Security,* Spring 2006, 7–44.

190 *"In questions of military-strategic stability":* Sergey Lavrov, press conference with Condoleezza Rice, Moscow, Russia, May 15, 2007.

190 *"destroying the strategic equilibrium":* Vladimir Putin, interview with newspaper journalists from G8 member countries, Rostock, Germany, June 4, 2007.

191 *"has not completed":* "Defense Acquisitions: Missile Defense Acquisition Strategy Generates Results but Delivers Less at a Higher Cost," Government Accountability Office, GAO-07-387, March 2007.

191 *"America did not change":* Robert Kagan, *Of Paradise and Power: America and Europe in the New World Order* (New York: Knopf, 2003), 83.

Chapter Six: APOTHEOSIS

192 *the immediate effects:* William C. Bell and Cham E. Dallas, "Vulnerability of Populations and the Urban Health Care Systems to Nuclear Weapon Attack: Examples from American Cities," *International Journal of Health Geographics,* February 28, 2007. David Howe, "National Planning Scenarios: Executive Summaries," The

Homeland Security Council, July 2004. "Black Dawn: Scenario-Based Exercise," CSIS, NTI, Strengthening the Global Partnership, Brussels, Belgium, May 3, 2004.

194 *One government study estimates:* "Thinking About the Unthinkable: Economic Consequences of a Nuclear Attack," Pacific Northwest Nuclear Laboratory, U.S. Department of Energy, January 27, 2006.

195 *"The personal loss":* Homeland Security Council, National Planning Scenarios, April 2005. As viewed April 12, 2007 on http://media.washingtonpost.com/ wp-srv/nation/nationalsecurity/earlywarning/NationalPlanningScenarios April2005.pdf.

196 *a mathematical model:* Matthew Bunn, "A Mathematical Model of the Risk of Nuclear Terrorism," *Annals of the American Academy of Political and Social Science,* September 2006.

196 *"I believe it's likely enough":* "CNN Presents: Nuclear Terror," CNN, September 12, 2004, as viewed on http://transcripts.cnn.com/transcripts/0409/12/cp.00 .html on December 15, 2007.

196 *George Tenet:* George Tenet, *At the Center of the Storm* (New York: HarperCollins, 2007), 272.

196 *Jonah Goldberg:* Jonah Goldberg, "What's Your Problem: What's the Problem Liberals Have with Israel?," *National Review Online,* June 21, 2007, available at http:// tv.nationalreview.com/whatsyourproblem/post?q=M2ZlYTczMjM2ZWQ2ZDM 1Mzg2YTUyNDU4MzQxYTRmNDY=.

196 *In 2004, Bush stated:* George W. Bush, the first Bush-Kerry presidential debate, University of Miami, Coral Gables, Florida, September 30, 2004.

197 *one of the world's leading weapons proliferators:* "Proliferation: Threat and Response," Department of Defense, 2001.

197 *the world's leading sponsor of terrorism:* "Patterns of Global Terrorism, 2002," Office of the Coordinator for Counterterrorism, State Department, April 30, 2003, available at www.state.gov/s/ct/rls/crt/2002/html/19988.htm.

198 *But when the* Washington Post *and "This administration is shaping up":* Dana Milbank and Ellen Nakashima, "Bush Team Has 'Right' Credentials," *Washington Post,* March 25, 2001, A1.

198 *"Oh, yes, I know your father":* As cited in Noam Scheiber, "Hero Worship," *New Republic,* October 11, 2004, 20.

198 *"What angered me":* Bill Minutaglio, *First Son: George W. Bush and the Bush Family Dynasty* (New York: Times Books, 1999), 85.

199 *Bush only read:* As cited in Scheiber, "Hero Worship."

199 *"we have a responsibility":* George W. Bush, "President's Remarks on Labor Day," Richfield, Ohio, September 1, 2003.

199 *During a few eventful months:* Mary Jacoby, "George W. Bush's Missing Year," *Salon,* September 2, 2004, as viewed at http://dir.salon.com/story/news/ feature/2004/09/02/allison/index.html on June 28, 2007.

199 *he was arrested:* Dan Balz, "Bush Acknowledges 1976 DUI Arrest," *Washington Post,* Novembetr 3, 2000, A1.

200 *Arbusto:* On Bush's oil record, see Susan Orlean, "A Place Called Midland," *New Yorker,* October 16–23, 2000, 128. See also Skip Hollandsworth, "Born to Run," *Texas Monthly,* May 1994, 112. Eric Pooley with S. C. Gwynne, "How George Got His Groove," *Time,* June 21, 1999, 34.

200 *Bible study group:* Howard Fineman, "Bush and God," *Newsweek,* March 10, 2003, 22.

200 *"Over the course of that weekend"*: George W. Bush, *A Charge to Keep* (New York: William Morrow, 1999), 136–37.

200 *"a very clear sense"*: Howard Fineman, "Bush and God."

201 told friends that God: Stephen Mansfield, *The Faith of George W. Bush* (Lake Mary, FL: Strang Publishing, 2004), 109.

201 *"I would not be president today"*: George W. Bush, as cited in Howard Fineman, "Bush and God." See also Paul Kengor, *God and George W. Bush: A Spiritual Life* (New York: HarperCollins, 2004), 25.

201 *"a monumental struggle"*: George W. Bush, "Remarks by the President in a Photo Opportunity with the National Security Team," Washington, D.C., September 12, 2001.

201 *"I don't believe there's many shades of gray"*: George W. Bush, "Remarks by the President at Scott McCallum for Governor Reception," Milwaukee, Wisconsin, February 11, 2002.

202 *"crusade"*: George W. Bush, "Remarks by the President upon Arrival, South Lawn, White House," September 16, 2001.

202 *"a struggle against evil"*: Dick Cheney, "Vice President Cheney Delivers Remarks at the 56th annual Alfred E. Smith Memorial Foundation Dinner," New York City, October 18, 2001.

202 *"We can never let the intricacies of"*: Condoleezza Rice, "Remarks by National Security Advisor Condoleezza Rice on Terrorism and Foreign Policy," Paul H. Nitze School of Advanced International Studies, Washington, D.C., April 29, 2002.

202 *"moral clarity"*: Dick Cheney, "Remarks by the Vice President to the Heritage Foundation," Washington, D.C., May 1, 2003.

202 *Rich Lowry . . . wrote approvingly:* Rich Lowry, "Faith-Based Warrior," *National Review Online*, January 30, 2002.

203 *"that the successor to the great ideological wars"*: Charles Krauthammer, "Iraq: What Lies Ahead," speech at the American Enterprise Institute, April 22, 2003.

203 *"the terrorists are successors"*: George W. Bush, President Discusses the Importance of Democracy in the Middle East," Washington, D.C., February 4, 2004. See also Geroge W. Bush, "President Bush Attends Dedication of Victims of Communism Memorial" (speech, Washington, D.C., June 12, 2007).

203 *"World War IV"* and *"World War III"*: On Woolsey, "Ex-CIA Director: U.S. Faces 'World War IV,'" CNN, April 3, 2003. On Podhoretz, John Podhoretz, *World War IV: The Long Strugle Against Islamofascism* (New York: Doubleday, 2007). On Peggy Noonan, Peggy Noonan, "What We Have Learned," *Wall Street Journal*, November 23, 2001. On Gingrich, "Newt Gingrich: This Is World War III," FOX News, June 18, 2006. On Steyn, Mark Steyn, "Happy Warrior," *National Review*, August 7, 2006. See also "War Count," *American Prospect*, September 2006.

203 *"I don't think you can win it"*: George W. Bush, "Exclusive Interview with President Bush," the *Today* show, September 2, 2004.

203 *John Kerry:* Matt Bai, "Kerry's Undeclared War," *New York Times Magazine*, October 10, 2004.

203 *"I know that some people"*: George W. Bush, State of the Union Address, Washington, D.C., January 20, 2004.

203 *"We'll fall back"*: Dick Cheney, "Vice President and Mrs. Cheney's Remarks and Q&A at a Town Hall Meeting," Des Moines, September 7, 2004.

204 *"We cannot deal with terror"*: Dick Cheney, "Vice President Cheney Delivers Remarks at the 56th Annual Alfred E. Smith Memorial Foundation Dinner."
204 *John Bolton added:* John R. Bolton, "Beyond the Axis of Evil: Additional Threats from Weapons of Mass Destruction," speech, Washington, D.C., May 6, 2002.
204 *"President Reagan went to Berlin":* George W. Bush, "President Bush Attends Dedication of Victims of Communism Memorial," speech, Washington, D.C., June 12, 2007.
205 *Osama bin Laden described* and *al Qaeda operatives:* Matthew Bunn and Anthony Wier, "Securing the Bomb," Nuclear Threat Initiative, July 2, 2006.
205 *Russian officials:* Bunn and Wier, "Securing the Bomb."
205 *two dozen known trafficking incidents:* Mark Fitzpatrick, *Nuclear Black Markets: Pakistan, A. Q. Khan and the Rise of Proliferation Networks,* International Institute of Strategic Studies, May 2007.
205 *"more than two hundred addresses":* Graham T. Allison, *Nuclear Terrorism: The Ultimate Preventable Catastrophe* (New York: Owl Books, 2004), 67.
205 *"virtual 'Home Depot'"* and subsequent quotes: Howard Baker and Lloyd Cutler, "Report Card on the Department of Energy's Nonproliferation Programs with Russia," Secretary of Energy Advisory Board, January 10, 2001.
206 *Energy Department programs* and *Pentagon projects:* James Kitfield, "Nuclear Nightmares," *National Journal,* December 15, 2001.
206 *an intelligence community assessment:* Alex Wagner, "Intelligence Estimate Upgrades Chinese, Iranian Missile Threats," *Arms Control Today,* March 2002.
207 *"ask the Congress to increase":* "The Candidates on Arms Control," *Arms Control Today,* September 2000, 6.
207 *report in the* Washington Post and subsequent quotes: Barton Gellman and Dafna Linzer, "Unprecedented Peril Forces Tough Calls," *Washington Post,* October 24, 2004, A1.
207 *"czar":* Steve Benen, "Wish Upon a Czar," *American Prospect Online,* May 9, 2007.
208 *enough material for two nuclear bombs:* See, for example, Philipp C. Bleek, "Project Vinca: Lessons for Securing Civil Nuclear Material Stockpiles," *Nonproliferation Review,* Fall-Winter 2003.
208 *the Nuclear Threat Initiative:* James Dao, "Nuclear Material Secretly Flown from Serbia to Russia for Safety," *New York Times,* August 23, 2002, 9.
208 *the Vinca success:* Author interview with NTI representative, July 2, 2007.
208 *six hundred tons* and *less material:* Bunn and Wier, "Securing the Bomb."
209 *"I don't believe that at this point":* As cited in Gellman and Linzer, "Unprecedented Peril Forces Tough Calls."
209 *54 percent* and *18 percent:* Bunn and Wier, "Securing the Bomb." July 2, 2006.
209 *refused to certify:* Philipp C. Bleek, "Bush Refuses to Certify Russian Chem-Bio Compliance," *Arms Control Today,* May 2002.
209 *The Bush administration (namely John Bolton):* Ultimately, a September 2006 agreement was concluded whereby a U.S. individual (but not the U.S. government or a firm) could be held liable in such an instance. Wade Boese, "US, Russia Sign Plutonium Accord," *Arms Control Today,* October 2006.
210 *"[W]e had to take":* George W. Bush, "President's Remarks at a Victory 2004 Rally," Wausau, Wisconsin, October 7, 2004.
210 *nuclear expert Graham Allison:* Graham Allison, "How to Stop Nuclear Terror," *Foreign Affairs,* January/February 2004.
210 *"In measuring the adequacy":* Sam Nunn, "The Day After an Attack, What Would

We Wish We Had Done? Why Aren't We Doing It Now?" testimony, 9/11 Public Discourse Project, Washington, D.C., June 27, 2005.

210 *a pathetic "D":* "Final Report on 9/11 Commission Recommendations," December 5, 2005, available at http://www.9-11pdp.org/press/2005-12-05 report.pdf.

210 *"ride herd":* Report on the Status of 9/11 Commission Recommendations, "Part III: Foreign Policy, Public Diplomacy, and Nonproliferation," November 14, 2005. Available at www.9-11pdp.org/press/2005-11-14_report.pdf.

211 *the shah of Iran:* This summary of Iran's early nuclear activities relies on Gordon Corera, *Shopping for Bombs: Nuclear Proliferation, Global Insecurity, and the Rise and Fall of the A. Q. Khan Network* (New York: Oxford University Press, 2006).

213 *shocked to find:* Paul Kerr, "IAEA 'Taken Aback' by Speed of Iran's Nuclear Program," *Arms Control Today,* April 2003. Joby Warrick and Glenn Kessler, "Iran's Nuclear Program Speeds Ahead," *Washington Post,* March 10, 2003, A1.

213 *building a commercial plant:* Corera, *Shopping for Bombs,* 57–58.

214 *George Tenet presented:* George J. Tenet, "Worldwide Threat 2001: National Security in a Changing World," testimony before the Senate Select Committee on Intelligence, Washington, D.C., February 7, 2001.

214 *"We believe Saddam":* George J. Tenet, "Worldwide Threat Briefing 2002: Converging Dangers in a Post 9/11 World," testimony before the Senate Armed Services Committee, Washington, D.C., March 19, 2002.

214 *"[W]e now know":* Dick Cheney, "Vice President Speaks at VFW 103rd National Convention," August 26, 2002.

215 *"unique":* George W. Bush, "President Bush Outlines Iraqi Threat," speech, Cincinnati, October 7, 2002.

215 *"we don't want the smoking gun":* See, for example, "Top Bush Officials Push Case Against Saddam," CNN, September 8, 2002.

215 *National Intelligence Estimate:* "Iraq's Continuing Progams for Weapons of Mass Destruction," NIE 2002-16HC, April 2004.

215 *One CIA analyst:* This analyst and others said no artillery rocket would be made with the specification of the discovered tubes, but in December 2002 the U.S. laboratories reported that Iraq was making copies of an Italian rocket (called the Medusa 81) whose specifications matched those of the tubes exactly. In early 2003, U.S. analysts discovered a Medusa 81 in Iraq, supporting that analysis. Barton Gellman and Walter Pincus, "Depiction of Threat Outgrew Supporting Evidence," *Washington Post,* August 10, 2003, A10.

215 *"More than a decade after":* Michael R. Gordon and Judith Miller, "U.S. Says Hussein Intensifies Quest for A-Bomb Parts," *New York Times,* September 8, 2002, 1.

215 *Bush himself:* George W. Bush, "President's Remarks at the United Nations General Assembly," New York City, September 12, 2002.

215–216 *pressured the CIA:* Spencer Ackerman and John B. Judis, "The First Casualty," *New Republic,* June 30, 2003.

216 *"We do know":* Dick Cheney, Tim Russert interview with Dick Cheney, *Meet the Press,* September 8, 2002.

216 *Jacques Baute:* Ackerman and Judis, "The First Casualty."

217 *admired by both Bush and Cheney:* Mark Leibovich, "The Strong, Silent Type," *Washington Post,* January 18, 2004, D01. Laura Secor, "The Farmer Classicist and Raisin-Grower," *Boston Globe,* May 25, 2003, D1.

217 *"utopian socialism"*: Victor Davis Hanson, "American Exceptionalism," *National Review Online*, November 5, 2004.

217 *"a return of inspectors"*: Dick Cheney, "Vice President Speaks at VFW 103rd National Convention."

217 *George F. Will compared*: George F. Will, "Innocents Abroad," *Washington Post*, October 1, 2002.

217 *"the 'international community'"*: Rich Lowry, "Inspections Questions," *National Review*, September 17, 2002.

217 *"aggressive UN inspections"*: See Report of the Iraq Study Group, as viewed on http://www.fas.org/nuke/guide/iraq/tsg_key.pdf on December 17, 2007.

219 *Bush cornered Richard Clarke*: Richard A. Clarke, *Against All Enemies: Inside America's War on Terror* (New York: Free Press, 2004).

219 *"I believe Iraq"*: George W. Bush, as cited in Bob Woodward, *Bush at War* (New York: Simon & Schuster, 2002), 99.

219 *Rumsfeld raised* and *as did Paul Wolfowitz*: Bob Woodward, *Plan of Attack* (New York: Simon & Schuster, 2004), 24–26.

219 *high-level interagency meeting*: As cited in Clarke, *Against All Enemies*, 231–32.

219 *"The so-called realist school"*: Jeffrey Goldberg, "A Little Learning," *New Yorker*, May 9, 2005.

220 *"[o]btain approval"*: Deputy Inspector General for Intelligence, "Review of the Pre-Iraqi War Activities of the Under Secretary of Defense for Policy," Report No. 07-INTEL-04, February 9, 2007, available at http://www.fas.org/irp/agency/dod/ig020907-decl.pdf.

220 *"allows [analysts]"*: As cited in Franklin Foer and Spencer Ackerman, "The Radical," *New Republic*, December 1, 2003.

220 *an essay in which*: Gary J. Schmitt and Abram N. Shulsky, "Leo Strauss and the World of Intelligence (by Which We Do Not Mean 'Nous')," in Kenneth L. Deutsch and John A. Murley, eds., *Leo Strauss, the Straussians, and the American Regime* (New York: Rowman & Littlefield, 1999), 410.

221 *"Assessing the Relationship"*: National Security Council briefing available at http://www.fas.org/irp/news/2007/04/feithslides.pdf.

221 *The intelligence community had found*: Peter Spiegel, "Investigation Fills in Blanks on How War Groundwork Was Laid: A Memo Calling for Progress on Linking Al Qaeda and Hussein Marked the Beginnings of a Pentagon Project," *Los Angeles Times*, April 2007, 10.

221 *"The first and preferred method"*: Deputy Inspector General for Intelligence, "Review of the Pre-Iraqi War Activities of the Under Secretary of Defense for Policy."

222 *"They so believed"*: Foer and Ackerman, "The Radical."

222 *intelligence community estimates*: Carl W. Ford, Jr., statement, "Assistant Secretary of State Before the Senate Committee on Foreign Relations Hearing on Reducing the Threat of Chemical and Biological Weapons," March 19, 2002. Department of Defense, "Proliferation: Threat and Response," January 2001.

223 *"Tens of thousands"*: George W. Bush, "President's Remarks at the United Nations General Assembly," New York City, September 12, 2002.

223 *network of gulags*: David Hawk, "The Hidden Gulag: Exposing North Korea's Prison Camps," U.S. Committee for Human Rights in North Korea, Washington, D.C., 2003.

223 *malnourished:* Dick K. Nanto and Emma Chanlett-Avery, "The North Korean Economy: Background and Policy Analysis," Congressional Research Service Report for Congress, February 9, 2005.

223 *killed between five hundred thousand:* Kay Seok, "North Korea Is Headed Toward Another Famine," *Human Rights Watch,* 2005.

223 *up to a quarter:* "Background Note: North Korea," U.S. Department of State, as viewed on http://www.state.gov/r/pa/ei/bgn/2792.htm on December 16, 2007.

224 *"a terrorism bubble":* Thomas L. Friedman, "Because We Could," *New York Times,* June 4, 2003.

224 *open letter:* "Letter to President Clinton on Iraq," Project for a New American Century, January 26, 1998, viewed on www.newamericancentury.org/iraq clintonletter.htm on November 25, 2007.

225 *first meeting:* Ron Suskind, *The Price of Loyalty: George W. Bush, the White House, and the Education of Paul O'Neill* (New York: Simon & Schuster, 2004), 70–75.

225 *"For much of the last century":* George W. Bush, "President Bush Delivers Graduation Speech at West Point," West Point, New York, June 1, 2002.

225 *"As we face this prospect":* Dick Cheney, "Vice President Honors Veterans of Korean War," speech, San Antonio, August 29, 2002.

225 *"In an age":* George W. Bush, "The National Security Strategy of the United States of America," September 2002, at www.whitehouse.gov/nsc/nss.pdf as viewed on January 4, 2008.

226 *three hundred thousand shells:* Robert D. Kaplan, "When North Korea Falls," *Atlantic Monthly,* October 2006.

226 *might well be armed:* Scott Stossel, "North Korea: The War Game," *Atlantic Monthly,* July/August 2005.

226 *Military options:* Kenneth M. Pollack, *The Persian Puzzle: The Conflict Between Iran and America* (New York: Random House, 2005), 392–93.

227 *Paul Wolfowitz fretted:* Romesh Ratnesar, "Paul Wolfowitz: Bush's Brainiest Hawk," *Time,* January 19, 2003.

227 *"a cakewalk":* Ken Adelman, "Cakewalk in Iraq," *Washington Post,* February 13, 2002, A27.

227 *"I admit there appears":* David E. Sanger, "Pyongyang Raises Only a Small Alarm," *International Herald Tribune,* May 25, 2004.

228 *28,000:* Iraqi Coalition Causalty Count, icasualties.org.

228 *650,000:* Tim Parsons, "Updated Iraq Study Affirms Earlier Mortality Estimates: Study Finds as Many as 654,965 Iraqis May Have Died as Result of Invasion," *Gazette* (Johns Hopkins University, October 16, 2006) at www.jhu.edu/ngazette/2006/16oct06/16rag.html as viewed on January 4, 2008.

228 *ignored the findings of the State Department:* James Fallows, "Blind into Baghdad," *Atlantic Monthly-,* January/February 2004.

228 *Feith mused* and subsequent quotes: Jeffrey Goldberg, "A Little Learning," *New Yorker,* May 9, 2005, 36.

229 *Shinseki:* General Eric K. Shinseki, "Testimony Before the Armed Servies Committee," Washington, D.C., February 25, 2003.

229 *"dangerous dependency":* Donald Rumsfeld, "Beyond Nation-Building," speech, New York City, February 14, 2003.

229 *"My thought was":* Author interview with John R. Bolton, June 29, 2007.

229 *Tuwaitha complex:* IAEA "Report by the Director General," Vienna, July 14, 2003.

Available at www.iaea.org/NewsCenter/Focus/IaeaIraq/Iraq UNSC14072003.pdf; Federation of American Scientists, "Tuwaitha—Iraq Special Weapons Facilities," available at www.fas.org/nuke/guide/Iraq/facility/Tuwaitha .htm; and Nuclear Threat Initiative, "NTI Country Overviews: Iraq: Nuclear Facilities," available at www.nti.org/e_research/profiles/Iraq/Nuclear/2117_3387.html.

229 *no guidance:* "Radiological Sources in Iraq," GAO Report, September 2005.
229 *hundreds of barrels:* Patrick E. Tyler, "Barrels Looted from Nuclear Site Raise Fears for Villagers in Iraq," *New York Times,* June 8, 2003. "Open Door Policy," *New Republic,* June 16, 2003. GlobalSecurity.org, "Tuwaitha–Iraq Special Weapons Facilities," as viewed on http://www.globalsecurity.org/wmd/world/iraq/tuwaitha.htm on December 16, 2007.
230 *"Iraq did not possess":* "Final Report," Iraq Survey Group, September 30, 2004.
230 *even telling ABC's Diane Sawyer:* "President George W. Bush: The Interview," *Primetime Live,* December 16, 2003.
230 *Richard Perle and David Frum asked:* David Frum and Richard Perle, *An End to Evil: How to Win the War on Terror* (New York: Random House, 2003), 28.
230 Gallucci quote, J. Peter Scoblic, "As I Say," *New Republic,* September 27, 2004.
230 *"a bit of troubling news":* George W. Bush, "President Discusses Foreign Policy Matters with NATO Secretary," Washington, D.C., October 21, 2002.

Chapter Seven: CATASTROPHE

232 *On a cold day:* Charles L. Pritchard, *Failed Diplomacy: The Tragic Story of How North Korea Got the Bomb* (Washington, D.C.: Brookings Institution, 2007), 52. Author interview with Charles L. Pritchard, June 28, 2007.
232 *"Moral clarity":* George W. Bush, "Bush's Commencement Address at West Point Graduation," West Point, New York, June 1, 2002.
232 *run by a brutal tyrant:* One North Korea policy maker said, "The president is given only the most basic notions about the Korea issue. They tell him, 'Above South Korea is a country called North Korea. It is an evil regime.' . . . So that translates into a presidential decision: Why enter into any agreement with an evil regime?" Robert Dreyfuss, "Vice Squad," *American Prospect,* May 2006, 30.
232 *"I loathe Kim Jong Il!"* and *"I've got a visceral":* George W. Bush, as cited in Bob Woodward, *Bush at War* (New York: Simon & Schuster, 2002), 340.
232 *"until he proves":* George W. Bush, "Remarks by President Bush and Kim Dae-jung in Press Availability," Seoul, South Korea, February 20, 2002.
233 *"tantalizingly close":* Wendy R. Sherman, "Talking to the North Koreans," *New York Times,* March 7, 2001.
233 *"appeasement":* John McCain, "A Good Deal?," *The McNeil/Lehrer NewsHour,* October 21, 1994.
233 *"dancing in Pyongyang":* John R. Bolton, as cited in Gellman and Linzer, "Unprecedented Peril Forces Tough Calls: President Faces Multi-Front Battle Against Threats Known, Unknown."
234 *"We don't negotiate with evil":* Dick Cheney, as cited in Warren P. Strobel, "Administration Struggles to Find Right Approach to N. Korea Talks," Knight Ridder, Washington bureau, December 20, 2003.

234 *"no carrot, no stick":* Gellman and Linzer, "Unprecedented Peril Forces Tough Calls: President Faces Multi-Front Battle Against Threats Known, Unknown."

234 *"I felt that":* James Brooke, "A Voice from North Korea Echoes in the White House," *New York Times,* June 18, 2005.

236 *"the light and opportunity":* George W. Bush, as cited in Michael Hirsh, Melinda Liu, and George Wherfritz, "We Are a Nuclear Power," *Newsweek,* October 23, 2006.

236 *"Except for my wife":* Donald Rumsfeld, "DOD News Briefing with Secretary Rumsfeld and General Casey," Arlington, Virginia, October 11, 2006.

236 *published a paper in 1999:* Richard L. Armitage, "A Comprehensive Approach to North Korea," National Defense University Strategic Forum, March 1999.

236 *"We do plan to engage":* Colin Powell, "March 6 Remarks on S. Korea, N. Korea, China," Washington, D.C., March 6, 2001.

236 *many who were willing:* Leon V. Sigal, "North Korea Is No Iraq: Pyongyang's Negotiating Strategy," *Arms Control Today,* December 2002.

236 *who had contributed:* "Rationale and Requirements for U.S. Nuclear Forces and Arms Control," National Institute for Public Policy, Vol. 1, Executive Report, January 2001.

236 *Rice herself was on record:* Condoleezza Rice, "Promoting the National Interest," *Foreign Affairs,* January/February 2000.

237 *"There was some suggestion":* Colin Powell, "Remarks by Secretary of State Colin Powell to the Pool," Washington, D.C., March 7, 2001.

237 *"I got a little far forward":* Colin Powell, "N. Korean Leader to Continue Sale of Missiles," *Washington Post,* May 5, 2001.

237 *"some skepticism":* George W. Bush, "Remarks by President Bush and President Kim Dae-jung of South Korea," Washington, D.C., March 7, 2001.

237 *dominated it:* Author interview with Charles L. Pritchard, June 28, 2007.

237 *"a less threatening":* George W. Bush, official statement, June 13, 2001. See also Michael R. Gordon, "U.S. Toughens Terms for North Korea Talks," *New York Times,* July 3, 2001, A9.

237 *felt the deterrent balance* and *100 percent verification:* Author interview with Pritchard.

237 *"improved implementation":* George W. Bush, official statement, June 13, 2001. See also Michael R. Gordon, "U.S. Toughens Terms for North Korea Talks," *New York Times,* July 3, 2001, A9.

237 *seemed to back away from:* Leon V. Sigal, "North Korea Is No Iraq: Pyongyang's Negotiating Strategy," *Arms Control Today,* December 2002. Some conservatives thought a "no hostile intent" pledge would constrain the United States. See Glenn Kessler, "Three Little Words Matter to North Korea," *Washington Post,* February 22, 2005, 10.

237 *"affirmatively"* and *"comprehensive approach":* Alex Wagner, "Bush Outlines Terms for Resuming Talks with North Korea," *Arms Control Today,* July/August 2001.

238 *a fear that had surfaced:* Representative Curt Weldon, who met with the North Koreans in 2003, reported that the Nuclear Posture Review "got their attention." Curt Weldon, "Congressional Delegation to North Korea Trip Report," presentation at the Strategic Nuclear Forum, February 22, 2005.

238 *"despotic regime"*: George W. Bush, "Remarks by President Bush and Kim Dae-jung in Press Availability," Seoul, South Korea, February 20, 2002.

238 *Pritchard was able*: Pritchard, *Failed Diplomacy*, 21.

238 *"bold approach"*: Michael R. Gordon, "Threats and Responses: Asian Arena; U.S. Readies Plan to Raise Pressure on North Koreans," *New York Times*, December 29, 2002.

238 *new National Intelligence Estimate*: CIA National Intelligence Estimate, November 19, 2002, as viewed on http://www.fas.org/nuke/guide/dprk/nuke/cia111902.html on December 15, 2007.

238 *In early October 2002*: Glenn Kessler, *The Confidante: Condoleezza Rice and the Creation of the Bush Legacy* (New York: St. Martin's Press, 2007), 68.

239 *a charge the North Koreans*: For more, see Glenn Kessler, "N. Korea Offers Evidence to Rebut Uranium Claims," *Washington Post*, November 10, 2007, A1.

239 *"will be ready to clear"*: Paul Kerr, "North Korea Admits Secret Nuclear Weapons Program," *Arms Control Today*, November 2002.

240 *"If the United States"*: Donald Gregg and Donald Oberdorfer, "A Moment to Seize with North Korea," *Washington Post*, June 22, 2005.

240 *"meet its obligations"*: Paul Kerr, "North Korea Quits NPT, Says It Will Restart Facilities," *Arms Control Today*, January/February 2003.

240 *"Of course we're going"*: Richard Armitage, testimony before the Senate Foreign Relations Committee, Washington, D.C., February 4, 2003.

240 *Bush became furious*: David E. Sanger, "U.S. Sees Quick Start of North Korea Nuclear Site," *New York Times*, March 1, 2003.

240 *Conservatives within the administration*: "[T]he U.S. Objective in Taking the Multilateral Approach Was to Avoid Bilateral Contact with Pyongyang," Pritchard, *Failed Diplomacy*, 57.

241 *under strict instructions*: Kessler, *The Confidante*, 69.

241 *"The American policy"*: "U.S. Policy on N. Korea Key Obstacle to Ending Nuclear Crisis, China Says Update," *China Focus*, September 1, 2003.

241 *"intention to coexist"* and *"I have been charged"*: Pritchard, *Failed Diplomacy*, 103.

241 *"strangulation"* and *"regime change"*: Lawrence F. Kaplan, "Split Personality," *New Republic*, July 7/July 14, 2003.

241 *"If we could have"*: Bill Keller, "The Thinkable," *New York Times*, May 4, 2003, 48.

241 *"teetering on the edge"*: Paul D. Wolfowitz in Michael Hirsh, "Neocons on the Line," *Newsweek*, June 23, 2003.

241 *"ultimate objective"*: John R. Bolton, FOX News interview, October 24, 2006.

241 *nicely summed up*: Aaron Friedberg, American Enterprise Institute panel discussion, February 2, 2006, as cited in Pritchard, *Failed Diplomacy*, 134–35.

242 *"If they test"* and *Bush seemed sanguine*: Colin Powell, as cited in J. Peter Scoblic, "As I Say."

242 *"This is quibbling"*: John R. Bolton, as cited in Gellman and Linzer, "Unprecedented Peril Forces Tough Calls: President Faces Multi-Front Battle Against Threats Known, Unknown."

242 *Having an extra*: See Ashton B. Carter, William J. Perry, and Michael M. May, "After the Bomb," *New York Times*, June 12, 2007, 23.

243 *"outposts of tyranny"*: Condoleezza Rice, "Opening Statement by Dr. Condoleezza Rice," Confirmation Hearing, Washington, D.C., January 18, 1005.

243 *"Kim Jong Il is a dangerous person"*: George W. Bush, "Press Conference of the President," Washington, D.C., April 28, 2005.

243 *"Mr. Kim"* and *"the tyrant"*: J. Peter Scoblic, "Moral Hazard," *New Republic,* August 8, 2005.

244 *Rice was well aware:* Kessler, *The Confidante,* 74.

244 *"the verifiable,"* *"stated that it has,"* *"other parties,"* and *"at an appropriate":* "Joint Statement of the Fifth Round of the Six Party Talks," Beijing, China, September 19, 2005.

244 *a hard-line statement:* "Assistant Secretary Christopher R. Hill's Statement at the Closing Plenary of the Fourth Round of the Six Party Talks," Beijing, China, September 14, 2005.

245 *"provide policy direction":* See Senate Democratic press release, "Reid, Biden, and Levin Hail Senate Passage of Legislation to Fix Bush Administration North Korean Policy," June 23, 2006.

245 *Tehran offered its support:* Ali Ansari, *Confronting Iran: The Failure of American Foreign Policy and the Next Great Conflict in the Middle East* (New York: Basic Books, 2006), 182–83. John H. Richardson, "The Secret History of the Impending War with Iran That the White House Doesn't Want You to Know," *Esquire,* October 18, 2007.

245 *what Western diplomats:* Gareth Porter, "Burnt Offering," *American Prospect,* May 21, 2006.

246 *Iranians specifically said:* Richardson, "The Secret History of the Impending War with Iran That the White House Doesn't Want You to Know."

246 *"We should liberate Iran":* Michael Ledeen, "The Temperature Rises," *National Review,* November 12, 2002.

246 *"The overthrow":* Eliot Cohen, "World War IV," *Wall Street Journal,* November 20, 2001.

246 *who wanted regime change:* See, for example, David E. Sanger, "Bush's Realization on Iran: No Good Choice Left Except Talks," *New York Times,* June 1, 2006, A8.

246 *In late 2001:* Flynt Leverett, "Illusion and Reality," *American Prospect,* September 2006, 29–33. Michael Dobbs, "Pressure Builds for President to Declare Strategy on Iran," *Washington Post,* June 15, 2003, A20.

247 *President Bush effectively:* See, for example, Alan Sipress, "Bush's Speech Shuts Door on Tenuous Opening to Iran," *Washington Post,* February 4, 2002, A10.

247 *"It is very important":* George W. Bush, as cited in Bob Woodward, *Plan of Attack,* 88.

247 *"[T]he thought":* Donald Rumsfeld interview with Newt Gingrich, FOX News, May 10, 2002.

247 *"The problem with Iran":* Condoleezza Rice, "Remarks by National Security Adviser Condoleezza Rice on Terrorism and Foreign Policy," Washington, D.C., April 29, 2002.

247 *issued a strong statement* and *leading then-president Mohammed Khatami:* Robin Wright, "Bush Endorses Reform in Iran," *Los Angeles Times,* July 13, 2002, 3. See also "Statement by the President," July 12, 2002. "Iran's President Blasts Bush," *Orlando Sentinel,* July 15, 2002, A6.

247 *"free Iran":* John R. Bolton, *Surrender Is Not an Option,* 139–40.

247 *A more shocking refusal:* Glenn Kessler, "2003 Memo Says Iranian Leaders Backed Talks," *Washington Post,* February 14, 2007, A14. See also "The Roadmap" as viewed on http://www.washingtonpost.com/wpsrv/world/documents/us_iran _1roadmap.pdf on December 15, 2007.

248 *wanted no part of it:* Gareth Porter, "Burnt Offering," *American Prospect*, May 21, 2006. Guy Dinmore, "U.S. Allies Urge Direct Dialogue with Iran," *Financial Times*, May 3, 2006.

248 *"We're not interested":* John R. Bolton, as cited in Gellman and Linzer, "Unprecedented Peril Forces Tough Calls: President Faces Multi-Front Battle Against Threats Known, Unknown."

248 *Iran offered to trade:* David Ignatius, "Lost Chances in Iran," *Washington Post*, July 9, 2004.

249 *while they would accept help:* Richardson, "The Secret History of the Impending War with Iran That the White House Doesn't Want You to Know."

249 *"There has to be":* Bolton, *Surrender Is Not an Option*, 139–40.

249 *"How many IAEA meetings":* Ibid.

249, 250 *The IAEA and the Europeans* and *"Look, John":* Kessler, *The Confidante*, 186–87.

250 *"leaving the driving":* Bolton, *Surrender Is Not an Option*, 130.

250 *"I don't do carrots":* John R. Bolton, as cited in Glenn Frankel, "Protests Loom in London for Visit by Bush," *Washington Post*, November 17, 2003, A1.

250 *"Oh, I think":* Condoleezza Rice, "Day One, Afternoon Session of a Hearing of the Senate Foreign Relations Committee," Washington, D.C., January 18, 2005.

251 *The Bush administration seized:* For a good discussion of the debate over the Libya success, see Bruce W. Jentleson and Christopher A. Whytock, "Who 'Won' Libya? The Force-Diplomacy Debate and Its Implications for Theory and Policy," *International Security*, Winter 2005/2006.

252 *not attempt to "undermine":* Robert S. Litwak, *Regime Change: U.S. Strategy Through the Prism of 9/11* (Baltimore: Johns Hopkins University Press, 2007), 181.

252 *"Libya's representatives":* Martin Indyk, "The Iraq War Did Not Force Gaddafi's Hand," *Financial Times*, March 9, 2004.

253 *on October 3, 2001:* Barbara Slavin, "Libya's Rehabilitation in the Works Since Early '90s," *USA Today*, April 27, 2004.

253 *"You don't want to reward":* Ron Suskind, *The One Percent Doctrine: Deep Inside America's Pursuit of Its Enemies Since 9/11* (New York: Simon & Schuster, 2006), 223.

253 *"President Bush does not deal":* Dick Cheney, "Speech at the Republican National Convention," New York City, September 1, 2004.

254 *"It's 'engagement' ":* As cited in Gellman and Linzer, "Unprecedented Peril Forces Tough Calls: President Faces Multi-Front Battle Against Threats Known, Unknown."

254 *"only that Libya's good faith":* Paula A. DeSutter, "Libya Renounces Weapons of Mass Destruction," *Foreign Policy Agenda*, March 2005.

254 *Libya had even offered:* Paul Kerr, "Libya's Disarmament: A Model for U.S. Policy?," *Arms Control Today*, June 2004.

254 *"explicit quid pro quo":* Flynt Leverett, "Why Libya Gave Up on the Bomb," *New York Times*, January 23, 2004.

254 *Qaddifi's son Saif:* Gellman and Linzer, "Unprecedented Peril Forces Tough Calls: President Faces Multi-Front Battle Against Threats Known, Unknown."

254 *evidence indicates:* See, for example, Martin Indyk, "The Iraq War Did Not Force Gaddafi's Hand," *Financial Times*, March 9, 2004.

255 *not to undermine Qaddafi:* John R. Bolton, "Appeasing Gadhafi," *Washington Post*, August 29, 2000.

255 *high-level British officials:* Michael Hirsh, "Bolton's British Problem," *Newsweek*, May 2, 2005, 30.

255 *"work to achieve":* Robert G. Joseph, Under Secretary for Arms Control and International Security, "Prepared Remarks Before the Senate Foreign Relations Committee," hearing on U.S.-India Civil Nuclear Cooperation Initiative, Washington, D.C., November 2, 2005.

256 *limited supply of uranium:* Zia Mian, A. H. Nayyar, R. Rajaraman, and M. V. Ramana, "Fissile Materials in South Asia: The Implications of the U.S.-India Nuclear Deal," International Panel on Fissile Materials, September 2006. Available at www.pfmlibrary.org/rr01.pdf as viewed on January 4, 2008.

256 *Foreign nuclear trade:* Joseph Cirincione and Daryl G. Kimball, "A Nonproliferation Disaster," Center for American Progress, December 11, 2006. Available at www.americanprogress.org/issues/2006/12/india_deal.html as viewed on January 4, 2008.

256 *experts consider it:* Bunn and Wier, "Securing the Bomb."

256 *"transform relations with India":* R. Nicholas Burns, "Remarks by Under Secretary of State for Political Affairs R. Nicholas Burns on U.S.-India Relations for the Senate Foreign Relations Committee," November 2, 2005.

257 *Rumsfeld and others:* Glenn Kessler, *The Confidante*, 57.

257 *"stop hectoring"* and *"nagging nannies":* Robert D. Blackwill, "The India Imperative," *National Interest*, Summer 2005.

257 *"We treat India":* David Ruppe, "U.S. Acknowledges Double Standard on Indian Deal," Global Security Newswire, April 12, 2006.

257 *"diplomatic triumph":* "Bush's Triumph in India," *National Review*, March 3, 2006.

257 *"no doubt"* and *"would be a terrible bargain":* Robert Kagan, "India Is Not a Precedent," *Washington Post*, March 12, 2006.

258 *one of the deal's architects:* Ashley J. Tellis, "India as a New Global Power: An Action Agenda for the United States," Carnegie Endowment for International Peace, 2005, 36–37.

258 *India did have a worrisome:* "A Game for All to Play: Nuclear Proliferation," *Economist*, October 9, 2004.

258 *India stated:* Leonard S. Spector, deputy director, Center for Nonproliferation Studies, Nuclear Cooperation with India, testimony before the House International Relations Committee, Washington, D.C., October 26, 2005.

258 *our perceived hypocrisy:* See George Perkovich, "'Democratic Bomb': Failed Strategy," Carnegie Endowment for International Peace, Policy Brief No. 49, November 2006.

259 *Charles Krauthammer and David Frum:* Charles Krauthammer, "World War II Is Over," *Washington Post*, October 20, 2006, A21. David Frum, "Mutually Assured Disruption," *International Herald Tribune*, October 10, 2006.

259 *Pakistan's nuclear weapons program:* Steve Coll, *Ghost Wars: The Secret History of the CIA, Afghanistan, and Bin Laden, from the Soviet Invasion to September 10, 2001* (New York: Penguin Press, 2004). Gordon Corera, *Shopping for Bombs: Nuclear Proliferation, Global Insecurity, and the Rise and Fall of the A. Q. Khan Network* (New York: Oxford University Press, 2006).

259 *"our security policy toward Pakistan":* Coll, *Ghost Wars*, 51.

259 *"His collection efforts"*: Ibid., 69.

260 *Khan had shifted:* Leonard Weiss, "Turning a Blind Eye Again?," *Arms Control Today,* March 2005, 12.

260 *fears that Khan's network continues to operate:* Matthew Bunn, Joseph, Cirincione, and Mark Hibbs, "The Next 5 Big Nuclear Stories: A Conversation with Mark Hibbs," 2007 Carnegie International Nonproliferation Conference, June 26, 2007. Available at http://www.carnegieendowment.org/events/index .cfm?fa=eventDetail&id=1012&&prog=zgp&proj=znpp.

Chapter Eight: FUTURE

263 *"The survival of liberty"*: George W. Bush, "Inaugural Address," Washington, D.C., January 20, 2005.

263 *A few conservatives:* Peter Robinson, "A Conservative President?," *National Review,* January 20, 2005.

263 *not a few liberals complained:* For example, Paul Starr, Michael Tomasky, and Robert Kuttner, "The Liberal Uses of Power," *American Prospect,* March 5, 2005.

264 *Peter Bergen and Paul Cruickshank:* Peter Bergen and Paul Cruickshank, "The Iraq Effect: War Has Increased Terrorism Sevenfold Worldwide," *Mother Jones,* March/April 2007, 64.

264 *"the most drastic political collapse"*: Peter Baker, "A President Besieged and Isolated, Yet at Ease," *Washington Post,* July 2, 2007, A1.

265 *"cut and run"*: See, for example, George W. Bush, "Press Conference by the President," Washington, D.C., October 11, 2006.

265 *"Choosing Victory"*: See Report of the Iraq Study Group, as viewed on http://www .fas.org/nuke/guide/iraq/isg_key.pdf on December 17, 2007.

265 *pragmatic Robert Gates:* Interestingly, the commission on ballistic missiles that Rumsfeld had led in 1998 was appointed not only because conservatives saw the 1995 NIE as too dovish, but also because their first attempt to Team B the report had largely reaffirmed the NIE's conclusions. That first Team B had been led by Gates.

266 *sent angry e-mails:* Glenn Kessler, "Conservatives Assail North Korea Accord," *Washington Post,* February 15, 2007, A1.

266 *"This obvious quid pro quo"*: Quote refers to Banco Delta Asia, from John R. Bolton, "Pyongyang's Perfidy," *Wall Street Journal,* May 18, 2007, A17. On fuel oil objections, see Bill Gertz, "Bolton Hits Agreement as 'Bad Signal' to Iran," *Washington Times,* February 14, 2007, 1.

266 *"I don't have a friend"*: Michael Abramowitz, "Conservative Anger Grows Over Bush's Foreign Policy," *Washington Post,* July 19, 2006.

266 *"How is it that Bush"*: Richard Perle, "Why Did Bush Blink on Iran? (Ask Condi)," *Washington Post,* June 25, 2006.

266 *"Is the Bush doctrine dead?"*: Norman Podhoretz, "Is the Bush Doctrine Dead?," *Commentary,* September 2006.

267 *the* Wall Street Journal *worried:* "Condi's Iran Gambit," *Wall Street Journal,* June 1, 2006. See also Danielle Pletka, "Diplomacy with the Devil," *New York Times,* November 19, 2007.

267 *"extraordinary failure"*: Jim Davenport, "Conservative Presidential Candidate Romney Criticizes UN, Calls for New Coalition of Nations," Associated Press, October 18, 2007.

267 *"I cannot support"*: Rudolph Giuliani, "Statement from Mayor Rudy Giuliani on the Law of the Sea Treaty," October 30, 2007, as viewed on http://www.join-rudy2008.com/article/pr/948 on November 22, 2007.

267 *"It's this century's nightmare,"*: See Romney for President ad campaign on http://www.mittromney.com/News/Press-Releases/Jihad_Ad as viewed on December 15, 2007.

267 *"It's a big thing"*: John McCain, speech, 2004 Republican National Convention, New York City, August 30, 2004.

267 *In an essay*: Rudolph W. Giuliani, "Toward a Realistic Peace," *Foreign Affairs*, September/October 2007.

268 *"That's the puzzle"*: Malcolm Gladwell, "Big and Bad: How the S.U.V. Ran Over Automotive Safety," *New Yorker*, January 12, 2004, 28.

268 *an innate tribalism*: For more on this topic, see Robert Wright, *The Moral Animal: Evolutionary Psychology and Everyday Life* (New York: Pantheon Books, 1994).

269 *a group of American college students*: John B. Judis, "Death Grip," *New Republic*, August 27, 2007.

269 *two death-related questions*: The questions are: "Please briefly describe the emotions that the thought of your own death arouses in you" and "Jot down, as specifically as you can, what you think will happen to you as you physically die and once you are physically dead." Lea Winerman, "The Politics of Mortality," *Monitor on Psychology*, January 2005, 32.

270 *"[R]esearch has shown"*: Florette Cohen, et al., "Fatal Attraction: The Effects of Mortality Salience on Evaluations of Charismatic, Task-Oriented, and Relationship-Oriented Leaders," *Psychological Science*, December 2004, 846–51.

270 *"worldviews that depict"*: Tom Pyszczynski, et al., "Mortality Salience, Martyrdom, and Military Might: The Great Satan Versus the Axis of Evil," *Personality and Social Psychology Bulletin*, April 2006, 525.

270 *final report concluded*: *The 9/11 Commission Report: Final Report of the National Commission on Terrorist Attacks on the United States* (New York: W. W. Norton, 2004).

270 *Political psychologists have found*: Mark Jordan Landau, et al., "Deliver Us from Evil: The Effects of Mortality Salience and Reminders of 9/11 on Support for President Bush," *Personality and Social Psychology Bulletin*, 2004, Vol. 30, No. 9, 1136–50.

271 *In one experiment*: Florette Cohen, et al., "American Roulette: The Effect of Reminders of Death on Support for George W. Bush in the 2004 Presidential Election," *Analyses of Social Issues and Public Policy*, 2005, Vol. 5, No. 1, 177–87.

271 *"From this perspective"*: Mark Jordan Landau, et al., "Deliver Us from Evil: The Effects of Mortality Salience and Reminders of 9/11 on Support for President Bush."

271 *"Jacksonian realism"*: Walter Russell Mead, *Special Providence: American Foreign Policy and How It Changed the World* (New York: Routledge, 2002), 245.

272 *"antithesis" of the American creed*: Anatol Lieven, *America Right or Wrong: An Anatomy of American Nationalism* (New York: Oxford University Press, 2005).

272 *against Bush critic Max Cleland*: As viewed on YouTube on http://www.youtube.com/watch?v=tKFYpd0q9nE on December 16, 2007.

272 *right-wing notion*: William Kristol, "They Don't Really Support the Troops,"

Weekly Standard, July 30, 2007. On the stab-in the-back narrative, Kevin Baker, "Stabbed in the Back! The Past and Future of a Right-Wing Myth," *Harper's Magazine,* June 2006. Spencer Ackerman, "War-Niks," *New Republic,* October 9, 2006, 10. Jonathan Chait, "Sub-Standard," *New Republic,* August 27, 2005, 5.

273 *Social research:* See Michael Shellenberger and Ted Nordhaus, *Break Through: From the Death of Environmentalism to the Politics of Possibility* (Boston: Houghton Mifflin, 2007).

273 *norms:* On the importance of norms, see, for example, Scott D. Sagan, "Realist Perspectives on Ethical Norms and Weapons of Mass Destruction," in Sohail H. Hashami and Steven P. Lee, eds., *Ethics and Weapons of Mass Destruction: Religious and Secular Perspectives* (Cambridge: Cambridge University Press, 2004), 73–95.

274 *"status quo, risk-averse adversary":* George W. Bush, "Prevent Our Enemies from Threatening Us, Our Allies, and Our Friends with Weapons of Mass Destruction," speech, West Point, New York, June 1, 2002.

274 *accidents and miscommunications:* See, for example, Scott D. Sagan, *The Limits of Safety: Organizations, Accidents, and Nuclear Weapons* (Princeton, NJ: Princeton University Press, 1993).

275 *"positive security assurances":* See, for example, Bill Clinton, "A Declaration by the President on Security Assurances for Non-Nuclear Weapon States Parties to the Treaty on the Non-Proliferation of Nuclear Weapons," April 5, 1995, as viewed on http://www.fas.org/nuke/control/npt/text/nonucwp.htm on December 15, 2007.

275 *"negative security assurances":* As explained in chapter 5, the George H. W. Bush and Bill Clinton administrations modified this assurance to allow for the possibility of nuclear retaliation in the event that a state attacks the United States or its allies with biological or chemical weapons. The George W. Bush administration, however, has, in effect, done away with negative security assurances. "U.S. Nuclear Policy? Negative Security Assurances," *Arms Control Today,* March 2002.

275 *Ukraine to retain its arsenal:* John J. Mearshimer, "The Case for a Ukrainian Nuclear Deterrent," *Foreign Affairs,* Summer 1993, 50–66.

275 *"Without the NPT":* Scott D. Sagan, "Why Do States Build Nuclear Weapons? Three Models in Search of a Bomb," *International Security,* Winter 1996/1997, 82.

276 *Bush's foreign policy manifesto:* Condoleezza Rice, "Campaign 2000: Promoting the National Interest," *Foreign Affairs,* July/August 2000.

277 *"The Senate vote against":* William Drozdiak, "Clinton's Star Wars Plan Undermining U.S. Arms Control Goals," *Washington Post,* June 15, 2000.

278 *"the troubling development":* See Marian Hobbs, minister for disarmament and arms control, New Zealand, statement on behalf of the coalition, 2005 Review Conference of the Parties to the Treaty on the Non-Proliferation of Nuclear Weapons, May 2, 2005, as viewed on http://www.un.org/events/npt2005/statements/npt02newzealand.pdf on December 15, 2007.

278 *"further steps towards":* See H. E. Nobutaka Machimura, minister for foreign affairs of Japan, statement, 2005 Review Conference of the Parties to the Treaty on the Non-Proliferation of Nuclear Weapons, May 2, 2005, as viewed on http://www.disarm.emb-japan.go.jp/statements/Statement/050502NPT.htm on December 15, 2007.

278 *"If governments simply ignore":* Peter Heinlein, "Nuclear Arms Meet Ends Without Agreement," Voice of America, correspondent report, United Nations, May 27, 2005.

278 *In an angry op-ed:* Robin Cook, "America's Broken Nuclear Promises Endanger Us All," *Guardian,* May 27, 2005.

279 *"The critics":* Stephen G. Rademaker, "Blame America First," *Wall Street Journal,* May 7, 2007, A15.

279 *"a greater U.S. readiness:* Lewis A. Dunn, Gregory Giles, Jeffrey Larsen, and Thomas Shypch, "Foreign Perspectives on U.S. Nuclear Policy and Posture," Science Applications International Corporation report prepared for the Defense Threat Reduction Agency, December 4, 2006, 3.

279 *conducted for Sandia National Laboratories:* Elizabeth A. Stanley, "International Perceptions of U.S. Nuclear Policy," *Sandia Report,* February 2007.

280 *"We are not approaching":* Stephen G. Rademaker, "Zeroing in on Noncompliance," interview with *Arms Control Today,* May 2005, as viewed on http://www.armscontrol.org/act/2005_05/Rademaker.asp on December 15, 2007.

280 *In other words:* "Armed and . . . ," *New Republic,* May 16, 2005, 7.

281 *we should not blame America first:* See, for example, Jimmy Carter, "Saving Nonproliferation," *Washington Post,* March 28, 2005, p. A17.

282 *"the civilian nuclear industry":* International Atomic Energy Agency, "Multilateral Approaches to the Nuclear Fuel Cycle: Expert Group Report to the Director General of the IAEA," Vienna, 2005.

283 *several countries:* Miles A. Pomper, "Vienna Meeting Airs New Nuclear Fuel Proposals," *Arms Control Today,* October 2006.

283, 284 *according to a study* and *Congressional Budget Office:* As cited in Miles A. Pomper, "Bush Nuclear Fuel-Cycle Program Suffers Blows," *Arms Control Today,* December 2007.

284 *the NPT divides those:* Lawrence Scheinman, "Equal Opportunity: Historical Challenges and Future Prospects of the Nuclear Fuel Cycle," *Arms Control Today,* May 2007.

284 *"We're not asking countries to sign":* Pomper, "Bush Nuclear Fuel-Cycle."

284 *ElBaradei has called:* Mohamed ElBaradei, "Seven Steps to Raise World Security," *Financial Times,* February 2, 2005.

284 *IAEA is focused:* Oliver Meier and Miles A. Pomper, "IAEA, Congress Tackle Nuclear Fuel Supply," *Arms Control Today,* July/August 2007.

284 *IAEA has also floated:* IAEA: Multilateral Approaches to the Nuclear Fuel Cycle: Expert Group Report to the Director General of the IAEA," Vienna, 2005.

284 *"It is not asking any State":* IAEA press release, "IAEA Seeks Guarantees of Nuclear Fuel," September 15, 2006 available at http://www.iaea.org/NewsCenter/PressReleases/2006/prn200615.html as viewed on January 24, 2008.

285 *"It proposes that* in this field": As cited in Kai Bird and Martin J. Sherwin, *American Prometheus: The Triumph and Tragedy of J. Robert Oppenheimer* (New York: Vintage Books, 2006), 347.

286 *The goal of nuclear disarmament:* Henry A. Kissinger, Sam Nunn, William J. Perry, and George P. Shultz, "A World Free of Nuclear Weapons," *Wall Street Journal,* January 4, 2007, A15; Mohamed ElBaradei, statement at the 2005 NPT Review Conference; Hans Blix, the Weapons of Mass Destruction Commission, *"Weapons of Terror: Freeing the World of Nuclear, Biological and Chemical Arms,"* June 1, 2006; and the High-Level Panel on Threats, Challenges and Change, "A More Secure World: Our Shared Responsibility," December 2, 2004.

287 *$5 billion:* See, for example, Steven Wingfield, "UBS Global Alternative Energy

Conference Presentation," New York, May 15, 2007, p. 7. Available at http://library
.corporate-ir.net/library/93/936/93662/items/245457/UBS507.pdf as viewed on
January 16, 2008.

288 *Princeton professors:* Stephen Pacala and Robert Socolow, "Stabilization Wedges:
Solving the Climate Problem for the Next 50 Years with Current Technologies,"
Science, August 13, 2004, pp. 968–72.

INDEX